Small Group Communication

Small Group Communication

Theory and Application

Arthur D. Jensen
Syracuse University

Joseph C. Chilberg
State University of New York College at Fredonia

Wadsworth Publishing Company
Belmont, California
A Division of Wadsworth, Inc.

Communications Editor: Peggy Randall
Editorial Assistant: Sharon Yablon
Production Editor: Sandra Craig
Managing Designer: Kaelin Chappell
Print Buyer: Karen Hunt
Permissions Editor: Robert M. Kauser
Cover and Text Designer: Paula Shuhert
Copy Editor: Pat Tompkins
Photo Researcher: Judy Mason
Illustrations: Wadsworth Production Art Department
Compositor: Monotype Composition Company, Inc., Baltimore
Signing Representative: Serina Beauparlant

Printed in the United States of America 49

1 2 3 4 5 6 7 8 9 10—95 94 93 92 91

Photo Credits

1, Leonard Freed/MAGNUM; 7, Owen Franken/Stock, Boston; 33, Photo Researchers, Inc.; 55, Alan Carey/The Image Works; 63, Strix Pix/Monkmeyer; 88, Shelley Gazin/The Image Works; 109, Alan Carey/The Image Works; 126, Peter Menzel/Stock, Boston; 151, Bob Daemmrich/The Image Works; 261, Roberta Hershenson/Photo Researchers, Inc.; 266, Jim Pickerell/Stock, Boston; 285, Eugene Richards/MAGNUM; 310, M. B. Warren/Photo Research, Inc.; 357, Mischa Erwitt/MAGNUM; 370, Leonard Freed/MAGNUM; 385, NASA; 395, Billy Barnes/Stock, Boston.

Library of Congress Cataloging-in-Publication Data

Jensen, Arthur D.
Small group communication / Arthur D. Jensen, Joseph C. Chilberg.
p. cm.
Includes bibliographical references and index.
ISBN 0-534-13140-9
1. Communication in small groups. 2. Group relations training.
I. Chilberg, Joseph C. II. Title.
HM133.J46 1991
302.3′4—dc20 90-41716
CIP

Contents in Brief

Contents

Preface

If there is such a thing as the five most dreaded words in the workplace, they would surely be "We are forming a committee." Nothing seems to strike greater fear in otherwise competent individuals than being forced to reach a group decision on some issue. The goal of *Small Group Communication: Theory and Application* is to reduce that fear by convincing students and professionals that they can become competent at group communication.

To develop group communication competence requires a combination of theoretical and practical knowledge. In this text you will find a wealth of theory and research that explains why groups succeed or fail. An understanding of those theories coupled with a practical knowledge of group techniques and skills will enable you to diagnose your group interaction problems and propose effective interventions.

The first course in small group communication should have an applied focus. This text will help you gain a working understanding of group communication by analyzing and practicing communication behaviors and procedures in a systematic framework.

Organization

The text is composed of four parts and a separate group project facilitation manual. Part I provides an overview of group communication and the complementary perspective. Chapter 1, "Investigating Group Interaction," reviews definitions, functions, issues, and attributes of groups. Chapter 2, "Prescriptive and Descriptive Group Process: Complementary Perspectives," establishes the book's dual perspective by defining and integrating the prescriptive and descriptive orientations of the group process. This is followed by a contextual model of group interaction and a review of the functional dimensions of group communication. The contextual model establishes the organization for the remaining chapters, while the functional dimensions provide a conceptual framework for understanding the role of communication in group dynamics.

Part II, "Group Communication Skills and Prescriptive Practices," includes Chapters 3 through 7. The placement of this part and the sequence of chapters were intended to introduce practical information early in the text to aid students who have been assigned semester-long group projects and to draw implications of theory to prescriptions in later chapters.

Chapter 3, "The Speech Act Level: Preparing for Group Participation," reviews the role of research skills, relevant knowledge, and members' attitudes in preparing for group communication. This is followed by a review of the types of speech acts and the emergence and performance of functional roles in Chapter 4, "The Speech Act Level: Communication Behaviors and Roles."

Chapter 5, "The Episode Level: Managing Task Group Meetings," describes and explains prescriptions for conducting learning-group and decision-making meetings. The chapter includes information on procedural steps and tips for structuring and managing meetings. Chapter 6, "The Episode Level: Managing Group Activities," provides specific techniques relevant to conducting various decision-making and problem-solving episodes. Each technique is presented in a step-by-step manner, followed by a list of functional advantages and disadvantages. Information and practices for developing and maintaining group relationships are presented in Chapter 7, "The Relationship Level: Cooperating to Manage Conflict." Emphasis is placed on the role of communication behavior in setting a climate for conflict management, followed by guidelines for managing conflict in groups.

The Group Project Facilitator, which follows Part II, is a manual to help project groups conduct careful group development and critical project decision making. The manual is divided into sections, corresponding to the four phases of a group project (forming the group, project identification, analysis and information search, and project synthesis and delivery). Each section includes instructions and discussion, brief lists of guidelines, and meeting preparation activities.

The Group Project Facilitator helps users refer to prescriptions in earlier skills chapters, provides additional guidelines for conducting project activities, and offers assistance with tasks that are not typically covered in textbooks on small group communication—such as goal setting, survey development, and the preparation of visual aids. What the manual really offers is a complete model for practicing critical, effective group communication that can be followed closely or consulted as a general reference. (Please consult the overview of the Group Project Facilitator, page 180, for additional information.)

Part III, "Analyzing Group Process from a Descriptive Perspective," covers six major areas of group research relevant to an understanding of group communication. Chapter 8, "The Individual Level: Managing Personalities in the Group," examines the role of group member personality and its impact on group interaction. The function and types of leadership are elaborated in Chapter 9, "The Relationship Level: Leaders and Followers." Chapter 10, "The Group Level: How Groups and Their Members Socialize Each Other," discusses the group socialization process, focusing on the role of norm development in shaping group culture and group membership. Chapter 11, "The Group Level: Decision Development," and Chapter 12, "The Group Level: Explaining Decision Shifts," examine group decision making, explaining decision paths, development, and shifts. Chapter 13, "The Cultural Level: Groups in Their Natural Habitats," looks at the group from a cultural perspective, addressing the influences of society and organizations on group culture and communication practices.

Part IV, "Future Directions," includes the final chapter, which introduces technological innovations used to facilitate and support group communication in organizational settings. The chapter describes several formal prescriptions for structuring problem-solving groups and uses of electronic technologies for group decision making.

Features

Small Group Communication was developed for a course that typically includes both a review of relevant knowledge and learning experiences that demonstrate and apply concepts, theories, and procedures. The book has drawn upon classic and contemporary research and practices, and it was designed for both analysis and application.

Briefly, the important concepts include:

- Integration of descriptive and prescriptive perspectives for understanding group interaction
- Updated research and current innovations in group practice and techniques
- Examination of the influence of culture on group communication
- The relationship of theory to practice and of practice to theory, and the implications of those relationships

Learning experiences include:

- A "user-friendly" organization of skills and prescriptions for easy access to encourage use and experimentation
- A variety of exercises, projects, and discussion activities in each chapter
- The Group Project Facilitator to model and guide group project management and decision making and thus enhance group project quality
- A case study in each chapter to demonstrate group process concepts and issues

Small Group Communication: Theory and Application offers more than information on group communication theory and practice. It is a learning aid designed to develop students' ability to assess and practice group communication. The selection and organization of material will help students increase their ability to apply group communication theory and prescriptions to achieve more satisfying experiences in groups and more productive results from group interaction.

Acknowledgments

We appreciate the contribution of the manuscript reviewers, including: Thomas E. Harris, University of Evansville; James Mancuso, Mesa Community College; Michael E. Mayer, Arizona State University; William Foster Owen, Texas A&M University; Patricia Palm, Mankato State University; Eileen Berlin Ray, Cleveland State University; Dan Robinette, Eastern Kentucky University; Joseph Scudder, Indiana University; Brant Short, Idaho State University; Doris Werkman, Portland State University; Thomas Wirkus, University of Wisconsin, La Crosse; and Stephanie Zimmerman, Northern Arizona University.

Arthur Jensen

Joseph Chilberg

Part I

Overview of the Group Process

Investigating Group Interaction

We live in a world beset by complex problems. Newspaper headlines simply chronicle the many unsolved dilemmas we face. Drug and alcohol abuse claim many lives. Entire families go hungry and homeless. A garbage glut and a dozen other environmental problems threaten our quality of life. Rape and other crimes haunt our cities and college campuses. The U.S. national debt and trade deficit grow larger each year, endangering our economy.

Even solutions to some of these problems have their bleak side. Innovations in medical technology have raised difficult ethical issues about rights to life and the right to die with dignity. The personal computer reduces the amount of time spent on menial tasks, but creates volumes of data that no one has time to interpret. In fact, experts have produced such a plethora of information that trying to keep up with the latest developments in a single field is enough to produce a state of information overload.

How can we use the information explosion to help solve some of our most perplexing problems (or even less perplexing ones)? Single individuals working alone can tackle such problems, but it is hard to be a "Renaissance person" in our time. In our society, the typical way to address such problems is by assigning them to small groups of people who analyze the problem, gather relevant information, and generate potential solutions. You are likely to be a member of many such task groups as a student or member of the work force.

However, working in groups is not always a satisfying experience. Many people complain about having to attend meetings where "nothing gets done," or where their efforts are an "exercise in futility" because the boss has already decided how to proceed. Others complain that only a few members do most of the work, which means that several people are unproductive "dead weight." It all adds up to a predominant attitude that groups are largely a waste of time.

We understand but do not share that view of small group work. We believe that, for most complex problems, small groups of people can produce far better solutions than can individuals working alone. In our view, the discrepancy between the potential and the typical outcome of group work is due to a lack of understanding of group communication and decision making, plus a lack of knowledge about the tools available to assist the group in making decisions. This book aims to provide you with a working knowledge of group concepts and tools and a systematic approach for using that knowledge to improve the quality of group interaction and decision making.

American industry is slowly coming to the same conclusion. The prominence of group decision making has slowly evolved since the early 1970s, when the concept of quality circles became widespread. A *quality circle* is a group of workers that meets as often as one hour per week to identify problems in its area and recommend solutions to management.[1] The success of quality circles led to the use of *special purpose teams*, in which groups of employees and managers collaborate to make decisions on operational procedures such as designing the flow of work from one subunit to another.[2] In recent years, some companies such as General Electric have used *self-managing teams*, which are given the responsibility of producing an entire product and making group decisions about work assignments and vacation schedules. A change from individual to team-based decision making can result in 40 to 50 percent increases in rates of productivity, depending on the type of work involved.[3]

For the concept of teamwork to succeed in the long run, both managers and employees will have to learn how to take advantage of the potential benefits of group effort and how to avoid the many pitfalls typical of group interaction. We will explore these aspects of the group process later in this chapter. For now, let us consider that this shift to the team concept, although an important step, will not work unless a corresponding shift occurs in the educational sector. Our schools have done a poor job of teaching group communication skills or promoting the value of teamwork. If you want to succeed in organizations, you will have to learn how largely on your own. We hope this text will be an important first step in helping you become more competent working with groups.

Task and Social Groups

Groups are social as well as task-oriented entities. To fully understand group decision making, we need to occasionally look at groups as purely social units and note the way people think about and behave in groups. We can usefully distinguish between social and task groups. A *social group* exists primarily to provide emotional support and a sense of identity to its members. A *task group* is organized for a specific and limited purpose, often to make decisions. Although this book is primarily about task groups, note that social groups make decisions and task groups offer some degree of social support. Most of the concepts in this text can help you understand both types of groups.

We start by briefly examining the role of the group in society, which has changed considerably from culture to culture and time to time. Historian Georges Duby describes life in a social group in medieval Europe:

> In feudal residences there was no room for individual solitude, except perhaps in the moment of death. When people ventured outside the domestic enclosure, they did so in groups. No journey could be made by fewer than two people, and if it happened that they were not related, they bound themselves by rites of brotherhood, creating an artificial family that lasted as long as the journey required. By age seven . . . young aristocratic males . . . embarked upon a life of adventure. Yet throughout their lives they remained surrounded, in the strong sense of the word . . . . Their apprenticeship over, new knights received their arms as a group. . . . From that time forth the young knights were always together, linked in glory and in shame, vouching for and standing as hostage for one another.[4]

Throughout most of history, the small group (three or more people) has been *the* unit of social life. Today, other units, the individual and the dyad (two people), have assumed official recognition. Earlier in this century, social scientists debated whether or not the concept of group even had any existence in reality. Many argued that only individuals could be considered as "real."[5] But do not be deceived. The small group is alive and well, perhaps all the more significant because of the subtlety of its influence.

In contrast to our culture's emphasis on the individual, it can be enlightening to examine the group as the basic social unit and individuals as the "products" of group interaction. As one group of scholars put it, "It is not really useful to think of individuals as the units out of which groups and societies are constructed; it is more fruitful to think of an individual [or the dyad] as the limiting case of a group when, for the moment, there is no one else around."[6] What does this mean? It suggests that every individual decision is at least partially influenced by the groups to which we belong. Both positive and negative examples of this influence are everywhere—in the streets, the dorm, or at home. A "generous and altruistic" adolescent buys blankets and food with her own money and delivers them personally to homeless members of her community—elaborating on a tradition started by fellow members of her church youth group. An "independent" college student decides he can pass tomorrow's exam without studying—because his friends are going out to their favorite haunt. A couple of "rebellious" teens decide to elope—a particular family habit that is three or four generations old.

Both task and social groups have a profound influence on our daily lives. But you may wonder if you really need to study group processes in order to understand and communicate more effectively in groups. Why not rely on your *experience* in groups to know what to do and what to avoid doing? Getting answers to this question may be a good place to start. After identifying reasons to study groups, we will clarify the concepts of *group* and *communication*. We will end the chapter by noting some of the major advantages and disadvantages of working in groups.

Why Study Group Interaction?

We want to explore with you the dynamics of group interaction for two reasons. First, improving your communication skills and being a better participant in groups is desirable. The following chapters contain many communication principles, strategies, and techniques that you can practice and employ. But there is a second, more important reason. We want to help you develop a perspective that will enable you to know *when* to employ those communication skills and *how* to help the group as a whole understand *what* it is doing that either facilitates or inhibits good decision making. That is why you will encounter a number of theories and many research findings about group communication in this text.

Perhaps you are one of the people who resist theory altogether and beg for "just the practical stuff." If so, we would like you to consider three arguments for our approach: (1) experience alone will not improve group decision-making skills, (2) your education has not prepared you adequately for group work, and (3) theories, whether they prove to be right or wrong, add a much needed perspective, a kind of wide-angled lens that helps us to see and reminds us that there is more to see.

Experience Alone Is Not Enough

Experience is the proverbial teacher. Practice makes perfect. We take these maxims for granted, but conventional wisdom about groups has not always held up under close scrutiny. For instance, most people believe they know the qualities necessary for effective leadership. Unfortunately, five decades of research has failed to substantiate claims that intelligence, assertiveness, and charisma are "the right stuff."[7] Most of us also respect the claim that we learn from our mistakes. We expect to make mistakes in our early group efforts and then learn how to correct them. But what usually happens is that "experience" reinforces most of the bad habits that groups develop. The fact that most people dread "another meeting" indicates that experience is not the answer.

Instruction in Group Skills Is Essential

Experience can be a good teacher only if you have been provided with a framework for evaluating that experience. For most of us, school has offered instruction in just a few basic communication skills: reading, writing, and

Like a team, chefs need to draw upon each member's special talents and coordinate task activities.

perhaps speaking. It is highly unlikely that you have received any formal instruction about group communication (leading discussions, listening, and critiquing ideas) prior to this course. Our educational system stresses individual effort so much that the idea of group work is often construed as cheating. Any effort to teach group skills has come on the basketball court or the softball diamond. In spite of inadequate instruction, college students and members of organizations are frequently required to participate in group projects, often with a major portion of their course grade or job success at stake. Working in groups without any training in group skills is an invitation to failure.

Knowledge of Group Dynamics Adds Perspective

Learning about the group process (not just the skills involved) helps you see "the big picture." Why do you need to understand the whole process? Because there is no single comprehensive recipe to follow in applying the skills once you have mastered them. Like any good chef, you need to know a range of alternatives to replace missing ingredients and respond to unforeseen circumstances. The theories of group communication in this text offer several alternative viewpoints to judge your experience against. You are invited to view groups as a real-life laboratory for confirming your own hypotheses about group decision making.

Finally, knowing about group process can influence decision-making outcomes. Once you develop a theoretical understanding of group interaction,

Some Defining Characteristics of Groups

Perception of common goals
A network of communication
Behavioral interdependence
Structured relations
Norms
Perception of wholeness

Figure 1.1

that knowledge will guide you in selecting among the tools available for managing group interaction. From the outset of a group project, you can anticipate problems and prospects and plan ahead for ways to manage them. We will describe various roles and rules for discussion management in Chapters 4, 5, and 6.

When Does a Group Become a Group?

The advantages of group interaction that we have described are tied directly to a collection of people's ability to become a group. But what defines the concept of groupness? Consider a dictionary's definition of a group: "when the persons or things in question are considered as one or as acting as one."[8] By this standard, several strangers meeting for the first time would not constitute a group. They have no history, no expectations of one another, and no guidelines for acting in concert. How does such a collection of individuals become a group? What must happen among them to create the impression that they can act as a unit? Research on group dynamics provides numerous characteristics that help us define the level of groupness members achieve (see Figure 1.1). Members constitute a group when they perceive themselves as having:

- Common goals
- A network of communication
- Behavioral interdependence
- Structured relations
- Shared norms
- A sense of wholeness

Taken together, these six characteristics flexibly define a group. We define a *group* as *a number of individuals whose communication behaviors are interdependent and structured, creating the perception of common goals, shared norms, and an identity as a collective whole.* Our term *groupness* indicates the degree to which each of these characteristics is present in group interaction. Let's look at each of these important characteristics.

Perception of Common Goals

Groups usually have specific reasons for their existence. A *group goal* is simply the common purpose group members strive to accomplish; it is often the reason a group gets organized. Suppose several tenants in the same building become concerned about slow or substandard maintenance of their apartments. Or perhaps they have heard rumors that the owner wants to convert the apartments to high-priced condominiums. These tenants share a common goal, which is often the impetus for group action. If each tenant decided to complain or take action as an individual, the commonality of goals would not lead to the perception of a group. Group perception can exist even when goals are vague. Much of our participation in social groups is simply to have fun. Or we may join a group for individual reasons that other members do not share. But these are exceptions; most groups can be defined as such precisely because members can point to their common goals.

In most cases, individuals bring many goals to a group discussion. Some of these goals are shared, others may be divergent and personal. One member may support a proposal because it favors a special interest group that he represents, another may be pushing a different idea simply to demonstrate her leadership potential. A third member may go along with the majority because the prestige of membership in the group is his only motive. But they still perceive themselves as a group because they share a primary goal—achieving some final product instead of a stalemate—that ties all their individual goals together. Box 1.1 reports a classic study of how primary goals can be created to help group members work with rather than against one another. The perception of groupness is directly related to the degree that a primary goal is shared in thought and action.

A Network of Communication

Individuals may share similar goals, but they are not likely to know that unless they have communicated with one another. In fact, the more frequently people communicate, the greater the opportunity to discover similar interests and common goals that might foster group activity. The perception of belonging to a group is further substantiated by the repeated use of a network of communication between members. By this we mean that members recognize and single each other out as appropriate recipients of certain kinds of information. They interact with one another regularly and frequently, especially on matters relating to their shared goals. In some cases, the network of communication is spelled out in formal job descriptions or assignment of special duties as in a company or institution that assigns people to form a specific group to investigate

Box 1.1

Creating Superordinate Goals: The Robbers Cave Study

In 1954, a research team headed by Muzafer Sherif conducted an elaborate experimental study of group behavior in a natural setting. A classic in the field of group dynamics, the study demonstrates how the creation of a superordinate group goal can help minimize hostile feelings between subgroups and forge a group bond.

Sherif and his associates formed a summer camp for boys ages eleven to twelve in the hills of southeastern Oklahoma. The criteria they used to select boys for the camp virtually eliminated the possibility that the boys would self-select into subgroups because of differences in race, social background, or physical appearance. All twenty-four campers were white, middle class, and Protestant. The camp's administrators, counselors, and staff were trained observers who helped set up particular aspects of the study and made unobtrusive notes on the boys' behavior.

The group was divided in half before the first day of camp; and each subgroup arrived in separate buses and stayed in cabins far apart from each other. For the first week of camp, neither subgroup knew the other existed. Each subgroup participated in activities such as camping out and cooking designed to require interdependent behavior, one of the key characteristics in developing groupness. As expected, roles and norms began to emerge in each subgroup. One group nicknamed itself the "Rattlers" and developed a norm for toughness that became so strong that many of the boys failed to treat their own cuts and bruises. The "Eagles," on the other hand, were the example of goodness; their norms included no swearing and lots of consideration for each other. Later, when introduced to the Rattlers, the Eagles would huddle in prayer before each athletic contest.

After a week, the two subgroups were allowed to interact, and the camp administrators acceded to the boys' demand for a tournament of games between the two groups. The tournament consisted of baseball, touch football, tug-of-war, a treasure hunt, tent pitching, skits, and cabin inspections, with prizes for the winning group. The researchers' goal was to create a degree of hostility between the two groups and then test several hypotheses about how such subgroup hostility could be reduced.

Although the researchers had planned to stage several events to promote hostility between the groups, they did not have to use them. After losing at tug-of-war, the Eagles stole and partially burned the Rattlers' makeshift flag. This was followed by several incidents of name-calling, pushing and shoving, and back-to-back raids on each other's cabins. As these events unfolded, counselors interviewed the campers through casual conversation. When asked to rate the personal qualities of other campers, the boys consistently rated their own group members as brave, tough, and friendly. Members of the

Box 1.1 (continued)

other group were perceived as sneaky and as smart alecks and stinkers. The observation and interview data confirmed four specific hypotheses:

1. Competition is likely to turn into hostility when each group has a goal (such as winning the tournament) that can only be obtained by one group at the expense of the other.
2. Conflict *between* groups tends to produce solidarity *within* each group.
3. Under competitive circumstances, each group forms unfavorable attitudes and stereotypes about the other group.
4. Intergroup hostility can be sufficient to change the social organization within a group. For instance, the Eagles' peacetime leader lost his role because he was reluctant to lead them in conflict; a member of the Rattlers who was initially labeled a "bully" became a "hero." Several norms changed also.

Once a sufficient degree of intergroup hostility had emerged, the researchers tested hypotheses concerned with reducing hostility between the groups. Previous research had ruled out several strategies that are often used in similar situations. For instance, the staff considered providing the boys with accurate and favorable information about members of the other group, but did not do so, because people usually respond to such information in a very selective fashion. In an earlier camp study in Connecticut, the researchers identified a strategy that worked temporarily. They brought in an outside team to face a camp-wide team in an athletic contest. But once the event was over, the between-group hostility reappeared.

Other strategies failed. Several camp-wide activities, such as going to the movies, eating together, and shooting off fireworks on the Fourth of July, actually produced more conflict. One reason for this is that the activities, while pleasant, did not require any interdependent or cooperative action by the subgroups.

The only strategy that worked was the creation of superordinate goals for the entire group. A *superordinate goal* has a compelling appeal for members of each group and is one that neither group can achieve without participation of the other. The researchers staged three incidents to create superordinate goals. The first was a breakdown in the camp's water supply system. Both groups volunteered to search for the source of the problem, but did not locate it until they had worked together to do so. The second situation arose when both groups indicated a desire to see a specific movie, but were told the camp could not afford it. As a group, the boys devised a plan in which each person chipped in part of the cost of the movie. They watched the movie together without any negative incidents. Finally, an outing was arranged for the whole group, but lunch was left back at the camp. When the

Box 1.1 (continued)

boys got hungry, the truck would not start and they could not return to camp. Again the boys decided what to do and, using the same rope from the infamous tug-of-war, worked together to pull the truck and get it started.

According to the researchers, these joint efforts *gradually* reduced hostility between the subgroups. They stopped pushing each other around, some group members began sitting with members of the opposite group, and eventually they performed skits for each other. At the close of camp, the boys chose to return home on one bus together rather than the two separate ones they arrived in.

This study demonstrates the necessity of creating superordinate goals any time there are important divisions within a group. One key seems to be the requirement of interdependent activity by members of the competing subgroups. Perhaps you can identify one or more superordinate goals that need to be stressed in the group you belong to.

Source: M. Sherif, O. J. Harvey, B. J. White, W. R. Hood, and C. W. Sherif, *Intergroup Conflict and Cooperation: The Robbers Cave Experiment* (Norman, Okla.: University Book Exchange, 1961).

a problem. In other instances, the network emerges as a result of happenstance or physical, social, or task attractiveness among individuals. For example, several people in the same company interested in innovative technology may be in different departments and have little contact with one another. Still, they may informally seek each other out and become a valuable network within the company. However it originates, the repeated use of particular communication channels among specific people fosters a sense of connection. When problem after problem arises and the same few people seek each other out to discuss solutions, they are creating a communication network.

Behavioral Interdependence

More evidence of a group's existence can be determined by observing whether or not individuals rely on and influence one another. Interdependence in a group takes two forms: task and relational interdependence. *Task interdependence* means that the work of each group member is related to and affects the work of the other members. Each person sees his or her job as a part of the larger group task. This requires the group to coordinate and integrate the knowledge, skills, and duties of its members; how well the group does this signals its interdependence. If the group's work can be subdivided so that each member can do his or her part without input from the others, members are essentially going it alone and are not demonstrating interdependence.

Relational interdependence refers to the emotional connections members make with one another *as persons*. The amount of energy, enthusiasm, respect, and support that members offer each other defines this type of mutual dependence. Some groups will exhibit more task interdependence and less relational interdependence and vice versa. This distinction may be the most significant difference between purely task and social groups. Relational interdependence is necessary for group harmony, cohesion, and commitment.

Consider the counterpart of interdependence—independence, which represents the absence of influence. When individuals seem unaffected by the actions of other people in their presence, their relationship is an independent one. This often happens even in established groups. On the basketball court, we use the term *showboat* for a player who abandons the structure of team play and tries to score without considering where his or her teammates are or what they are doing. Interdependence, on the other hand, is characterized by talk that takes into account other members' comments and joint actions that enable members to do things they could not do as well by themselves. Perhaps the simplest example of interdependence is a person who modifies his or her own idea because another member questioned some aspect of it.

Structured Relations

Another factor that promotes the perception of groupness is the creation of *structured relationships* among members—an extension of the interdependence concept. A highly interdependent group will most likely have some structure for managing its coordinated activities. The most common type of structure in a group is a *role structure*. A *role* is a position in the group defined by a set of behaviors that the group usually expects the person in that position to perform. Members may expect their leader, for instance, to call the meeting to order, remind them of the agenda to be discussed, and summarize their progress. If a member breaks the ice at the first group meeting and then helps smooth out an argument between two members at the second meeting, then the group may unconsciously look to that person to reduce tension later. Other members may take on roles such as information provider, recorder, or questioner. Chapter 4 details these and many other roles. A role structure helps members perceive some sense of order emerging from their interactions. If members continue to act in somewhat predictable ways, it becomes easier to work in concert. This fosters the impression that members can think and act interdependently as a group. In addition, it creates a sense of stability and projects what the group might expect in the future. A group may structure itself in many ways. Closely tied to roles is the *status structure* of the group—how members rank each other in terms of importance and influence. A leader is usually perceived as the highest status person, but this is not necessarily the case. You may be able to think of other ways that group members relate to one another and create their social hierarchy. People often begin to feel more like a group once roles emerge and stabilize.

Shared Norms

Whereas role relations establish expectations for individual members, *norms* are expectations for the group as a whole. A leader is expected to talk more than a recorder does, but both may be expected to attend meetings, show up on time, be cordial, and perhaps even show enthusiasm about the group's project. Norms are standards or guidelines for acceptable behavior. They help differentiate full members from nonmembers or marginal members. It is difficult for people to see themselves as a group if they cannot distinguish how they are different from anyone else in the vicinity. Sometimes groups use highly visible means of distinguishing themselves, such as wearing uniforms. Usually the markings are more subtle: similar vocabulary, attitudes, levels of effort, and practices. The importance of norms in designing and using effective group communication processes will be more fully discussed in Chapter 10.

Perception of Wholeness

Wholeness, the final characteristic that identifies a group, refers to whether or not individuals perceive themselves as parts of a whole. If they do, they are likely to talk about themselves using collective terminology: "we," "us," "the group." Furthermore, members may smile or flinch at each other's behavior in public because of the perception that such behavior reflects on the group as a whole. A reprimand like, "Stop shouting! You're making us all look bad," is evidence that at least one person has the perception of wholeness. If other members nod in agreement, you can be fairly certain that the outlook is shared.

Communication: Creating the Group Reality

We have already identified the linking of people through communication as one of the key components in the creation of a group. There is no group if there is no communication. But what is communication?

One popular definition is to think of communication as a channel that carries messages from a source to one or more receivers. In this view, one person conceives an idea and passes it on to others via an oral, written, or nonverbal communication channel. The only impediment to a message being received correctly is some mechanical failure in the channel (a muffled voice, poor handwriting, a bad connection on the telephone). Communication is seen primarily as a way of exchanging information. Group communication would thus involve an exchange of information and viewpoints by several senders and receivers at one time. Most communication scholars today consider such a view overly simplistic.

Another way is to define communication as a transaction in which people collectively create and manage social realities.[9] *Transaction* means that messages are being sent and received simultaneously by each party involved in a conversation or discussion. It also implies that messages are open to interpretation by the receiver. People frequently misunderstand the meanings of the words they exchange, but as two (or more) people interact, the number of possible interpretations for each message is usually reduced. This happens because each person begins to make sense of the conversation by taking into account such contextual features as the setting, circumstances, and previous messages.

Together, they begin to construct a particular *social reality*, a coherent sense of what they are doing together and how they relate to one another. In some cases, the social reality created might be something as simple as the kind of conversation such as an argument or gossip. Eventually, a series of interactions will produce some sense of the kind of relationship emerging—allies or rivals, for example. Or the conversation may result in an agreement about how to view a given topic. For example, say that a group is discussing the homeless in America. A member introduces a particular "fact" to the group (for example, that 2.5 million Americans are homeless). The group discusses this "fact":

Joe: Most of them are alcoholics, drug addicts, or people who used to live in mental institutions.

Jan: Yeah, a lot of people want to live on the street. They're willing to sue city governments that try to force them into shelters.

Pete: Can we get information on that? We'll need it to support our views.

Jan: Sure we can. It was in all the papers.

Contrast this discussion with that of another group talking about the same "fact":

Tom: Two and half million? That's a lot of people. Do we know why most of them are homeless?

Pat: The stereotype is that a homeless person is a middle-aged male alcoholic, but I've read that the number of homeless women and children is rapidly increasing.

Kate: A lot of people do actually want to live on the street, though.

Tom: Yes, but there are many more who simply can't find affordable housing.

In each case, the group's communication is more than simply exchanging facts or opinions. Collectively, each group reinforces a different image of the homeless, making the "reality" of the 2.5 million homeless people different for each group. Group communication is a process of using information, understanding or misunderstanding each other's positions, marshaling arguments, and negotiating social relationships so that some ideas, facts, opinions, or values are seen as "more real" than others. It is not merely *passing* meaning from person to person but *making* meaning and creating reality. As already suggested, when group members communicate effectively enough to create common goals, interdependence, shared norms, specialized roles, and a sense of wholeness, they have collectively created the social reality of groupness.

Another social reality that a group creates is its task reality. As members talk about their goals and plans, they negotiate a shared vision of what their task is. From the reality-creating perspective, a group decision is not a logical conclusion based on an objective exchange of information. It is the product of a complex social process inevitably involving bias, distortion, and politics as well as clarity, vision, and hope. This suggests all the more reason to seek as full an understanding of the communication process as possible.

With an idea of the importance of groups in society and with basic definitions under our belt, we are now ready to consider when to employ groups as the decision makers of choice. We also need to identify some of the pitfalls and promises that make working in groups so exciting and frustrating at the same time.

Why Work in Groups?

Although groups are interwoven in the fabric of our lives, there are clearly times when we see ourselves as acting alone and deciding things without the assistance of others. We do not expect a family to convene at the breakfast table and reach a consensus on what clothing each member should wear that day. We like to think adults are capable of making some decisions on their own. Still, it is important to remember the influence of groups on supposedly individual decisions. Then when the question is asked, "Should the decision be a *group* or an *individual* one?" we will know that the distinction is a matter of degree more than of kind.

There are practical reasons for deciding why and when to sound the horn and call a group together. People generally do not like meetings, so we should know the advantages and disadvantages of deciding things by group. Some decisions have aspects that make group deliberation more likely to produce superior judgments; others do not require the assets of a group at all. The following discussion should help you to differentiate when group decision making is in order.

Advantages of Group Decision Making

Knowing the pros and cons of group decision making is absolutely essential to effectively solve problems. If you know what the group process can and cannot do, you will make much wiser decisions about when to ask for group help (see

Some Potential Advantages of Group Decision Making

Division of labor
Greater comprehension of decisions
- Pooled information base
- Multiple perspectives on issues
- Creativity stimulated

Enhanced commitment

Figure 1.2

Figure 1.2). We start with three major advantages of groups: division of labor, increased comprehension, and enhanced commitment.

Groups Can Do More: The Division of Labor An obvious reason to use group decision making is the power inherent in numbers. If managed well, more people can get more work done. Group members who specialize in various aspects of the decision-making task create a *division of labor.* Once a group realizes what information it needs, some members may prefer to handle certain tasks: interviewing experts, doing library research, or polling people on the street, for example. As the group begins to evaluate the information it has, members may differ in their ability to identify the validity or relevance of specific information or to interpret and integrate those facts. When the group turns to generating and evaluating decisions or solutions, one member with political savvy can help the group see whether or not its preferred choice will be acceptable to other groups that may be affected. In short, members typically develop one or more role specialties within the group. The clear advantages of specialization and divided labor do have a price. Groups require much more time to process and integrate information than do individuals. We will say more about time constraints when we discuss the disadvantages of groups.

Groups Can Comprehend More Than Individuals Can Groups have the potential for making decisions of a higher quality because of their greater capacity to comprehend a problem's complexities and its alternative solutions. One reason for this greater capacity is the *pooled information base* that results from the combined knowledge and wisdom of all its members. Five people usually know more about a problem than any one of them would individually. The cognitive limitations we have as individuals prevent us from retrieving all of the ideas and information stored in our memory. Group members are able to remind each other of what they know collectively. But remember that this is only a *potential* advantage. The group must turn that potential into reality. Apathy, fear, or lack of commitment on the part of even a few members can severely limit any advantage groups have over individuals. Obviously, the pool of information shrinks when only a few members participate.

In addition to a greater information base, group members bring *multiple perspectives* to bear on what the facts mean, how ideas can be related to one another, and what the implications are in any given alternative. Because they often represent different perspectives and approaches to problems, group members can correct each other's blind spots and jolt each other out of rigid patterns of thinking. To make sure that new products will be successful, organizations often assign people from different units to task forces to ensure that multiple perspectives are represented. People from operations, research and development, marketing, and accounting departments simply see the world through different lenses. And they can help each other see the big picture a lot more clearly. A person making decisions alone will find this very hard to do.

Once members pool information and break the tendency to think in old, secure, but stereotyped ways, the group has a broader view of the issue under consideration. A comprehensive understanding of the group's task can stimulate creativity, which in turn expands the group's knowledge as it explores new options. If members listen to one another carefully, they can "piggyback" on each other's ideas, modifying or altering them in some way. Edward de Bono talks about ideas as having a "forward effect"—one idea becomes the stepping stone to another.[10] The result is often the discovery of the *un*usual solution to a routine problem.

Group members frequently have to implement the decisions they make. Knowing how the decision was reached and the logic behind it can be extremely helpful when conditions make it difficult to carry out a decision exactly as it was rendered. Having a comprehensive knowledge of the decision process enables one to make the necessary adjustments in keeping with the spirit of the group's original intent.

In sum, groups can increase their comprehension of the decision-making situation in three different ways:

- By pooling the wisdom and knowledge of individual members
- By exploring the multiple perspectives that members bring to the group
- By listening carefully and responding creatively to each other's ideas during discussion

All of these are important to a thorough understanding of the issues at hand and set the stage for greater commitment to the ultimate solution.

Groups Can Enhance Commitment Over the past several decades, researchers have demonstrated that participation in group decisions affects how group members feel about decisions and alters their subsequent behavior. Many U.S. organizations have instituted "participatory decision-making" programs because they recognize the impact of group involvement on employee performance. The commitment to carrying out a decision is increased significantly when people believe they are at least partly responsible for the decision.

This increase in commitment can be explained in several ways. First, participation can result in improved attitudes and performance on the part of group members. Even the *perception* that one feels free to say what one thinks can produce feelings of satisfaction with group outcomes.[11] In his research on high- versus low-participation groups in organizations, F. B. Chaney found that attitudes became more positive and performance levels increased for members who participated in making decisions.[12]

Of course, the quality of group interaction affects the level of commitment. One of the surprising features of high-quality communication is the frequent expression and management of conflict. Without disagreement ideas remain untested. The willingness to engage in conflict is itself an expression of commitment to stick it out during tough times. Individuals who are not willing to express or listen to differences tend to be less committed to quality outcomes and to the group itself. Any group that can successfully manage conflict is likely to remain committed to the final decision it has reached. We will deal with the many benefits and pitfalls of group conflict in Chapter 7.

Disadvantages of Group Interaction

It would be unfair to suggest that group decision making is a panacea. Too often the advantages just listed give way to specific pressures that haunt group behavior. In Figure 1.3 we have categorized the disadvantages of group interaction into three types of pressures that every group must learn to manage in order to succeed: time pressure, social pressure, and ego pressure.

Time Pressure No matter how you look at it, groups take a lot of time to make high-quality decisions. At the simplest level, people can think faster than they can talk, so any form of oral communication will be more time-consuming than thinking through a problem. Add the time necessary for critically testing ideas, questioning facts, summarizing positions, soothing bruised egos, and reaching consensus, and you will recognize the slow nature of group process. The trade-off is that the slower group process can often result in better decisions. Even so, group members are likely to feel the pressure of time and may rush through a discussion without close scrutiny of ideas and opinions. A good group will often remind itself of the progress being made to counteract the feeling that things are moving too slowly.

Another pitfall to avoid is the use of arbitrary deadlines. Too often groups fail to think carefully about how to manage their time. The end result is usually one of two extremes. Either no deadlines are set and work never gets done, or the deadlines do not fit the nature of the work assigned and the quality of work suffers as members try to complete tasks in an impossible time frame. The best thing a group can do at the outset of a project is to assess the demands of the task realistically before proceeding. This means allowing sufficient time for

Some Potential Disadvantages of Group Decision Making

Time pressure
- Slow nature of group process
- Arbitrary deadlines

Social pressure
- Pressure to conform
- Groupthink tendencies
- Social loafing
- Reserve productivity

Ego pressure
- Fear of being dependent
- Individual domination
- Status apprehension
- Competitive climate
- Egocentric communication

Figure 1.3

each phase: establishing goals, defining the issues, finding the relevant facts, and creating and exploring potential solutions, for example. The common practice of setting arbitrary limits (usually one hour) for most meetings may be unrealistic. The number and length of meetings should match the nature of the task, with the understanding that many unexpected issues will probably be raised. Group process takes time. If proper time cannot be allotted, you should abandon the group process as the mode of decision making or modify the goals of the task to make it more manageable. Although some individuals may thrive on stress and only work well under the pressure of a deadline, the group is more likely to suffer a breakdown if it pursues impossible goals.

Social Pressures Time is not the only enemy of group decision making. Groups, as we know, are social units, and they constantly face social pressures. One of the major ones is the pressure to conform to group norms. Groups will frequently accept the first feasible solution that seems acceptable to the majority of members, while other, perhaps superior, solutions go unexamined. In an early study, L. R. Hoffman and Norman Maier found that the first solution that received a substantial positive response ended up being the group's choice 85 percent of the time, regardless of its quality.[13]

Closely linked to the pressure to conform is a phenomenon known as *groupthink*, the tendency of a group to minimize the critical testing of ideas because of a fear that such conflicts will create disharmony. Groupthink usually happens in very close-knit groups; their history of intimacy heightens the pressure to conform beyond normal levels. (Chapter 12 says more about groupthink.) Sometimes the social pressure moves in the direction of goofing off more than working. Researchers point to *social loafing* as the outcome when group members believe that their own individual effort will not be recognized or cannot be identified, so they put less energy into their work.[14] One way to counteract this tendency is to use the group's division of labor. By assigning separate and identifiable tasks to each person, members will receive greater recognition and be less likely to loaf.

Finally, the group itself may develop a norm of *reserve productivity*. This occurs when group members know they can be highly productive, but implicitly or explicitly agree to limit their output, often to reduce the expectations of those in authority.[15] Workers on an assembly line, for instance, often pace themselves so that they achieve the minimum rather than the maximum quota set by management. Any individual who overproduces is likely to be chided and urged to conform to the group norm.

Ego Pressures In spite of the social pressures just mentioned, individuals in groups still need to protect their self-concepts and maintain a level of self-esteem. To succumb repeatedly to group pressure threatens one's sense of self. As a result, the group may become a stage where members play out a variety of ego-defensive strategies. You may have already experienced the fear of being dependent that dooms many groups right from the start. Some individuals simply cannot stand to have their fate determined by a group. The loss of control is too much for them to handle. This frequently happens in the classroom, and it often afflicts some of the brightest students. They would rather do the whole project on their own than risk failure in a group they cannot control.

You have also probably seen groups suffering from domination by a single individual. Some people find the group arena the perfect place to satisfy their personal needs for control or leadership and so feel compelled to initiate most of the conversation and to respond with the last word to every proposal. Unfortunately, the person who talks the most is not necessarily the one with the best ideas. Other group members often play into the hands of such people by not acknowledging their own responsibility to present alternative points of view and to challenge the ideas of "the talker." Nothing saps a group's energy like a dominating member.

Inhibiting factors are often more subtle. *Status apprehension* is the raised anxiety level that group members experience when they anticipate communication with someone perceived as having higher status. The result is often silence or acquiescence to the ideas of members seen as having more status. A number of research studies demonstrate the negative effects of status distinctions among group members.[16] In this case it is the silent member who is ego defensive, who fears judgment and rejection. He or she will usually withdraw unless the status barrier is broken down.

Not every group suffers from an imbalance in participation, but any group may experience other ego problems. Sometimes the essential airing of conflicting viewpoints develops into a competitive climate that destroys group effectiveness. This happens when group members allow the individual goal of winning the argument to take priority over the shared goal of solving the problem. People become committed to their own ideas before a thorough effort has been made to critique those ideas. This is one of the most difficult tendencies to overcome because ideas are often treated as personal property. When someone attacks or ignores your idea, it is difficult not to feel personally affronted.

A final tendency noted in group behavior is *egocentric communication.* You have no doubt been in groups where it seemed as if members were politely talking past one another or simply taking turns giving private speeches on the topic at hand. Dean Hewes has offered a recent explanation for this phenomenon.[17] According to Hewes, groups often engage in a pretense of communication because each individual has limited information-processing capabilities. Group members are involved in the multigoal task of reasoning their own way through a problem, listening to the ideas of others, managing fragile social relations, and trying to integrate all that is said and done. It is an impossible cognitive task. So members compromise in two ways:

- They manage the task by engaging in *egocentric speech* (only thinking and talking about their own private line of reasoning).
- They manage taking turns and social relations through the use of *vacuous acknowledgments* (statements that recognize the previous speaker but do not indicate comprehension of the point he or she made).

Hewes offers an example of such a vacuous statement:

> C: How about building an underpass for bikes on Sierra?
>
> D: *I can see your point, but* how about more money being put into traffic lights?[18]

In short, groups frequently circumvent effective communication and make decisions not on the basis of thoroughly examined arguments and proposals but simply according to who pushes their own private reasoning the hardest. Most of the advantages of group decision making we have discussed all but disappear when this happens.

Group Versus Individual Decision Making

The advantages of divided labor, comprehension, and commitment will not always be reason enough to choose group over individual decision making. Likewise, the fact that groups often get in their own way and create obstacles to good decisions should not dissuade us from using the group mode. What we need are some guidelines for distinguishing *when* groups are preferred. The best evidence to date suggests that we should carefully review some basic tasks

When Is Group Decision Making Superior to Individual Decision Making?

Decision/Task Requirements	Individual	Group
Routine decisions: Decision is relatively simple or guidelines already exist.	✔	
Time constraints: Decision needs to be made quickly; extremely negative consequences if decision is not immediate.	✔	
Technical expertise: Decision requires the knowledge or analysis of highly trained specialists.	✔	
Idea generation: Task requires that many creative ideas be generated.	✔	✔
Group commitment: Decision will require group acceptance before it can be successfully implemented.		✔
Integrative tasks: Decision will require knowledge, perceptions, or skills that a single individual is unlikely to have.		✔

Figure 1.4 Use these guidelines to assess any decision-making task. The particular requirements of the task should help you determine whether or not group decisions are likely to be superior to individual ones. (Note that idea generation can be accomplished efficiently by individuals or in groups using the "ideawriting" technique. See Chapter 6.)

(see Figure 1.4) and determine whether they apply to our particular decision-making situation. Let us look at each of these requirements briefly.

In many situations, a group can expect some tasks to recur with irritating frequency. The group may have already established some procedure for handling the task and can therefore leave the decision to the judgment of individuals, assuming that they will employ the recognized procedure in a reasonable manner. Decisions that require high degrees of precision and coordination in pressured situations do not permit discussion. Military exercises are a good example; decisions are usually made by the book or at the discretion of the commander in the field. The longer you work with a group, the more adept you will become at understanding what a group considers to be simple or routine decisions.

As noted earlier, group decision making takes time. You should always assess the amount of time you can afford to work through a group decision and weigh that against the group's desired goal. If time is of the essence or quality is not crucial, then you can probably live with the decision of the most qualified individual. On the other hand, if group commitment to the decision is essential, the possibility of modifying the goal to fit the time constraints is worth considering.

Some individuals have been trained to deal with certain problems. If the decision task falls clearly within the domain of an expert, and such a person is available, you may not want to waste time employing the efforts of the group. You should, however, always question the match between the complexity of the problem and the range of the expert's knowledge. Most problems in our society are beyond the grasp of single individuals with narrow specializations.

If the task requires broad perspective, fresh ideas, or a novel approach to an old problem, the group would seem to be the best form of attack. In the late 1950s, Alex Osborn championed the use of "brainstorming," a technique in which a group generates ideas in a fast and furious manner, withholding evaluation until later. Conventional wisdom held that brainstorming groups produced a greater number of and more creative ideas. But this assumption has been questioned recently. In trying to demonstrate the superiority of the brainstorming technique, researchers have discovered that it has some pitfalls as well. In short, those people who are comfortable in group settings seem to produce more ideas as a result of interaction, but apprehensive members are often inhibited by the process.[19] The latter do better in "nominal group" settings where members individually generate ideas on paper prior to discussion. We will look at the details of these specific techniques in Chapter 6. Thus the question of how to generate more creative ideas depends on fitting the idea-generating practice to the people in the group. If the group has overcome the inhibitory effects of status and member apprehensions, then group discussion will probably improve the number and perhaps even the quality of ideas. Otherwise, silent generation of ideas by individuals followed by thorough discussion will be more productive.

Any time you size up a decision-making task, you should consider this question carefully: Will you need the group's enthusiasm or its cooperation once the decision is announced? If the answer is yes, then the group needs to feel that it played an important part in making the decision. Commitment from the group is necessary any time the group sees an issue as important, especially if group members will be responsible for carrying out the decision. Similarly, group decisions are preferable when issues are especially controversial or of a sensitive nature. Such a decision may have far-reaching consequences on other groups in an organization or the community at large. Any issue that seems to involve office politics may have to be decided by a group to avoid the appearance of the decision maker playing favorites. In such situations, the group should be composed of members representing different backgrounds and points of view to ensure greater commitment. As a group participant, you need to be sensitive to the politics within your group and within the larger organization or community of which the group is a part.

The final consideration for group versus individual decision making is the question of whether or not the task rquires the integration of knowledge, perceptions, or skills held by different group members. For instance, a company's decision to change a product that it has produced for years would require a knowledge of product design, marketing, and cost factors as well as perceptions about how the change might affect employee morale and consumer loyalty.

All of these task requirements are important. There is no set rule about which concerns matter more than others. You will have to weigh each of them and find the appropriate balance in each case. But these general guidelines will at least help you focus on one of the most important first questions about the group decision-making process: Is the issue an appropriate one for group discussion?

Summary

This chapter has focused on the advantages and drawbacks of group interaction. We have noted the major characteristics that define groupness and help build a sense of teamwork: common goals, a network of communication, interdependence in accomplishing tasks, unique roles that define each member's contribution, a set of shared norms, and a sense of wholeness to unify members. We have also pointed out the need to take advantage of group factors such as the division of labor, the greater ability to comprehend issues by pooling information, sharing perspectives on issues, and inspiring more creative ideas. At the same time, we recognize that groups can foster negative tendencies such as impatience with the group process, social pressure to conform to the majority view, and ego pressures. In addition, we have stressed the group process as one of the most viable forms of decision making, especially when tasks require integration and widespread commitment is needed to carry out a decision.

Frequent participation in group decision making will not automatically qualify you as a capable member. You must begin now to acquaint yourself with the underlying dynamics of group communication. We will help you do that in the following chapters, just as your instructor will help you put this knowledge to work in the classroom. You have already considered what it means to be a group and what happens when we portray communication as a powerful and active process of creating task and social realities. What you do with these ideas and future ones that you encounter in this text is up to you. They afford you an opportunity to make a real difference in the groups in which you work and socialize.

GroupQuests: Discussion Questions

1. At the beginning of the chapter, we raised the issue of which comes first—the individual or the group? Which is the most basic social unit? Think of as many reasons as you can for why the individual should be considered primary. Then identify reasons why the group is primary. Is there any way to resolve this chicken-and-egg problem? Does it matter which view we adopt?
2. We have described several advantages and disadvantages of working in groups. Compare your experience in groups with these characteristics. Can you think of additional advantages or disadvantages? Can you think of ways to turn any of the disadvantages into a plus for the group?
3. Try defining the concepts of *group* and *communication*. Compare your definitions with those in the chapter.

GroupWorks: Group Activities

1. Brainstorm a list of ten problems that need to be solved on your campus or in your city. Then analyze each problem in terms of the six task characteristics listed in Figure 1.4 and conclude whether or not the problem requires individual or group deliberation. Did you discover any important characteristics not listed in Figure 1.4 that should be considered when making such a decision?
2. Form groups of five or six members. Have each person write a definition of a group on a large sheet of newsprint or posterboard. Post these definitions where everyone in the group can see them. Discuss each definition in turn, focusing on how that definition helps you to understand what it takes to "become a group." You may want to combine your ideas into a single definition. Conclude by discussing what a newly formed group might do to help itself become a full-fledged group.
3. Choose a decision-making group on campus or at work that you can observe without your presence disturbing the group too much. If the group agrees, audiotape the meeting for further study. Select three negative and three positive group tendencies and record instances of these tendencies occurring in the group. For instance, record statements of *egocentric speech* or *vacuous acknowledgments* as a pretense of communication. Try to determine any consequences of these actions (a poor-quality decision or low group morale, for example). Write your observations in a separate journal or share them with the class.
4. Rent a videotape of the movie *The Breakfast Club* or a similar movie that focuses on the behavior of a small group of people. As you watch the film, look for evidence of the defining characteristics of a group discussed in the chapter. Ask yourself whether the people involved have really *become* a group. How well do they measure up to the prototype? Is the group likely to continue intact beyond the end of the film? Why or why not?

GroupActs: Practical Applications

Your professor will place you in a group to begin a group project. The group should meet and identify its project and discuss what members expect from each other in terms of:

1. *Project goals:* What does each person envision as the outcome(s) of the task?
2. *Working relationship goals:* What kind of working atmosphere would each person like to see established?

3. *Group norms:* What norms need to be established? Which ones should be avoided?

As you discuss each person's view of these issues, work toward consensus on what is desirable for the group as a whole.

CHAPTER 2

Prescriptive and Descriptive Group Process: Complementary Perspectives

Traditionally, experts in small group communication have proposed that groups adopt one of two approaches to decision making. In the first approach some elements are predetermined. The expert identifies the skills that group members will need and the discussion methods the group can use. The expert then prescribes a series of steps that *should* be followed (an agenda), who *should* perform specific communication behaviors (roles), and what format (technique) *should* be used to maximize high-quality decision making. This is a *prescriptive group process*. The emphasis is on members' developing and applying communication skills within some specified framework.

The second approach is a *descriptive group process*.[1] Proponents of this perspective generally believe that the prescriptive approach does not convey a truly comprehensive understanding of how groups develop and change. Its users acquire a smorgasbord of techniques and communication skills, which they tend to apply indiscriminately. In contrast, advocates of the descriptive approach emphasize the need for research and theory that describes the communication patterns that are most indicative of high-quality decision making. They believe that well-informed group members will implicitly understand and recognize which roles, techniques, and communication skills a given situation requires.

Those who subscribe to one of these approaches tend to consider the other one unsatisfactory. This is unfortunate because the two approaches can complement each other with effective results. After we look more closely at each of these perspectives, we will suggest some principles for integrating the two points of view.

The Prescriptive Group Process

The history of civilization is the story of human development. Daniel Boorstin's book *The Discoverers* chronicles some of our most significant inventions: the clock, compass, telescope, and printing press. These tools have changed the way we live by prescribing in new ways how we should think about life. For example, the calendar and the clock freed us forever from the "cyclical monotony of nature."[2] The clock sets the beginning and end of the workday; it assists us in deciding when to eat, when to make phone calls, and when to shop. Although the study of group interaction over the past fifty years has not yet produced any tools of this magnitude, it has led to the development of practices that enhance group performance and achievement.

To be prescriptive means to provide instructions or guidelines. When group practitioners offer such prescriptions, they are attempting to make the process of making decisions easier and more effective. Most prescriptive tools are either general outlines or specific techniques. For example, most problem-solving agendas include a series of steps to be followed—identify the problem, define it, gather relevant information—but do not tell the group *how* to perform each step. Specific techniques have been developed for accomplishing different aspects of decision making—for example, brainstorming to generate ideas—but very few systems have been designed that prescribe the entire group process. One exception is the group project facilitator (GPF), a system you will encounter in the special insert after Chapter 7. To give you some idea of the prescriptive approach, however, we will describe the most typical example of that approach, the standard agenda.

The Standard Agenda

The prescriptive approach has a long history and tradition in the study of group communication. Early in this century, John Dewey wrote *How We Think*, a book that indirectly influenced teachers of group discussion for decades.[3] Dewey analyzed the process of *reflective thinking*, or how individuals approach problem solving in a logical fashion. He speculated that once an individual perceives a problem, he or she will reflect on the nature of the problem for a while, identifying its causes or symptoms. This is followed by several logical steps, including listing possible solutions, mulling over advantages and disadvantages, selecting the best solution, and finally taking steps to implement the solution.

In the 1940s, Dewey's analysis was shaped into an agenda for leading small groups through the problem-solving process. Over the years, the steps have been modified a number of times, but the essential elements have been retained. You will encounter a standard agenda in our discussion of problem solving in Chapter 6.

If tackling a problem or making decisions by following these steps sounds logical, you may wonder if it is really necessary to inscribe them in stone and follow them so carefully. Don't these steps reflect a commonsense approach to decision making? Yes, but proponents of the prescriptive approach argue that groups do not always follow their own common sense. They need reminders to keep them on the straight and narrow path. As mentioned in Chapter 1, groups all too frequently follow the first good solution they generate and fail to consider other options carefully. The standard agenda reminds them to be more thorough in their analysis. A well-designed agenda is at the heart of the prescriptive approach.

Strengths of the Prescriptive Perspective

What is the value of following prescriptive processes such as the standard agenda and other techniques? First, *prescriptions provide the group with an organized plan of attack.* An agenda structures the way a group spends its time and serves as a reference point for maintaining progress toward goals. A group member, sensing that others are going off on tangents, can call the group back to the task by asking what step of the agenda is being discussed. The rules for brainstorming (see Chapter 6) or conflict management (see Chapter 7) serve as similar reference points. Researchers have demonstrated that some people prefer more structure than others do, so some groups may follow prescriptions by the book, while others use them as guidelines. But prescriptions do give the group a sense of confidence that they are proceeding in a manner that others have found to be successful.

A second strength is that *prescriptive designs make members more conscious of the group process.* In *The Care and Feeding of Ideas*, James L. Adams argues that formal decision-making techniques help override the brain's tendency to process information in a largely unconscious (but highly efficient) manner. He thinks that formal procedures help us focus *consciously* on what we are attempting to do and remind us to evaluate difficult choices in a more systematic way. In the absence of formal procedures, we are much more likely to rely on long-held and often untested assumptions, which tend to be very conservative and uncreative.[4]

Prescriptions can also save time once the techniques are mastered. Of course, the complexity of the prescriptive design will determine how much time you save. Some techniques take ten minutes to learn; more comprehensive systems may require considerably longer. Someone must evaluate the time needed to learn the system versus the number of times the system will be employed and its perceived benefit to the group in the long run.

Weaknesses of the Prescriptive Perspective

The prescriptive approach is not without its shortcomings. Several critics have noted that most prescriptive tools assume rationality and ignore the social-emotional dimension of group interaction. Decision making is characterized as a process of focusing only on the facts and the most logical way of organizing those facts. Most agenda systems treat the social dimension as something to be eradicated. Members' emotional reactions to ideas and to each other are viewed as unimportant. This is a serious problem because building a strong social dimension is crucial if a group is going to sustain the high motivational level needed to do a good job. But it need not be an inherent problem. A group might, for example, dispense with its task agenda occasionally and take a five-minute social break. Or group members can joke with each other while they perform task operations. Remember that groups should use (and modify, if necessary) prescriptive tools to fit the group's needs. It is detrimental to have the tail wagging the dog.

Another weakness of the prescriptive approach is closely related to the first. The prescriptive assumption that the best path to a decision is always a linear, step-by-step approach is inadequate. If a group does not consider ideas in the order specified by the agenda, it does not necessarily mean something is wrong with the group's approach. Suppose a group is attempting to define its problem as specified in the standard agenda. One member, intrigued by a particular way of looking at the problem, gets excited about a possible solution. Strict adherence to the step-by-step sequence would forbid comments about solutions. But *not* mentioning the idea may mean losing it. Most of us may forget an idea in two minutes, let alone the two weeks or longer it may take the group to reach the solution phase. In a now classic study, Thomas Scheidel and Laura Crowell discovered that groups rarely discuss and evaluate single ideas in such a lockstep fashion. Members are more likely to introduce ideas spontaneously, or alter each other's ideas, or change the topic, and go back and modify an earlier idea.[5] In fact, research has consistently shown that groups seldom spend more than sixty to ninety seconds on any given idea or theme before they shift gears and go on to something else.[6] From the prescriptive perspective, this short attention span is viewed as a logical flaw. Proponents of the descriptive approach see it as a virtue. Topic shifts can defuse mounting tensions, and the relatively slow process of emerging consensus allows the group to build commitment to the idea and to each other.

A final criticism is that using an agenda may produce overconfidence in group members such that they subsequently fail to do their best work. Dennis Gouran points out:

> Although (a systematic decision-making scheme) can be very useful in keeping a decision-making discussion focused on the requirements of the question, you can fall prey to the belief that the sequence itself, rather than the quality of mind it represents, is what determines a group's effectiveness . . . it would be

> a mistake to assume that by simply going through a set of steps a group will automatically make a good decision. What happens at each stage and how well necessary functions are executed are the real determinants of success.[7]

A group using an agenda should remember this caution every time it checks its progress.

In contrast to the prescriptive approach, other experts believe that general knowledge about communication and group dynamics is the best way to produce high-quality decisions. They prefer the descriptive approach.

The Descriptive Group Process

The goal of the descriptive perspective is to inform us about communication patterns and other group dynamics that make a difference in the quality of group decisions. The better our understanding of these patterns, the greater the likelihood that we can more accurately diagnose group situations and therefore help our groups make better decisions. The late Aubrey Fisher was one of the leading proponents of approaching group decision making from a descriptive point of view. He believed that groups could be equally effective with or without instruction in the use of agendas. According to Fisher, there is a common and identifiable pattern of communication concerning task and social issues that emerges in nearly all successful groups, a pattern we will describe later in this chapter. Fisher discovered the importance of this pattern quite by accident.

> As an instructor in a group decision-making class in which I taught the use of the agenda, I soon found that members of the groups seemed to be making decisions *despite*, rather than *because of*, their step-by-step outline-agendas. I even attempted an experiment in one class in which I assigned the same task to different groups and asked one set of groups to use an agenda based on Dewey's reflective-thinking pattern. I gave no such instructions to the other groups but left them on their own. All of the groups arrived at consensus on similar decisions. More important, each group appeared to reach those consensus decisions in a similar manner, with or without the assistance of an agenda. . . . I came to believe that a natural process is present in all or nearly all successful decision-making groups, whether they use an agenda or not.[8]

Fisher believed that the best way to improve group decision making was for researchers to observe and describe the communication behavior of groups that made high-quality decisions (rated by expert judges) and compare their group process to that of groups that produced lower-quality decisions. Let's look at how Fisher conducted his research in support of the descriptive process.

Fisher's Leaderless Group Discussion

To know what an effective group looks like without any prescriptive aids, it makes sense to look first at the totally autonomous group as an example of that process. Fisher offered the leaderless group discussion (LGD) as the best place

A group project involves both task and social communication.

to start describing group process. An LGD is "a group with 100% capacity for and freedom of self-regulation."[9] This does not mean that no one exerts leadership in the group. It simply means that no external force has imposed leadership or any other structure on the group. A "pure" group of this type would have no assigned leader, no agenda, no history, and no member starting with higher status than any other member. All of these characteristics would have to be achieved through members' actions within the group. Under these conditions, the group process could be observed in its most natural state, because there would not be any unnatural restrictions impeding its development.

Fisher acknowledges that the "pure state" is realistically impossible. No group exists in such a vacuum. Most working groups in society have a number of imposed structures—a chairperson, an agenda, and a defined goal, for example. Even a largely autonomous group made up of volunteer members, such as a quality circle, must take into account the organizational context in which it exists. But to argue that the LGD is unrealistic is to miss the point. Every group is leaderless to some extent. Classroom groups probably come closest to a pure LGD situation. But some, if not many, aspects of group structure are not prescribed. Often the leadership position is assigned, but the degree of authority, leadership style, and other matters (norms, work routines) remain to be worked out by the group. Even in the most formal group, an informal network of roles tends to develop. You may have participated in groups where the assigned leader was largely ineffective, but the group found ways to work around him or her. In such a group, you can see the group process evolving.

The study of essentially leaderless groups has produced some very useful knowledge about group process. Let us look at the communication patterns that tend to distinguish effective groups.

The Phases of Group Development

One of the earliest and most consistent research findings is the observation that leaderless groups tend to follow their own kind of natural agenda. Fisher and others have identified a four-phase sequence of focused interaction characteristic of effective groups.[10] We will describe the basic pattern here and discuss variations of it in more detail in Chapter 11. The typical pattern consists of periods of time devoted to orientation, conflict, emergence, and reinforcement.

Most new groups spend their first meeting or two just getting acquainted with themselves and their task. This *orientation phase* enables group members to reduce some of the uncertainties they have about each other and begin to build a social dimension. One of the initial difficulties a group has is overcoming primary tension. *Primary tension* is the uneasiness that members feel when they first meet.[11] It is the "ice" that has to be broken before members can start to feel comfortable with each other. Nervous laughter, overly polite behavior, and avoidance of disagreement are typical of this first phase. Primary tension usually (but not always) subsides after one or two meetings. At the same time, communication also focuses on building a clearer understanding of the group's task or charge. Effective group members try to clarify what their goals are during this phase. Fisher found that during orientation members tend to respond to each other's idea proposals with ambiguous feedback.[12] In other words, members avoid making their true feelings known because they are not yet comfortable enough to take a stand on any issue.

Many ineffective groups will minimize the need to develop a strong social dimension and jump right into the task at hand. In the long run, they pay a heavy price for this inattention to group building, as motivation and interest wane. And as we said earlier, many prescribed agendas (such as the standard agenda) also downplay the social dimension, encouraging the group to tackle its task immediately. Some ineffective groups go too far in the opposite extreme. They overemphasize the social dimension so much that negative patterns such as social loafing and extreme pressure to conform get established. Effective groups strike a balance between socializing and developing a consensus on the nature of the task ahead of them. In most groups, the orientation phase lasts one or two meetings.

Once group members begin to feel comfortable with each other and their understanding of the task, they are ready to manage the *conflict phase*. In this phase, members argue about how the problem should be defined and about the relative merits of relevant ideas, information, and proposals for solutions. This is the phase in which most groups succeed or fail. If members fail to successfully orient themselves, most groups back off when disagreements arise. If they have not built any positive identification as a group, their social bonds are too fragile to withstand conflict. If they do not clearly understand their task, disagreements become disruptive and the group seems to flounder aimlessly. Or if the group has become too socially oriented, conflict may be seen as a threat to cohesiveness.

The group that has managed the orientation phase well is more likely to feel free to disagree because members are comfortable as a group but have not lost their individuality to the emerging social dimension. The ambiguity of the orientation phase disappears as members state how they really feel about various issues under discussion. Similarly, the greater the clarity and comprehension of the task, the better group members will be at understanding and resolving their differences of opinion. Effective groups tend to spend a lot of time in the conflict phase, as they try to carefully and thoroughly test ideas and proposals. In contrast to the primary tension of the orientation phase, the conflict phase is characterized by *secondary tension*, the feelings of uneasiness sparked by disagreements or critical evaluations of one's ideas.[13] Note that effective groups learn to manage secondary tensions—not by squelching them, but by encouraging disagreement until it begins to threaten relationships, then allowing some time for the tension to subside. Chapter 7 presents more specific techniques for managing conflicts.

The *emergence phase* is a transition from the heated conflicts of the previous period to the back-patting congratulations of the final phase. It reflects how effective groups resolve their differences and maintain good social relations among members. In this phase, the decision on a major issue or the solution to the problem becomes clear to everyone in the group. Decisions are not usually announced, but emerge slowly as a consensus is being built. Effective groups move slowly enough for everyone to become comfortable with the ultimate decision, especially those who might have opposed the idea during the conflict phase. Fisher discovered that some group members (who earlier disagreed with the emerging consensus) respond to the idea ambiguously for a while, before finally offering their full support.[14] Why? Apparently, ambiguous responses allow members to change their opinion while keeping their dignity intact. For example, a member might say, "I still have some reservations, but you've convinced me that this idea has more potential than I originally thought." Such a statement is not a wholesale endorsement, but it indicates that the member is willing to give the idea more thought.

Many times the ineffective group will resort to compromise or voting too early in its deliberations and short-circuit the process by which commitment is built for a decision. Imagine that you were strongly opposed to one aspect of a proposed solution; for example, given the current state of the treasury, you are bothered by the cost of a new bus to transport your church's youth group. How would you feel if the group summarily voted to buy the new bus without giving your objection its due consideration?

The final phase of decision making is the *reinforcement phase*. This is when members celebrate their decision and commit themselves to working out the details of their plan and how it will be implemented. Ineffective groups have often used up all their motivation by the time this phase rolls around.

Effective groups learn to manage all four of these phases. Ineffective groups tend to mismanage, skip, or get bogged down in one or more of the phases. To the extent that this happens, the group has veered off the natural course of group decision making.

Although this simple four-phase model accurately describes the path that many successful decision-making groups follow, there are exceptions and variations. Research by Marshall Scott Poole and his associates reveals that there may be several different paths to success, depending on the complexity of the group's situation and how the group manages its task and social dimensions.[15] Poole's work questions the simple movement of a group through the phases in blocks of time, but it does not question the importance of social orientation, conflict management, and the emergence of decisions. As an example, a group that has been together for a while but is tackling a new problem will not require much social orientation, but may need considerable time to orient itself to the new task. Thus its "orientation" period may be disjointed. Socially, the group may have moved on to the conflict stage, as members feel comfortable enough to disagree, but the exact nature of their conflict is not clear because they have not yet figured out exactly what they are supposed to be doing. Likewise, some fairly simple decisions may not create as much conflict as usual. The implications of Poole's research will be examined more thoroughly in Chapter 11.

Descriptive Communication Patterns in Effective Group Process

It is rare to observe the group process in its "pure state," but several descriptive features will help you recognize effectiveness at work. One of these features is the relatively slow process of organizing the group. It takes time for group members to adapt to one another and to develop an understanding of what they are trying to accomplish. Once the group gets down to the business of making decisions, it also takes time for those decisions to emerge naturally. This is why successful groups rarely short-circuit the four-phase pattern of group interaction altogether. Members are sensitive to the amount of time it takes to build a commitment to the group and to a winning proposal.

Another key aspect is the development of a group culture, which includes the behavior patterns, beliefs, rituals, and general way of doing things that make members feel that their particular group is unique. As with most group processes, it takes time for members to get to know one another and to create communication rules that will govern their social and task interaction. Mutual attraction among members and participation in group rituals and norms helps create a cohesive group culture.

A third key element is the natural emergence of leadership and other roles. In contrast to the prescriptive approach of formally establishing roles and rules, these entities emerge as the result of members' task and social communication and feedback. Remember that informal leadership can emerge even when the leader's role is formally assigned.

Finally, you should see the emergence of a vigilant communication climate in the group. Group members in such a climate demonstrate "a sensitivity to the need for careful and thorough examination of the information on which a choice rests."[16] A number of group researchers have begun to pinpoint specific communication behaviors that contribute to a vigilant climate. An effective group:

- Thoroughly investigates a wide range of alternative courses of action
- Carefully considers the negative as well as positive consequences that could result from each alternative
- Questions members' statements for hidden or inaccurate assumptions
- Intensively searches for new information to help evaluate each alternative
- Takes new information into account even when it does not support the course of action the group favors
- Bases decisions on accurate and reasonable premises
- Reexamines all the alternatives before making a final decision
- Makes detailed plans for implementing the chosen solution, including contingency plans if circumstances change[17]

In short, the descriptive approach to group process has identified some aspects of group communication that tend to produce high-quality outcomes. As research continues, other patterns will no doubt be discovered. Recognizing these patterns will help you determine particular communication behaviors to encourage or discourage as you work in groups. In time you will become more sensitive to the complexities of group interaction. Do not try to understand everything about groups at once. For now, just realize that you are learning to perceive the hidden dimensions of group interaction; later, you will be able to see even more.

Strengths of the Descriptive Perspective

As you might expect, some of the weaknesses of the prescriptive approach are seen as strengths from the vantage point of the descriptive group process. *Advocates of the descriptive approach see the social and task dimensions as equally important* to a group's success. This perspective focuses on such issues as how a group handles primary and secondary tension and how members are allowed to save face through the strategic use of ambiguous communication. How group members feel about their group affects their motivation to produce solid, high-quality outcomes.

Perhaps the most important aspect of this viewpoint is that *it encourages group members to be full-time participant observers.* Each participant is inspired to continue to learn from every new encounter with a decision-making group. This open-ended approach essentially says, "We do not yet know all of the differences between effective and ineffective groups, but here is what we know so far." This is no doubt harder than simply following the prescriptions of experts, but it can be more enlightening. You may discover something new and exciting about how groups can work more effectively.

Another advantage of the descriptive perspective is that *it focuses attention on changes in communication behaviors over time.* Each of the phases of natural group development is defined in terms of the communication that occurs within that phase. This makes it relatively easy for participants to translate theory into practice. Your knowledge of what the overall pattern is like gives you a better idea of when it is appropriate to be tentative, conciliatory, or argumentative; when to seek or provide information; and when to work hardest at integrating ideas.

Weaknesses of the Descriptive Perspective

Although it overcomes some of the weaknesses of the prescriptive approach, the descriptive approach is not a comprehensive alternative to prescriptive practices. To date, advocates of the approach have left the impression that knowledge about group process is equivalent to producing an effective group process. In their distaste for an overly prescriptive approach, descriptive proponents have generally avoided the issue of application altogether. While descriptive findings suggest when some communication behaviors might be appropriate, there are very few specific guidelines for how a group could proceed through periods of orientation, conflict, emergence, or reinforcement. Even when armed with an extensive knowledge of group process, members need signposts that remind them to look for the presence or absence of specific kinds of interaction. We have witnessed too many groups that can explain their failure to be productive, but cannot find ways *on their own* to overcome an ineffective process. The necessary guidelines (from a descriptive perspective) have not yet been developed in any coherent fashion.

A second weakness is due to the first. Because the use of prescriptive tools is often eschewed, leaderless groups often make poor use of a very valuable commodity: time. In raising this criticism, we recognize that groups take time to develop a strong social dimension. But much of the floundering that goes on is unnecessary; the use of an agenda system coupled with an awareness of its limitations would help the group develop a healthy respect for time constraints. Most decision-making groups in a business organization or volunteer agency are short on time and expect formal systems of operation to be used. These factors make it highly unlikely that a purely descriptive approach will be adopted anywhere other than the classroom.

The strengths and weaknesses of both perspectives enhance the prospects for a combined approach. To date, the two approaches have been depicted as adversaries rather than teammates that complement one another. In the next section, we suggest some ways to use both perspectives, keeping their strengths and weaknesses in mind.

Integrating the Two Perspectives

Knowledge of group process and the use of prescriptive group designs can complement each other. An emphasis on either one without the other compromises effective decision making. Although descriptive knowledge of group process is invaluable, we are all subject to the limits of human memory. Well-designed prescriptions can serve as reminders. In addition, new knowledge about group interaction should lead to better prescriptions. To use prescriptive tools effectively in the context of our increasing knowledge of group process, we offer the following five principles for a combined approach:

1. *Adopt a prescriptive agenda system as a useful starting point.* None of the research reviewed earlier indicates that following an agenda system hurts the group's chances of making wise decisions. The choice of which agenda to follow is an important consideration and should be discussed during the initial meeting.
2. *Evaluate the agenda system thoroughly to make sure each phase includes adequate concern for the social dimension of the group, and modify it accordingly if it does not.* This might be a good assignment for a subgroup. Once an agenda system is chosen, have the subgroup create some modifications that allow the social dimension an opportunity to flourish. For instance, the subgroup might propose a rule of thumb that spontaneous socializing be permitted as long as it does not become excessive. The group would have to define what "excessive" is and perhaps assign someone to monitor such behavior. It would be counterproductive to dictate when and how much socializing should take place; what is needed is an understanding that a mixture of task and social interaction is healthy. Groups can do both at the same time if members relate to each other and the task with a sense of humor. There is really no need to stop doing the task in order to socialize.
3. *Develop a working knowledge of alternative prescriptive tools for generating ideas, sharing information, and making decisions.* Chapters 5 and 6 provide an overview of such tools. The effective group will know both how and when to use these tools. Remember that prescriptive tools do not make decisions—they only assist group members who make decisions.
4. *Analyze each prescriptive tool regarding potential positive or detrimental effects it might have on the group.* Descriptive knowledge of group process should be used to determine possible effects. The use of any prescriptive tool alters the pattern of interaction within the group. When a group brainstorms, for instance, members agree not to communicate negative reactions to ideas. When communication patterns change, there are usually both advantages and disadvantages associated with the new pattern. The group should realize how any tool can affect both the task and social dimension. This is especially critical if a particular tool will be used frequently or for a prolonged time. It might help to have a group member monitor the

effects that different tools seem to have on the group's spontaneity, energy level, seriousness, and other factors.

5. *Assign at least one member the role of process observer and schedule regular feedback sessions to talk about those observations.* This role, discussed more fully in Chapter 4, is very significant. Learning the principles stated here does little good if the group does not make a concerted effort to implement and sustain use of them. The best way to do this is to build into the agenda time to talk about how well you are doing as a group. Development of individual skills is important, but groups succeed or fail *as groups.* The only way to improve as a group is to set goals and monitor how well you are achieving them.

If your group takes these recommendations to heart, you can successfully integrate the best of the prescriptive and descriptive perspectives.

A Model of the Group Communication Process

To fully implement the combined approach just described, group members need to understand how communication works, especially in the group context. In this section, we describe a model of group communication that not only highlights its most crucial aspects but also serves as an organizing scheme for the rest of the text. This model and the succeeding chapters that focus on its parts are a full-fledged description of the group process and the role of prescriptive practices within it.

Defining Communication

We have already defined *communication* as a process in which people collectively create and regulate their social realities. What does this mean? A quick examination of the key terms will clarify our meaning. The idea of *process* implies events unfolding over time. Even the simple act of one person, Smith, greeting another, Jones, involves a sequence of events in time. Smith must first become aware of Jones's presence and then size up the situation and determine that a greeting is appropriate. That much accomplished, Smith has to encode or formulate a particular greeting ("Hi," "Hello, Ms. Jones," or "Hey there") and then verbalize the message with the proper intonation and other gestures. For her part, Jones must hear the message and decode its meaning (What did he say? Was he sneering at me?). At the same time, her nonverbal behavior provides feedback to Smith indicating whether she understood his message (a quizzical look) and how she feels about it (a slightly superior smirk on her face). Finally, she encodes a verbal response ("Oh—hello"). The sequence (message-feedback-response) may take less than two seconds, but it qualifies as a process. You can imagine how much more complicated a whole dialogue becomes, not to mention a conversation involving several people at once.

Another intriguing aspect of a process is that it does not have a definite beginning or ending. No one can pinpoint when a collection of people starts becoming a group. You may perceive that the group started to show signs of cohesion during its second meeting; someone else may say it was more like the fifth meeting. A third person may argue the group is not cohesive at all. The important point is that individuals act on their perceptions of the process.

People are always the most interesting part of the group process. Each of us brings different experiences, perceptions, and biases to an encounter. We are forever interpreting each other's messages in similar and dissimilar ways. We collectively create new meanings, new fads and fashions, and new group norms. Communication is a joint effort. A group member cannot create the reality of himself or herself as a leader without other members acknowledging it. Once a pattern of interaction is established, group members collectively regulate each other's behavior to conform to expectations. We do this through feedback that serves to sanction deviant behavior and reward conformity.

All of this collective action results in shared social realities, or beliefs, assumptions, and behavioral habits that are taken for granted. One leading social theorist has defined a social reality as "that which people believe that other people believe."[18] For group communication, three particular kinds of realities are significant: task, social, and procedural realities. How the group defines the nature of its various tasks reflects its *task reality*. This shapes the group's goals, the type of information it seeks, and ultimately, how well solutions work. The *social reality* encompasses all the relationships among members as well as the group as a whole; the social climate affects members' satisfaction and motivation to complete the task. Finally, the group that establishes a coherent *procedural reality* will be in charge of its own group process rather than the victim of it. Procedural reality refers to techniques and routines that the group assumes are the natural way to do group work. We will discuss these three functions of group communication at the conclusion of this chapter.

In addition to the assumptions implicit in our definition of communication, two additional ones are important: the nature of making meaning and the importance of context. They are crucial to an understanding of how communication works.

A group communication pattern is the joint creation of its members. These patterns consist of observable behaviors occurring in a predictable sequence. What the observable pattern means to each member is another story. Individuals often have very different interpretations of what is happening in their group. For instance, one group exhibits a regular pattern of about ten minutes of small talk at the beginning of each meeting. All of the members participate in this ritual, some more than others. But the *meaning* of the ritual is not the same for each member. Some believe that this period of small talk is essential to the group's cohesiveness. Others view it as a waste of time, but tolerate it because others seem to enjoy it. Another member interprets it as an opportunity to "get the goods" on members who "run off at the mouth." This person keeps mental records of information that group members believe they are expressing in confidence, and he waits for a chance to use it to his advantage. Messages have meaning on several levels. Similarly, the negative response to an idea ("That won't work on this campus!") can be interpreted as a statement of fact, as a prediction, as a criticism of the person who suggested the idea, or as an indication of the speaker's dislike for his own school. Even when meaning is highly shared at one level, members may disagree at other levels. And they may or may not realize it. It is probably a good idea to assume that misunderstanding is the rule to which understanding is the exception. Communication has always been a double-edged sword. Messages are frequently misunderstood, yet communication directed at avoiding or addressing a misunderstanding can promote shared meaning.

One reason people misinterpret each other's meanings is that they see the behavior in a different context. Edward and Mildred Hall define *context* as "the information that surrounds an event and is inextricably bound up with the meaning of that event."[19] For instance, messages exchanged in an executive board meeting are typically given more credence and status than messages exchanged in a hallway chat. In many cases, people simply do not know the history of a situation and lack all the information necessary to fill in the context. In other cases, they have the information but choose not to attend to it for one reason or another. The model depicted in Figure 2.1 represents some relevant aspects of group life that often surround interaction. As such, they are contexts—that is, information—that must be taken into account if we hope to understand our fellow group members' messages.

The Contexts of Group Interaction

The idea that context is important to communication is one most communication scholars share. The particular organizing scheme used here is derived from the theoretical work of Barnett Pearce and Vernon Cronen.[20] Their approach is very useful for diagnosing why a particular communication situation succeeded or failed.

Figure 2.1 depicts a typical group of six members. The round table in the center represents the level at which observable communication behavior takes place (the act level). All group members share this level of activity because they can see, feel, and hear nonverbal and verbal messages. The messages themselves are indicated by the symbol "∼∼." Each member has unique (as well as shared) ways in which he or she puts communication into context and thus interprets messages. Six levels or contexts are depicted: speech act, episode, individual, relationship, group, and cultural levels.

The relationships between different levels are a flexible hierarchy. In other words, one level usually serves as context for the levels below it in the diagram. For instance, acts are usually interpreted in the context of an episode, which is interpreted in the context of members' relationships and group structures. Note in the diagram that two of the levels (group and cultural) form continuous circles. This illustrates that knowledge at these levels of context is usually shared to a much greater extent than is knowledge at other levels. Group and

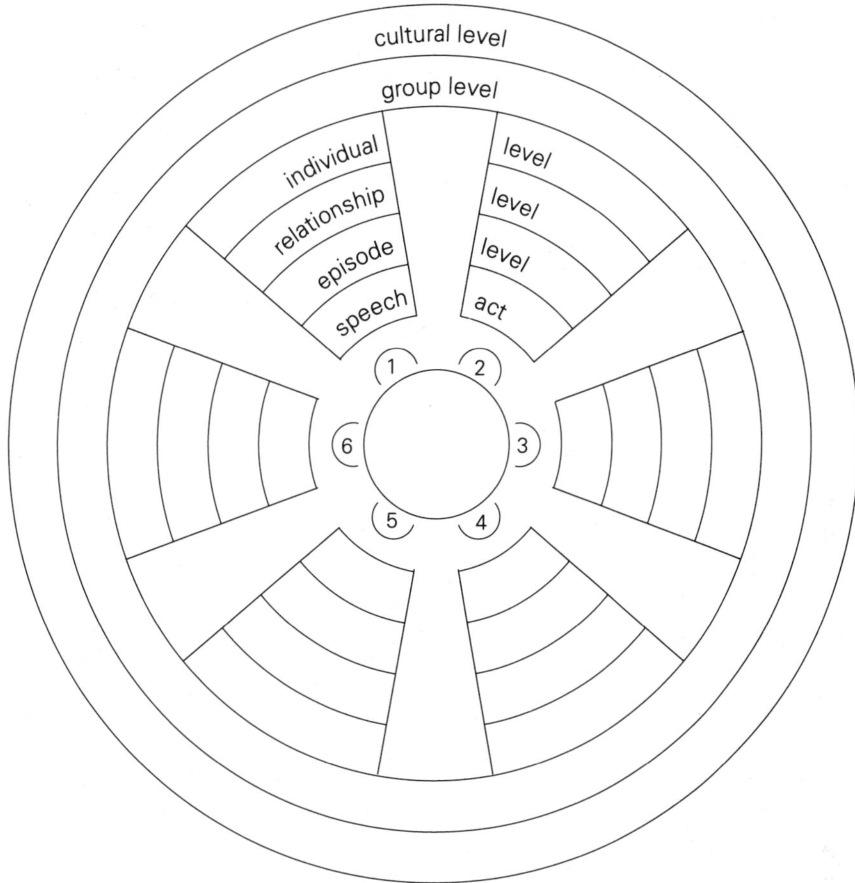

Figure 2.1 A model of the small group communication process.

cultural information is often taken for granted. Some group members might have highly shared views at other levels. For instance, two members may be close friends and would therefore know a lot about each other at the individual and relationship levels. Or a subgroup of three members who wrote and conducted a survey for the group would have more refined expectations for episodes of doing research.

In the following sections, we describe briefly the kinds of information that can come into play at each of the levels of group context. We start with the most observable level: speech.

Speech Act Level: Labeling Behavior This level of analysis is the *focal point* of meaning. All of the other contexts we have mentioned help us determine what meaning to attach to a specific action. At this level, we label speech and nonverbal behaviors act by act. The distinction between "speech" and "speech act" is crucial. *Speech* refers to the specific words used and *nonverbal behavior* indicates the gestures performed. The *speech act* is the summary label we place on speech plus attendant nonverbal behavior. For instance, the verbal statement "You don't have the slightest idea of what we are talking about, do you?" may have been intended as the speech act of "insulting one's intelligence." The recipient may have interpreted the message in the same way it was intended or may have taken it as a "joke" or a "reprimand" for not listening carefully. Other group members may have reached other conclusions. As we stressed earlier, the behavior may imply meanings at higher levels of context as well. When we send a message, the important component is what we intend our act to mean. Ideally, this means we have considered how other group members will likely interpret our action. When we receive a message, we interpret the other's act. A more detailed examination of the types of group speech acts follows in Chapter 4.

Episode Level: Situation as Context The meaning of a message also depends on how group members define the situational context. Some people think of a situation as all the relevant information of the moment (who is present, how they feel, what happened earlier in the day). We prefer the more specific term *episode* because it narrows our focus. An episode is a sequence of speech acts that are perceived as a whole, as part of the same general activity.[21] Some common group episodes include small talk, generating ideas, and evaluating solutions. Most episodes have clearly recognizable opening and closing routines. For instance, the question "What do you think of this nasty weather?" is an invitation to engage in an episode of small talk. Awareness of the episode helps group members realize when particular information or comments are relevant. Take the episode of "defining the problem." As the discussion unfolds, a member who suggests a solution is clearly not tuned into the episode. Other members can legitimately reply, "How can we push for a solution when we don't even know what the problem is?" People commonly misread the nature of the episode the group has engaged in. The tools and techniques for managing group episodes successfully are discussed in Chapters 5, 6 and 7, while the *Group Project Facilitator* describes a comprehensive (and highly prescriptive) system for conducting group projects episode by episode.

Individual Level: Persons as Context We often misunderstand each other because we bring such different backgrounds and expectations to group situations. Personality is the most obvious individual difference, and it affects how people send and receive messages. A person who defines himself as an aggressive "go-getter" rarely cautions a group to be conservative and may even find the group process stifling. People also bring different skills, knowledge, and experience to the variety of problems and concerns the group must face. Chapter 8 explores the significance of these factors.

Relationship Level: Interpersonal Relations as Context Group members act on the basis of both their individual and their group identity, but they also interact with each other on a one-to-one basis. Group members thus form more specific dyadic relationships that influence the group discussion. Some members will become friends; others will antagonize each other repeatedly. A difference of opinion may be interpreted as a personal insult because one friend assumed that another would support him on an important issue. Many of the following chapters comment on how to maintain positive relationships and manage conflicts between particular group members. Chapter 9 will focus on one unique group relationship, that of leader and follower.

Group Level: Group Process and History as Context The group process and the unique history of a particular group are also contexts that influence meanings at the act level. In addition, any prescriptive practices a group might use have their own built-in rules for how members should behave. Most groups are unaware that they fall prey to a dozen different group tendencies every day. The information is available in the group's own history and in its members' collective knowledge of all the different groups they have participated in. We can see it in the many bad habits and in the repeated successes of group after group. But most people do not use such information. You have the chance to become more aware as you study the group process. Chapters 10, 11, and 12 focus on the specific group processes of socialization, decision emergence, and managing social pressure.

Cultural Level: Society as Context A group inherits a great deal from its culture: basic values, patterns of thinking, personalities, a concept of time, views on topics, even beliefs about how people should behave in groups. As we saw at the outset of Chapter 1, the very concept of a group is more important in some cultures than in others. Culture represents the shared codes of communication that we assume are our foundation. Even though we realize that some groups behave differently from others, and that every individual is unique, some patterns are so ingrained in us that we do not question their meaning. These are cultural patterns. The cultural context can be as large as East versus West, or as small as an organization or group. In Chapter 13 we look more closely at some of these cultural patterns and how they influence group decisions. The influence of culture is so overwhelming that we usually do not recognize it until we encounter someone from a totally different culture.

We strongly encourage you to think of the context of your everyday group interactions. Use this model to analyze a specific group episode in which everything seemed to fall apart. Or analyze a situation that seemed very productive. Figure 2.2 provides some diagnostic questions to help you apply the model. Look at the discussion from each group member's point of view. How do you think each person labeled the others' actions? Did each one frame the discussion as part of the same episode? Was there evidence of problems in relationships? In what way did the group's history or process contribute to the

Diagnostic Questions for Analyzing Group Communication

Context	*Questions to Consider*
Speech Act	**Descriptive Questions** 1. What do you think was the speaker's *intended* meaning in the message given? Could messages have been made clearer? How? 2. How do you think the message was *interpreted* by the various members of the group? Were some interpretations out of line? How so? 3. Was the message focused more on task, social, or procedural concerns? Did a problem arise because members focused on different concerns? **Prescriptive Questions** 1. What do you *intend* to convey to the group? How many different ways can you get the message across? (Focus on organization of ideas, examples you can use, and word choices.) 2. How are other members likely to *interpret* what you say? Will interpretations change if you alter some aspect of the message? 3. How will the message affect the group's progress on the task, its cohesiveness, and its procedural organization?
Episode	**Descriptive Questions** 1. Were all members concentrating on the topic of discussion or were there lapses of attention? If so, why? 2. How did group members define the episode in which the message/action took place? Did any one state his or her understanding of what the group was doing or was it taken for granted that everyone knew the situation? How might some members have defined the situation differently? **Prescriptive Questions** 1. How long can the group comfortably focus on one issue at a time? What can you do to help the group focus on its topic? 2. Given the meeting's agenda, what is the most appropriate time during the discussion to present your information, idea, or concern? 3. Do you need to remind the group about how your message fits the flow of discussion? Some members may forget the discussion's context.
Relationship	**Descriptive Questions** 1. Are there any ongoing relational problems between group members that might have contributed to the misunderstanding? 2. Could one or more members have misinterpreted the "relational" meaning of the message?

Figure 2.2 These questions are designed to help you apply the model of group communication in Figure 2.1. Use the descriptive questions to analyze communication behaviors from recent meetings and the prescriptive questions to help you plan important messages for future meetings.

Context	*Questions to Consider*
	Prescriptive Questions 1. How will the topic of discussion or the specific message you are planning be interpreted relationally? Will someone be offended? Feel left out? Picked on? Will someone feel honored or glad he or she came to the meeting? 2. Are there relational concerns that need to be dealt with so the group can concentrate on its task? How can these concerns best be handled?
Group	**Descriptive Questions** 1. Are there any group habits (norms, roles, methods of decision making) that might have influenced how members intended or interpreted messages? 2. Where is the group in terms of the phases of group development? Were messages exchanged today consistent with the current phase of development?
	Prescriptive questions 1. What significant features (values, working habits) about this group set it apart from other groups you have worked with? How will you need to adapt your usual style of communication to be effective with this group? 2. Do any group habits, norms, or roles need to be reconsidered?
Individual	**Descriptive Questions** 1. Are there any personal biases (beliefs, professional affiliations, communication styles) of group members that might have influenced how they reacted to each other's messages? 2. Did anyone have a bad day or seem otherwise preoccupied and unable to concentrate on the group?
	Prescriptive Questions 1. Which personality characteristics of various members seem most likely to either facilitate or inhibit the group's efforts? How can the members best manage each other's personality quirks? 2. Given the personality of each individual, how do you think each person can best be motivated to help the group achieve its goals?
Cultural	**Descriptive Questions** 1. Are there differences in the cultural backgrounds of group members that might have influenced how they reacted to each other's messages? 2. Is there any external pressure that might be partially responsible for what is happening in the group? Is this good or bad? Can it be controlled in the future?
	Prescriptive Questions 1. If group members are similar in cultural background, are there any assumptions that might be producing blind spots in the group's thinking? 2. Of the cultural values and customs that group members share, which are most likely to facilitate (or hinder) the group's task and social dimensions?

Box 2.1

The Coca-Cola Classic Caper: Analysis of a Decision

On April 23, 1985, the Coca-Cola Company shocked the country by announcing, "The best has been made even better." Coke, the world's best-selling soft drink, was to appear in a new formula known as "the new Coke." The decision was followed by three months of consumer outrage. On July 11, 1985, the company apologized and reintroduced the old formula under a new name, Coke Classic.

How could such a decision-making fiasco happen to a company of Coca-Cola's stature? Some people believe that the company planned the whole thing in the hope that lagging sales of the "old Coke" would skyrocket once it was reintroduced. Coca-Cola's response: "The truth is we are not that dumb and we are not that smart." But the case, as chronicled by Thomas Oliver in *The Real Coke, The Real Story*, is an instructive one for decision-making groups of any size. It illustrates many of the key factors in the model of group communication introduced in this chapter.

Cultural Level Influences

The decision-making process is always affected by external factors. This decision was no different. First, the key players were all high-ranking executives. As such, their attention was frequently diverted by other problems facing the company: regulative battles with the Federal Trade Commission, a major contract dispute with bottlers, and a new venture into the wine industry, among them. In addition, the organizational culture at Coca-Cola valued loyalty above all, which made it difficult for those who had reservations about the decision to disagree with top management; this led to a form of groupthink. The larger culture of consumers was changing also. Baby Boomers were more diverse in their values and tastes than previous generations, making it harder to promote Coke as the one drink for everyone. Another key external factor was the success of the competitor's nationwide taste tests known as the "Pepsi Challenge." This factor almost single-handedly narrowed Coca-Cola executives' focus to the issue of "taste" as the definition of their problem. Finally, several of the company's top executives were foreign born and could not possibly have known how deeply rooted the Coke image was in the American psyche. This combination of factors may have prevented the group from realizing the impact of their decision on the public.

Individual Level Influences

In every group, hidden agendas and personal views of individual members either augment or inhibit the quality of discussion. In this case, the group

Box 2.1 (continued)

that made the ultimate decision was composed of several key executives, each of whom brought different strengths and biases to the group. Two of them, Robert Goizueta (chairman and CEO) and Brian Dyson (president of Coca-Cola USA) had been highly involved in two previous decisions (the purchase of Columbia Pictures and the introduction of Diet Coke). The phenomenal success of these two decisions had built the two men's confidence levels to the point where they were willing to take further risks. One year earlier, Goizueta had made a prophetic statement, "There is a danger when a company is doing as well as we are. And that is, to think we can do no wrong." A third member, Donald Keough (president of Coca-Cola), originally lectured his fellow colleagues not to meddle with the taste of Coke, but later confessed that his original instincts "got lost in my mind." Here we see personal feelings of pride or instinct that somehow rose to the surface or got muddied in the waters of group discussion.

Group Level Influences

Several factors identified in Chapter 1 as negative tendencies were apparent in the decision-making process at Coca-Cola. The executives shared an ego obsession that Coke had to be the top-selling soft drink. This pressure prevented them from considering the option of having two products (old Coke and new Coke) on the market at the same time. The reason: Two Cokes would split the company's market share and Pepsi would most likely become number one. That outcome was intolerable to their collective ego. In addition, the fact that Pepsi was winning the taste tests led the group to accept the first best solution (the new formula) even though they could not anticipate the reaction. And contrary to their own conventional wisdom, the group's discussion of a fallback plan was inadequate. "Everyone was so infatuated with the project that no one would develop contingency plans," said one insider later.

Relationship Level Influences

Personality clashes and other relational problems between group members also had an impact. During an earlier dispute on syrup contracts with bottlers, the two then highest-ranking officers of the company, J. Paul Austin and Luke Smith, clashed so strongly that they literally stopped speaking to one another. The impact on the organizational climate was significant. Later, a minor group success story took place as the decision to bring back the old Coke was taking shape. The two top men, Goizueta and Keough, had already decided to bring the old formula back, but Keough

Box 2.1 (continued)

insisted that they wait a little longer to give Dyson, the most ardent defender of the new Coke, a chance to come to the same conclusion. Dyson did come around, and the senior executives avoided undermining his authority over American operations.

Episode and Act Level Influences

Our ability to analyze the episode and act levels of Coke's decision is limited because we do not know the details of actual conversation during crucial meetings. But one situational factor that the group overlooked bears mention. The glaring oversight was in the group's consideration of its own taste-test research. The company knew all along that approximately 10 to 12 percent of die-hard Coke drinkers would be upset at *any* change in the product, but tests showed that most people liked the taste of the new formula even better than Pepsi or the old Coke. What the researchers failed to do (and the decision makers failed to notice) was to tell those tested that the old Coke would no longer be available. So they never knew (from the research) how people would react to the loss of the old Coke as a national icon, as a symbol of American culture. In other words, they defined the problem too narrowly as a matter of taste alone.

In all fairness to Coca-Cola, it did survive its decision and has since flourished. What may well have been the saving grace was the decision makers' flexibility once they realized their mistake. And no doubt they have learned from that mistake.

Source: Thomas Oliver, *The Real Coke, The Real Story* (New York: Penguin Books, 1986).

problem (or its management)? What individual factors affected each member's behavior? Before long, we think you'll be able to identify what is going right and wrong in your group. To see how some of these questions can be used to analyze a real decision-making case, see Box 2.1.

The model is also useful for integrating the prescriptive and descriptive perspectives discussed earlier in this chapter. As a general principle, the lower levels of context are more amenable to prescriptive practices. Most of the prescriptive tools you will learn about were designed to operate at the speech act and episode levels. Prescribing small segments of behavioral interaction is much easier than designing the whole process. For the most part, an effective group process will enable the appropriate patterns to develop at the relational and group levels. Rather than prescribe interaction at these levels, it is probably best to periodically evaluate these levels (during feedback sessions led by the process observer) and talk about needed changes in more general terms or design your own group-specific prescriptions. Although not as easily accessible to the group, the individual and cultural levels also can be periodically discussed. Look for cultural patterns and individual needs that limit how the group defines a problem or inhibits the exploration of creative alternatives.

Functional Dimensions of Group Interaction

For some time now researchers have been most interested in what we have called the speech act level of group interaction. They have identified three general classes of communication behaviors and the speech acts they perform. We consider them functional dimensions of group interaction because most of these behaviors contribute to the achievement of group goals. We introduce the dimensions here and describe the specific behaviors related to each dimension in Chapter 4.

The social dimension includes all those behaviors that keep the group operating in a cohesive fashion. One or more individuals must assume the duties of helping the group manage tensions and promote an enjoyable atmosphere. Some people view the social dimension as a distraction that prevents the group from working on its task. This does happen, but most groups need a moderately successful social dimension. It usually helps motivate the group to work harder.

Most of a group's interaction is focused on the task it has been assigned. Some communication behaviors help the group do its job more thoroughly and make progress more rapidly. Most of these behaviors center on finding the most relevant information, asking the right questions, testing ideas, and contrasting or integrating different points of view. Fisher has demonstrated that not only does cohesiveness contribute to accomplishing tasks but that success in completing tasks can also foster feelings of cohesiveness.[22] It is surprising how often dissension among the members of a sports team, for instance begins to dissolve in the midst of a winning streak. The group's success in the task dimension begins to spill over into the social arena.

The third dimension of group interaction is concerned with how a group organizes itself to manage the other two dimensions. Procedural behaviors include setting goals and using the various tools and procedures identified in Chapters 5 and 6. Many groups do not pay enough attention to the procedural dimension, and the quality of decision making suffers as a result. Group members need to keep an eye on all three dimensions as the group process evolves.

Summary

This chapter presents the heart and soul of our approach to group decision making. At the outset we presented the strengths and weaknesses of both a prescriptive and a descriptive approach to group decision making. The prescriptive approach offers a group a detailed agenda to follow, but plays down the importance of the group's social dimension. The descriptive approach tells us a lot about how the social and task dimensions of groups work, but offers few concrete suggestions for acting on that knowledge. We offered a combined approach that stresses the need to choose prescriptive techniques based on your continually improving knowledge of group process. A thorough knowledge of group process will enable you to design your own procedures and produce a better fit between any particular group and the array of techniques available. Finally, we explored a model of group communication. This model offers a framework for understanding group discussions and the often unpredictable directions they take. It outlines the influence of a variety of contexts on the meaning of messages. Among these contexts are the speech acts themselves, the episode in which the acts take place, individual members' backgrounds and personalities, group members' relations, group process factors such as norms and phases of decision making, and organizational and cultural beliefs we often take for granted. We hope this model gives you new eyes to see beneath the surface of group interactions. With more perception, you should be able to make a difference in the groups to which you belong.

GroupQuests: Discussion Questions

1. What are the essential differences between the descriptive group and prescriptive group process? How are the two perspectives related? When should a group allow the natural group process to unfold? When should the group be more prescriptive? Does it make sense to integrate the two approaches?
2. Can you think of ways (other than those mentioned in the text) in which the prescriptive and descriptive approaches can complement each other?
3. Can you think of other contexts (besides those mentioned in the text) that might influence how members interpret each other's speech acts?

GroupWorks: Group Activities

1. Your instructor will divide the class into five small groups. Each group will be assigned one of the following contexts of group interaction as a topic for discussion: episode, relationship, individual, group, and culture. For its assigned topic, each group should create a list of different ways in which that context can affect how well the group is able to communicate. For instance, a discussion of episodes could focus on identifying the many different situations or tasks a group could find itself focusing on—for example, making decisions, solving problems, brainstorming, socializing. Once the list is complete, discuss each item in terms of how it might be mishandled or handled effectively by a group. When finished, a group spokesperson can share the list with the rest of the class or a legible copy of each list can be given to your instructor, who will make copies for everyone in class. This exercise can help you identify potential communication problems and be on the alert for ways of managing those problems.
2. Observe or audiotape a group meeting (or videotape an episode of family or group decision making from a TV show). Select for analysis an interesting segment of the meeting, perhaps one in which a disagreement, a misunderstanding, or even

an especially effective example of decision making takes place. Use the diagnostic questions from Figure 2.2 to help you analyze how the group's communication went awry or how it worked well. Record your observations in a journal or prepare a brief oral report for the class.

3. Plan an important message that you want to convey to a group of friends or co-workers. Use the prescriptive questions from Figure 2.2 to help you plan what to say and how to say it to the group. After you have discussed the topic or issue with the group, write a brief analysis of how effective the message was and whether or not the planning session seemed to help.

GroupActs: Practical Applications

If your group has already been assigned to a term project, take a few minutes to discuss any aspects of the natural group process that you have recognized at work in your group so far:

1. Discuss the extent to which the group has followed the typical phases of orientation, conflict, emergence, and reinforcement. At what phase is the group currently?
2. Consider any problems related to the fast or slow nature of the group's development. Is the group moving too quickly or too slowly for everyone?
3. Identify any aspects of group culture. Do members have a sense of being a group yet?
4. Examine the emergence or absence of leadership and other important roles. Have these roles helped or hindered? Why or why not?
5. Determine the extent to which the group has established a vigilant climate. Is the group careful in examining information, opinions, and ideas?

Part II

Group Communication Skills and Prescriptive Practices

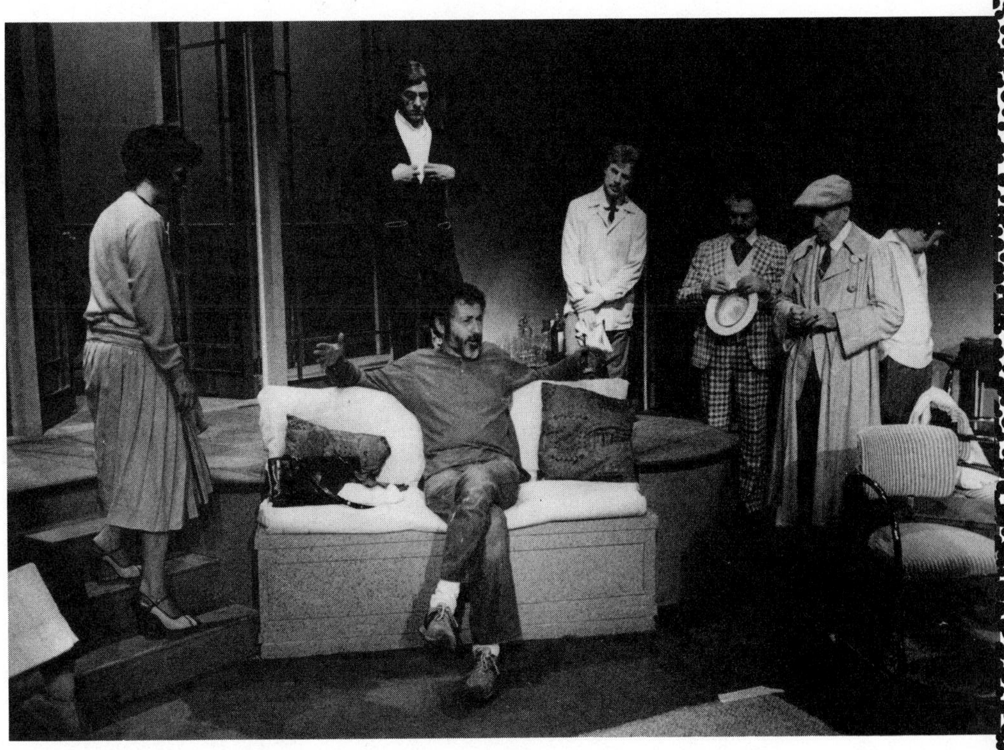

CHAPTER 3

The Speech Act Level: Preparing for Group Participation

Although much of a group's success in decision making is a direct result of how well members communicate their views, preparation for meetings has an obvious effect on the quality of each member's communication during meetings. Without adequate preparation, group discussions become little more than coffee klatches or opinion-sharing sessions. Anyone can have an opinion on a topic. It is something else to develop an informed opinion based on a realistic assessment of all the facts, statistics, and expert testimony available. In the narrow sense of the term, being prepared means finding information relevant to the next discussion topic, digesting it, and organizing it for presentation to the group. In a broader sense, being prepared means developing your research and reasoning skills, becoming informed on a wide variety of topics and issues, and bringing a proper attitude to group meetings. In this chapter, we review several ways that you can better prepare yourself for working in groups.

If you have worked in groups before, you know that not all group members are equally informed. Some people bring an enviable range of general knowledge with them. Others seem to know so little that you begin to question their qualifications. Some people can rattle off information from memory. Others have a facility for finding the needed facts from the library and other sources. Still others have a knack for asking the right questions to help the group decide if certain information is really valid or relevant to the problem under discussion.

All of these different skills are important to a group. Together, they contribute to the group's comprehension of its task, one of the advantages of group effort discussed in Chapter 1.

Ultimately, it helps if most group members can do all of these things well. When everyone has at least some knowledge of the topic, respectable research skills, and good reasoning skills, the group is still able to function when a given specialist cannot make it to a meeting. It is very frustrating to sit in a meeting when the "idea person" or the member who has all the information is not present. Many organizations now train workers as teams so that each member learns all of the skills necessary to perform the job. Thus while members specialize, they are also well versed about the total process. Members of successful decision-making groups need the same kind of general knowledge about the group process and overlapping skills that enable the group to work around problems like absent members. Let us look briefly at what it takes to improve our skills in each of these areas.

Research Skills

We are all easily impressed by the person who recites reams of information from memory, and more impressed when that person can offer a clear summary of that information. Such a person can be invaluable to a group when it takes stock of its knowledge on a given topic. Even so, a group would not want to rely solely on the memory of any one person. Such information would have to be checked and documented for use in formal reports and presentations. *The single most important research skill is knowing how to find information.* Toward that end, there are several things you can do to improve your chances of finding the right information quickly.

Learn how to use your library's resources. You may assume you already have this one covered. But you might be surprised at how much more proficient you can become in this regard. Every college library offers some form of guided tour of its facilities. Take the tour and take notes. Note every index, its purpose, its location, and how to use it. If you do not have enough time during the tour, retrace your steps afterward and ask a librarian for help. If your group has identified a topic to research, you may be able to schedule a group tour.

Develop your own mini-library of reference works. You can use numerous self-help books to refresh your memory or find unusual sources. You should probably purchase one or more books that address the following topics: planning research projects, finding information (guides to indexes and abstracts), evaluating information or arguments, and organizing and writing research papers. You also need general works: a dictionary, thesaurus, and style manual. We have included several suggestions in Figure 3.1.

Improve your skills at collecting information. Many group projects will need information that is simply not available in books or periodicals. For example, a college group was investigating the prevalence on its campus of

Reference Works for Group Members

Planning Research Projects

Rebecca Rubin, Alan Rubin, and Linda Piele, *Communication Research: Strategies and Sources* (Belmont, Calif.: Wadsworth, 1986).

Information Search

Alden Todd, *Finding Facts Fast,* 2nd ed. (Berkeley, Calif.: Ten Speed Press, 1979).

Charles Stewart and William Cash, *Interviewing: Principles and Practices,* 3rd ed. (Dubuque, Iowa: Wm. C. Brown, 1982).

Organizing/Writing/Presenting Project Reports

Marya Holcombe and Judith Stein, *Writing for Decision Makers* (Belmont, Calif.: Lifetime Learning Publications, 1981).

Marya Holcombe and Judith Stein, *Presentations for Decision Makers* (Belmont, Calif.: Lifetime Learning Publications, 1983).

Theodore Cheney, *Getting the Words Right: How to Revise, Edit and Rewrite,* 4th ed. (Cincinnati: Writer's Digest Books, 1987).

William Strunk and E. B. White, *The Elements of Style,* 3rd ed. (New York: Macmillan, 1979).

General References

Reference Books: A Brief Guide (Baltimore: Enoch Pratt Free Library).

The World Almanac (New York: Pharos Books, published annually).

Statistical Abstract of the United States (U. S. Bureau of the Census, published annually).

Figure 3.1

"the freshman fifteen" (the average freshman gains about fifteen pounds during his or her initial year at school). The members had plenty of data from nationwide surveys, but they did not know much about the habits of freshmen at their own college. More importantly, the group wanted to know what factors caused the problem (cafeteria food, too many late-night snacks, increased alcohol intake, lack of exercise). The group had to uncover this information on its own. The minimum skills they found necessary included designing a valid survey questionnaire, analyzing the data, evaluating published menus for caloric information, and interviewing a variety of health and nutrition experts. Fortunately, the group members had acquired the needed skills from their coursework in social science methods, statistics, and principles of interviewing. It might be worth your while to develop a plan of study that includes such courses if you expect to do a lot of group decision making in your future. For the short term, locate sources that can provide assistance in these areas in case you need to conduct interviews or surveys. Again, Figure 3.1 can help you get started.

Box 3.1

Put on Your Thinking Cap: Six Hats for Thinking

If you think there is only one way to think correctly, think again. According to Edward de Bono, perhaps the world's foremost thinker on thinking, there are at least six distinctive modes of thinking. And the sooner we learn to distinguish among them, the better our decision making. In *Six Thinking Hats*, de Bono identifies each mode and suggests ways to make sure you get the most mileage out of each one. He describes a process (complete with rules to follow) that allows group members to change hats without placing their fragile egos on the table every time they suggest an idea or comment on someone else's proposal.

One of the risks of a vigilant group is that members may overemphasize critical thinking in an effort to be thorough decision makers. De Bono rightly points out that it is often too easy to be critical. The usual result is what he calls "negative indulgence," or the satisfaction of proving someone else wrong.

To counteract this threat, group members need to know what other options are available to them and necessary to balance critical thinking. They also need to learn when to employ the various modes of thinking. Each mode is briefly summarized here. Visualize group members asking each other to put on the hat most appropriate for the task at hand. De Bono believes it is easier to shift gears if you associate each mode of thinking with a different color of hat.

1. *The White Hat.* This hat represents the neutral and objective kind of thinking we associate with computers. It is the Sergeant Friday approach, "Just the facts, ma'am." But not all facts are equal. At least two types of facts must be distinguished: first- and second-class facts. A first-class fact has been verified by documentation from credible sources. A second-class fact is one that a person believes to be true, but has not yet checked. Both are legitimate, as long as their class level is acknowledged. Opinions, on the other hand, are forbidden while the speaker is wearing the white hat. Opinions are not facts.

2. *The Red Hat.* The complement to the cool, detached white hat is the emotional perspective of the red hat. An easy way to remember the function of the red hat is to associate it with anger or seeing red. This hat allows members to express how they feel about a problem, idea, or solution. It is a license to describe one's own hunches, intuitions, and feelings without having to defend them at once. De Bono argues convincingly that this type of thinking has a place in group discussions. It helps the individual discover how he or she really feels about an issue, and it helps the group discuss reasons for decisions directly and honestly. De Bono offers a number of valuable suggestions for managing and communicating red hat thinking.

Box 3.1 (continued)

3. *The Black Hat.* This is the gloom and doom approach. When someone puts on the black hat, he or she can legitimately explore all the reasons why a solution might fail. In contrast to red hat thinking, the black hat thinker must go beyond feeling and search for logical reasons behind an emotional reaction. The black hat challenges facts identified under white hat thinking.

4. *The Yellow Hat.* Positive thinking is reserved for the sunny disposition of the yellow hat. It is the opposite of the black hat and should, in most cases, be worn *prior* to the black hat. Too much negative critique can kill an idea before it has a chance to prove itself. The yellow hat looks at the overall vision, the best possible scenario, the value of "if," and the logic of what is practical and beneficial.

5. *The Green Hat.* The color of fertility and creativity, this hat is put on deliberately to create new ideas, new alternatives, and new solutions to old problems. De Bono notes that this is the one hat that most people have trouble wearing. Creative thinking is difficult because we tend to become mired in the ruts of traditional thinking. The key to green hat thinking is learning the language or idioms of creative thinking: provocation, forward movement, random thinking, and other forms of what de Bono calls "lateral thinking." This type of thinking involves jumping from one frame of reference to another and searching for new ideas and concepts in such movement. De Bono's book *Lateral Thinking* describes techniques for creating and exploring this mode of thought.

6. *The Blue Hat.* The color blue represents the sky and its position over and above everything else. The blue hat is for controlling and organizing the whole thinking process. It is thinking about thinking. The blue hat thinker is both the procedural leader and the process observer. He or she helps plan or choreograph the thinking process and then critiques its evolution. ("We're spending too much time wearing our black hats. Could someone take a yellow hat view on this issue?") In effect, the blue hat thinker signals when it is time to switch hats.

De Bono visualizes using the six hats in much the same way that mapmakers use colors to highlight different features. Blue hat thinking lays out the map and oversees its construction. The red hat can be used to propose various routes to a destination ("Let's go by way of Orlando"). The white hat checks the facts concerning the trip and indicates whether or not the signposts exist. The black and yellow hats take turns pointing out the pitfalls and promises of scenic routes and potholes along the way. Finally, the green hat allows the mapmaker to overcome significant roadblocks and explore new routes.

The overall approach de Bono advocates runs the risk of being perceived as too cute. Some may not take it seriously. But such a view would be a mistake. This system has the potential to channel a group's thinking in a

Box 3.1 (continued)

productive manner and manage many of the conflicts inherent in group decision making. We strongly recommend his little volume as must reading for every potential group member. Ideally, every group should master this book before it establishes its ground rules for operation.

Source: Edward de Bono, *Six Thinking Hats* (Boston: Little, Brown, 1985).
Suggested reading: Edward de Bono, *Lateral Thinking: Creativity Step by Step* (New York: Harper & Row, 1970).

Reasoning Skills

The information your group collects will not speak for itself. The group must test the quality of any information and draw inferences from it. There are a variety of ways to think about the ideas, arguments, proposals, and data before and during meetings. Box 3.1 identifies six different modes of thinking used in group decision making. Note how the use of different colored "hats" to represent each type of thinking can be used as code words to stimulate the appropriate mode of thought. Two of these reasoning skills are developed more fully in the next two sections.

Creative Thinking Abilities

Creative thinking requires that you deviate from the routine or common ways of doing things. Creativity is seeing things that others do not. James L. Adams defines it as "the combining of seemingly disparate parts into a functioning and useful whole."[1] In other words, the creative thinker takes ideas or issues that others dismiss as conflicting or irrelevant to each other and relates them in new ways.

How should we assess creativity? Is it a personal trait unique to some individuals? Or does it involve different patterns of thought and behavior that anyone can master? Maybe both assessments are partially correct. We will identify some of the things that set creative people apart from others and then look at the hallmarks of creative behavior. Notice, however, that creativity consists largely of behaviors that can be learned. It will do you no good to write yourself off as uncreative just because the following profile does not sound like you. Experts on creativity agree that most of us do not make enough use of our natural, creative talents.

One approach to improving group problem solving is for leaders to identify

Research is one of many important tasks conducted independently by group members in preparation for meetings.

and recruit people who have already begun to develop their creative gifts. But what kind of person would you look for? Researchers have studied creative (and uncreative) people, attempting to profile the "creative personality." Psychologist Frank Barron mentions several personal factors associated with creativity:[2]

- Superior general intelligence—they are born with greater brain capacity and can hold and compare many ideas at once.
- Vigorous physical constitution—they have exceptionally high levels of physical and psychic energy.
- Strong ego, forcefulness of opinion, and highly independent—they resist conforming readily to the consensus of opinion.
- Highly perceptive and precise in their observations—they tell themselves the truth more than most people do.
- Responsive to challenge—they look for the unknown, the contradictory, the exception to the rule.
- Preference for dealing with things and abstractions rather than people—somewhat detached in their relationships, though not without insight or sensitivity.
- Choose to live in a more complex universe than most people—they do not oversimplify life.

Thinking: A Reading List

Creative Thinking

James L. Adams, *Conceptual Blockbusting: A Guide to Better Ideas*, 2nd ed. (New York: W. W. Norton, 1979).

Edward de Bono, *Lateral Thinking: Creativity Step by Step* (New York: Harper & Row, 1970).

Arthur Koestler, *The Act of Creation* (New York: Macmillan, 1964).

Critical Thinking

S. Morris Engel, *With Good Reason: An Introduction to Informal Fallacies* (New York: St. Martin's Press, 1976).

Jeffrey Katzer, Kenneth Cook, and Wayne Crouch, *Evaluating Information: A Guide for Users of Social Science Research* (Reading, Mass.: Addison-Wesley, 1976).

Comprehensive Thinking

Edward de Bono, *Six Thinking Hats* (Boston: Little, Brown, 1985).

Figure 3.2

If you were responsible for selecting members for a decision-making group, think of questions you could ask prospective group members to determine their creative potential.

Many people believe that creativity is a gift from the gods. You either have it or you do not. But there is good evidence that we can be taught to be a lot more creative than we usually are. Experts agree that to become more creative we need to (1) identify the common perceptual, emotional, and cultural blocks that limit our ability to connect ideas in new ways, (2) learn to think with all our senses (sight, sound, touch, smell, taste), and (3) practice a lot using exercises especially designed to release our natural, but hidden talent. Organizations can do more to promote and reward the creative effort needed to spawn ideas. Figure 3.2 lists some excellent books to help you become more creative and foster an environment that nurtures creative potential.

One aspect of creativity that most of us can already exercise is greater reliance on our own intuitions. *Intuition* is "a spontaneous, unexpected, intensely clear inner awareness, which occurs without aid of intellectual reasoning, and is experienced as 'right' or fitting to the person."[3] It is the sudden insight or hunch that produces an "aha" reaction, even though we cannot explain to ourselves how we arrived at such a conclusion. Our point is that the hunches that group members have should not be quickly written off. They can and should be explored for their potential. The tendency in groups is to shift to an evaluative mode before creative ideas have been fully developed. Such exploration may take more time and will result in frequent dead ends, but it has the potential to produce more than its share of big ideas in the long run. Only a few research studies have investigated that potential. Two studies tested groups composed of members who scored either high or low on measures of intuition. Groups discussed a simulated building expansion and other managerial situations. The high-intuition groups made decisions that were judged to be significantly better than those of the low-intuition groups.[4] Another study tested intuition indirectly by training one group in meditation techniques that enhance inner awareness. The meditation group improved its problem-solving ability more than did the two control groups.[5]

Should your group make such a concerted effort to follow its hunches? The trade-offs are significant. Before you commit your group to this kind of process, you need to assess the group's goals. Is the group charged with discovering big ideas or just producing competent, routine solutions? Are workable solutions already available? Has the group been given the time to explore more creative avenues? Will the group remain intact long enough for its creative process to pay long-range dividends? The answers to those questions should dictate your approach.

In sum, the nature of the task will dictate how much creative effort is needed for effectively solving problems in groups. But it makes sense to identify and recruit creative people when possible and to tap the creative potential of all group members as often as possible. Any improvement in releasing your creative energies will make you a more valuable participant to your group.

Critical Thinking Abilities

Individuals' creative efforts produce fertile ideas and potential solutions to problems, but they are not finished products. Effective decision making requires "critical testing" of ideas, arguments, and proposals until they represent the group's best efforts. Critical thinking generally includes two skills: (1) logical reasoning based on credible information and ideas and (2) recognition and refutation of any logical fallacies in arguments for or against a proposal. Let us examine each of these aspects of critical thinking.

In a formal sense, logical thinking is the ability to reach a sound conclusion by making valid inferences from premises that are considered factual or true. A *conclusion* can be any kind of claim or proposal the group is asked to believe. The *premise* of an argument is any reason implicitly relied upon or verbally stated in support of the conclusion. For instance, a group member may suggest:

> "We should organize a student escort service [conclusion] because such services have reduced crime on other campuses [premise]."

The *inference* links a particular premise to a given conclusion. As such, inferences can involve either valid or invalid reasoning. When group members disagree about proposed ideas or actions, a close look at their arguments may reveal weak or strong premises, valid or invalid inferences, accurate or inaccurate conclusions, or some combination of all three.

When considering an argument, identify the premises and verify them. You might ask yourself the following questions:

- What assumptions are being made? Are they assumptions of fact or value?
- If a premise is an assumed fact, do we have a sufficient amount of reliable evidence to verify that the facts are true?
- If a premise reflects a particular set of values, do group members share those values? Will others affected by the decision find these values acceptable?

The premise in the argument for an escort service may be true. The group may have factual evidence demonstrating that escort services have worked well on many campuses. Members of the group may agree with the implicit value premise that "reducing campus crime is a good thing." Even so, others on campus may not perceive crime to be a serious problem, undermining acceptance of the premise.

Much critical thinking must be done at the inference level. Inferences are either inductive or deductive. An *inductive inference* is one in which we project a probable conclusion based on one or more known facts or experiences. If our group has already successfully solved one problem using a particular approach to problem solving (the known), we might conclude that the approach will work on the next problem we tackle. This is an example of an inductive inference. A *deductive inference*, on the other hand, is derived necessarily from a given set of premises that we believe to be true. There is no probability involved in a deductive inference. If the premises are true, then the conclusion has to be true. For instance, a task force is charged with establishing a company policy that will advance more women into management positions. One member of the task force made the following argument:

> "Women are just as capable as the men in this company [premise 1]. We know that our workforce is now 50 percent female [premise 2]. If we give those women just as many opportunities to prove themselves [premise 3] and reward the achievements of men and women equally [premise 4], and always promote on the basis of those achievements [premise 5], we will have as many new female managers as we do males [conclusion]."

Note the deductive nature of this argument. If the string of premises are all true, the conclusion would follow logically. As with many deductive arguments, if we show one of the premises to be false, the argument falls apart.

To critically test the inferences made in arguments, you might ask questions such as:

- What inferences are being made? Are they inductive or deductive?
- If an inference is inductive, can we show how the premise is directly relevant to the conclusion?

- If an inference is deductive, is each premise meaningfully related to the other premises and to the conclusion? Are the classes of behavior or events under consideration mutually exclusive (for example, males cannot also be females)?

Let us return to the example of the escort service. The inference "if it works on other campuses, it will probably work here" is an inductive one. To test the relevance of this inference to the conclusion, you might want to know how similar the target campus is to the other campuses studied. Are they the same size? Would size of campus make a difference in managing the problem? Are the types and rate of crime similar? Would an escort service offer equal protection for all types of crime? Would students on this campus really use the service if available? Evidence may not be available to answer all of these questions, but raising and considering them in putting together a solution means that the idea of an escort service has been more thoroughly tested and not simply accepted in blind faith. Any group member can improve his or her critical thinking by identifying and analyzing the inferences often hidden in arguments.

Recognizing logical fallacies in arguments is another useful skill in groups. It is probably easier to find holes in other people's logic than it is to produce sound arguments of our own. Even so, many group members are lax in evaluating the arguments produced in group discussions. Sometimes people avoid tearing apart each other's arguments to avoid making enemies. People are sensitive about their ideas, so it is important to evaluate ideas rather than the people who initiate them. As much as possible, a group should consider an idea as a separate entity that belongs to no one once it enters group discussion. The transition can be eased somewhat if the group initially looks for the positive aspects of an idea before proceeding to the critical testing stage. This provides a little distance between the time the person volunteers the idea and the beginning of criticisms. Other group members' additions of potential benefits also make the idea more of a group idea. Moreover, the positive response to an idea encourages creative thinking. Once the criticism begins, it is harder to see an idea's potential. When the group is ready to shift to critical thinking, it often helps if the person who initiated the idea signals the shift. Being the first to criticize his or her own idea, the idea generator opens the door for others to do so without fear of offense.

With all these ground rules operating, the group can ask its members to use their critical testing skills more thoroughly. As each proposal is considered, the reasons for supporting it can be evaluated. In addition to the general approach to analyzing premises, inferences, and conclusions, group members also need to be on the alert for a variety of logical fallacies that are often accepted because they sound like good reasoning. Figure 3.3 lists some of the more common logical fallacies encountered in group discussions. You can improve your own skill at recognizing such fallacies by listening for examples in everyday conversation as well as reading some of the books suggested in Figure 3.2. One word of caution. Just because someone forwards an argument

Logical Fallacies in Thinking

Fallacy	*Example*
1. **The Sweeping Generalization:** A general rule is applied to a specific case in which the rule is not applicable because of the special features of the case.	"Republicans favor increases in defense spending; therefore, the new Republican administration will increase spending on defense." (Budget deficit may invalidate the rule.)
2. **The Hasty Generalization:** An isolated case is used as the basis for an unwarranted general conclusion, or only evidence that supports an argument is used while contrary evidence is ignored.	"The escort service at campus X reduced attacks on students by 30 percent. Therefore, escort services are a proven method of reducing crime on U. S. campuses."
3. **Bifurcation:** An argument is presented in either/or fashion, falsely assuming that the alternatives are contradictory and that no other alternatives exist.	"Either we stop the spread of communism or communism will take over the world."
4. **Circular Argument:** Instead of offering proof for a conclusion, the argument only reasserts the conclusion in a slightly altered form.	"The vast majority of people are conservative because they are not willing to change the status quo."
5. **Special Pleading:** Applies one standard to a favored group and another (stricter) standard to other groups.	"He is firm; she is not being reasonable."
6. **False Analogy:** Results from comparisons of things that may be alike in relatively unimportant ways but different in significant ways, thus making the analogy erroneous.	"In the world of academe, the student-teacher relationship is the same as the employee-employer relationship in the real world. Therefore, grades are as negotiable as salary."

Figure 3.3 You can use this sampling of logical fallacies to begin developing your critical thinking skills. Remember that an argument based on a logical fallacy does not prove that an idea is unsound. Look for other, more reasonable arguments before rejecting the idea. [Adapted from S. Morris Engel, *With Good Reason: An Introduction to Informal Fallacies* (New York: St. Martin's Press, 1976). Used with permission of St. Martin's Press, Inc.]

Fallacy	*Example*
7. **False Cause:** An argument that suggests events are causally connected when no such causal relationship has been established.	"The stock market performs better in years when an NFC team wins the Super Bowl. Go NFC!"
8. **Irrelevant Thesis (red herring):** An argument that either supports or refutes a somewhat different thesis or conclusion than the one it purportedly deals with.	"I fail to see why gambling should be considered an addiction when it gives tremendous pleasure to many people, employment to even more, and substantial tax revenues to the state.
9. **Personal Attack:** Diverts attention away from the argument by focusing on the credibility of the person who supports the idea. Another form of the fallacy is the "practice what you preach" response, which fails to acknowledge that an idea can have merit whether or not it is practiced.	"I don't care how good the idea is, Smith is an East Coast liberal whose ideas cannot be trusted."
10. **Mob Appeal:** An appeal to the emotions of the crowd rather than rational reasoning. It usually involves emotionally charged language that fails to address the issues. Also known as the "bandwagon effect," which argues that "everybody's doing it" without providing reasons for doing so.	"Groups all over this country are rising up to stop the mass murder of the innocent unborn. We must stop this kind of moral treachery dead in its tracks."
11. **Appeal to Authority:** Attempts to persuade by linking arguments to famous people, time-honored traditions, or widely held beliefs that are actually irrelevant to the argument.	"Several speech professors we talked to agreed that our budget plan was a good one."
12. **Ignorance:** Claims that as long as no one has disproven a conclusion, it should be considered true. In logical argument, the burden of proof always belongs to the person making the claim.	"No hard evidence has ever linked radiation leaks from nuclear power plants to the detrimental health of a single nearby resident. Therefore, the nuclear energy industry is as safe as any on earth."

based on a logical fallacy does not mean that idea is not a sound one. There may be other, more reasonable arguments that have not yet been conceived. Good critical thinking requires that we explore as many bases for acceptance or rejection as we can.

Relevant Knowledge

Individuals are frequently selected for membership in a group because they possess knowledge or expertise that the group will need to tackle specific projects or problems. This is especially true of task forces or ad hoc groups (those created for a specific purpose and disbanded once their goal has been accomplished). Members of ongoing groups generally need a broader base of knowledge because they may face a variety of tasks over time. This is one reason that universities have always stressed the importance of the liberal arts. Students who have been exposed to general knowledge in various fields (history, literature, economics, sociology) have an advantage over others who are trained more narrowly.

Exposure to the variety of ideas that have led to different cultural traditions and different forms of government makes creative thinking easier. It helps a person realize that the tried and true ways of doing things are not the only options. Someone who has learned to make connections between events in history or patterns in world religions is trained in the art of linking ideas together. Knowledge of problems that humans have faced over and over again in different cultures and in different eras aids critical thinking because it makes more information relevant to the problem at hand. George Santayana's observation that "those who do not remember the past are condemned to relive it" is especially true for groups that are making decisions not just for themselves but for a whole organization, city, state, or country. The individual who can bring relevant knowledge to the group's attention will help that group immensely.

Relevant Attitudes

The attitudes that members bring with them to meetings can have a great impact on the communication patterns that evolve. We consider here seven attitudes that often make or break a group's spirit; they involve commitment, responsibility, motivation, participation, respect, willingness to disagree, and being open minded.

Commitment to Group Goals and Decisions

For many reasons, people do not always find the work of a task group exhilarating or inherently motivating. If the group has a hand in choosing a topic to discuss, the final decision will inevitably fail to please some members.

Nonetheless, a negative attitude and a lack of commitment to the group will not improve things. If you cannot commit yourself to work hard and put the group's goals first, you are better off withdrawing completely from the project. If you commit yourself right off the bat, most of the other positive attitudes will fall in line.

Responsibility for Attending Meetings

Nothing slows a group down or saps its energy more than people missing meetings. The group is placed in a situation where it can make little or no progress until all members are present, or it must make decisions without those absent. Either way, the group loses precious time or valuable input. When you miss meetings, you are risking your credibility with the group. Make sure that you do not put the group or yourself in such a situation. When you absolutely must miss a meeting, call another member ahead of time, arrange to get your completed assignments to the group, and volunteer to do extra work to make up for not being there.

Responsibility for Accomplishing Assignments

Failure to complete work on time also slows group progress. An entire agenda may hinge on your bringing information or a proposal to the table for discussion. The common attitude that "I'll get it done in time to write my part of the proposal" misses the point of doing group work. If the individual (rather than the group) makes the decision about the value or possible use of the information, then the advantages of multiple perspectives is lost. The only way to make group decisions is for the group as a whole to discuss the information or ideas that individuals bring to meetings. Therefore, individual tasks must be organized and presented on time.

Active Participation

As we saw in Chapter 1, social loafing is a common hazard of group work. It is likely to happen when one member observes another slacking off or not participating and decides "if he or she can get away with it, so can I." Such an attitude can snowball until only a few are doing the work of the many. A commitment by all members to be actively involved in every discussion is crucial to curbing such tendencies. Active participation means more than just offering your opinion occasionally; it means listening carefully, questioning assumptions, and building on the ideas of others. In short, it means participating in every way possible to produce better decisions.

Respect for Group Members

You may have been in a group where an active participant slowly became a nonparticipant. This is often the result of the feeling that other members do not value what someone has to say. A lack of respect can be communicated nonverbally such as by a lack of eye contact or through unenthusiastic responses. But such communication often stems from an attitude that only higher status members have anything important to say. We all have to remind ourselves to respect another's right to an opinion even when we disagree with that opinion.

Willingness to Engage in Conflict

Most people believe the proper attitude for group decision making should be cooperation rather than conflict. It is important to realize, however, that a cooperative spirit must value disagreement as the means to reaching high-quality decisions. When you believe the quality of the group's project is in jeopardy, you have an obligation to disagree with the rest of the group. And when someone objects to your proposal, the group has an obligation not only to respect you but also to challenge your position. Without the willingness to experience a little disagreement and conflict, the group cannot possibly evaluate ideas in a thorough manner.

An Open Mind

One attitude that seems to accompany individuals who join groups is an open or closed mind about the topic under discussion. The open-minded person approaches the topic and the group without prejudging the meaning of information or the kind of experience the group will provide. The closed-minded person has seen it all before and usually *knows* what decision should be made or has already concluded that every group is a waste of time and effort. By judging the group before it ever gets started, the closed-minded attitude sets a negative tone that is hard to overcome. Other attitudes never get a chance to develop.

Aubrey Fisher believed that most attitudes toward group interaction are created in the group itself.[6] Attitudes like the seven just listed tend to develop (or fail to develop) over time. Individuals rarely bring these attitudes with them to the group. More often, they take a "wait-and-see" approach. Although we agree with Fisher that attitudes do take time to emerge, a group's initial discussion can focus on what it will take for the group to be successful. This is an opportunity for the group to identify attitudes that members would like to see develop. In effect, these attitudes become part of the group's goal.

Summary

Anyone who has ever helped stage a play or some other production knows how much work goes on behind the scenes. In small group decision making, preparing for discussion is the "behind the scenes" assignment of each group member. For the group to look good on stage, each member must complete his or her individual work assignments, as well as saving some energy for listening and responding to the contributions of others. Unless members are already experts on the subject (which means they have spent years preparing for such meetings), a good deal of effort is required between every group meeting.

You can become better prepared for group meetings by locating and organizing relevant information for group consumption. In addition, you can enhance your creative thinking skills by working at them. Read some of the suggested books in Figure 3.2 and use the exercises in them to hone your skills. You will also find some group activities in Chapter 6 that aid creativity. The discussion of critical thinking includes questions to pose when examining ideas and information from a more critical point of view. Improving your overall knowledge base, one of the primary reasons you are in college, will also improve your group participation. Finally, bring a proper set of attitudes to the group setting. Armed with this preparation, communicating and achieving good decisions becomes much easier. With a commitment to being prepared for meetings, we are now ready to look more closely at the kinds of messages that help group members make better decisions.

GroupQuests: Discussion Questions

1. Individuals can work on four basic skills to better prepare themselves for group interaction: adding research skills, strengthening reasoning skills, improving general knowledge, and adopting appropriate attitudes. What would you add to this list? More specifically, how do you think a person can best prepare himself or herself during the twenty-four hours prior to the group's next meeting?
2. Think of a recent group discussion that you participated in and try to identify aspects of general knowledge (for example, history, literature, philosophy) that could have been used to aid the group's understanding of the topic or issue. How can we make better use of such knowledge on a regular basis? How can we remind groups to think in terms of the liberal arts?
3. If you wanted to help a new group to develop the norm of being prepared, what would you say to the members during their first meeting?

GroupWorks: Group Activities

1. Box 3.1 suggests one way that groups can better manage the thinking process by using the vocabulary of the six thinking hats. Discuss the value of such an approach and talk about other aspects of group work that might benefit from a clever vocabulary. For instance, how could you label different types of conflict in a group in order to manage them better?
2. Assign each member of your group to look through the catalog describing courses at your college or university and list courses that are most relevant to developing the research and reasoning skills introduced in this chapter. Bring these lists to your next group meeting and develop a study plan that would help students acquire these skills. Think about the sequence in which courses should be taken and identify any gaps in the curriculum.
3. If you are a member of a decision-making group outside of class, attend one meeting in which you are especially well prepared

for the discussion and another meeting in which you wing it. Note how group members respond to you under these different conditions and how you felt as a result. Write a short paper describing the differences in the quantity and quality of your participation, the feedback you received, and how your state of preparation affected the overall group effort.

4. Tape-record a group discussion and evaluate the quality of critical and creative thinking exhibited by the group. List ways group members could have better prepared themselves for the discussion.

GroupActs: Practical Applications

At your next group meeting, assign one member to wear the "blue thinking hat" (see Box 3.1). This person should follow the flow of discussion and ask other members to put on different colored hats at appropriate times. At the conclusion of the meeting, take a few minutes to discuss how well this approach works. What could improve the use of the six hats?

CHAPTER 4

The Speech Act Level: Communication Behaviors and Roles

The jury had been deliberating for close to three hours. Their first vote to convict or acquit the accused murderer had not been unanimous. The jurors have still to determine why the suspect went to see the victim's husband, Dr. Collins, shortly after the murder. Once they decide this, they will take another vote.

> "The thing that bothers me is why he went to the hospital. I don't believe it was to treat his scratches."
>
> "He said it was to see Dr. Collins."
>
> "I know, but if he really had just stabbed that woman forty-seven times . . . how could he go see this woman's husband right after that?"
>
> "Unless he was nuts."
>
> "Well, we don't have evidence of that."
>
> "The only thing that makes sense is . . . that he was going to tell him he wasn't going to be her bodyguard anymore."
>
> "Maybe he's such a cold-blooded killer he figured out a jury like us might believe he didn't do it if he went straight to see Dr. Collins."[1]

This dialogue is from Seymour Wishman's *Anatomy of a Jury*, an account of an actual jury case. We have chosen this segment to introduce the role of communication behavior in decision making. The jurors are exchanging more than mere words about a puzzling event. They are engaging in speech acts that help them define their task, their relationships, and the manner in which they ought to proceed. This chapter focuses on the types of communication behaviors necessary for effective group functioning. In addition, we will examine the types of group roles that often emerge as a result of members' abilities and willingness to perform certain behaviors consistently. First, we describe some basic principles for effective group communication.

Ten Principles for Effective Group Communication

What individual members say and do and how they act shape the group. Because every group, task, and situation differ in unique ways, there is an endless variety of communication behaviors that could contribute to an effective outcome. But some general principles can make group communication behaviors more manageable and productive.[2] In the following list, the primary function (task, relational, or procedural) that each principle addresses appears in parentheses.

- *Principle 1.* The group establishes a set of operating procedures and follows them judiciously. (procedural)
- *Principle 2.* The group formulates a comprehensive understanding of the nature, extent, possible causes, and symptoms of the problem. (task)
- *Principle 3.* The group carefully examines the validity of opinions and assumptions introduced into the discussion. (task)
- *Principle 4.* Members evaluate the idea under consideration rather than the person who initiated the idea. (relational)
- *Principle 5.* The group generates a large number of feasible alternative solutions to the problem. (task)
- *Principle 6.* Group members thoroughly (not just superficially) test each alternative solution in terms of any set criteria and speculate about the likely consequences of implementing each solution. (task)
- *Principle 7.* The group bases its final decision on apparently reasonable and accurate facts, assumptions, and inferences. (task)
- *Principle 8.* The group resists the influence of authority figures, opinion givers, and other high-profile participants when they forward erroneous assumptions, inferior ideas, or irrelevant topics. (relational)
- *Principle 9.* The group maintains a supportive climate that encourages all members to participate. (relational)
- *Principle 10.* To accomplish the other principles, group members need to make sure they have done all they can to be prepared for group meetings (procedural; see Chapter 3).

As we describe the various communication behaviors in this chapter, keep in mind that their goal is to make group interaction more effective by involving one or more of these principles.

Speech Act Analysis of Group Communication

One way of thinking about group discussion is to view a meeting as a string of speech acts, with the potential for multiple meanings attached to each act. Every speech act has both content and a relational meaning attached to it. The *content* of a message is the information about an idea, topic, or issue conveyed through the actual words, while the *relational meaning* refers to anything said or implied about how the speaker sees himself, the other person, and their relationship to one another—for example, as superior-inferior or as equals.

Suppose Tom recommends that his group go to the library and do some research rather than hold a meeting during class time. Janet's response, "We're supposed to have our research done *before* we get to class," can be interpreted in several ways. The content reminds members that the purpose of meetings is to explore the relevance and validity of information already collected. The group might improve on the content of her message by proposing a policy that information from all research assignments be collected, summarized, and distributed to all members two days before the meeting at which the information will be discussed. There are always ways to modify and improve the content of group discussion. On the relational side, Tom might take Janet's message as an attempt to make him the chief culprit, holding back the group's progress. Or he might not give it a second thought, simply telling himself that Janet wants to have a meeting so she can hear herself talk. However we interpret Janet's message, the ultimate value of her speech act is the reaction it gets from Tom and the rest of the group. If they ignore or overrule her plea, she has been unsuccessful. But if the group subsequently alters the way it manages its meetings, she has made a significant contribution. As this example illustrates, effective communication involves all the members of the group. A single speech act means very little in itself; the pattern of interaction (speech act-feedback-response) tells the real story of what is happening in a group.

As you participate in group discussions, note members' specific types of speech acts and the group's responses to those acts. This will give you a better understanding of what motivates different members as you see the types of responses that discourage or encourage them. You may also begin to anticipate what needs to happen next as the discussion unfolds. The first step in developing this kind of insight about group process is learning to label the individual speech acts that are most relevant in group decision making. To help you remember them, we have classified each act according to the dimension of group interaction it most fully addresses: procedural, task, or relational. Keep in mind, however, that messages that appear to emphasize task or procedure also carry some relational meaning.

Procedural Acts

When group members engage in procedural communication, they are attempting to shape or alter the way the group conducts its interaction. Procedural acts range from setting goals and objectives to deciding which method of decision making is most appropriate. We have identified nine different communication behaviors that focus on procedures. Add to the list if you find a distinct behavior that makes a difference in how the group operates.

Goal Setting Every decision-making group has a set of goals to achieve. These goals often are established for the group by some external authority, but achieving the goals depends upon members communicating their understanding of overall objectives, setting short-range goals to ensure the accomplishment of long-term ones, frequently reminding each other what the goal is, checking progress in relation to goals, and occasionally modifying goals in light of new information. Many groups expect this kind of behavior of a leader, but these acts can be performed by any member who recognizes the need for them. "What this campus really needs is a little less student apathy" and "I think we can produce a better product at a third of the cost" are examples of goal-setting statements. "How does this information help us reduce apathy?" tries to measure progress toward the goal. But perhaps the most important contribution group members can make in this category is to help break down the overall goal into a series of short-term, achievable subgoals or objectives. The group concerned about student apathy was floundering until one member suggested creating objectives to reach the goal. The members came up with the following short-range goals:

- Develop a working definition of what students (and other experts) mean when they use the term *apathy* in relation to campus activities.
- Create a survey to measure:
  a. the level of student apathy on this campus,
  b. the perceived reasons for one's own and others' apathy,
  c. whether or not students want to see apathy reduced, and
  d. how students feel apathy could best be reduced.
- Summarize psychological and other literature related to apathy, anomie, and purpose in life.
- Integrate survey data and research literature into a statement of the problem.
- Generate ideas for solutions (brainstorming).
- Develop best ideas into detailed proposed solutions. (Subgroups prepare position papers for each proposal.)
- Conduct internal evaluation of proposed solutions.
- Interview students for reactions to proposed solutions.
- Select and develop implementation plan for best overall solution.

- Develop outline and write final report.
- Prepare oral presentation for class.

All of this was the result of one member's prompting. The importance of setting goals should be obvious.

Orientation To orient means to become familiar with or adjust to a new situation or set of facts. Sometimes such a general overview is necessary to discover what the group's goals ought to be. At other times, it follows the targeting of a goal. For instance, someone may have to translate the new goal into a way for the group to proceed. Likewise, when the group encounters a problem or some unexpected difficulty, orientation is necessary to make sure everyone defines the new situation similarly. Orientation behavior can be as specific as suggesting an agenda to follow or as general as a simple overview of what tasks or issues need to be addressed. Sometimes the focus of orientation behavior is talk about desirable norms, procedures, and other ground rules. Researchers have demonstrated that groups high in orientation behavior tend to reach agreement more often than do groups that do not orient themselves.[3]

Focusing This type of behavior involves concentrating on a single discussion topic for a time. Group members may suggest a focus ("Should we start by discussing what information we need from our survey?") or remind the group to maintain its focus ("I think we're getting ahead of ourselves. We don't want to write the specific questions until we know the purposes of our survey."). Either way, focusing is important for managing the flow of group interaction. Knowing when to suggest a new focus requires good judgment about what group members understand, how much conflict the group can handle, and whether or not the topic has been thoroughly examined.

Tooling At various times during meetings, members may suggest or direct the group to use a particular procedure. For instance, once the group focuses on a topic, any member can suggest the use of a discussion format (round-robin, open discussion) or a tool for generating ideas (writing down ideas, brainstorming). Similarly, concrete decision-making moments may prompt a member to invoke a scheme for making decisions (majority vote, decision by expert). Chapters 5 and 6 say more about these procedures. When a member performs a speech act of this nature, he or she is establishing procedure or tooling. As with most acts, this one may be performed in various ways with different relational consequences. A member may assume he or she has the authority to direct procedure ("It's time for us to vote on this issue"), may simply suggest its use ("How shall we decide this? Do you guys want to vote or what?"), or may supervise the use of the tool ("Hold it! We need to be careful not to evaluate ideas while we brainstorm.").

Clarifying or Modifying Procedures Sometimes a procedure works poorly and needs to be modified to fit the group or its situation. If some members do not understand how to use the technique, someone who does may simply clarify it. If the procedure itself does not fit the group's personality or skills, it may have to be altered. Suppose several members are reticent and do not feel comfortable criticizing other members' ideas orally. A sensitive member notices this and says, "To make sure we have thoroughly evaluated each idea, let's spend the last five minutes of our critical testing sessions with each member summarizing the discussion in *writing* and adding any criticisms they didn't mention during the discussion. That way we won't miss anything really important." This modification of the usual group practice makes a better fit between the group and the procedure it has adopted.

Regulating Interaction Speech acts that regulate interaction are often called "gate-opening" and "gate-closing" acts. Group members do this all the time, often without realizing it. At any given time, the member speaking is in a position to select the next speaker through eye contact or verbal address. When Ann finishes what she has to say and looks only at Peter, Peter will most likely be the next speaker. This behavior simultaneously "opens the gate" for Peter to talk and closes it to everyone else. Of course, another member (Janet) may force the gate open by jumping in ahead of Peter or interrupting him. But that act may be costly for Janet. If she frequently forces her way into the discussion, she may be perceived as too aggressive or pushy. Or she may begin to feel that others do not regard her very highly. The sensitive group member tries to keep as many lines of communication open as possible. An easy way to do this is to scan the whole group while talking and then "select" the person who appears most eager to talk next or someone who has not had a chance for a while.

Referencing the Record Most groups appoint a recorder to take minutes and organize the information gathered, but very few use this information beyond a ceremonial reading of the minutes at the outset of each meeting. When a member "references the record," he or she calls attention to the minutes to make use of some earlier information, argument, or decision. For this procedure to be successful, the group must specify what kind of information the recorder should be prepared to provide during meetings. Some experts recommend that the group tag information it wants to go in the record, much like items are entered into evidence in the courtroom. Otherwise, members will ask for information that is not readily available. If carefully orchestrated, the record can be a valuable resource for a group, and referencing the record in a timely fashion can be an important speech act.

Reporting on Process In Chapter 2, we noted the importance of observing your group's habits and tendencies and reporting those observations to the group. Suppose members frequently miss meetings. No single individual is missing more than the others, but at least one member is absent every meeting. Everybody views it as a problem and several have openly complained ("Where's Jim? He said he'd be here."), but only Andrea is willing to make it a group process issue. She says to the group, "We always seem to gripe about people missing meetings when they're not here, but we don't do anything about it. By doing nothing, we're saying it's really no big deal. Is that what we want?"

Some aspects of group process are easier to see than others. Absences are more noticeable than the fact that the group consults Mary about simple decisions such as where to hold the next meeting, but ignores her input on more important decisions. To sharpen your observational skills, remind yourself of the negative group tendencies mentioned in Chapter 1. Such tendencies must be brought to the group's attention early on. And members should report (and thus reinforce) positive developments as well. Reporting on process depends on one's powers of observation, but also involves the risky business of telling the group what it may not want to hear. Nonetheless, progress cannot be made without such risks.

Modifying Group Process It does little good for members to identify negative aspects of their group process unless they follow up with appropriate changes. Once a group recognizes that it displays several symptoms of groupthink, for instance, members will need to suggest strategies to overcome the problem. Chapter 12 includes several strategies for counteracting specific problems (and thus modifying group process). You may see some similarity between this speech act and an earlier one labeled "modifying procedures." The difference is that group process problems occur repeatedly in different situations and when using different tools. For instance, members may feel extreme pressure to conform to group norms during general discussions, when voting, and even during brainstorming. Modifying the procedures would not get at the real problem. The group would have to take on and overcome a much larger tendency.

Procedural speech acts are perhaps the most significant contributors to efficient group decision making. They set the table so that equally important task contributions can be made in a timely and orderly fashion. Without an organized procedure, the group may waste a lot of time. Additionally, attention to group procedures can improve decision making by eliminating bad habits and highlighting good ones.

Task-Oriented Acts

While procedural acts organize the group and keep it functioning smoothly, task-oriented speech acts provide the substance of group interaction. In fact, some groups hire third-party facilitators to perform many of the procedural and relational functions so the group can focus almost exclusively on the task. Most of the task-oriented acts listed here should be easy to identify during group decision making. How well they are performed will be a major key to group success.

Contributing Ideas or Information An important function of a group member is to produce fresh ideas for the group to explore. One source of ideas is exposure to new information. A major purpose of conducting research is to see what ideas others have had about a topic. In many cases, the new information will be a full-fledged idea; in other cases, the information can stimulate us to form new ideas. Without new ideas or information, a group may simply rehash the same old ground. Recognizing the importance of new ideas should be impetus for group members to spend some time before meetings reading about and reflecting on their topic or problem. If members prepare themselves and use the many techniques developed for generating ideas during meetings, there is no reason to experience a shortage of ideas to solve problems.

Seeking Ideas or Information Even the best groups have occasions when ideas and information just will not flow. Some shy members may be reluctant to volunteer their ideas. Normally outgoing members may be intimidated by the presence of their supervisor or some other high-ranking individual. At such times, a little coaxing becomes necessary. Sometimes members will respond to direct requests, but the seeking function can be more difficult to pull off. You may have to till the soil a bit by redefining the problem or specifying the nature of the information needed. In addition, take care not to embarrass or threaten members when you ask for their contribution. Realize that seeking information may take time as well. A simple question—"Do we have any information about registration procedures on other campuses?"—may result in a research assignment that takes two or three weeks to complete.

Clarifying Ideas or Information Communication is inherently difficult. A single message uttered in a group of five people may be interpreted in five different ways. As a result, ideas and information cannot be expected to stand on their own. To achieve a relative consensus about the meaning of a fact or an idea, group members must clarify what they mean. They can offer clarification by defining or drawing distinctions, paraphrasing, generalizing from a specific idea, or providing concrete examples of more abstract ideas. Look at the following group discussion about a possible project topic, and note how members try to clarify the original idea:

Lynn: Why don't we tackle the problem of stress on campus?

Judy: [seeking clarification] What do you mean? Are you talking about academic or social pressure or what? [drawing a distinction]

Lynn: Well, both really . . . and maybe more. I did a paper for my psych class on biological and psychosocial stressors and found that there are a lot of things that frustrate us and interfere with our ability to function. [definition]

Treva: So what would you look for—how many exams in a day it takes to drive a person over the edge? Or how depressed people get when they haven't had a date in a month? [checking for specific examples]

Rodney: Yeah, but isn't some stress good for you? How do you know if a stressor is bad or not? [seeking clarification]

Greg: If I heard Lynn correctly, a negative stressor would be one that prevented a person from going about his normal routine. [paraphrase] Negative stressors probably cause headaches, upset stomachs, and things like that, right?

Lynn: Exactly. I've got more information at home. . . .

Seeking and offering clarification can clear up much of the confusion surrounding new ideas. But be careful how you ask for clarification. If you allow critical evaluation to masquerade as clarification, you put people on the defensive. The goal is to see things more clearly, not to destroy them.

Substantiating a Claim In the preceding example, Lynn and her fellow group members have made several claims about the nature of stress. One goal of a group's research effort is to find information, statistics, solid reasoning, and other evidence that supports the major claims put forward. Ideally, a group member has already found information that will substantiate a claim before he or she makes that claim during group discussion. This is not always possible, so a group will probably produce an ongoing list of claims that have to be substantiated. You should begin to worry, however, when unsubstantiated claims start to dominate a group discussion. Not only is quality being jeopardized, but chances are that someone down the line will question those claims and embarrass the group. Make sure that complete citations for evidence are entered in the record of meetings for future reference when writing reports.

Developing an Idea or Line of Reasoning This speech act usually requires the creativity and comprehension of the whole group. People sometimes describe this process as "taking an idea and running with it." It often happens as members seek clarification of others' ideas. One person's attempt to clarify may not be accurate, but will push the idea in a different direction. As group members build on others' ideas, proposals start to take shape. Examples of full-fledged proposals include statements of problems or discussion questions, well-defined criteria, proposed solutions, position papers, implementation plans, and outlines for reports. Rarely are such proposals hammered out quickly. They are nurtured through numerous starts and stops. Undeveloped ideas fail because members do not understand the idea well enough to draw out its potential or predict any negative consequences. A final suggestion: Do not overlook the need to develop unpopular ideas. Expressing and developing unpopular or opposing viewpoints has two important benefits. First, the dissenting idea may prove valuable upon closer scrutiny. Second, dissent often forces the majority to reevaluate their beliefs and think through the issues more carefully.[4]

Evaluating Ideas or Information When ideas have been clarified and fully developed, they are ready to be tested. If evaluation of ideas begins too soon, further development is likely to be squelched. If the group has been careful not to allow criticism during brainstorming and idea development, the shift to evaluation can be a significant jolt. One way to make the transition smoother is for someone to summarize the idea or proposal and then remind the group that it is time to shift gears. Until members get comfortable criticizing the ideas they have spent so much time developing, the group may need someone to seek evaluation. For the group to be thorough, evaluation may have to be encouraged repeatedly. ("OK. One more time. What have we overlooked here? What could possibly go wrong with this plan?")

The critical testing of information and ideas should involve both positive and negative aspects (strengths and weaknesses, possibilities and limitations). Members can test ideas by questioning or showing:

- *The relevance of the idea/information to the situation, problem, or solution.* The group may have interesting evidence that appears to substantiate a claim, but closer scrutiny may reveal that the information is not that relevant to the group's problem.
- *The degree of objectivity or bias of sources.* When examining proposals put forward by students, teachers, or administrators, keep in mind the special interests and biases of each group that might be reflected in their ideas. Likewise, the reputation of a particular newspaper or magazine should help you interpret information obtained from that source.
- *How dated the information or idea is.* Generally, the more recent the information the more faith we place in it, especially if it concerns social trends that are subject to change.
- *The degree of consistency with known facts and opinions.* If information from different sources with different biases is very similar, we can usually feel confident. When new information contradicts previous findings, we need to seek additional sources to help us make a good judgment.
- *The logical fallacies in an argument.* Review Figure 3.3 to help identify some of the more common ones.
- *Whether the amount of information is sufficient to base a decision on.* "Do we have enough information?" is always a hard question to answer. Generally, you want to collect as much information from as many different sources as you can. But you have to make judgments based on the difficulty of getting additional information and the time it will take versus the added confidence such information will provide.

Evaluating ideas and information is the crux of effective decision making. It must be done carefully, following guidelines such as those just listed.

Summarizing Studies of listening behavior demonstrate that people retain only about 50 percent of the new information they hear in lectures and group discussions, even when they know they will be tested for retention.[5] If we assume that every member of our group is interested and motivated to follow the discussion, we still cannot be sure which ideas, arguments, or decisions will be remembered. As a result, group members need frequent summaries to highlight the most important facts, to follow the logical progression of ideas, and to check for flaws in thinking. Providing a summary requires better-than-average listening skills and a good sense of timing. Summaries are often needed when members seem to be losing interest or are confused about where the discussion is headed. Ask for a summary when you are confused. Chances are that other group members are just as lost but hesitant to admit it.

Verbalizing Consensus This speech act is often a good follow-up to summarizing. Just as members need summaries to capture the gist of a discussion, they also need to have areas of agreement brought into the open. Because consensus is often a very desirable group outcome, it is important to recognize when your group has achieved it. You might think that consensus would be obvious to group members, especially if it is a group goal. But research demonstrates that decisions emerge slowly and are often not recognized quickly—as the emergence phase of the group process illustrates. Verbalizing consensus can improve efficiency by helping the group draw more quickly and clearly the lines between areas of agreement and disagreement. Once a consensus has been reached, the group can anchor that decision and move on to explore other related issues. If consensus cannot be achieved on the new issue, the group can always return to the earlier anchor point and start again. But if anchor points have not been verbalized, group members are likely to feel lost at sea.

Task-oriented communication behaviors are the "substance" of group decision making, so members will benefit from performing these eight acts well.

Relationship-Oriented Acts

The social dimension of group interaction is concerned with the relationships that exist between group members and the level of cohesion they experience as a whole. Three categories of communication behavior affect the development and maintenance of a group's relationships: climate making, climate busting, and climate control.

Climate Making Active listening, showing support, and expressing solidarity are climate-building acts that tend to produce a trusting and supportive climate for work. *Active listening* makes others feel that the group values their ideas and them. To improve your listening skills, try to listen for comprehension before you listen to evaluate. Listening to comprehend means that you:

- Listen for main points.
- Suppress your own emotional reactions to the idea.
- Avoid prejudging what you think the speaker is going to say.
- Ignore any distractions, including the tendency to rehearse what you will say next.
- Paraphrase the speaker's point if your mind starts to wander.

Once you understand what the other person is saying, you (and other members) can begin listening to evaluate. You must adjust the type of listening you do to the situation at hand. But active listening also requires that you communicate your interest and understanding to the person speaking. Eye contact, nodding the head, and verbal reinforcement ("I see." "OK. Go ahead") exemplify active listening. Good listening tends to produce other important task behaviors, such as clarification of ideas.

Group members also enhance the social climate by *showing support* and encouraging one another to do more. Positive feedback such as "That's a good idea" or "I like the way you phrased that" can be very reinforcing if they are perceived to be genuine reactions. You can even be supportive when giving negative feedback. ("I don't agree with a thing you said, but I like your style. You've got real potential.")

Finally, *expressions of solidarity* can forge positive relationships and enhance the group climate. Examples of such expressions include frequent references to "our" group, invitations to be together outside of formal meetings, and statements of hyperbole like, "Could there possibly be a better group on the planet?" Together, these kinds of communication behavior help members feel good about themselves and their group.

Climate Busting Just as a climate can be built up through members' prosocial acts, it can also be brought down by negative behaviors that create tension and despair. We call such behavior "climate busting." Group members stall cohesive efforts by dominating, blocking progress, disconfirming others, or being defensive. A member may target negative behavior at another group member or at the whole group. But either way, all members feed the tension and are responsible for extinguishing the behavior.

One frequent climate buster is the *dominating* of discussions or decisions by a single individual or coalition. Talking more than your fair share and always having the last word are common examples. Some members act as if their own personal stamp of approval or disapproval must be given to every idea mentioned. Others do not dominate talk time, but simply assert themselves forcefully when decisions are made. They assume that others will give in to such intimidation.

To dominate a discussion requires a willing or at least a timid audience. When other group members are not easy marks, a dissatisfied member may resort to *blocking progress*, an exercise in dragging one's feet. The member usually remains inflexible on issues, raises minor objections to group preferences, and may say things like, "Well, we're supposed to be critical evaluators, aren't we? I'm just doing my job." By exhibiting this behavior, the member acknowledges that he or she will not sway the group to his or her view, but seems to derive satisfaction from the stance, "If I can't win, you won't either."

An especially difficult relational problem to handle is the use of *disconfirming behavior*. To disconfirm means to devalue a person's sense of self-worth. Sarcasm or insults are obvious forms of this behavior. But we run the risk of disconfirming another member any time we ignore, interrupt, or make irrelevant comments to him or her. A vacuous acknowledgment is also disconfirming; it says in essence, "I heard what you said, but I didn't think much of it, so I'm taking this conversation in another direction." As with other behaviors, you can disconfirm an individual member or the whole group. Not participating in discussions can be interpreted as saying, "I don't respect you people enough to bother giving you any input. I don't care about you or this project." Indifference can hurt more than insults.

Negative behavior makes others feel tense and defensive. And *being defensive* produces problems of its own. No one enjoys being around others who constantly have their guard up, justify every move they make, and interpret comments in the most negative way. The real problem with climate-busting behaviors is that they snowball. One negative behavior leads to another. A disconfirming act by Paul produces a defensive reaction by Jeri, who takes Carl's friendly insult the wrong way, and so on.

A certain degree of climate busting is inevitable. Human beings are prone to misunderstanding as well as occasional malicious intent. To counter these destructive forces, group members need to engage in what we call "climate-control" behaviors.

Climate Control The metaphor of climate that we use to describe the group's relational atmosphere is perhaps most appropriate now. Managing group tension is somewhat like managing the climate-control system in a house. When a house gets too hot (a deviation from the desired state), the system reacts by producing enough cool air to return to the desired temperature. A thermostat registers the desired temperature and a governor turns the cool air on and off. Think of your group's social climate as operating in a similar way. You use climate-making behaviors to produce the kind of atmosphere in which most members can be comfortable. You may even talk about what temperature setting you want to maintain. A major difference between your group and a mechanical climate-control system is that no governor automatically monitors the tension level in your group. You will have to monitor that yourselves and engage in climate-control behaviors to maintain the desired state by showing deference, demonstrating equivalence, and mediating disagreements.

Showing deference simply means being courteous and remaining respectful of others, especially when you do not feel like it. When another group member sends disconfirming messages, dominates, or blocks progress, your initial reaction will be defensiveness. You will want to do unto others as they have

A member with expert knowledge can coordinate members' interaction during specialized tasks.

done unto you. Remaining level-headed at the relational level preserves options and breaks the cycle of defensive interaction. You can still disagree with the content of the other's message and with how it was said. But the moment you challenge the other person's dignity, you will have made climate control almost impossible. Showing deference is not easy, but it can be done. Suppose Al just interrupted you for the third time in the past five minutes. You might respond to his disconfirmations, "Al, I know you are enthusiastic about our project. But please give me a chance to finish making my point before adding your contribution." To formulate such messages on the spot, remember that every person deserves to be shown respect.

When group members threaten the social climate by dominating or otherwise placing themselves in a superior position, *demonstrating equivalence* is an appropriate response. It places all group members on equal footing: "We're all in this together" or "I'd like to see if we have consensus on this issue. How does everyone else feel about? . . . " Sometimes you can even compliment the dominator and remind the others that they are responsible for what is happening. "Come on, folks. We've all been so quiet that Jack has had to carry the load the past five minutes." This allows Jack to maintain his dignity and reinforces an equality of responsibility.

Members in heated conflict may be unable to provide their own climate control. Then a third group member must step in and *mediate the disagreement.* Timing is very important here. As a third party, you do not want to squelch disagreement that will test ideas more thoroughly. But often members lose sight of the real issue, and disagreements become more personal than substantive. If you pay close attention to the nonverbal communication of those involved, you will recognize the telltale signs of people about to lose control: tense gestures, clenched teeth, throbbing veins. Be ready to deflate the tension by calmly asking the members in conflict to summarize their differences on one substantive issue at a time or by moving the discussion to other issues if the tension is too great. Chapter 7 describes specific ways to mediate conflict.

The goal of a moderately cohesive climate is not an end in itself, although it is more pleasant to enjoy one another's company than to merely tolerate each other. But a healthy dose of cohesion enables better working relationships because group members are more motivated to accomplish goals for the sake of the group and are less preoccupied with relational problems.

A Major Concern: Look for Patterns of Speech Acts

Group communication, like all forms of communication, is a joint activity. The outcome is never determined by the single speech act of any one individual. Suppose you have been listening to several members of your group praise a proposal to require any sponsor of concerts or dances on campus to hire two roving security officers to check for underage drinkers. You think the group is overlooking some issues like who will pay for the officers and how effectively they will be able to curb underage consumption. Even though your concerns are appropriate and well intentioned, they do not guarantee good results. If other members ignore your warnings or rationalize them away, your speech act will fall short of its goal. To create effective patterns of interaction, appropriate speech acts need other complementary speech acts to complete the pattern. For example, group members could respond to your evaluation of the idea with other related evaluations or serious rebuttals to your concerns; they might demonstrate that your evaluation, while important, has not been well timed. Perhaps you jumped the gun before the idea had been fully developed. You cannot make other group members respond to you as you think they should, any more than they can make you respond as they would like. The best you can all do is *recognize the significance of the whole pattern of interaction the group is creating and cooperate to improve it.*

Roles and Their Emergence

When an individual group member begins to perform specific communication behaviors consistently, he or she is on the verge of adopting a role in the overall group structure. A group's role structure is best understood as a division of labor. From the first moment of the first group meeting, members begin trying on different "job descriptions" until they find one that fits. Ideally, the job each one ends up with will match his or her skills and personality as well as the group's needs. Each role or job description will include behaviors necessary to accomplish a specific function related to the task, procedural, or social dimension of the group. When a group member displays communication behaviors aimed at achieving one of these functions, we say that person has taken on a role.

One way to define a *role* is to say that it is "a part, function, or position necessary to maintain the group." A role also refers to the expected behavior of a particular individual in the group. If we focus on the first definition, we will initially observe whether or not the primary functions of group decision making are being carried out and then perhaps notice who (if anyone) is performing those functions on a regular basis. Let us call this a *functional role.* Notice how the second definition draws our attention to the positive (or negative) contributions of specific group members. Because the emphasis here is on how each person distinguishes himself or herself from the rest of the group, we call this a *personal role* in the group. We think an emphasis on functional roles is more valuable. If crucial role behavior is enacted in a timely and competent fashion, it does not matter who gets credit for performing the behavior.

The way roles are divided up constitutes the group's *role structure.* Some groups develop clearly distinct roles for each member. Other groups have more overlap—members specialize but do not "own" the role. Imagine a group of aeronautical engineers trying to determine the cause of an airplane crash. One member of the investigating team may have the expertise to take charge of a discussion about specific equipment failure, while another may know more about possible sabotage. Each may take over the leadership role on a specific issue, but no one threatens the acknowledged leader's position. As we investigate the structure of roles in groups, we will focus on the types of roles that develop and how they emerge.

Types of Group Roles

Recognizing the variety of roles members play is half the fun of observing group interaction. We would not attend the theater expecting every member of the cast to play the role of hero. Nor would we be satisfied if the villain was always the same type of character. Variety is also the spice of life in group decision making. Some researchers have studied the variety in role behavior and have classified common types of characters. Perhaps the best-known classification is that of Kenneth Benne and Paul Sheats.[6] We have modified their scheme and have integrated some of the roles identified by John Cragan and David Wright.[7] The result is thirty-four role descriptions (see Figure 4.1) in one of four categories: task, social, procedural, or individual.

Task Roles Many of the roles people specialize in are oriented toward accomplishing tasks. The *task leader's* behavior frequently encompasses most of the task roles in Figure 4.1. Even in groups where several members share leadership, there is usually one person whom group members are most likely to turn to in a crisis. The person able to guide the group when it most needs guidance is the task leader.

Aside from the task leader, the information provider, questioner, and evaluator-critic roles are most often needed to get things done. Information is the primary energy source that fuels high-caliber decision making. Without people who provide this information, group discussions would consist of the membership's uninformed opinions. Every member should play the role of *information provider*. If we believe that groups are superior to individuals because of the differing perspectives of group members, then it would be foolish to leave information gathering to one person's limited perspective.

The best answers are often those that raise more questions. If we apply that wisdom to group roles, we can recognize the value of a person who raises the right questions for the group to pursue. The *questioner* can prompt people to play other important task roles simply by the questions he or she asks: "Something about our implementation plan doesn't feel right to me. Can anyone pinpoint the problem?" or "The information we've looked at seems to support Alternative B, but is it as current as we'd like it to be?"

The *evaluator-critic* is one role often elicited by the questioner. In fact, the more often the group requests this role, the easier it is on the person playing it. The evaluator always runs the risk of becoming disliked because he or she must pick apart the ideas of others. Asking the evaluator to "put on her black hat" (see Box 3.1) allows some distance between herself and the role and also softens the blow to the information provider's ego.

Social-Emotional Roles The effectiveness of a group's social dimension can be measured by the presence of role behavior devoted to building, maintaining, and repairing relationships among group members. The *social-emotional leader* supervises the social dimension. He or she makes sure that the roles listed in Figure 4.1 are performed when needed. Sometimes the same individual plays the roles of social and task leader, thereby giving the group a single all-around leader. In other groups, the task leader is complemented by a social leader who does not contend for overall leadership, but assists the leader in a variety of ways. For instance, an overzealous task leader might suggest several assignments for specific group members to complete before their next meeting. The social leader, noting a look of quiet disappointment by the one member who was overlooked, might inquire of the task leader, "And what did you have in mind for Joe?"

There is some debate among group scholars about the frequency and nature of dual leadership—when different people occupy the task and social leadership positions. Using an observation scheme that separates task from social behavior, Robert Bales and Philip Slater noted that dual leadership occurred often and that the single leader was the exception to the rule.[8] Others argue that this finding may be an artifact of the observation scheme used. Because a message could only be placed in one category, observers may have recorded a leader's act ("Tom, get us going on the Fisk proposal") as a task behavior even though the act may have implied a social message as well ("I know you will do a good job, Tom"). Stephen Wilson took a different approach, noting that dual leadership occurred most often when some group members were less involved

Group Roles and Associated Communication Behaviors

Role	*Typical Communication Behaviors*
Task Roles	
1. Task leader	Behaviors include goal setting; agenda making; initiating, seeking, and evaluating ideas and opinions; regulating participation of members; summarizing discussions
2. Initiator-contributor	Proposes new ideas or approaches to problem solving
3. Information seeker	Asks for facts and information as needed; seeks clarification of ideas and suggestions
4. Opinion seeker	Asks for evaluation of ideas under discussion; seeks values and beliefs of members
5. Information provider	Gathers information (statistics, examples) and organizes it for presentation to group; provides group with evidence it needs to support or refute ideas and proposals
6. Opinion giver	Offers own interpretation of ideas and proposals under discussion
7. Elaborator	Draws inferences from information presented; uses own experience to show how ideas would work if adopted; visualizes ideas
8. Questioner	Probes the value of ideas by raising concerns and questions for others to answer; does so without putting others on the defensive
9. Evaluator-critic	Critically tests soundness of ideas, information, and inferences; reinforces good ideas; points out logical fallacies or inadequate evidence
10. Devil's advocate or central negative	Responds negatively to most ideas of group; generally counters view of majority with own ideas; often takes opposite point of view for sake of argument
11. Energizer	Motivates group by dramatizing progress and trying to stimulate productive effort; makes upbeat comments and pushes group to do its best work

Figure 4.1 This classification system includes four general types of roles that group members play: task roles, social-emotional roles, procedural roles, and individual roles. Observation and analysis of the roles people play can help you facilitate small group interaction and decision making. [Adapted from Kenneth Benne and Paul Sheats, "Functional Roles of Group Members," *Journal of Social Issues*, 1948, *4*, 41–49, and from John Cragan and David Wright, *Communication in Small Group Discussions: An Integrated Approach*, 2nd ed. (St. Paul: West, 1986), pp. 159–165.]

Social-Emotional Roles

12. Social-emotional leader	Usually most well-liked member of group; plays many of roles 13 to 17 in an effort to keep group functioning smoothly
13. Encourager	Shows acceptance of others' ideas and praises their efforts; engages in active listening; shows understanding; serves as sounding board
14. Follower	Follows orders carefully and does assigned tasks or routine chores no one else wants to do; goes along with group consensus
15. Tension releaser	Breaks ice and manages conflict by using well-timed humor or changing discussion topic
16. Harmonizer	Mediates disagreements between members by emphasizing importance of getting along; tries to play down differences
17. Compromise	Mediates disagreements by encouraging parties to give in on minor points until they find a suitable solution

Procedural Roles

18. Facilitator	Performs several procedural roles in an effort to manage overall traffic flow of group interaction; keeps group on focus and aware of procedural options
19. Orienter	Helps group clarify its goals, establish a manageable agenda, summarize its progress, and keep moving forward
20. Coordinator	Tries to identify relationship among various ideas and suggestions discussed; may assign or keep track of individual tasks
21. Gatekeeper and expediter	Manages flow of interaction by encouraging quieter members and curtailing talkative ones; may also be primary contact person for group between meetings and between group and external groups or supervisors
22. Procedural technician	Assists leader or group through such tasks as arranging meeting room, securing needed materials, and running errands
23. Recorder	Keeps a written record of all major ideas, proposals, decisions, and rationales behind those decisions; makes record available to group as necessary; may assist group deliberations by making previous record visible during discussion (on board or easel)
24. Group observer	Makes mental (or written) notes concerning group's process (roles and rules, norms, and other routines); offers feedback and suggestions for improvement

(continued)

Individual Roles

25. Self-centered follower	Engages in many of following roles because of self-interest
26. Aggressor	Puts others on defensive by criticizing or taking credit for their ideas; inhibits quieter members and instigates conflict with more assertive members
27. Dominator	Tries to control flow of ideas and content of discussion; manipulates others into submission
28. Blocker	Acts stubborn and contrary usually; prolongs decision making by foot-dragging and nitpicking about procedure
29. Recognition seeker	Tries to gain the group's attention by boasting and recounting own accomplishments; needs to be center of attention
30. Self-confessor	Distracts group by disclosing personal problems unrelated to task; uses group to relieve guilt
31. Help-seeker	Expresses feelings of inadequacy or apologizes for quality of work in an attempt to gain sympathy or reassurance
32. Special interest pleader	Tries to maneuver group outcomes so that they favor interests of some other group he or she represents; brings a hidden agenda or bias to discussion
33. Playboy or playgirl	Displays general lack of interest in group and its task; behaves in cynical or carefree manner
34. Joker or clown	Uses excessive and often inappropriate humor to divert group from its task

Figure 4.1 (continued)

in the task and sought a social leader to divert attention from the task.[9] Although we agree that messages exchanged in the group can carry both task and social meaning simultaneously, members may "read" a message as being primarily task or socially oriented.

Of the specific social roles, the *tension releaser* is perhaps the most essential. The person playing this role is needed during the orientation phase of group interaction to help manage the uncertainty and awkwardness the group inevitably experiences. He or she is equally important during periods of conflict, trying to prevent the escalation of emotional outbursts.

Procedural Roles Procedural role players help the group decide when to tackle the topic, what format to use, and how to remain on track. Perhaps the most difficult of these tasks is keeping the group focused. Groups are

Box 4.1

Selling Good Art and Bad Wine: Changing Communication Behavior in a Sales Group

One of our students analyzed the communication behavior and roles of several small groups within a publishing company that produces fine art books and signed limited edition prints of some thirty U.S. artists. The primary group she observed was the sales staff, which included the sales manager and several sales representatives. The initial observations revealed that most of the group meetings throughout the company were largely for sharing information. The president of the company had a highly authoritarian leadership style that intimidated the majority of members. Reports on work in progress were the most common information-sharing routines in both the general staff meetings and in the sales group. Decision by authority was the only decision-making routine practiced company-wide. Members always tried to put a good face on their reports and almost never spoke about any problems.

In one sales meeting, the staff was notified of the president's decision that they would be introducing a new concept to the art collector market, called Gifts of the Land. The idea was to offer a signed print of a timber wolf to art dealers and a reproduction of the same image on a wine label to local wine dealers. A California winery would be producing a limited edition wine, and art dealers would be told where customers could purchase the wine in their area. The sales staff saw many difficulties with the project. They knew art dealers would be confused about why they were suddenly getting into the wine business and how they could secure the wine for their customers. Other objections were raised, but the sales manager, who employed the same leadership style and decision-making routine as the president, simply stated that the project was underway and moving ahead.

Several weeks later, the sales staff's worst fears were realized. The prints were not selling and many dealers had difficulty understanding the concept and how it was supposed to work. At this point an outside consultant was brought in to help resolve some of the problems. The consultant was given the authority to run the group meetings and immediately introduced several new routines. A polling technique generated a list of all the problems with the program. Brainstorming was used to stimulate possible solutions, which were written down and assigned to different group members for follow-up. Several solutions were put in place, including the assignment of a single member of the sales group to act as liaison to the winery and a phone survey of the art dealers to find out what had gone wrong and how to improve it. Within a couple of days, the entire mood had changed, as had a significant part of the group structure.

Box 4.1 (continued)

Most groups do not have the luxury of hiring outside consultants to introduce a needed change in roles or communication routines. But the experience of this group shows that it can be done successfully.

Source: Carol Mills, "Comparing the Dynamics of Small Group Meetings Conducted with and without Innovative Behavior" (Unpublished paper, Fairfield University, December 1988). Used with permission of Carol Mills.

notorious for digressing into irrelevant discussions, pushing through an agenda without finishing important issues, and failing to apply criteria in evaluating alternatives.[10] The person who helps the group manage these procedural difficulties is called the *facilitator*. In a sense, the facilitator has to understand the group process better than he or she understands the group's task. Much has been written about how to facilitate roles, but there has been little research to indicate which strategies and tactics are really effective.[11] But two studies by Randy Hirokawa are worth mentioning. Hirokawa discovered that members of effective task groups made (and agreed on) more procedural statements than did ineffective groups.[12] In another study, groups that had difficulty agreeing on which procedures to follow squandered precious time that they could have devoted to their task.[13] These studies point out the need for skillful procedural role players.

The *recorder* role qualifies for the Rodney Dangerfield Award because the person playing it never gets any respect. If groups regard the role as significant and demand quality work from its occupant, the benefits will be obvious. A description of how to play this role effectively is in Chapter 5. The other significant procedural role is the *group observer*. Groups using this role have a decided advantage because they can profit from their mistakes as well as their successes. The effective group observer, a mirror that talks back, identifies and describes to the group its role structure, norms, decision-making habits, and other tendencies. A good group will tell the observer what it wants her to report on and then give her the freedom to do so, warts and all. Some groups schedule a periodic episode devoted exclusively to feedback from the observer. Other groups try to make feedback a regular part of every meeting by encouraging the observer to comment any time she feels it is necessary.

Make sure the groups you belong to discuss and decide on an approach that will ensure attention to procedure. For your own part, practice the various procedural roles until you feel comfortable with them.

Individual Roles Any role that detracts from group goals and emphasizes personal goals is an individual role, which is not beneficial to the group. You need to recognize such role behavior and curb its use. Familiarize yourself with the individual role descriptions in Figure 4.1. You may find that some individual role playing is only a temporary extension of an otherwise valuable task or social role. For instance, the tension releaser can sometimes go too far and start to function as the joker; an overzealous task leader may become a dominator. You need to know the difference between these temporary excursions and the long-term variety. Someone who temporarily steps out of bounds needs to be handled carefully. You do not want to turn a productive group member into an outcast. Rather than reprimanding such behavior, you might try turning the discussion back to a task issue. But you need to stifle special interest pleaders, perennial blockers, and other detractors. Perhaps the best way to handle these problems is by addressing them directly. "It would be inappropriate for us to make a decision that favored one group over another" can draw the whole group's attention to attempts at special interest pleading. Likewise, "Our deadline is really breathing down our necks. Can we limit discussion to the task at hand?" cuts off a variety of individual roles, including the self-confessor, playboy, and joker.

After reviewing the role descriptions in Figure 4.1 and the suggestions in each of the four categories just presented, you are ready to observe roles in action. As a member of an ongoing group, periodically assess the roles played by members of your group. One way is to conduct a person-by-person analysis, noting the combinations of personal roles that each member plays. Or take a group perspective and analyze which functional roles are present or absent on each dimension, which ones are shared or owned by individuals, and how well the group is doing on each dimension. Once you can identify typical role behavior, you will be ready to look more closely at how those roles came into being.

Role Emergence

How do individuals come to occupy their place in a group's role structure? Formal organizations often make role assignments and prescribe group designs. But even when this happens, informal roles tend to develop alongside more formal ones.

Many people believe that roles simply reflect group members' personalities. According to this view, assertive and talkative people become natural task leaders, friendly types take on social roles, and the precise and orderly Felix Ungers of the world attend to procedure. If this were true, the process of emergence would be a simple matter of the right personality type taking on the appropriate role when the group task calls for it. Members certainly have preferences and unique skills that predispose them to play some roles better than others. But personality is not the only or the most significant influence on the emergence of roles.

The most significant factor affecting role emergence is the communication process itself. The messages that group members send, receive, and return to each other are at the heart of role development. Each member works out his or her role jointly with the whole group. Role emergence begins at a point in group discussion where the group needs a specific role to be played. As an example, suppose a group has to choose a topic for a semester-long group project. After twenty minutes of discussing options, the group really needs someone to summarize the discussion and narrow the choice to the two or three most favored topics. The group needs an orienter.

Recognizing this need, member A tries his hand at a summary statement. The group's response to member A's summary is a crucial factor in the role emergence process. Several possibilities exist. The group's response will fall somewhere along a continuum from wholehearted *approval* to total *disapproval* of member A's role behavior. In between those two extremes, the group may give an *ambiguous* message that neither confirms nor disconfirms the behavior. The key is member A's *perception* of the group's feedback. If he views it as essentially supportive, he is more likely to provide additional summaries in the future and expand his role into other related behaviors. If he thinks the group has ignored his statement because members continued to introduce new project ideas, he will be less likely to repeat the same role behavior later. Rather he will try to find another role the group supports him in.

Ambiguous responses are likely to prolong role emergence. Member A may keep trying until he gets a clear indication from the group, and other members may be encouraged to vie for that particular role. But why would a group respond ambiguously to role performances? Perhaps the quality of the role performance did not indicate whether the person fits the role. Or some members may want to play that role themselves and so offer only lukewarm feedback to any performance, no matter how good. Finally, the group may be punishing a member for some earlier behavior, such as violating a group norm to be on time for meetings.

Role emergence is the joint product of all the members in the group, not just the individual who occupies a given role. Aubrey Fisher suggests that "each member's role 'belongs' less to the individual member than to the group as a whole."[14]

Role Conflict

Role emergence can involve some conflict among members. Scholars have identified three different kinds of role conflict that occur in groups: role strain, interrole conflict, and interpersonal role conflict.[15]

Sometimes the burden of role performance can cause an internal conflict for a group member. A leader may feel the pressure of too many role responsibilities and begin to lose enthusiasm for performing them. Unless she learns to delegate some of these duties, a leader may never regain the emotional health necessary to function effectively in her role. External perceptions of the group can induce role strain as well. If expectations are too high or the group's reputation is tainted, members may feel pressure that diminishes their role capacity. At the height of the Iran-Contra scandal when President Ronald Reagan's popularity was at its lowest, many sources reported the president to be "depressed" and unable to perform his role very effectively. He may have been experiencing role strain.

When a person must play two or more roles at the same time, he or she experiences interrole conflict. This can happen when a procedural or social role specialist engages in some task behavior that requires comment on his or her own behavior. For instance, the group harmonizer may discover a role conflict when he must defend a position as information provider and then try to manage the ensuing disagreement among members. Such conflicts can lead to ineffective role performance and the neglect of much-needed role behaviors. Such role conflict could be reduced if a group develops a shared role structure. As long as the group has at least one member (in addition to the role specialist) who can play a given role, interrole conflict can be minimized. A third-party process facilitator can also reduce conflict between procedural and decision-making roles.

The most common kind of role conflict occurs between members struggling to play the same role. Most groups go through a period in which several contenders vie for the leadership position. This can be very healthy for a group, because it prevents premature role emergence and allows the group to see that it has some overlap in a crucial skill. It is probably not healthy if the group fails to resolve the conflict and members continually invest energy in a role struggle rather than other important tasks. Interpersonal role conflicts usually get worked out as a result of feedback. The group tends to offer more support for one of the members involved in the role struggle and the other member eventually looks for another role to fill.

Members are more likely to compete for roles that have the highest status in a group. The task leader, social-emotional leader, tension releaser, and devil's advocate are usually accorded high status. Groups can minimize such struggles if they stress the importance of such roles as facilitator, recorder, active listener, questioner, and observer when setting ground rules or discussing the goals of their project. Members who feel that their roles have the group's respect will not try to move in on someone else's territory.

Guidelines for Managing Role Structure

We have summarized the major issues regarding roles and offer five guidelines for you and your group to consider:

1. As you follow the flow of discussion, make it a habit to ask yourself what functional role needs to be performed next. If you do not feel qualified to play the role yourself, ask someone else to.
2. Conduct an inventory of personal roles. Are some members overburdened?

Are some underemployed? Given their skills, should some members switch roles?

3. As a group, periodically assess some of the more important role functions (task leader, facilitator, social leader) in terms of quality of role performance. Do not ask who is doing well or poorly; ask if the group is paying enough attention to each role function.
4. Evaluate the feedback you give others for their role performance. Are you reinforcing poor performances? Are you not reinforcing good performances? Are you being too ambiguous at the wrong time?
5. If your group experiences interpersonal role conflict, try to determine why. Is one person better qualified for the role? How much is each person's ego at stake?

Learning to manage the role structure requires every member's involvement. You can encourage involvement by bringing these matters to the group's attention. Understanding your group's role structure is equivalent to knowing how the parts of an engine work together to move your car. This knowledge enables you to be a group mechanic who can recognize which parts need lubrication and which ones can cause the most damage if they fail. Groups do not come with a manufacturer's warranty, so a good mechanic is more a necessity than a luxury.

Summary

The ten general principles that enable groups to communicate more effectively and generate high-quality decisions can be realized when group members perform task, procedural, and relational communication behaviors at appropriate times during discussions. Task behaviors enable the group to progress by introducing, clarifying, substantiating, evaluating, summarizing, and verbalizing consensus about relevant ideas and information. Procedural behaviors keep the group "on track" by verbalizing goals, focusing on one issue at a time, selecting the proper discussion tools, regulating participation, and referencing the written record when necessary. Relationship-oriented acts such as climate-making and climate-control behaviors enhance motivation and minimize the chances that task discussion will get sidetracked by personal concerns.

The chapter concludes by showing how the types of communication behaviors that an individual performs best and most often establish his or her role in the group. We described how these roles emerge, how roles can sometimes be stressful, and how you can manage roles more carefully. No group member can be expected to master all of these communication skills, but knowing the range of skills needed can help as members remind each other of what needs to be done. You can assess your own strengths and weaknesses in terms of the skills you have and offer to help your group in the best way you can.

GroupQuests: Discussion Questions

1. Review the list of procedural, task, and relational speech acts and try to identify additional speech acts that you think need to be included. Discuss how your proposed speech acts differ from those in the text and why they should not be omitted.
2. Why is identifying the *pattern* of speech acts so important? Why is it necessary to know when a speech act occurred and what act(s) preceded or followed it? How is such knowledge more helpful than knowing, for instance, that group members engaged in fifteen evaluations of ideas during the last meeting?
3. Do you think groups should develop highly specialized roles in which each person virtually owns a particular role? Or do you think that members should have a shared role structure, taking turns performing the various roles? What are the advantages and disadvantages of specialization versus sharing?

GroupWorks: Group Activities

1. The jury dialogue at the opening of the chapter is from chapter 9 of Seymour Wishman's *Anatomy of a Jury*. Select a longer segment of his chapter or a section of dialogue from Reginald Rose's play, *Twelve Angry Men* (in "Twelve Angry Men and Other Plays," *American Scholastic Scope Magazine*, 1971), or some other group discussion. Each member should photocopy and read the dialogue and identify (write in the margins) the kind of speech act that best describes each juror's turn at speaking. (You may do this as a group if you want to save some time.) As a group, compare interpretations and then discuss the *pattern* (sequence) of speech acts and determine which ones seem inappropriate or poorly timed. Replace these ineffective speech acts with more appropriate ones. You may also want to evaluate the *quality* of specific speech acts and try improving the wording of specific messages.

2. Although we have presented procedural, task, and relational speech acts as if they were performed independently, they are obviously related. For instance, the act of modifying a procedure is a form of evaluation because it implies that the idea of using that procedure can be improved. In addition, such evaluation could be perceived by some as climate busting. As a group, identify similar ways in which speech acts from one category might affect acts in the other two categories. Discuss what a group could do to manage some of the potential problems or take advantage of positive relationships among speech acts.

3. Your instructor will show a movie like *Lifeboat* or *Twelve Angry Men* or a video of another classroom group in a decision-making meeting. As you view the film, write down the roles that various group members played. In addition, take notes on one or two of the following aspects of role performances:
   a. Note specific behaviors that exemplified ideal role performance; also note how roles could have been played more effectively.
   b. Identify "missing" role behavior that could have helped the group improve its decision making.
   c. Follow the path of role emergence for one of the more important roles (task leader, tension releaser, devil's advocate).
   d. Describe how group members were able to draw out the appropriate role behavior when it was needed (if they did) and how they *could have* drawn it out (if they did not).

Organize your notes for a brief oral or written assignment.

4. Choose another group (in or outside class) and focus your observations exclusively on the *procedural* dimension of interaction. Identify effective and ineffective examples of procedural communication acts and propose several ways that the group could improve the way it manages the procedural domain.

GroupActs: Practical Applications

Purchase a pack of three-by-five-inch note cards and write each of the speech acts identified in the chapter on a separate card. Shuffle the deck and place it in the middle of the group at the beginning of the next meeting. Reserve about fifteen minutes at the conclusion of the meeting for this exercise. When the meeting is over, have each member take turns drawing a card from the deck, announce the speech act drawn, and then recall some point during the discussion when that speech act was performed especially well or poorly. Other group members may help by adding their perceptions of the event. If someone draws an act that was not performed during the meeting, the group should discuss whether or not there was a point in the discussion when such an act needed to be performed. Conclude by identifying communication behaviors that the group needs to work on or affirm those that are being performed well and in a timely fashion. Doing this exercise on a regular basis may serve as a useful tool for discussing group process.

CHAPTER 5

The Episode Level: Managing Task Group Meetings

The study of task group interaction over the past fifty years has led to the development of practices to enhance group performance and achievement. This chapter and the next introduce specific procedures for conducting the various activities of task groups. They will provide you with the basic tools of the trade for group decision making.

As Chapter 1 pointed out, most of us will be involved in numerous task groups without knowing the practices or tools available to guide group communication. This ignorance is costly. Ivan Steiner points out that a group's actual productivity is equal to its potential productivity minus losses due to faulty processes.[1] In other words, group effectiveness is contingent on effective practices. We could liken ourselves to bridge builders who do not know about contemporary engineering practices. We can make bridges but not of the same quality as those by a trained engineer. It would be foolish not to draw on engineering knowledge and practices in building a bridge, just as it would be foolish not to use the basic knowledge and skills for effective communication in meetings.

This skills chapter will describe and explain procedures for managing group meetings concerned with sharing information and making decisions. Because most of you will be involved in a group project, this information is presented early in the text to offer guidance. Later chapters will provide additional theoretical information to further your understanding of the significance of these skills and practices. The information of this chapter has been integrated into the group project facilitator at the end of Part II to provide guidance in applying the decision-making meeting practices discussed here.

Managing Meeting Communication

Group communication generally functions at three levels: task, relational, and procedural. This third level involves the first two levels. Procedures guide communication practices for conducting group tasks and developing group members' relationships. They can also reduce confusion and provide a common focus for group members that supports productive relationships and enhances group satisfaction. Rules can prescribe appropriate relational interaction.

Procedures manage meetings through establishing communication behaviors and patterns of interaction. The extent to which procedures govern communication vary. (This will be discussed further in Chapter 14.) The important consideration in adopting or deviating from any procedure is whether such a move is productive, considering the procedure's task and relational consequences. Whether or not a group discusses procedural matters, it is still proceeding. Communication is the ultimate procedure, whether it is guided by a formally adopted procedure or occurs spontaneously.

The meeting, the largest unit of analysis for examining group communication, is composed of episodes involving tasks and communication practices. Episodes can establish the content focus, type and order of tasks, and manner of participation. An agenda, a common procedural practice to manage meeting communication, establishes the content focus of an episode. The goal of an agenda item—sharing information, for example—will imply, if not establish, what communication acts are appropriate. However, an agenda item does not direct the order of communication acts such as when to give or evaluate ideas. With the exception of reports, an agenda seldom indicates who can speak and when during a meeting. It never establishes how people should act toward one another.

Procedures are usually established when the group decides on how to do something before doing it. As the meeting progresses, someone suggests a discussion focus or technique for the group to adopt. For example, a member may recommend that the group discuss how to develop a comprehensive list of questions for a survey. This is a request for a procedural episode: How should the group develop the questions? Regardless of how meeting procedures are adopted, they all depend on rules and roles.

Procedures as Rules and Roles

Procedures structure group communication through rules and roles. *Rules* determine the who, what, how, and when of communication. Rules determine *roles*—who is to perform an act, when, and how. Although some members may have specific roles (group coordinator, recorder, meeting facilitator), procedures may require members to perform several distinct role behaviors. For example, an idea-generating episode using brainstorming (see Chapter 6) requires members to first perform the role of idea generator, followed by idea clarifier, then idea evaluator. Even though these three roles occur during the same activity, they are distinct and expected of all group members. At the same time, the group chairperson usually has the role of procedural leader—making sure the members follow the rules of brainstorming. Thus roles can be specified for meetings (for example, chairperson) to guide episodes and activities (generating ideas using brainstorming) by establishing specific practices for members to perform during episode interaction (ideas followed by clarification).

Following the rules determines whether the group will achieve the intended purpose of the procedure and reap its benefits. The four elements of any rule involve identifying (1) the desired practice, (2) who the rules apply to, (3) the appropriate occasion for performing the practice of a rule, and (4) how initiation and compliance is established. This fourth element is in the hands of the group leader, a facilitator, or the group members.

With these considerations in mind, let us look at procedures for conducting information-sharing and decision-making meetings.

Procedures for Managing Meetings

Groups share information and make decisions. Information-sharing groups are for learning and personal enrichment. Decision-making groups typically identify and make choices regarding future action or a solution to a problem. Administrators, representatives, experts, and affected parties gather to share information and opinions to reach a decision. All decision-making groups share information, but all information-sharing meetings are not directly concerned with making decisions.

Information-Sharing Meetings

Information sharing enables members to develop a critical understanding of a topic or issue through comparing data and options and evaluating options. The goal of information-sharing meetings is to learn, not to decide. A panel of experts on a community problem at a public hearing or on a broadcast news program to discuss economic policy are information-sharing meetings. Typically such groups are *ad hoc*—formed for a single specific task and disbanded upon completing it. Information-sharing ad hoc groups may not be true groups in that the members may not be a group before or after the information-sharing meeting. They meet once to share information and never develop a sense of groupness or go through the group development process discussed in Chapter 2. In contrast, decision-making groups meet several times to work toward a decision. Such groups invariably experience the natural group process and achieve some degree of groupness.

Common information-sharing meeting procedures are the panel discussion, forum discussion, and the roundtable group. Panel and forum discussions are for public review of issues, perspectives, and opinions about a problem, whereas roundtable groups are designed for private learning. Public information-sharing groups address social or community issues for public discussion and have an audience. They usually address a problem, but are not required to develop or reach consensus on a solution. Private information-sharing groups promote personal learning. They are typically organized around a theme, topic, or purpose (for example, a literary club, women's support group, or hobby group). Membership in these groups may be limited to those who formed it or open to persons interested in it.

Specific roles and rules distinguish responsibilities, agenda, and communication practices for the information-sharing meeting's participants. Two, sometimes three, distinct roles are involved in conducting information-sharing groups: discussion members, moderator or discussion leader, and audience participants if the meeting is public. The members provide information and opinions regarding the topic under discussion. The moderator or leader organizes and coordinates the steps or episodes of the discussion. The audience participants can ask questions or comment on the topic and members' contributions. In the following consideration of the procedures for conducting each of these three formats, specific attention is given to the moderator's key role.

Panel Discussion Panel groups share information with an audience about a current problem or policy issue needing resolution. An organization concerned with a public or community problem usually sponsors a panel discussion group and establishes its focus or theme. For example, the student government might sponsor a panel about whether security should be increased in the dormitories and select persons who are informed or directly involved in the issue (dean of students, dormitory director, head of campus security, and chairperson of the residence council). The panel's designated moderator is responsible for coordinating the preparation and presentation of the panel discussion.

The moderator organizes or establishes procedure and should not get involved in the discussion. The following guidelines will help the moderator develop and conduct a panel discussion.

Panel Discussion Guidelines

Preparation

1. Contact desired panel members; establish topic, time, date; and solicit major topic questions and issues.
2. Identify three to five major questions or issues relevant to the topic and forward them to the panelists so they may consider their responses.

3. Obtain biographical information on the panelists and their connection to the topic.
4. Create name cards for the panelists and a visual display of the topic and questions or issues to be covered to orient the audience.
5. Prepare the room or hall for the panel discussion:
   - Make sure seating arrangements are adequate.
   - Arrange panelists so they are visible to each other and to the audience; seat the moderator at the end or middle of the panel.
   - Display name cards unobtrusively on the table and set up the visual display of the topic and questions or issues.
   - Set up and test microphones, if needed.
   - Fill water pitchers and set out glasses.

Conducting the Panel Discussion

6. Introduce the topic, relevant background, panelists and any ground rules about time limits for speakers, order of panelists, and audience questions.
7. Take the audience's perspective and solicit clarification, elaboration, or definitions of terms or ideas that appear ambiguous or unclear.
8. Summarize each panelist's contribution or solicit a summary from her or him before moving on to the next speaker;
9. Specify the procedures for audience questions and comments when the panel discussion is completed. (See forum discussion guidelines later in this chapter.)
10. After the question and answer session, summarize the panel presentation's highlights and thank the participants.

In addition to these requirements, the moderator must know what is happening at all times to ensure that the discussion is on track and manage heated exchanges between panelists diplomatically. Organization can help eliminate arguments. For instance, establishing procedures that require each member to present his or her views on the specific issue one at a time in turn followed by questions and comments offers more control than allowing panelists to question or respond to each other at will. Keep in mind that the panel members' contributions are largely impromptu; they are not scripted or planned speeches. Panelists who speak first may set the agenda for succeeding panelists, creating a desire to respond to criticisms or different views. Managing speaker interaction is perhaps the most difficult task for the moderator. The basic issue is to determine the degree and placement of panelist interaction.

The main tools for managing the discussion are topic questions or issues. They give the moderator control over what is discussed and the right to intervene if the discussion gets off the track. Managing a discussion also involves how much and when panelists' interaction is permitted. These decisions are based on how controversial the topic is and the relationship of the panelists.

You should consider two ways to control interaction when the topic is hot and the panelists are highly involved adversaries. First, require panelists to present their response to a question or issue one at a time in turn without addressing other members' presentations. This can be followed by a question and comment period, then repeating the process with the next question or issue. A second, more restrictive approach requires the panelists to respond to all the questions in turn followed by a single question and comment period; this approach is most appropriate if there are only two or three questions or issues. When many issues are addressed, it is difficult for the audience and moderator to keep track of what is covered.

An experienced moderator may allow panelists to approach each issue or question as they wish and permit reactions to other panelists' views. This approach can stimulate lively debate and enhance the drama of the discussion. However, you must allow panelists to respond to criticisms in a timely manner while ensuring that all panelists have a relatively equal opportunity to speak. You can observe some good examples of panel discussion moderation weeknights on "The MacNeil/Lehrer NewsHour" broadcast over your local PBS affiliate.

Forum Discussion Forums involve the audience in the discussion of an identified topic or public presentation. For example, a forum can follow a panel discussion, lecture, film, or a public interview. The moderator opens a forum on a public topic or community problem by announcing the topic, providing general background information related to the forum's purpose, reviews ground rules, and turns the floor over to the audience.

Forums require the moderator to establish procedures for conducting them, especially when the audience is large or the topic is controversial. The ground rules for participation must be established before opening discussion to the audience. Several guidelines should be considered when setting ground rules.

Forum Discussion Guidelines

1. Announce the amount of time available for questions and comments.
2. Require audience members to raise their hand to be recognized.
3. State that additional turns at speaking will be permitted after all persons desiring to speak have had the opportunity.
4. Establish whether comments are permissible or questions only. This is especially important if the forum's purpose is to consider expert information and not public opinion on the topic. (Even when participation is restricted to questions, some audience members invariably launch long-winded monologues.)
5. Have the audience member identify who the question is directed to and repeat the question for the audience.
6. When comments and opinions are permitted, be sure to solicit different points of view.

Interpreting ideas and their relationships in visual terms gives group members a common reference point for understanding complex information.

7. Cue the audience at the end of the forum by announcing time for two or three last questions or comments.

You can see numerous examples of forums following talk show interviews or after guest lectures. Although a forum discussion is easy to conduct, it becomes demanding when the audience is emotionally involved. In such circumstances, the moderator must maintain the ground rules and request that audience members respect the rights of guests and fellow audience members.

Roundtable Discussion The roundtable discussion is used for learning groups that typically exist for more than one meeting. A roundtable goes through a group development process. Members belong to such groups for the sake of personal development and growth in some professional or personal area of interest. At the turn of the century, literary groups were common. Such groups would select a book to read and meet to discuss the work and its merits. Most learning groups are specialized or focused on some general area (film, music, hobbies) and identify a specific focus for the roundtable discussion (for example, new movies or albums).

A cooperative atmosphere is important. The roundtable discussion is for sharing information, not competing to see who has the best information or opinion. All members have the opportunity to present views or solicit information. The "round table" is a symbol of unity. Discussion goes around the table, enabling all members to participate, although you do not have to use a circular table. John Brilhart's research on learning groups indicates that they not only provide an effective method for learning through information sharing but also contribute to social development.[2]

Roundtable discussions need to be focused, provide an equal opportunity for participation, and be open to a variety of viewpoints. A discussion leader can facilitate these requirements. The leader can be chosen from the group members, rotated among members, or solicited from outside the group. Regardless of how the discussion leader is selected, several procedural guidelines can maximize a productive roundtable discussion.

Roundtable Discussion Guidelines

1. Establish the specific focus of the learning discussion and how long the meeting will last.
2. Prior to the discussion identify the questions or issues for discussion at the meeting and arrange in a logical order (information questions before related opinion-seeking questions). Use questions or issues to monitor the discussion to keep it on track.
3. Cover questions or issues one at a time, providing all members an opportunity to speak before moving on to the next one.
4. Be sure participation is distributed relatively equally, and consider using time limits for each question or issue or restricting each member's turn. Such limits can increase the amount of information covered because they encourage members to get to the point.

These procedures, designed to maximize the cooperative exchange of information and opinions, can be modified to suit the situation of the group or meeting. However, changes should encourage participants' involvement, maintain a clear focus for discussion, and fulfill the specific goal of the meeting.

A detailed guide for learning discussion groups by William Hill has been successfully implemented in classroom settings and study groups.[3] This procedural guide is well worth consulting if your group's goal is to learn through sharing information.

Decision-Making Meetings

Decision-making groups need to share some information prior to making a decision. An informed decision maximizes its chances for success. Thus the procedures for information-sharing meetings may be adopted in part or whole to prepare for group decision making. However, decision making presents additional considerations to a group. It requires the same needs for participation, involvement, cooperation, focused discussion, and goal achievement as information-sharing meetings. But the group has the added task of identifying the best decision, ideally one that all members can accept.

The difficulties in conducting decision-making meetings include reconciling differences of opinion or outright conflict; identifying, sharing, and managing relevant information; identifying and evaluating decision choices; and perhaps most important, conducting such activities in the most efficient and effective manner. The remainder of this chapter provides a procedure for conducting decision-making meetings.

Parliamentary procedure is a familiar decision-making meeting format. It is, in simplest terms, a set of rules and roles designed to facilitate decision making in large groups.[4] The rules and roles provide a means for orderly discussion and debate. Although decisions are made through majority vote, numerous rules and procedures protect members aligned with the minority vote. Parliamentary rules were designed to establish the rights of all members to participate in open discussion and to be consistently and equitably applied.

A review of the specific rules and role responsibilities of parliamentary procedure is beyond the scope of this chapter. However, note that parliamentary procedure reflects the same emphasis as small information-sharing and decision-making groups: managing interaction, promoting participation, and efficient and effective goal attainment.

The Interaction Method for Conducting Meetings

After observing numerous meetings and conducting interviews with participants, Michael Doyle and David Straus designed a procedure—the Interaction Method—to facilitate effective decision-making meetings.[5] They identified four common problems that contributed to ineffective meetings: lack of discussion focus, forgetting the how, forgetting the group, and personal attacks.

Meeting Problems

The *focus problem* identifies the wandering and unproductive discussion. It has two aspects: not identifying what is to be accomplished during a given discussion and not maintaining the identified discussion focus.

If left unchecked, the focus problem can undermine decision-making effectiveness and groupness. For example, knowing what the objective of discussion is at a given point of the meeting contributes to productivity. A wandering discussion wastes time and sidetracks productivity. Focused discussion reduces the frustration and dissatisfaction that unfocused discussion creates. Unfocused discussion contributes to poor morale, undermines group cohesion, and promotes apathy or hostility among members.

Forgetting the how is the problem of not identifying the best procedure or technique for conducting a selected discussion focus. This is probably the most overlooked and ignored issue in group decision making. By not knowing what they are trying to accomplish and how to accomplish it, groups become ineffective.

This common problem is largely the result of members not knowing or using available techniques or practices for conducting the various meeting tasks.

There are two considerations for selecting a tool for a discussion focus: It must (1) be appropriate to the task at hand and (2) fit the participatory and relational needs of the group. For instance, if the group's immediate task is to develop a comprehensive list of potential solutions to a problem, it needs to generate ideas and draw on all members' suggestions. The manner in which ideas are generated would be determined by the degree to which there is relational tension, an open communication climate, and the need to manage inappropriate behavior.

Forgetting the group is another common and debilitating problem that occurs when one or more members dominate discussions, do not participate, or make unilateral decisions. When the whole group is not involved in the decision-making process, the value and quality of group decision making is undermined in several ways. First, it does not capitalize on the main advantage of groups: to provide greater comprehension of decisions. For decisions on matters or problems that are unstructured, complex, and unfamiliar, several heads are usually better than one or two. Second, if the members feel they have not been involved in making the decision, they may be less committed to the group and the decision. This can reduce participation, group morale, and compliance with the decision.

If a group is to effectively solve a problem or make decisions, then its members must feel and act as a group. This requires consistent (not necessarily equal) and active participation by all group members in discussion and decision-making activities. This calls for a safe communication environment, one in which members are free to express themselves and do not fear personal attack. Overcoming the problem of forgetting the group requires meeting practices that encourage participation and promote a supportive communication climate.

Personal attacks in the form of aggressive responses and criticism of a person through verbal and nonverbal messages promote defensive reactions and contribute to a defensive communication climate.[6] Group members should evaluate ideas, not other members. Constructive criticism of ideas is legitimate. Harsh criticism of fellow members—"If you knew what you were talking about, we might get somewhere!"—can derail the group. Even more subtle personal criticism—"What would you like us to do, Joe?"—said sarcastically can undermine supportive working relationships.

Personal attacks can create an atmosphere of fear, which tends to silence less assertive or apathetic members, thus reducing the variety of inputs. The value of group decisions is premised on the contributions and involvement of all the members; variety of information and opinions contributes to quality decisions. A group's ability to prevent attacks on members will help develop and maintain supportive relationships and contribute to group productivity.

Meeting Rules

Doyle and Straus's Interaction Method for conducting meetings is designed to eliminate or at least reduce the incidence of the preceding four problems through the use of several rules and roles. The rules establish practices to counter the meeting problems; the roles are members' special responsibilities to implement them. Together they provide procedures for group communication in decision-making meetings. The four essential rules are the focus rule, tool rule, consensus rule, and no-attack rule.

The *focus rule* requires the group to identify the specific task to be accomplished for each meeting activity. A focus is a specific agenda item that clearly establishes a desired outcome. This specificity identifies not only the desired outcome but also the type of activity—for example, generating ideas, evaluating, or reporting information. Knowing the specific focus of discussion provides direction for selecting the appropriate tool for conducting the focus. The group can identify the various meeting focuses before or during the meeting as long as it identifies the desired outcome. Once a focus has been selected, it is to be maintained until it is completed, postponed, or dropped. Then the group moves on to the next focus. Groups commonly change a focus because they did not recognize a preliminary subtask needing treatment to complete the task they are working on. For example, groups faced with doing a survey may try to develop survey questions before they have identified the information they need from the survey. Each subtask is a specific focus that should receive independent attention in a logical order.

Of course, the group needs to know what its goal is before identifying a specific focus. It might be a project with dozens of focuses to be addressed over several meetings or a meeting to reach a single decision involving two or three focuses. Regardless of how complex the group's goal is, the relevant focuses must be identified. This may be accomplished through an open discussion among the members followed by agreement on the first focus for treatment or through more comprehensive efforts to identify all the project focuses using idea-generating techniques (discussed in Chapter 6).

Following on the heels of the focus decision, the *tool rule* requires the group to determine how it is going to conduct the focus of discussion. Tool selection is determined by the nature of the activity indicated or required by the focus. For example, if the group's focus is to identify standards for evaluating teaching effectiveness (assuming the issue has already been researched), the group could use brainstorming as a tool for generating a comprehensive list of standards. Perhaps another technique could be used to decide on the next logical focus concerned with deciding on which standards to select. As with a focus, the tool can be changed if the group feels it is unproductive; another tool can be selected.

The relational situation of the group should also be considered in the selection of a tool. The need to encourage participation and reduce the occurrence of unproductive interaction such as premature evaluation and sarcastic comments should enter into the tool selection decision. The review of the various procedures in Chapter 6 emphasizes both the task and relational advantages and disadvantages.

The *consensus rule* requires all members to be involved in making decisions and to accept the final decision. Unanimous agreement is not necessary, but members should accept the reasoning underlying the decision.

Basically, consensus is an approach that attempts to keep the group together and arrive at the best decision by drawing upon the members' collective resources. It identifies all perspectives and conflicting viewpoints to test all options. Decisions regarding the selection of a focus, tool, or problem solution should be arrived at consensually. Most focus and tool decisions are usually obvious and easy to agree on. Substantive decisions, those concerned with the content and issues under deliberation, may give rise to several viewpoints that need to be discussed and evaluated carefully before a decision is reached. Guidelines for consensus decision making are presented in Chapter 6. If consensus is not reached after initial efforts, the group may need to consider voting or using conflict management strategies. (See Chapter 7.)

The *no-attack rule* requires members to refrain from behavior that negatively evaluates another group member. The rule establishes a desired communication practice that has members watching their own behavior, and it allows members to interrupt and remind members who stray from the rule to evaluate ideas, not people. Beware of nonverbal gestures that may suggest a personal attack such as a cocky smirk or stern stares while speaking. Furthermore, remember that many people tend to perceive a criticism of their idea as an attack on them. Establish that your concern is with the merits of the idea and not the worth of the person.

Together, the Interaction Method rules reduce the incidence of common problems that undermine productive group meetings. The rules generally follow an order, and each has its own decision points. For example, the focus rule is first followed by the consensus rule, then by the tool rule followed by the consensus rule again. At each of these points, there is either a focus or not and a tool or not. The next decision point is whether the group follows through and stays on focus and uses the selected tool. If the group is off the focus or is not using the tool, it can either change or get back on track. The no-attack rule is operative at all times.

Meeting Roles

The four rules of the Interaction Method are implemented through establishing four roles: facilitator, recorder, member, and manager/member. Role specialization has two purposes. First, it reduces the number of tasks that need to be performed by one person, thus freeing certain members' attention for specific tasks. For example, it is easier and more effective to engage in an activity such as brainstorming without having to also think about whether it is being conducted properly, which creates another task. Groups often have trouble brainstorming properly because members get so involved with the ideas that they forget about the proper procedures of brainstorming. The second and related purpose of role specialization is to improve the quality of attention and performance of a specific task or activity. Thus when you only have to work on generating ideas and someone else is keeping an eye on the process, both of you are more likely to do better with your individual tasks in the overall idea-generating activity.

A description of each role and its responsibilities will clarify the value of role specialization and the relationship of rules and roles. But first, a few words of caution. The Interaction Method requires being more systematic than is typical of most group experiences. It takes effort and vigilance to learn new ways of performing effectively in groups. The roles discussed here provide a way to help groups use the preceding rules. Although some of the roles described may not be feasible or directly relevant in class project groups, they are appropriate in other settings. Regardless of how feasible it is to establish these roles, the duties associated with each role need to be performed. Keep in mind that the problems with meetings discussed earlier are real; the rules developed to overcome them are effective only if they are implemented. Establishing roles and responsibilities to ensure rule compliance is a major way to implement adopted meeting procedures as well as other group duties and tasks.

The *facilitator role* is strictly procedural. That is, he or she is responsible for making sure that the group follows the four rules and any other guidelines it adopts, including the procedures of any tool adopted for conducting a selected focus. The facilitator may also suggest techniques or practices for consideration when selecting a tool for a focus but cannot contribute to the content of the group meeting. This restriction keeps the facilitator's mind on the meeting's process.

The facilitator role should be performed by a neutral third party, someone uninvolved in the group or its project. Such a person, one who is already versed in the Interaction Method, is a luxury. Ideally, your group could seek a person interested in developing facilitation skills and have him or her work with the group in performing the four rules. Another option is to assign a member to perform the role. But keeping him out of the meeting content could be difficult and might not be desirable if he has ideas to contribute. A third option is to have all members play the facilitation role: self-facilitate. This has the same problems as the second option but has the advantage of everyone performing the role. At any given time, any member can let the group know it is violating a rule or not using a tool properly. One group member is likely to recognize what is going on at any given point of the meeting. The group project facilitator at the end of Part II is designed to self-facilitate project group meetings in a systematic manner.

The *recorder role* performs the secretarial duties for the group. This person should ideally be a neutral third party, although a member could be assigned the task or it can be rotated. The recorder must keep his mind on what is being said and track the meeting flow by using a group memory. This is merely a visual display of the meeting's progress on large sheets of paper. It frees members from having to take notes, keeps attention on the discussion, and provides a review of the meeting. Copies of the group memory can be reproduced for later distribution. The use of paper is much better than a chalkboard, which can fill up and have to be erased.

The recorder must track the meeting without slowing it down and avoid putting words in a member's mouth. He or she must seek clarification when

Box 5.1

Teacher as Member: Using the Interaction Method

Professor Dokes did not want to dominate the group meeting, especially because he was the teacher, the expert on the project, and the project's director. It was important that the student members of the group be involved and participating throughout the project meetings. He knew that the student members would let him take over the meetings. The project had to do with diagnosis of the staff meetings of the campus radio station. The students' experience and background with student groups and their responsibility for conducting the diagnosis and making the recommendations report made their active participation crucial to the project's success.

This course project was a good opportunity to demonstrate and test the usefulness of the Interaction Method for conducting participatory meetings. The class members had read about the method and observed a videotape of a meeting using it. They were familiar with the rules and roles. The question was who would facilitate and record the meetings. Dokes knew he could do so if necessary, but this would defeat his purpose. It would promote the group's tendency to defer to him and wait for his leadership. He wanted the student members to initiate ideas, opinions, and suggestions for meeting procedures. Playing the role of the facilitator, recorder, member, and manager would certainly compromise the performance of all four roles—too many jobs to manage well. Dokes wanted to work as a member, as a team. He needed a neutral third-party facilitator and recorder so he could devote his attention to working as a manager/member.

The "great participator" was looking kindly upon Dokes. A former student, who was available to facilitate meetings, was experienced in using the Interaction Method, and his work study assistant could record the meetings.

At the first meeting, Dokes charged the project to the group. He established the goal of the project, background information, specifications, the time frame, and constraints. He then sat with the group members in a semicircle and let the facilitator review the rules and roles for conducting the meetings.

Professor Dokes had mixed emotions as he sat down with the group. He was relieved to focus his attention on the project and not have to perform so many roles. He was anxious about the Interaction Method and completing the project successfully. The demonstration of facilitation practices and effective project achievement were on the line.

The facilitator had the group identify the first focus and tool and made sure all were in agreement. The group decided to identify all the potential tasks involved in the project using brainstorming. The facilitator briefly

Box 5.1 (continued)

reviewed the brainstorming procedures, then monitored the interaction, making sure members stayed on focus and used the selected tool. The six group members began calling out ideas as the recorder tracked the group's progress on large sheets of paper. The first meeting went surprisingly well, even though Joe, one of the more enthusiastic personalities in the group, had to be brought back to the focus a few times. Dokes attributed the meeting's success to the fact that all participants knew and followed the rules and roles. The facilitator was able to recognize when a member lost focus or was not using the selected tool. He gently but firmly brought this to the attention of the member. He even had to bring Professor Dokes in line a couple of times. Because the facilitator's actions were understood, no one, including Dokes, resented his interventions when a rule or role was broken. He also made sure that all members were involved with each group decision and had opportunities to participate throughout the meeting.

The group had six meetings using the Interaction Method. They were all smooth and productive. The Interaction Method kept the group highly task centered. There was little socializing during the meeting, but there was some kidding around. The most satisfying aspect was that the students did participate in all aspects of decision making. The collective contributions of all the group members enhanced the quality of decisions and task completion. The project goal was successfully achieved. The method demonstrated that groups can work effectively together when they use practices to enhance participation and effective decision making. Most important, the experience demonstrated that "the boss," Professor Dokes, could be a member.

uncertain either by asking the member to repeat or explain a statement or by paraphrasing it to check for comprehension. Different colored markers can be useful in highlighting or emphasizing different types of information. For example, if the group lists ideas using a black marker, the rank order numbers can be written in red alongside the ideas. The recorder should have clear handwriting; printing is preferred.

The *member role* is devoted to following the meeting's content, making decisions, and keeping the facilitator and recorder in their respective roles. When the facilitator and recorder are well versed in their role duties, the others can devote their attention to the task at hand. Once the members have decided on the appropriate focus and tool for tackling it, they can direct their energies to completing the task with the support of the facilitator and recorder.

The *manager/member role* is concerned with redefining the role of the group's leader or manager in an effort to eliminate dominance, increase member participation, and develop group ownership of the meeting. Although the leader is responsible for establishing goals and identifying constraints and the group's role in the decision, once the leader has set the direction and limits of the task or goal, he or she becomes a participating member subject to all the rules of the meeting process. This role may appear to be irrelevant for groups without a formal designated leader or manager. However, as Chapter 4 points out, someone typically emerges as a perceived leader in the natural group process. Regardless of how the leader is determined, that person is to work as a member.

Developing such role specialization may seem unnecessary, but keep in mind that the roles are designed to make sure that the four rules are performed. The observance of these rules will contribute to the group's procedural effectiveness, which can translate into effective performance.

The Interaction Method provides a format for conducting decision-making meetings. The types of meeting tasks and procedures for conducting them provide another area for consideration. The tool rule requires the group to decide on the best way to tackle a focus. The tools for the tasks are taken up in the next chapter.

Designing Group Meetings

In Chapter 2 you read about the stages of group development. The first stage, orientation, when members get to know one another and form the group, is the time to consider developing and adopting rules and roles. Rules and roles need to be established before setting out on the group's project and put into operation before making major decisions. Not all general meeting rules and role duties will be identified in the first group meetings. The project and meeting process will likely raise problems and tasks leading to additional procedures or role duties.

The value of rules and roles depends on their purpose. They are designed and implemented to overcome practices and behaviors that undermine a group's task effectiveness and relational satisfaction. To the extent that groups do not anticipate and plan to manage unproductive group behaviors, such behaviors become entrenched practices or unwritten rules. The unfortunate consequence is that the group carries two burdens: the group project and the unproductive meeting practices.

The remainder of this chapter will provide suggestions for designing your group's meeting process by identifying meeting problems, designing rules and roles, and evaluating meeting effectiveness. These suggestions are part of the group project facilitator at the end of Part II.

Identifying Problems with Groups and Meetings

The earlier discussion on meeting problems provides a starting point. However, you have probably encountered other problems in your experience with meetings. All groups begin by focusing on their task. Few groups ever consider how they want to work together or identify what problems they wish to avoid. These two issues can be especially important for new groups because they have no history.

Ideally, group members could discuss the types of unproductive practices and behaviors they have experienced in other groups (or with the group if it has met several times). Consider their effects on task effectiveness, participation, and group cohesion. Seek consensus on the importance of managing the identified problems and explore ways to avoid them. Consider possible rules and role responsibilities for carrying them out.

Designing Rules and Roles

Rules and roles go hand in hand. Rules provide guides for practice; roles indicate who is to practice them. The rules of the Interaction Method prescribe specific practices to be conducted by one or more people. Although role specialization is desirable, it may not be feasible. In such cases the members must monitor themselves and other members for rule compliance. This is easier said than done. Even when groups establish rules, members forget them, fail to recognize when they are being violated, or are anxious about stopping a rule infraction. The group must firmly commit itself to the rules and reinforce members who invoke them.

The clarity and specificity of a rule is critical in effective rule compliance. An ambiguous, unclear rule does not manage a problem but creates one. Besides suggesting that the rule is unimportant, thus worth ignoring, it can also lead to confused or inappropriate applications. Create rules that clearly establish what behaviors are to be performed.

When a group decides to handle a meeting practice problem, it needs to identify the behavior or activity it does not want and what it prefers. Say that your group's discussion wanders and is unfocused. It decides to create a rule that requires members to agree on a direction and purpose before discussion. Furthermore, any member can invoke the rule if he or she perceives that another member has wandered from the set direction of discussion. If a member thinks he is on track, he can explain why he thinks so.

Most rules are perceived in a negative light, unless they are in games. In a way, group decision making is like a game in which the members create the rules as they go. Imagine playing football or Scrabble this way. It would be chaotic and probably lead to arguments and resentment. Unlike a game, the results of group decision making can have serious consequences. The development and use of rules and roles can eliminate problems and maximize successful decisions.

Evaluating Meeting Effectiveness

Whether or not a group chooses to implement rules and roles, it should spend a few minutes at the end of its meeting to evaluate practices and progress. This feedback can be used to assess the effectiveness of adopted rules and roles or the emergence of unanticipated problems. Without such information, the group cannot begin to alter the unproductive situation and is likely to repeat the problem. Unproductive meeting behaviors and problems steal from the group's energy and hinder effective goal achievement.

Conduct evaluations at the end of the first few meetings if the group is newly formed and occasional evaluations if the group appears to be working smoothly. Any member should be free to request such an evaluation. Focus on your observations and meeting experiences as the initial source for identifying what is or is not working well. You can use the itemized response described in Chapter 6 to evaluate meetings.

Assessing the effectiveness of meeting practices is only as useful as the group's interest and motivation to work effectively. Frequently, members feel that spending time on developing rules and evaluating meetings cuts into working on the group's task. It does take a little time. The trade-off is that the group avoids unproductive practices that waste time, enhances positive relationships that strengthen motivation and commitment, and ultimately improves the quality of its decisions.

Summary

This chapter has built on Chapter 4 by providing prescriptions for roles and rules for both information-sharing and decision-making meetings. These prescriptions enhance both task and relationship communication practices and outcomes.

Information-sharing meetings—panel, forum, and roundtable discussions in public and private settings—require clear gound rules for discussion. These rules are largely determined by the type, purpose, and circumstances of the information-sharing session and facilitated by a designated moderator.

Decision-making meetings are more complex events requiring groups to make choices based on information. We identified four group communication practices that hinder productive group meetings: focus problem, forgetting the how, forgetting the group, and personal attacks. To prevent these basic meeting problems, groups can adopt the focus rule, tool rule, consensus rule, and no-attack rule. The effectiveness of such procedures for dealing with problematic communication depends on the willingness of members to adopt and use them. The successful use of procedures is dependent on the clarity of the rules, specific role responsibilities of a designated member or members, and members' compliance with the rules.

Meeting rules and roles should be designed as the group forms, but can be adapted at any time a group perceives meeting problems. A group cannot anticipate every task or relational situation that creates problems. With evaluations at the end of meetings, the group can identify problematic communication practices and consider ways to prevent their occurrence.

These prescriptions may seem like a lot of work, especially those recommended for decision-making groups. However, they are based on practices known to be useful for conducting effective meetings. Planning can prevent poor performance.

GroupQuests: Discussion Questions

1. What do you think of the Interaction Method—the use of rules and roles to avoid and overcome typical meeting problems—as a way to improve the effectiveness of decision-making meetings? What are its advantages and disadvantages?
2. Think about the group meetings you have participated in and list all the practices and behaviors that you have found to be particularly unproductive and productive. Then consider why they were effective or ineffective in terms of the task and relationship dimensions of group communication. Would the use of a specific rule or role have been helpful in overcoming the ineffective behaviors and practices?

GroupWorks: Group Activities

1. Form groups of three to five members. Imagine that your group has been assigned the task of organizing and moderating a campus discussion on the "parking problem." What would you do specifically to fulfill this assignment for your campus? Consider the types of questions that you might use to organize the panel discussion.
2. Form groups of four to six members and select a film, text chapter, article, or album as the topic for a learning group discussion. As a group, develop a plan to organize and conduct the learning group discussion. Select a moderator and set a time for the learning group to meet. After the meeting conduct a roundtable to solicit members' perceptions: How did the selected plan and procedures work? Was the moderator able to maintain the discussion focus? What could improve future learning group meetings?
3. Observe a public or televised panel discussion. Identify the topic of the panel and the moderator's questions. Note how the moderator managed the discussion, panelist interaction, and controversy. Evaluate the moderator's ability and provide the reasons for your views.
4. Attend a meeting of a campus organization or class project group. (Seek permission if it is not open to the public.) Observe the meeting for the typical meeting problems identified by Michael Doyle and David Straus, the developers of the Interaction Method. Were they evident? How so? Were there any apparent consequences?

GroupActs: Practical Applications

This assignment is for groups working on a term project. Prior to your next meeting, answer Discussion Question 2. Be prepared to discuss the meeting's problems with your group and to decide how to prevent and manage them during the project. Consider adopting rules and roles of the Interaction Method or devising your own particular rules. Be sure to be specific and clear on the who, what, when, and where of each rule or practice you develop for use in the meeting. Do not merely discuss the problems without establishing specific practices for dealing with them.

CHAPTER 6

The Episode Level: Managing Group Activities

Tools are made for specific tasks. For example, using a regular hammer to pound delicate finishing nails is a disaster. If the nail is not bent by the weight of the hammering, the wood will certainly show marks. A smaller, lightweight hammer is appropriate for fine nailing jobs. Knowing the tools and when and where to apply them during meetings poses critical procedural decisions for groups. The two main considerations are matching the tool to the task and social needs of the group.

This chapter identifies the types of meeting tasks encountered by groups and describes procedures or tools for conducting them. As discussed in Chapter 5, groups typically proceed without considering the best way to conduct an activity. This can lead to inefficiency or poor decisions and may undermine the development of productive and satisfying working relationships. The following sections introduce specific techniques and guidelines for your task group's toolbox.

Types of Group Tasks

Decision-making groups conduct five general types of tasks: information gathering, information sharing, idea generating, idea evaluation, and problem solving. The first four tasks occur in virtually all groups concerned with decision making. Problem solving, a specific complex type of decision making, may occur during decision making or be the group's specific goal. The steps of problem solving, as you will see later, correspond to the four types of tasks.

Recall that procedural communication serves both task and relationship functions. Thus the group can and should consider its immediate task and social needs in selecting a tool. For instance, two or three members may dominate a project group, but the opinions of the whole group need to be obtained before making a final decision to ensure involvement and support. The group could select an activity that would require participation and opinions from all members. Using a procedure that creates an opportunity to participate could reduce domination by the few and increase involvement of others. The chosen tool should ideally fulfill these requirements.

Tools for Information Gathering

Information gathering is concerned with inquiry and research for the sake of answering questions. It helps if you know what questions need answering. The question is the most fundamental and powerful tool for analyzing an issue or problem.

Four types of questions are used for conducting the group's detective work: questions of definition, fact, value, and policy. These questions build upon each other and are sequential in that questions of definition typically precede questions of fact, questions of fact precede those of value, and so on. Questions of policy are the most complex and involve all the other questions.

Questions of definition are concerned with establishing and justifying what a concept or term refers to. The first problem of communicating something is to establish what that something is. This becomes particularly important when there are competing definitions, abstract concepts, and the potential for multiple meanings or interpretations.

Ultimately, the group is faced with establishing a definition so it can clearly communicate with its members and others. The group can use standard definitions from dictionaries or subject-specific encyclopedias from such fields as psychology and economics. Experience can be a source of creating definitions in cases where there is a new or original view of a concept. For example, a knowledge of the "campus funding process"—not typical of all funding processes—would serve as a basis for defining it.

Defining is only half the battle: justifying is the other half. This poses no problem when you share definitions of common concepts, such as transportation, gravity, and popular election. Defining becomes problematic when there are competing, controversial, or no appropriate definitions of abstract concepts such as love, faith, and socialism. To establish the legitimacy of your definition, identify the expert source or develop an argument that supports the definition. For example, the definition of *socialism* used by political scientists would be a legitimizing source for that term. Situation-specific terms such as *campus funding process* could be established using documents about the process. Regardless of how a definition is established, make it as clear and concrete as possible.

Imagine that you belong to a student group charged with evaluating funding for chartered student organizations on campus. This project immediately raises two questions of definition: "What is a chartered student organization?" and "What is the funding process?" The group will likely come across other questions of definition as it conducts its inquiry.

The goal of defining a concept is to provide the group and its audience with the information needed to understand when it appears in questions of fact, value, and policy or in answers to them.

Questions of fact are concerned with whether something "is": Does it exist? Questions of definition emphasize identifying something. Questions of fact, the most prevalent type, emphasize whether that something has occurred or is occurring.

Group projects are loaded with such questions. Although a question of fact ideally seeks the "truth" of the matter, the absolute truth of something is virtually always debatable. Therefore, the answers to most questions of fact are statements of probability. They are the most reasonable answers after examining all relevant data. Because we are usually unable to secure all relevant data and cannot predict the future with absolute certainty, the answer needs to be qualified. *Most*, *some*, *likely*, *possible*, *probable* and similar terms acknowledge the probable nature of factual statements, especially those concerned with the future.

Questions of fact can be classified in terms of time or the type of answer sought. Those concerned with time are questions of past, present, and future fact. Questions of past fact are historical and are a constant matter of concern in courts of law. Questions of present fact involve matters of ongoing concern that have not been resolved. "What are the ways to get funding?" or "How many sources of funding are available on campus?" reflect concerns about the present. Questions of future fact involve prediction using information about past and present facts: "Will funding increase next year?"

Virtually all projects involve several other types of basic fact questions, including these common ones:

- *When* questions are concerned with time relationships, such as "When can an organization apply for funding?"
- *Who* questions focus on persons or groups as they relate to something, for example, "Who can submit funding proposals?"
- *Why* questions address the cause of an outcome or effect: "Why are organizations denied funding?"
- *Where* questions involve matters of place or location: "Where do you submit proposals for funding?"
- *Extent/degree* questions are about how something relates to other objects, events, and people: "How detailed is a funding proposal?"

Questions of duration ("How long?"), process, method, or procedure ("how to"), and comparison-contrast are just a few other types of fact questions. Your group should always look for other types to thoroughly explore relevant needs for information.

Sources for answers to questions of fact are many. Although most of such answers are found in print in newspapers, books, magazines, and reports, some may have to be generated through interviews, observation, or surveys conducted by the group when questions of fact have no available answers in print. For example, "What do campus organizations think about the funding process?" probably requires interviews to answer.

Another important matter is the legitimacy of the answer to questions of fact. The credibility of the source, procedures for arriving at an answer, and the age of the data are factors to consider. Look for all available answers to a question of fact to compare them and obtain the most current information. Too often people accept the first answers they find, only to discover that they do not have the most recent data. Such situations undermine the credibility of the answers, the project, and the group.

The relevance of facts derived from information searches requires scrutiny. Groups often become enamored with the volume of information collected and force it into the presentation or report. The report then appears confusing because the information, although clearly connected to the topic, does not clearly relate to the project goal. An opposite problem can occur when groups discard or overlook information because it appears irrelevant. The group needs to ask itself whether information is relevant: Does it answer a key question directly related to the project's goal?

Questions of value are concerned with decisions and evaluation. They involve judgment about right and wrong, beauty and ugliness, and good and bad. For example, the questions "What is the *best* way to write a proposal?" or "Does funding *improve* student organizations' membership recruitment?" require assessments. Such questions are slippery in that they are tied to matters of taste and personal needs and vary with different people and different times. To make matters worse, value terms (*beautiful*, *fair*, *effective*) are subjective and have no specific meaning. The challenge is to specify or qualify the value term as it relates to the object being evaluated—for example, what is meant by a "good" proposal?

You can handle questions of value by identifying common or expert standards for making a judgment about something and then applying them to the specific object of evaluation. You could, for example, consult books about effective practices for writing proposals. You can also use ideal cases of the object of judgment to assess and identify value standards. For instance, a review of successful proposals could be used to establish the standards for an effective proposal.

Value term criteria range from simple to complex, depending on the focus of judgment. They are largely determined by the interplay of the specific person, time, place, situation, and goals. Often the values of the intended or affected target audience must be considered when developing criteria to answer questions of value. As in questions of definition and fact, the legitimacy of a

Ideawriting, although conducted individually, requires members to share and build upon each other's ideas.

set of value standards or criteria is critical. It is important to establish the validity and reasoning behind the qualifications used to answer a value question.

Questions of policy are a special type of complex value question. They are typically the result of a problem or situation needing change. Policy questions are constantly emerging in the social, governmental, scientific, and health arenas, where matters of public policy arise from changes that create actual or potential problems. Such questions spotlight a given situation in an effort to determine if it is acceptable, effective, or productive. If not, an alternative is sought. The policy question is always judging how to best fulfill a goal.

The typical policy question is the should or ought question. "Should funding procedures be simplified?" is a question that could be raised if many organizations failed to receive funds due to procedural errors. The question "What type of events should be funded by student government?" may arise because of the lack of funding of academic-oriented events. Policy questions may be raised to anticipate or prevent problems, even if there is no perceived problem. For example, if the student government wanted to review its funding policy to determine whether it was meeting student needs, it could ask, "What activities should the student government be funding?"

The answer to a question of policy requires the investigator, who raises the question, to examine the status quo—the present policy or state of affairs. If there is a problem with the existing situation, the investigator must establish

Information-Gathering Questions

Group Goal:	***Determine if campus radio station programming needs to be altered or changed.***
Question of Policy	What type of programming should be aired on the campus radio station? (Note: This provides the goal and basis for identifying all information needed—questions to ask—to answer the policy question.)
Question of Definition	What is radio programming?
Questions of Fact	What is the present radio station programming? Is the programming targeted to specific audiences? Why are the present programs being aired? What are the possible types of programs? (This question may lead to defining each type of programming.) Who determines radio programming? Who listens to the radio station? Why do people listen to the radio station?
Questions of Value	What is desirable radio programming? What is good radio programming?

Figure 6.1 Four types of questions are used for gathering information: questions of policy, questions of definition, questions of fact, and questions of value. The questions listed here in three of the categories (definition, fact, value) are only a few of the relevant questions that could be asked. Also, gathering answers to these initial questions may raise new questions.

it. All recommended changes or solutions should be workable and clearly improve the identified problem.

Questions of policy require the identification of and answers to questions of value, fact, and definition that underlie it (see Figure 6.1). A thorough analysis of any policy, value, or complex fact question depends on identifying the inherent questions that need to be answered before you can proceed with the investigation. The investigation should ideally lead you to the best policy decision or answer. Just as there are few if any absolute fact answers, there are no absolute policy answers. The goal is to develop the most reasonable and feasible answer possible.

Once a group has identified its specific task or goal, it needs to know what it needs to know and decide on ways to find out. Be careful that the first few questions do not lull you into thinking that all the relevant questions have been identified. Some questions give rise to other questions and additional research. The search for answers frequently reveals a few more questions. By arranging all questions in a logical order, some answers will provide the basis for understanding other questions and their answers. When no new questions emerge, you have reached the end of questioning. You know when to stop searching for answers when the same answers recur.

Tools for Information Sharing

Information sharing is specifically concerned with the exchange of information or views regarding some matter of discussion. Although all tasks involve the exchange of information, some are devoted specifically to this activity. Reviewing members' opinions, presenting information or research findings, and sharing feelings or thoughts are common examples of sharing information, usually done through the open discussion. But other information-sharing practices may be more appropriate, depending on the information-sharing task and the relational situation of the group. Some information-sharing practices encourage involvement, while others can discourage it.

There are three fundamental ways a group can share information: open discussion, round-robin, and reports. An interactive computer program, electronic mail (E-mail) can be used to share information outside of meetings efficiently. Let us now consider each tool, its purpose, and its advantages and disadvantages.

Members use *open discussion* to gain information or views on a focus of discussion; it supplies a comprehensive understanding or variety of opinions on some topic. Any member can speak when he or she has information or an opinion to offer. There is no order or particular organization to who speaks. This often-used discussion format is the starting point for any group activity in which there is no adopted procedure. Groups typically use open discussion to identify meeting focuses and tool selection.

Open discussion is fine as long as the group does not allow a few members to dominate discussions. Members need to solicit input from all members. The lack of structure and order to open discussion can contribute to heated and hostile interaction that may detract from effective group relationships. The group may need to slow down interaction by taking turns speaking or use conflict-reducing procedures (see Chapter 7) to clarify the discussion and maintain a productive working relationship.

Open Discussion

Advantages

- Allows for spontaneous presentation of ideas.
- Is easy to use—no specific procedure.
- Does not restrict individual members' expression.

Disadvantages

- Dominant and extroverted members can monopolize discussion.
- Unassertive members may become dissatisfied and alienated from the group.
- The quantity of information may be reduced because of lack of participation.
- Discussion gets off focus easily.

The *round-robin* is a systematic discussion tool that allows each member to briefly address an issue or focus in turn. For instance, if the focus of discussion is to find out members' preferences on how to administer a survey, each member would take a turn presenting his or her views. Members are not required to speak and may pass, but all are given the opportunity to voice their thoughts without being interrupted. It is an especially useful tool for promoting involvement, scanning members for information or opinions, and controlling meeting interaction.

Round-Robin Guidelines

1. Establish a specific issue or focus for discussion.
2. Allow each member to have a turn to speak on the focus without interruption. You can set time limits.
3. Seek clarification of a member's input after his or her turn or once all members have had their turn.
4. After all clarifications and questions have been answered, other meeting tools may be used.

Advantages

- Promotes involvement through participation.
- Provides reconnaissance of group members' positions on issue or focus.
- Reduces heated discussion and tension.
- Can increase the quantity of information and ideas.
- Enhances understanding and reduces confusion among members.

Disadvantages

- Some members may talk excessively, wasting time and frustrating those who are anxious to move on.
- May not be appropriate if time is short.

The round-robin is easy to conduct but can readily be sidetracked into open discussion before it is completed if members are permitted to interrupt the speaker for questions or clarification. Questions are appropriate only after the speaker is finished or all members have spoken. If questions or clarification are permitted during the speaker's turn, the group must make sure that it does not slip into open discussion. These procedural options must be clear before conducting the round-robin.

Reports are the most common and effective way to deliver specific information to a group. An individual member, subcommittee, or a team of experts can be assigned a task for investigation or a request for information. Written reports can be distributed before meetings, which enables members to study the information and can save meeting time for questions and interpretation. Remember these tips when delegating and receiving oral or written reports:

Report Guidelines

1. Make assignments for information specific (questions to be answered, desired and potential sources, and manner of delivery).
2. Establish the due date for the report.
3. Schedule reports at the beginning of meetings or just before a related agenda item.
4. Listen or read carefully and seek clarification of the report's facts, opinions, and implications for group decisions.

Advantages

- Provides systematic tool for information exchange (research, plans, recommendations).
- Separates information from group decision tasks.
- Uses time efficiently and provides a record of information if written.

Disadvantages

- May include irrelevant or unneeded information and waste time.
- May create confusion if disorganized.

Reports must be assigned in a timely fashion so the information is available when the group needs it. Late reports could stall the group's progress. Distributing reports before meetings can save meeting time and prepare members for discussion. College student groups do not have the use of interoffice memos and fax machines to exchange written information between members, but most campuses have computer systems equipped with electronic messaging programs (E-mail). Members can use E-mail to exchange reports or share ideas so meeting time can be spent on tasks needing face-to-face interaction.

E-mail is a computer program that can be used to share information between meetings. It provides the group members with another channel for sending or receiving written information or graphics. It allows users to send or receive messages without having to be present. Messages are stored in each user's electronic mailbox until he or she signs on and reviews them. It does not require knowledge of computers to learn how to use it.

E-mail lets members conduct information-sharing tasks without having to meet. For example, if all members are to individually list questions in preparation for information gathering, they could send them to one member who could compile a master list electronically and forward it to the group members before the meeting. Then meeting time could be devoted to fine-tuning and selection. E-mail offers other efficiency advantages. Once you type information on E-mail it is done, ready to send to all group members with a single command. There are no duplicating costs, and no time is spent on distributing information. Also members can seek clarification of a report, allowing its author to respond before the meeting or prepare responses for the meeting, thus saving meeting time for matters requiring face-to-face deliberations. E-mail is a useful skill to develop because its use in organizations is increasing. A visit to your campus computer center will provide you with the needed information to get on line.

Tools for Idea Generating

Idea-generating communication in groups is a special form of sharing information; the same tools can be used for both activities, especially if the issue or focus is routine. For example, if the group needed to develop ideas on where to find information on a well-known topic with many obvious resources, an open discussion could do the job. On the other hand, if the focus is to generate a comprehensive list of creative decision options or possible solutions to a difficult problem, then a more task-specific tool is desirable. Although open discussion can be used to generate ideas, it usually gets bogged down in premature evaluation. This can hinder the identification of many useful ideas and lead to resentment if members do not get to contribute their ideas.

Brainstorming is a popular technique for generating ideas.[1] All evaluation or criticism is held off until all ideas are listed. Members are urged to offer ideas and to build on those of others. Even weird and unusual ideas are acceptable for listing because they might trigger a usable idea or solution. Remember, the group is looking for a large pool of ideas, and evaluation before the pool is generated undermines this goal.

In idea writing, a variation of brainstorming, each member generates a list of ideas on paper silently for ten to fifteen minutes.[2] Then all the listed ideas are placed in the center of the table and each member selects a list to make comments and additions until each member has reviewed and added ideas to all the members' lists. In a round-robin, members present the ideas from their list until all members' ideas are on a master list. Research has shown that the silent generation of ideas increases their quantity, reduces conformity pressures, and can control conflict.[3] Idea writing can be conducted through E-mail.

The steps of brainstorming are easy to understand but difficult to follow. The tendency to prematurely evaluate ideas is natural. Group members need to adhere to the following steps:

Brainstorming Guidelines

1. Establish a clear focus for the brainstorming session: What is the group seeking ideas about?

2. Select a member or third party to record all ideas by writing as clearly and as fast as possible and displaying ideas on large sheets of paper. Use members' words.
3. Ask members to call out their ideas and remember to not evaluate or seek clarification at this time. They should feel free to express any idea (the wilder the better) at any time during the session, combine or build on others' ideas, and maximize quantity, not quality.
4. Once all ideas are listed, seek clarification of unclear or unusual ideas.
5. Decide on the most acceptable idea options, using an appropriate decision-making tool.

Advantages

- Maximizes the pool of ideas available for consideration.
- Helps elicit creative ideas to difficult problems.
- Reduces the tension among members due to premature evaluation.
- Idea-generating phase of idea writing can be done before meeting.

Disadvantages

- Takes time to conduct correctly.
- Volume of ideas may create information overload.
- Idea writing reduces verbal interaction needed for developing groupness and cohesion.

Idea generating can be aided by using questions to trigger ideas, especially solutions to problems. Questions may even be used during the idea-generating step of brainstorming to help stimulate ideas. *Idea-spurring questions* can also help analyze a problem by broadening the perspective from which it can be viewed.[4] This question technique is easy to implement and adapt. Simply have a member read each question and allow the members to write their own ideas silently or record verbalized ideas on a master list. As in brainstorming, postpone clarification and evaluation until all questions are asked and all ideas are listed.

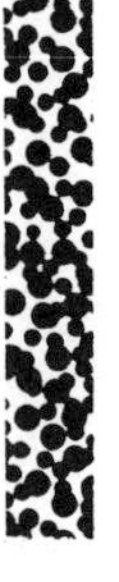

Idea-Spurring Question Guidelines

1. Identify the triggering question based on the specific idea-generating task. For example, problem analysis requires ideas on what causes the problem; if solution ideas are needed, the question searches for ways to solve the problem.
2. State the triggering question to the group using one of the following idea-spurring terms: adapting, magnifying, substituting, reversing, modifying, minimizing, rearranging, combining. For example, "Is this a problem due to adapting?" Record all the members' ideas triggered by the question on a list, and then restate the question using the next term.

3. After using these or other relevant terms, review the list of ideas for clarification and selection.

Advantages

- Broadens perspective on problem and can stimulate variety of ideas.
- Can help solicit ideas when stuck during brainstorming.

Disadvantage

- Systematic procedure takes time to implement.

The value of these idea-generating tools depends on the value, quantity, and variety of ideas. After all, group decision making is supposed to maximize the quality of decisions through a variety of perspectives and ideas. It would seem that the variety of individuals in a group would naturally contribute to the quantity and variety of ideas, but as you will read later on, numerous factors undermine this possibility. The preceding tools can help expand the pool of ideas through stimulating ideas and participation.

Tools for Idea Evaluation and Decision Making

The last set of basic meeting tools are for decision making, which requires group members to evaluate something and compare options to make an informed choice. The challenge is to establish a basis for making reasonable judgments to make the best decision.

Open discussion can be used during decision-making activities, but it does not provide a critical and systematic approach to selecting among decision options. There are two general approaches to making informed decisions—based on criteria or on preference. Criteria-referenced decisions or solutions must satisfy identified standards or criteria. For example, an acceptable decision for a company training program may require low costs, short implementation time, and use of existing personnel. These three requirements could serve as criteria for choosing among decision options. Such criteria often are elaborated during decision-making discussion. Identify such decision criteria before making decisions so decision makers are aware of constraints and requirements.

The second type of decision making is conducted by personal preference: Each member selects decision options based on his or her standards. Others may also hold standards, but they need not be publicly shared or agreed upon among members. A clear example of preference-based decision making is voting. Regardless of what reasons people give for a preference, it is never certain what standards motivated their vote. Frequently, personal criteria are revealed through discussion and may become acknowledged as the group's criteria for making or accepting a decision.

There are three reasons why it is useful, when time permits, to identify criteria for an acceptable decision before making a final choice. First, it establishes the standards by which to judge or modify decision options. Second, by using the collective wisdom of the group, the quality of the decision is maximized. Third, decisions made with shared criteria enhance group commitment to them and foster group cohesion. On the down side, criteria-referenced decisions may lead to an ineffective decision if all relevant criteria are not identified, the importance of a criterion is overrated, or the criteria were not based on knowledge and reason.

The following techniques for evaluating ideas emphasize either criteria-referenced or personal-referenced decisions. Three criteria-referenced techniques are consensus decision making, the itemized response, and weighting. The preference-based techniques are ranking, nominal group technique, and voting.

Consensus decision making requires that all members of the group find the decision acceptable—not necessarily the best one, but workable. This means any one member can block the decision if it is perceived to be illogical or unfeasible or if it does not fulfill a major criterion. Recall that one of the major problems in group decision making is forgetting the group; a dominant few make the decisions, ignoring the views of the less vocal. This not only wastes the group's brain power but also alienates members from the group, undermining cooperation and cohesion. Consensus decision making can reduce the likelihood of this occurring.

The value of this approach to decision making is its requirement that a member present the reason and logic for a preference when there are differences between members' preferences. The reasons for a member's preference directly or indirectly reveal standards or criteria governing the preference. Establishing the reasons for preferences can help the group identify and discuss essential attributes of a good choice or solution.

The following guidelines, adopted from Jay Hall, will provide you with ground rules for conducting decision making by consensus.[5]

Consensus Decision Making Guidelines

1. Do not argue for your own position. Present your views and reasons and consider others' reactions before pressing your point.
2. Do not assume that you are in a contest and someone must win or lose. Look for the next most acceptable option for all members.
3. Do not avoid conflict or differences of opinion. Explore reasons for views and agreement. Yield only to views that make sense and are well founded. Differences of opinion are natural and the most valuable resource for critical decision making.
4. Avoid conflict-reducing techniques such as flipping a coin, voting, compromising, and averaging. These techniques require someone to lose and do not ensure reasoned decisions.
5. If open discussion seems to leave out certain members, be sure to ask their opinion. Use the round-robin to be sure all members have a final say if

you doubt all views have been aired. The wider the range of information and opinions, the greater the chance of high-quality decisions.

Advantages

- Broadens information base.
- Promotes cohesion through participation.
- Contributes to member satisfaction.
- Increases decision quality.

Disadvantages

- Open discussion alone does not ensure participation.
- Takes time, especially when opinions differ on acceptable decision criteria.
- Promotes false agreement—members say yes, but really disagree.

The *itemized response* is used to constructively evaluate an idea or solution by first identifying its strengths and then its weaknesses.[6] The weaknesses should ideally be stated in a proactive form—what is needed or desired rather than what is wrong. For example, if cost is a concern, you could say, "I would like a more economical way to develop the training program." The more typically evaluative statement is "It's not a cost-effective program. We'll go broke!" Unlike negative statements, proactive evaluation helps reduce the sting and anxiety that evaluating others' ideas often creates, while providing direction for improving an idea. As in consensus decision making, the criteria for a good solution are indirectly implied in the identified positive and desired attributes of the idea. However, be careful. General and vague statements—"It was a good meeting"—do not provide useful information. The itemized response requires members to be specific—"Participation by all members made the analysis comprehensive." Regardless of what the group is evaluating, it needs to know specifically what was and would be useful. The following example, using the itemized response to evaluate a group's meeting, will illustrate.

Strengths	*Requirements*
Members listened to each other	More ideas from all members
Brainstorming was productive	Quieter meeting room
Recorder kept up with meeting	Have meetings start on time
Project appears to be on track	Remember to stick to the discussion focus
Joking around did not stop meeting progress	

The itemized response can be conducted as a group or individually depending on the circumstances and needs of the group. It offers a simple and efficient way to review ideas or solutions for acceptability and provides direction for modification and improvement.

Itemized Response Guidelines

1. Establish the focus or object of evaluation.
2. Solicit all positive evaluation first—things members like about the idea or solution.
3. Solicit all concerns and/or weaknesses with the idea or solution in proactive form—things members would like to see.
4. Address needs for clarification and discuss next steps.

Advantages

- Identifies desirable attributes of idea or solution.
- Establishes perceived needs for more acceptable idea; provides basis for modification.
- Promotes supportive and sensitive evaluation and positive relationships; prevents defensiveness.

Disadvantages

- Takes practice and monitoring use to perform correctly.
- Vague and general statements reduce utility of procedure.

Ranking is a useful tool for reducing options or identifying the best ones. It is easy to use and can sometimes be conducted outside of meeting time. Ranking can be used to make choices, but is not meant to replace thoughtful discussion of options. It is especially useful for narrowing the field of options developed through brainstorming or idea writing and can be followed by other decision-making techniques. When ranking, remember to:

Ranking Guidelines

1. Have a clear list of decision options and code them (A,B,C, for example). Review all options for clarity.
2. Determine how many of the listed options are to be selected for ranking.
3. Hand out three-by-five-inch note cards, one card for each idea to be selected and ranked. Instruct members to place the idea code in the upper left-hand corner of a card. Write the idea in the center of the card and the rank in the upper right-hand corner; use 1 to indicate your first choice, 2 for your second favorite, and so on.
4. Record members' preferences on a master list and tally the ranking for each item to obtain an idea score. Order the ideas based on each idea's score; the idea with the lowest score (receiving the most 1's) would be first.
5. Review the ranked ideas and share impressions. Discuss the need for modifications and next steps.

Advantages

- Efficient method for reducing options for discussion.
- Establishes group's perceptions of preferred options.

Disadvantages

- May substitute for discussion, undermining quality of decisions.
- May eliminate viable options because of lack of discussion before ranking.
- Large differences between members' rankings may weaken or eliminate some members' preferences from final ranking.

The tool of *Nominal group technique* combines idea writing, the round-robin, and ranking to arrive at group decisions.[7] It begins with a focus question from which participants silently brainstorm ideas on paper. This is followed by a round-robin in which each member presents one idea from his or her list until all members' ideas are on a master list. Members can add any ideas stimulated by the round-robin, but must refrain from discussion of ideas until all ideas are on the master list. Once the comprehensive list of ideas is completed, members can seek clarification of the ideas to establish understanding of them, not to evaluate them. Ranking is then employed to narrow or select the idea options. This three-step technique is best used for tasks that require generating a large list of ideas that have to be narrowed down to a few choices for further discussion and evaluation. The advantages and disadvantages of idea writing and ranking apply in the use of nominal group technique as well.

Weighting requires identifying the criteria or standards for making a decision, giving them numeric values in terms of importance, and then applying them to rank decision choices.[8] The group can select a tool such as brainstorming to identify the possible list of relevant criteria or use criteria obtained from external sources. It then consensually decides on the important standards and their comparative value by giving them numeric weight. All these steps must be conducted before the group can evaluate each decision option.

There is no one way to set up a weighting system for decision options. The following guidelines list the steps for both *basic* and *complex* weighting. Review the examples in Figure 6.2 to help you understand the guidelines.

Weighting Guidelines

1. List the specific decision options or choices to be evaluated vertically on the left-hand margin of the paper in front of the group.
2. Develop the list of criteria deemed relevant to an acceptable decision or solution and list them horizontally on the paper. (For a complex option, weight each criterion in terms of importance, 1 being unimportant to 7 very important.)
3. Examine each idea or option and discuss whether it fulfills the criteria and how well. (This can be done silently on paper and compiled later.) Decide

Basic Weighting

Solution / Ideas	Criteria: Reduce Noise Source	Easy/Fast to Do	Low Demand on Resources (staff, $, materials, etc.)	Accommodates Student Needs/Wants	Total Score
Restrict group meetings to enclosed meeting rooms	7	7	7	0	21
Designate "quiet zones" away from public areas	7	7	7	7	28
Install acoustic ceiling panels	4	3	1	7	15
Relocate noisy machines (copiers, microfilm, etc.) to enclosed room	7	6	6	7	26
Install acoustic partitions between public and study areas	5	4	1	7	17
"Quiet library" campaign	4	5	5	7	21
Restrict "Walkmans" from quiet areas	7	7	7	3	24
Library staff monitor and enforce quiet policy in designated areas	5	7	5	7	24

Key: 1= low fit 7= high fit

Figure 6.2 Basic and complex weighting techniques.

on the degree to which it fulfills each criterion, using 1 for poor fulfillment to 7 for complete fulfillment. (For a complex option: If criteria are also weighted, multiply each criterion weight by the idea weight.)

4. Total the weights for each idea across all the criteria to obtain an idea score. Rank the ideas by order of scores, the largest being first.
5. Examine decision options for the degree of similarity between them. Note where there appears to be agreement and difference. Discuss differences between idea scores to determine the basis of the difference.

Advantages

- Provides systematic method for critical decision making.

Complex Weighting

Solution / Ideas	Reduce Noise Source	Easy/Fast to Do	Low Demand on Resources (staff, $, materials, etc.)	Accommodates Student Needs/Wants	Total Score
Criterion Weightings	7	3	6	4	
Restrict group meetings to enclosed meeting rooms	7 / 49	7 / 21	7 / 42	0 / 0	112
Designate "quiet zones" away from public areas	7 / 49	7 / 21	7 / 42	7 / 28	140
Install acoustic ceiling panels	4 / 28	3 / 91	1 / 6	7 / 28	71
Relocate noisy machines (copiers, microfilm, etc.) to enclosed room	7 / 49	6 / 18	6 / 36	7 / 28	131
Install acoustic partitions between public and study areas	5 / 35	4 / 12	1 / 6	7 / 28	81
"Quiet library" campaign	4 / 28	5 / 15	5 / 30	7 / 28	101
Restrict "Walkmans" from quiet areas	7 / 49	7 / 21	7 / 42	3 / 12	124
Library staff monitor and enforce quiet policy in designated areas	5 / 35	7 / 21	5 / 30	7 / 28	114

Key: 1= low fit 7= high fit

- Establishes clear basis for decision making, which can enhance commitment.
- Can be conducted in part outside of meeting.

Disadvantages

- Time-consuming.
- Comparatively complex tool.
- Inappropriate or biased weightings can lead to low-quality decisions.

Weighting can help the group make decisions based on clear and mutually accepted standards. Having such standards, especially before idea evaluation begins, can help reduce the possibility of conflicts during discussion. Although disagreement may occur over establishing the appropriate criteria, such discussion can be critical to effective decision making. Note that the numeric rankings do not always feel right. The group may actually prefer lower ranked decisions. This may be due to some inflated weightings, a lot of divergence in members' weightings, or important criteria that are operating in members' minds but are not identified in the weighting activity. Discussion usually helps the group discover the problem and guides the final decision. The story in Box 6.1 illustrates how using the weighting technique can solve a decision-making problem.

Voting, a popular decision-making practice, contrasts sharply with decisions by consensus. Although discussion typically precedes voting, it does not necessarily determine voting outcomes. Voting hides as much as it reveals about the reasons for a choice, especially if no discussion takes place. A disaffected minority is an ever-present threat to group cohesion. Nonetheless, voting is an efficient means of arriving at decisions, especially when there are time pressures. There are several considerations to note when voting:

Voting Guidelines

1. Determine the minimum number of members needed to conduct an acceptable vote. This is the *quorum*. The larger the quorum, the more members' attendance becomes important.
2. Set the voting margin or percentage of votes needed to accept a choice. It can be a simple majority or more. The larger the percentage, the more votes needed and the more members committed to the decision.
3. Thoroughly discuss the decision options before voting, balancing discussion of different positions and preferences.
4. If a vote is close, find out the reasons or objections to the issue and consider revoting if any new issues are raised.

Advantages

- Allows for timely decisions.
- Establishes decision preferences.
- Can reduce options.

Disadvantages

- May cause group polarization and loser dissatisfaction.
- Can reduce the quality of decisions.
- May lessen group cohesion and commitment.

The preceding tools are a basic set of procedures for use in decision-making meetings. Most of them are easy to use, although some may require a review of the guidelines provided here prior to use. Remember that the selection of tools should be based on the task at hand, relational needs, and given situation. The thoughtful selection of tools can enhance effective working relationships

Selection Considerations for Decision-Making Techniques

	Selection Criteria					
Techniques	Task Focus	Time Cost	Conflict Potential	Social Needs	Promote Cohesion	Pressure to Conform
Open discussion	M	M	H	H	L/M	H
Round-robin	H	M	L	L	M	L
Reporting	H	L	L	L	L	L
Brainstorming	H	L	M	H	H	L
Idea writing	H	M	L	L/M	M	L
Idea-spurring questions	H	M	M	H	M	L
Ranking	H	M	L	L	M	L
Weighting	H	H	M/H	H	M/H	M/H
Voting	H	L	H	L	L	L
Itemized response	H	M	M	M	M	M

Key: L = low
M = moderate
H = high

Figure 6.3 To help you select the appropriate decision-making technique for your group's needs, each technique has been given a rating—low, moderate, or high—for several task and relationship factors: task focus, time cost, conflict potential, social needs, promotion of cohesion, and pressure to conform. The evaluation of two techniques, weighting and itemized response, will vary depending on the manner of conducting the technique—for example, individual versus interactive generation of ideas.

and task achievement. Figure 6.3 summarizes the strengths and weaknesses of each technique in terms of several basic task and relationship factors: task focus, time cost, conflict potential, social needs, cohesion, and pressure to conform. The table can help you select tools based on your group's circumstance and needs.

Nongroup Decision-Making Methods

The preceding tools encourage participation and draw upon group members' knowledge and skills. No matter how well a group makes a decision, the group

Box 6.1

Group Decision Making: Finding the Right Tool

The search committee was having considerable difficulty selecting one of the top four candidates for the Medical Assistant position. The job description and qualifications document made narrowing the thirty-six applicants to four finalists easy. But from the difficulty agreeing on the finalist, tempers were beginning to flare and feelings were negative at the latest meeting. No one was looking forward to the next session.

Tom Styles, the committee chairman, recognized that every time a committee member raised a point in support of a candidate, someone else would either raise a negative point or remind the committee that another candidate also had the same quality. It was difficult to keep the candidates' strengths and weaknesses clear. They all had a number of strong qualifications, but none of the members felt certain about any one candidate.

Tom decided to discuss the problem with the organizational development specialist, Susan Mangano, at the hospital training center. She listened to Tom's description of the committee's quandary and asked Tom what he wanted to accomplish. Tom said he wanted the committee to make the best possible choice and to avoid any hard feelings among the members. He stressed this last point because the committee members worked as an administrative team on a daily basis and the person selected would be working with them. Tom did not want their decision to divide the team.

Susan asked Tom if they had tried to identify the criteria or standards of a "good" candidate. Tom immediately responded, "We're using the job description and qualifications to review each candidate." Susan then asked, "Do you think all the important qualifications are spelled out by the written qualifications? And are the qualifications of equal importance?" Tom hesitated. "I don't think so." Susan suggested that the committee use a weighting technique to help them clearly establish all written and unwritten standards of the position. From there the committee could determine the comparative importance of each standard and then evaluate the degree to which each candidate fulfilled each standard. The committee would weight each qualification and each candidate's ability to satisfy them. Impressed with the idea, Tom asked Susan to attend the next meeting.

Susan explained the weighting technique to the committee members, who had not thought of the unwritten standards that might be operating in their individual thinking or of the possible differences in the importance of qualifications.

The members were first asked to idea write all the essential qualifications. Each member's list was compiled on a master list, followed by questions of clarification to make sure everyone understood each qualification.

Box 6.1 (continued)

Candidates	Position Qualifications →	Medical Records/ Bookkeeping Education	Interpersonal Skills	Experience in Hospital Setting	Computer Info/ Management Experience	Total
	Criterion Weightings	3	3	2	1	
	Randall	2 / 6	2 / 6	2 / 4	1 / 1	16
	Munoz	3 / 9	2 / 6	2 / 4	1 / 1	20
	Siefert	3 / 9	3 / 6	2 / 6	1 / 1	22
	Fabretti	2 / 6	2 / 6	0 / 0	1 / 1	13

Key: 1= low 3= high

Figure 6.4 Chart of candidates' weighted scores.

The following discussion led to some rewording and combinations of similar or related qualifications. Once the committee had agreed on the list of qualifications, Susan had them discuss the comparative importance of each qualification by weighting them as either 3 (most important), 2 (important), or 1 (desirable). The committee decided to leave out all qualifications that the position absolutely required such as administrative health certification because all the candidates had to fulfill them.

A lively discussion followed, covering one qualification at a time. After all the criteria were weighted, the committee reviewed them together to make adjustments for qualifications that may have received too much or not enough weight. Then the committee began reviewing each candidate's degree of fulfillment of each qualification. They agreed to use a 3 for complete fulfillment, 2 for partial fulfillment, and 1 for no fulfillment. It was relatively

Box 6.1 (continued)

easy to determine each candidate's fulfillment of a qualification because all members had interviewed the four finalists and seen their application files.

Each candidate's qualification score was multiplied by the position qualification weight (see Figure 6.4) and totaled. The higher the score, the better the qualifications. The highest score was 22 followed by 20. The group narrowed their discussion to the two highest scoring candidates because they were so close, especially on the most important qualifications. The position went to the candidate with the second highest score because that person qualified as a minority and the hospital was committed to affirmative action hiring practices.

The long task was completed, and all the members felt the committee had selected the best candidate. The careful identification of all important qualifications and the weighting of them and the candidates helped the committee make a careful and thoughtful decision. The members were pleased with their success in working together and were so impressed with Susan's ability to facilitate decision making that they invited her to observe their next meeting for possible tips to improve the meeting process.

itself may not have the power to make a final decision. A decision may be attributed to or associated with a group, but is not truely the group's decision or satisfactory to the whole group when decisions are made by authority, compromise, or a minority of group members.

Decision by authority occurs in many formal groups. The lines of authority are clear, and the group only serves to advise. Decisions are made by the leader, but are often based on input from group members. Quality control circles, which are problem-solving groups of employees used to improve work processes and performance, operate in this manner.

Sometimes leaders pretend that the group is involved in decision making. In such cases, members often parrot what they think the leader wants to hear, knowing that their input is not really valued. In other words, members who can influence decisions seem to give this right to an "expert" or other high-status member of the group, for reasons addressed in Chapter 9. Members may vote, but as nonverbal communication in the group may indicate, the group may be "falling in line" behind the authority or expert.

Decision by compromise is a barter method of group decision making. Members representing one point of view give up some aspect of their favored preference in order to garner needed support. Often a compromise combines ideas from each of the leading alternative ideas. This is not necessarily bad, unless the final decision is weakened or the group members find the decision dissatisfying. The worst compromises occur without much discussion. Group members have been known to express their individual opinions at the outset of a meeting and then just "average out" their differences. The often-quoted remark that "a camel is a horse designed by committee" reflects the kind of inane compromises that groups sometimes make. Group decisions by compromise reflect individual members' preferences but not necessarily the group's as a whole. The compromise decision method is most appropriate when differences between members are clearly incompatible and there is no decision that the group finds acceptable and satisfying.

Decisions by minority are determined by a subgroup or clique within a group. Often the "silent majority" resents these subgroups, but not enough to create any significant opposition. Those who find themselves in a less powerful minority may try to swing the decision their way by attempting to push a proposal through at the end of a meeting when people are tired and inattentive, a technique known as *railroading*. Or they may convene a meeting when the advocates of the majority view cannot be present. Such practices lead to decisions not based on the whole group. Decisions by the minority are most appropriate when the majority is dragging its feet on an important matter. We have seen this in many class project groups where two or three members are compelled to make decisions because of the lack of conscientious participation by the majority.

Tools for Problem-Solving Steps

Problem solving occurs when a group's task is to find a solution to an undesirable state of affairs or when the group is blocked in trying to fulfill a task or goal. When the group perceives no immediately apparent way to accomplish something, it should use problem-solving steps to conduct the meeting.

The standard problem-solving agenda involves several sequential steps that focus discussion on assessing and solving the problem. Careful problem solving requires a clear view of the problem, critical analysis, a variety of options for solutions, reasoned selection of a solution, and a feasible plan for its implementation. Use these five steps to guide the problem-solving process:

1. *Problem identification*. Define the problem and review available background information. Explore all possible ways of looking at the problem, and develop several alternative problem statements before selecting one as "the" problem.
2. *Problem analysis*. Identify issues and questions related to the problem. What are possible causes? Consequences? How does it differ from the desired condition? Redefine the problem if analysis suggests a more appropriate definition.
3. *Solution generation*. Develop a comprehensive list of possible solutions to

Techniques for Problem-Solving Steps

Problem-Solving Steps	Techniques
Problem identification (information gathering)	Brainstorming Idea writing
Problem analysis (information gathering)	Questions of definition, fact, value, and policy
Solution generation (idea generating)	Brainstorming Idea writing Idea-spurring questions
Solution selection (idea evaluation)	Consensus decision making Itemized response Ranking Weighting Voting Nominal group technique
Solution implementation techniques	Use methods for idea generating and evaluation

Figure 6.5 These problem-solving techniques are merely a place to begin. You can find many additional suggestions in the references at the end of the chapter.

the problem. Review the list after exhausting all possibilities, and make sure all solutions are clear. Narrow the options using an appropriate decision tool.

4. *Solution selection.* Identify the criteria for evaluating a solution. Then apply them to the solutions. (Note: You may wish to generate these criteria prior to generating solutions and combine steps, particularly if time is limited.)
5. *Solution implementation.* Although your group may not have to implement the solution it identifies, it should provide an implementation process or plan. Implementation may raise new problems. A good solution is legitimate and workable. A solution is always tentative until it is successfully implemented.

The problem-solving agenda does not provide any specific guidelines for conducting the steps. However, the decision-making tools already discussed can be readily used. For example you could use brainstorming or idea writing to generate a list of problems or when developing possible solutions. Ranking and weighting are obvious tools for narrowing and evaluating solution choices. See Figure 6.5 for tools corresponding to the steps of problem solving.

Note that the problem-solving steps are sequential but not necessarily linear. That is, steps can be repeated. Problem solving is typically a back-and-forth movement between steps that gradually moves forward. It is common to find information or ideas in one step that affect a previous step. For example, a group working on the problem of ineffective employee motivation could find out that workers' performances were largely due to ineffective training and lack of performance feedback. The problem changed from "how to motivate employees" to "how to improve employee performance." Sometimes problems raise secondary problems that must be solved before working on the original problem. This frequently occurs in implementation, where a proposed solution raises problems in putting it to work. This problem must then be solved if the solution is to fix the original problem. For example, a one-legged design for a portable solar mirror for camping posed a problem because the wind might move it. The mirror had to be stabilized. The solution was to place two loops on the frame for string to anchor it with stakes in the ground.

The tools just described are the basic tools of the task group. Many people, when first exposed to them, wonder why they never heard of them. Others have avoided such procedures because they feel that systematic, rule-governed interaction cramps their style. Frequently, leaders or members with domineering personalities do not want to share decision-making authority. Procedures that encourage participation just get in the way of their agendas. But ignoring these tools can undermine effective group interaction and decision making.

Summary

This chapter described procedures for the basic tasks of decision-making groups: information gathering and sharing, idea generating, evaluation for decision making, and problem solving. The tools we reviewed are designed for various types of decision-making tasks. However, tools for a given type of task vary in how they shape participation and members' interaction. Decision-making groups will proceed in some manner by the mere fact that they will communicate. The challenge they face is in selecting and using procedures that serve both task and relational needs toward effective decisions. Choosing appropriate tools depends on being able to perceive or diagnose what is going on in the group in general and at the specific moment. The remaining chapters will build upon and deepen your understanding of group dynamics and communication.

GroupQuests: Discussion Questions

1. Describe a situation or specific task that you have experienced in a group meeting that was particularly unproductive. What type of task was it? Why was it unproductive? What tools would have been useful?

2. Imagine that you are a member of a group that has just brainstormed a large list of potential questions related to a topic under investigation. The members are beginning to get restless and show signs of frustration. The group must reduce the list to the most essential questions so research assignments can be delegated before the meeting ends. What would you recommend that the group do next? Why?

GroupWorks: Group Activities

1. In groups of four to six members, select an idea-generating tool for developing a list of possible project topics. Use an evaluation tool to select a project topic. Provide some time to discuss the merits of each tool. Were they useful? Why?
2. Form groups of four to six members and identify all the possible questions of definition, fact, and value relevant to the policy question "Should the grading of courses be eliminated from higher education?"
3. Attend a meeting of a group you do not belong to (seek permission if it is not open to the public) and observe the members' behaviors and meeting practices. Focus on how they performed such decision-making procedures as information sharing and idea generating. Take note of the specific techniques used to perform each type of task and what occurred. Evaluate the effectiveness of the meeting and your reasons for your judgments. What would you specifically recommend to this group to improve its meeting and why?
4. Form three groups of four to six members each. Have each group complete Group Discussion Activity 2; instruct one group to use idea writing, another brainstorming, and the third open discussion. Be sure each group knows how to use each technique. Assign one to three observers to each group to take notes on the group's activity. Provide enough room to prevent distractions around each group and give it twenty minutes to develop a list of questions. Then have each group report on the number of questions it generated. Have the observers describe what they saw and how the groups use of the tool worked. Did the tool contribute to the number of questions generated? The quality of questions? Did the tool affect interaction? How so? How did it contribute to the task? To the relationships?

GroupActs: Practical Applications

1. If your term project group has not been delegated a specific project, use the nominal group technique to develop a list of three to five possible topics. Be sure to review the procedures before using the technique. Once you have narrowed the choices down to the top three to five, use the weighting technique to evaluate and decide on the one topic your group wishes to pursue. You may want to use an idea-generating technique to develop the criteria the group will use in weighting the topic options.
2. Select a tool for identifying all the possible questions of definition, fact, value, and policy related to the goal of your group's project. Once a list of questions has been developed, review it for their relevance to the topic. Which ones must be answered? Which ones are secondary or tangential? In what order should the questions be answered?

CHAPTER 7

The Relationship Level: Cooperating to Manage Conflict

Susan thought her recommendation to use electronic dorm keys was the way to solve the security problem in the dormitories. The committee members were very interested in her idea and asked many questions. Joe, the supervisor of resident assistants, thought that the resident assistants at the front desk could maintain security if they implemented a sign-in procedure with ID cards. No one could get into the dorm unless accompanied by a resident with a card. Susan and Joe, arguing over the merits of their respective proposals, began dominating the meeting's discussion, which was getting heated and personal. The group members listened to the same points being repeated. The issues were becoming unclear and time was running out. After the meeting was adjourned, Don remarked, "I hate getting involved in conflicts."

When we ask our students to free-associate words or phrases that come to mind when they think of *conflict*, the list is invariably pejorative in tone. When asked why conflict is perceived as a negative and undesirable experience, students say it is uncomfortable, threatens the stability of a relationship or group, and prevents things getting done. They also say they are afraid of losing. No wonder there is such reluctance to engage in conflict communication.

In *The Magic of Conflict*, Thomas Crum poses a very different view.[1] First, he claims that conflict is neither good nor bad: "Conflict just is." He suggests that how you approach conflict makes the difference in whether it turns out positively or negatively. The conflict is a motivator of change and offers the opportunity for success if we find ways to blend the energies of the parties involved without making it a contest. Perhaps our negative reaction to conflict is really a response to our inability to manage conflict in a satisfying manner.

Conflict between groups, organizations, and nations is inherent in the human condition—people will have differences. Recall that the second phase of the group development process is the conflict phase. How should a person or group manage conflict? How do we blend energies to achieve satisfying and productive results?

Managing Group Conflict

Conflict is inherent in task groups. The value of groups for decision making depends on the differing information, values, ideas, and perspectives that members bring to a group decision or problem. Ideally, the collective wisdom of the members should achieve an assembly bonus effect—group decisions that are better than those of any individual member working alone.[2] Groups enhance the possibility of high-quality decisions, but pose the prospect of conflict. Yet when members do not raise different opinions or question decisions, the group process is jeopardized. Conflict is a sign of an effective group. The hard part is finding the way to encourage and handle conflicts so that they pose an opportunity for successful and satisfying group decisions.

As noted before, a high-quality decision is a major goal of group communication. However, attention to the task dimension alone will not suffice. The role of relationships is also a major factor operating in group communication and decision-making outcomes. Members need to promote an open and trusting communication environment so all members share relevant information and tackle the conflict constructively. This is in contrast to defensive and judgmental behavior that demonstrates a disregard for others; this produces a closed and distrustful atmosphere that reduces the perceived freedom to participate and encourages competition. Competition among members and lack of participation reduce relevant information that can help resolve the conflict and pit members against each other. How we communicate shapes relationships, which in turn shapes how we communicate.

The procedural dimension of communication, the focus for conflict management, incorporates both the relational and task dimensions by stressing communication episodes, activities, and acts that increase the possibility of both effective relationship and task outcomes. This involves communication practices that foster cooperative relationships and careful examination of the conflict. Conflict is productive if we maintain constructive relationships for achieving goals.

This chapter will increase your understanding of the nature and practice of conflict in general and in groups particularly. It gives specific attention to identifying styles and types of communication behavior and procedures for managing group conflict.

If members' concerns are not aired, they can break out into open hostilities.

The Nature of Conflict

What do we mean by conflict? What types of communication practices contribute to or prevent conflicts? How do members differ in their approaches to conflict interaction? Answers to these questions will provide us with a foundation for understanding conflict in groups.

A Definition of Conflict

Joseph Folger and Marshall Scott Poole have defined *conflict* as the "interaction of interdependent people who perceive incompatible goals and interference from each other in achieving those goals."[3] The four I's of this definition contain the inherent conditions of conflict: interaction, interdependence, incompatibility, and interference. A brief explanation of these attributes will clarify our understanding of conflict.

Communication researchers recognize the importance of interaction in conflict in at least three respects. First, conflict is perceived and maintained through interaction; we discern irreconcilable differences by talking with others. This perceived conflict may remain perceived—unexpressed and kept to oneself. Second, interaction moves conflict from the private to the public sphere. Communicating the perceived conflict is essential for recognizing that a conflict exists between members. Unexpressed conflicts are usually rationalized away or left to fester and perhaps emerge in other ways (taking it out on the dog, developing stress-based illness, complaining chronically). Third, conflict communication is conducted through interaction. Therefore, we need to look at the characteristics of communication to understand how it can help or hinder effective conflict communication.

Interdependence is an essential condition of human conflict. There would be no conflict with another if you did not depend on her to satisfy your goal in some manner. This mutual dependence is especially critical in task groups, which depend on their members to fulfill the task, get along, and agree with decisions. Even when a group gives up on a member who is unwilling to do his or her fair share, it still is affected by the situation. Whether we like it or not, we are connected to each other in group relationships. All members invariably have an impact on the group to some degree.

Incompatibility and interference are at the heart of conflict, which arises when you perceive an incompatibility with another person and he or she is interfering with your efforts to achieve a reward or goal. You see the conflicting positions as mutually exclusive—some must lose. Such perceptions are exacerbated in situations where rewards—respect, money, power, land—are actually or believed to be scarce. We stress the "perceived" aspect of conflict. Often people leave a perceived conflict unexpressed only to find out later that there was no conflict at all. The perception may have been the result of misinterpretation, incomplete information, or any number of obstacles to clear communication and understanding. Frequently, a conflict is actually a response to the fear that another person's preference will interfere with achieving your own needs. You get locked into a position and see the other as an adversary. Ironically, there may be ways to satisfy the interests of both parties if they can get beyond holding on to their positions and seeing each other as obstacles. In short, we may see conflicts that do not exist or not see solutions that do exist.

This brings us full circle, back to interaction and the role of communication in the conflict process. Communication gives rise to the perception and expression of conflict. Communication can also reveal misperceptions that lead to conflict or contribute to identifying ways to resolve incompatible positions. Most important, we are faced with communicating in a manner that recognizes the interdependence of group members and establishes relationships that tackle conflicts, not people or their positions.

The Focus of Conflict

Conflicts between group members are either over ideas or relationships and the difference in value of something, somebody, or both. Conflicts over ideas—*ideational conflict*—involve choices among interpretations, evaluations, solutions, proposals, or procedures. For instance, a group may encounter conflicting views on the meaning of a set of facts, the best solution to correct a problem, or a procedure to obtain needed information. The more decisions that have to be made, the greater the possiblity for conflict to occur.

Relational, or *interpersonal conflict*, is over the relative value or worth of a person. That is, it ultimately questions the self-concept of an individual, threatens self-esteem, and may lead to loss of face. Interpersonal conflict is commonly associated with status and role performance. Sometimes members vie for leadership or other prestigious roles and become locked in aggressive exchanges that frequently appear to be ideational conflicts on the surface. For example, the conflict between Susan and Joe at the opening of the chapter may not have been about the use of a sign-in procedure versus electronic dorm keys but over leadership of the group. It had all the markings of a conflict between ideas. However, the conflict became interpersonal when Susan and Joe began attacking each other's worth and ability to offer good ideas and lead the group.

Even when roles are resolved the performance of them can raise conflict. Issues regarding the proper conduct or timing of role behaviors can fuel interpersonal conflict. This is evident in the increased scrutiny devoted to the ethical conduct of politicians. Unethical personal or political behavior raises doubts about the politician's ability to perform the role effectively. The ensuing conflict is over whether he or she is fit to perform the role.

The most destructive attribute of interpersonal conflict is the disrespect and disregard for others simply because they are different or do not share a similar perspective. Rolling one's eyes or using a sarcastic tone of voice conveys the same kind of message as a direct insult on a person's intelligence: "You're stupid" or "What do men know?" Such behaviors never get at the specific focus of the conflict and ultimately undermine the development of productive interdependent relationships so vital to task groups. Lewis Coser calls conflicts characterized by aggression intended to defeat and even hurt others "nonrealistic."[4] They are not directed toward a substantive resolution of the conflict.

Recognizing the focus of a conflict helps you begin managing the conflict by identifying what is at issue: ideas or relationships. It helps the group limit discussion to specific issues. If the conflict is over procedure, then discussion can be limited to information and issues relevant to procedures. If the conflict is over role performance, then discussion can focus on needed performance and ways to obtain it.

Constructive and Destructive Conflict

Conflict communication has been characterized as constructive or destructive.[5] Although most conflict communication is neither solely constuctive nor destructive, certain practices contribute to one or the other. Two fundamental issues determine the differences between these forms of conflict: conflict interaction and its consequences.

Constructive conflict is distinguished by interaction that focuses on issues, is flexible and varied, preserves the rights and dignity of the involved parties, and considers the common good. The ideal is to arrive at outcomes that establish an aceptable resolution and preserve, if not enhance, the relationship of those in conflict. Productive group conflict establishes decisions that further the group's task goal, maintains and contributes to each member's self-esteem, and supports the development of group cohesion. Members should not avoid conflict to maintain friendly relationships or maintain cohesive feelings, as with groupthink (discussed in Chapter 12). The group must work on preserving positive relationships and achieving high-quality decisions.

Constructive conflict is particularly concerned with the individual and relational outcomes of conflict because it emphasizes the satisfactory fulfillment of all parties' interests: the win-win outcome. This outcome in group conflicts should also serve the group's interests. Sometimes conflicts lead groups to focus on the immediate conflict between members and forget that the issue in conflict concerns the group's goal.

Destructive conflict poses an opposite scenario. Interaction is characterized by emphasis on personal interests, inflexible attitudes and behaviors, defensiveness, polarizing positions, and an unwillingness to negotiate. It is driven by a fear that something of value—such as resources, status, or self-esteem—will be lost. Conflict is understood as a battle with only one winner. Thus it is competitive; the outcome must be win-lose.

The emphasis on self-interest alone is destructive in two respects. First, the quality of decisions is likely to be compromised or jeopardized. Decisions based on one or two members' personal interests that do not clearly satisfy the group's interests may not be productive. Second, to achieve personal interests at the expense of other members' interests and self-esteem undermines relational satisfaction, group cohesion, and commitment to decisions. Destructive conflict reflects a disregard for individuals and their relationships, undermining the very wellspring of group effectiveness. If groups expect to do their best, they need to have the involvement and commitment of their members and supportive relationships.

We will now look at the types of communication that contribute to the development of a climate that supports individuals, effective working relationships, and a collaborative style of conflict interaction. We will then identify specific procedures and practices that contribute to the cooperative management of a conflict's task dimensions.

Communication Acts, Activities, and Episodes in Conflict Situations

The literature on conflict management has many prescriptions for effective practice. The practices focus on three distinct areas of communication: acts, activities, and episodes. Act prescriptions examine types of message behaviors and their effect on the relational dimension of group experience. We will focus on the types of messages that act to create competitive and cooperative group communication climates before and during conflict interventions.

Competitive and Cooperative Communication Acts

In describing the message behaviors associated with competitive and cooperative communication acts, we will consider their implications and consequences for conflict management. As we will see, the nature of group member interaction in general and especially during conflict shapes the prospect for cooperative or competitive group conflict.

As indicated in Chapter 4, how members communicate creates a *communication climate*, a mood or atmosphere that affects ongoing communication. According to Ronald Adler, a communication climate represents the degree to which members perceive they are valued, trusted, and appreciated.[6] A communication climate can be open or closed to varying extents based on the degree to which members feel free to communicate. The mutual respect in an open communication climate encourages participation, expression, and risk taking. The disregard of others in closed communication climates discourages participation and willingness to share ideas. Severely closed communication climates are perpetuated through fear of personal attacks and reprisals. In such climates, members use power and various communication strategies to dominate group members.

The collective communication of group members develops this communication climate, which influences all group decision making, including conflict situations. The more open the climate, the more members are able to collaborate and manage conflict. For example, the members' willingness to listen to and evaluate different proposals to resolve a conflict is a collaborative activity that helps to control the conflict. The more closed the climate, the more members either avoid conflict or fight. That is, members will become apathetic and give up or grow angry if they feel threatened or suppressed by other members' dominant and aggressive behaviors. How members communicate their conflict can change a relatively open climate into a more closed one.

Let us now turn to specific types of communication acts that contribute to open and closed climates. You can use these descriptions of specific verbal and nonverbal behaviors as guidelines in developing a cooperative communication climate for conflict management.

Confirming and Disconfirming Messages Confirming communication acts validate the other's idea or self-concept. Disconfirming messages do the opposite; they invalidate the idea or individual.[7] A confirming message does not mean you agree with another, but that you respect his or her right to an opinion, value him or her as an information source, and acknowledge receiving the message. Confirming and disconfirming acts occur as responses to another's message and frequently indicate how well you have been listening. A disconfirming message can be very subtle and overlooked by the uninvolved observer but felt deeply by the recipient of it. A common disconfirming message is when you propose an idea or opinion only to have the next speaker ignore your contribution by raising an entirely different issue. Add insult to

Disconfirming and Confirming Messages

Disconfirming Messages

Impervious responses: ignoring a member's attempts to communicate by not responding to the message—a question, problem, or request. This can occur by not returning phone calls or using some of the disconfirming behaviors that change the subject or focus of discussion.

Interrupting responses: cutting off the sender before he completes his statement. Such behaviors suggest that what the responder has to say is more important and relevant than the sender's message.

Irrelevant responses: not relating to the sender's message. For example, a member may ask the group whether it should conduct a survey to obtain needed information. The group's leader responds by reporting on what he found from his review of research articles.

Tangential responses: acknowledging the sender's topic or subject but changing the focus of discussion. A member outlining the presentation of the group's report to the boss followed by a member suggesting the types of visual aids to use exemplifies this subtle change. Although the visual aids are related to the presentation, it is not the same issue as outlining the presentation content, which will largely determine what should be visualized.

Impersonal responses: not acknowledging the sender's feelings or perceptions. Cliched, superficial, or overly intellectualized responses are typical. For example, a member says, "I've been doing some serious thinking on our project goal and feel I've got it nailed down." The project leader responds, "We all should be doing serious thinking."

Ambiguous responses: obscuring the discussion's focus and increasing uncertainty. A member asks for specific direction for her research assignment on dormitory security. The response, "Just find out what's happening," ignores her need for clarity.

Incongruous responses: posing contradictory messages between a statement's verbal and nonverbal cues. A member who responds to a request for clarification by saying in a sarcastic tone, "We *all must understand everything* before we go to the next point," says one thing verbally and another nonverbally. While the verbal message emphasizes the value of seeking clarification, the nonverbal message devalues the request and the person requesting it.

Figure 7.1 Group members can communicate either confirming messages, which validate a member's idea or self-concept, or disconfirming messages, which invalidate a member's idea or self-image. Group members need to recognize the difference and strive to communicate confirming messages to promote the group's effectiveness. [Adapted from R. B. Adler, *Communicating at Work* (New York: Random House, 1983).]

Confirming Messages

Acknowledgment of the other's existence: letting people know you recognize them. Returning calls, giving sincere greetings, using names, and responding to requests are ways to accomplish this.

Acknowledgment of the other's position: communicating your understanding of the sender's view. It does not require agreement and may explain a disagreement. Acknowledgment can be conveyed through paraphrasing the content of the other's statement in your own words or providing a thoughtful response to the points the sender presented. Each demonstrates interest in the other's contribution.

Recognition of the other's feelings: emphasizing the feelings of the sender regarding the issue raised. Recognizing a member's feelings shows a personal regard for his experience and a deeper level of understanding. Paraphrasing feelings and acknowledging their significance demonstrates your understanding of the sender's emotions:

> "I sense that you have worked hard on the graphs. No wonder you're so disappointed that we can't use them."
> "You should be excited! You found the missing information and saved us from missing our deadline."

Support of the other's performance: acknowledging contributions, praising completion of a job, or offering to help with a difficult assignment . Such actions show your interest and concern for the individual.

---

injury when someone else later gets credit for your initial idea. Ignoring contributions with vacuous responses, passing over them, or showing a lack of interest does not validate the contributor. Figure 7.1 provides several categories of confirming and disconfirming messages. Review them and see if you can remember instances when they have occurred in your group experiences. Were they obvious? Was there a pattern of behavior? What effect did they have on the communication climate and on the quality of the decisions?

Defensive and Supportive Message Behaviors Jack Gibb's work on defensive and supportive group communication climates describes several types of behaviors that contribute to either competitive or cooperative relationships.[8] Gibb defines defensive behavior as what occurs when a member perceives or anticipates a threat in the group. This situation creates defensive listening and reactions to other members through a variety of verbal and nonverbal cues. The more members experience and engage in defensive behaviors, the less they are able to accurately perceive others' motives, values, and emotions. This increases distortion, which makes task communication inefficient. Defensive

Behaviors That Lead to Defensive and Supportive Climates

Defensive Acts	Supportive Acts
Evaluation	Description
Control	Problem orientation
Strategy	Spontaneity
Neutrality	Empathy
Superiority	Equality
Certainty	Provisionalism

Figure 7.2 A supportive climate encourages open, constructive, effective interaction, whereas a defensive environment can lead to competition and destructive conflict. [From Jack R. Gibb, "Defensive Communication," *Journal of Communication, 1961, 11*, 141–148.]

behaviors emerge easily in conflict situations and can lead to interpersonal conflict. Supportive behaviors reduce defensiveness by conveying openness to a member's participation, ideas, and worth. Supportive messages are acts of cooperation; defensive messages are competitive acts.

Gibb identified six pairs of defensive and supportive categories based on extensive examinations of discussions in a variety of group settings (see Figure 7.2). The six sets are interactive. That is, a defensive act such as evaluation can be neutralized if supportive acts of equality, empathy, or spontaneity are prevalent.

Gibb's *evaluation* and *description* categories distinguish between speech that is judgmental and evaluative and that which is open to and seeking information. The recipient of evaluative messages feels judged and expected to comply with the speaker's value system. For example, a question asked in an irritated tone, "Didn't you know we needed the information for this meeting?" implies fault and the violation of an expectation. Although stated as a question, it is really an attack on an individual's performance. The message does not seek information; it puts down the person.

An individual who is prone to defensiveness—has low self-esteem or observes attacks on other's ideas—may perceive evaluation of his or her idea even when no judgment was intended. If a general question was asked of the group in an inquiring tone ("Do we need all reports for the meeting?"), a defensive person might perceive being judged, even if the question was not directed toward him or her. Descriptive statements usually arouse a minimum of defensiveness. Descriptions of feelings ("I'm getting nervous about finishing our project"), opinions ("Our conclusion could include suggestions for future research"), or processes ("We might outline the presentation before selecting visual aids") present thoughts without judging or blaming. Their tentative or open manner invites others to contribute to the focus of discussion. In contrast, confrontation-orientated evaluative messages present an indictment ("Do you consider this competent work?") or a verdict ("This group doesn't know what it's doing!").

Being evaluative is easy and natural; being descriptive takes thought and awareness. Deborah Borisoff and David Victor offer several useful suggestions when making descriptive statements:

1. Admit your own assertions. Use "I" statements to attribute perceptions to yourself: "I believe we need to establish our goal before identifying research questions."
2. Make statements clear and specific: avoid generalizations and exaggeration. The more ambiguous and oblique a statement is, the more members can misinterpret it.
3. Word selection should promote shared perceptions, not personal or private meanings. Watch for words or phrases that are loaded ("When's this group going to get serious?") or biased ("You girls can do the tabulations, the men will do the analysis"). Avoid words or phrases that are hurtful and emotionally arousing ("That was a dumb move, Jim!").
4. Beware of judgmental nonverbal cues that convey hostile feelings. Voice qualities, gestures, and facial expressions frequently convey evaluations in the form of sarcasm, anger, hostility, indifference, and annoyance. The words may be very descriptive, but the tone of voice may be harshly judgmental.[9]

These suggestions are basic ways to promote descriptive speech acts and reduce evaluative perceptions. It is not easy to overcome the habit of evaluation or even perceiving evaluation where it was not intended. The first step to changing this habit is awareness. Reflect on your past experience in groups to determine when you have been especially judgmental. Note the situation and feelings that gave rise to the judgmental statements. They can serve as an early warning system to cue caution and remind you to phrase statements descriptively. Try to phrase past evaluative statements in a descriptive manner to recognize the difference and practice this more supportive way of communicating. You will not be able to change overnight, but awareness and attention to your speech acts can make this productive practice part of your supportive communication repertoire.

Control and *problem orientation* statements reflect the difference between attempting to persuade and gain compliance and seeking collaboration in decision making. Acts of control are efforts to impose one's will upon another, which can lead to resistance ("If we were smart, we would make recommendations based on the needs of the audience"). A problem orientation poses an invitation to the group to work together on finding a solution or answer to a situation ("How can we make recommendations that will be acceptable to our audience?"). The problem orientation depends on being descriptive, focusing on issues, and incorporating members' interests through soliciting alternative positions. Although you may already have an idea on how to solve a problem or achieve a goal, you are not imposing it and are open to exploring it or other options with the group.

Strategy and *spontaneity* characterize the difference between ulterior or hidden motives and open and forthright acts. When people perceive they are being manipulated through deception, withholding information, or putting on an act, they get suspicious and defensive. We have experienced such suspicion even when we were sincere about using these very suggestions for supportive communication. This illustrates that receivers control the interpretation of speech acts. Meanings may be determined more by the receiver's personality, self-concept, and past experiences than by the speaker's intentions. Examples of reactions to strategic messages are common in the political arena, where the public perceives the politician as a strategist whose messages say one thing but are intended for something else.

Spontaneity is the opposite of strategy. Strategy is planned; spontaneity is unplanned and free of ulterior motives. Spontaneity is speaking your mind in response to a situation, in a straightforward and honest manner. Some of our students have questioned being spontaneous when we recommend using practices such as description or problem orientation. Certainly, it would seem strategic to do so. However, we can initially view this situation as a matter of attitude. Are you practicing the behavior to influence members for personal gain or to promote a supportive climate? What is your intention? Once you choose to practice supportive and confirming behaviors, they will become part of your communication repertoire. Over time they will become second nature and spontaneously expressed.

Neutrality and *empathy* are acts that contrast indifference with understanding. Responses that show a lack of interest or concern for an idea or person instigate defensiveness. Messages that convey low involvement, disinterest, or detachment can communicate rejection. For example, the verbal statement, "I don't care what we do," suggests detachment. Said in a monotone, this statement could also convey disinterest.

Empathy, on the other hand, is responsive to others' feelings and thoughts in a manner that conveys interest and understanding. Empathic messages acknowledge the speaker's feelings and perceptions at face value. This is accomplished through responses that solicit or demonstrate understanding. Figure 7.1 suggests the use of paraphrasing the ideas and feelings of others in confirming messages. You can also seek clarification by asking questions. Sometimes role reversal—acting out the situation from the other person's viewpoint and communication style—can demonstrate and develop understanding.[10] Sincere paraphrasing, questioning, and role reversal are highly supportive and reduce defensiveness.

Superiority and *equality* are self-explanatory. Messages that cast the speaker as superior in worth, ability, wealth, or power arouse defensiveness. Such messages not only emphasize the speaker's worth but also directly or indirectly portray the listener as inadequate or inferior. Furthermore, the sender of such messages communicates that he or she does not need help, desire feedback, want involvement, or care to support the receiver's need for power, status, or worth. Messages of superiority may arouse feelings of resentment, jealousy, and competition and stimulate disconfirming and defensive responses.

Of the many ways to express the attitude of equality, perhaps the simplest and most direct is to ask members for their input and to follow up with confirming responses and other supportive messages as the situation warrants. This implies the worth of the receivers and an interest in their participation.

Certainty and *provisionalism* reflect the difference between messages that portray something as absolute or tentative. Messages of certainty are typically perceived as authoritarian and dogmatic. They raise our defenses and, depending on the circumstances and personality tendencies, give rise to the fight-or-flight response. Messages of certainty convey the attitude of superiority, self-righteousness, competitiveness, and an unwillingness to explore alternatives.

Provisional messages pose a point of view but with an open attitude. They offer ideas but invite investigation, exploration, and alternatives. They do not challenge or debate issues but offer a perspective ("We can consider using a chronological method for organizing our report" or "Research indicates that recycling will become a major way to manage household waste"). Basically, provisional messages leave the door open for input and discussion, which is essential if small groups are to have an advantage over an individual in the quality of decision making.

Aggressive, Nonassertive, and Assertive Communication Styles

Another way of looking at competitive and cooperative communication acts is the style of communication people use in groups. We can get a fix on a person's style by examining the types of communication acts they perform in general and specifically during conflicts. Identifying your own or others' conflict style provides information on whether opposing parties are engaging in competitive and destructive conflict or cooperative and constructive conflict. This information can be useful in selecting an appropriate style for the situation or confronting the group about its method of managing or not managing group conflict.

Three prevalent communication styles are aggressive, nonassertive, and assertive.[11] An *aggressive* communication style is defined by disconfirming and defensive types of messages emphasizing control through threats, coercion, and other strategies used to gain compliance. The key attribute of the aggressive style is an emphasis on personal goals at the expense of others' self-respect and goals: the win-lose outcome. Aggressive styles are destructive to group cohesion in most situations. (Aggressive behaviors might, however, be needed to keep a disruptive, self-serving, and aggressive member from jeopardizing progress.)

The *nonassertive* style has two types: avoidance and accommodation. *Avoidance* is merely saying nothing and not confronting each other. *Accommodation* is giving in to the other instead of asserting your position. You let the other win at your or the group's expense. Nonassertive styles lead to win-lose outcomes: you lose, the other person wins. Nonassertiveness may be appropriate if the conflict is minor, time is short, and it is not worth the personal or relational risk. However, when group members rely on the nonassertive style at the expense of positive and satisfying work relationships, it becomes destructive and undermines group cohesion.

The *assertive* style is distinguished by the confirming and supportive types of communication acts discussed earlier. Assertiveness expresses regard for one's self and the other: the win-win outcome. It is a desirable style in that it emphasizes cooperation, positive relational outcomes, and group productivity. The ideal assertive act has four parts:

1. *Describe the problem:* Use descriptive and problem-oriented statements regarding the issue in conflict. Be *specific* and use *descriptive* language; avoid judging or accusing others.
2. *Explain your perceptions:* Describe your interpretation and feelings about the conflict. Do not blame or accuse the other for your perceptions of the conflict ("Why are you so evasive?" or "If you would be reasonable about the costs, we could solve this problem!"). Use "I" statements to describe your perceptions and feelings ("I think we are not sticking to the issues. It frustrates me" or "I get the impression you think I don't care about cost issues"). Be provisional and open to discussing perception, and be clear and specific about your feelings.
3. *Make requests:* Seek action from others regarding the issue or the process of conflict itself. Requests should be specific and feasible (Can we agree to stick to the issues, one at a time?" or "I'm not certain what you consider acceptable costs—would you explain?"). Avoid demands or commands and making too many requests at one time.
4. *Describe the consequences:* State the outcomes or payoffs for fulfilling requests or resolutions. What are the possible tangible or intangible achievements, which may involve time, or personal satisfaction? Consequence statements should emphasize positive outcomes. If they focus on punishment— "If we don't stick to the issues, I won't discuss the conflict!"—they become aggressive acts, not assertive.[12]

A fourth and less distinct style is *compromise*, which is clearer as an outcome than as a specific style. It typically combines confirming/disconfirming and supportive/defensive acts. Both parties win and lose a little. The compromise outcome has the advantage of giving something to each side and may contribute to preserving group cohesion. At the same time, compromise sows seeds of discontent in that the resolution of the conflict is not completely satisfying to the involved parties, although the group as a whole may find it satisfying. The outcome may appear to be win-win but feel like a lose-lose to those directly involved in the conflict. The dissatisfied members may erupt later. The limitation of the compromise style is that it involves competition over trade-offs, not a cooperative effort at finding a mutually acceptable solution in which the parties in conflict and the group win. Although we do not recommend a compromise style as an intitial way to resolve group conflicts, it may be the lesser of two evils when it is clear there are "real" incompatibilities between members.

Confirming and supportive communication acts are at the core of cooperative conflict management. You will also find the four styles just presented useful in helping individual members and groups discern trends and patterns of conflict interaction. Recognizing styles can help people avoid destructive styles and select constructive practices for conflict communication. Your group can talk about how members will talk with each other during the conflict, either before taking on a conflict or during a destructive interaction.

The ideal goal of communication at the act level is to enact cooperative and collaborative attitudes and behaviors for the sake of positive working relationships and effective task outcomes. This goal may be unattainable in some situations (for example, held by an aggressive person) or inappropriate in others (insufficient time to collaborate or an uncontrolled competition). Yet the ideal is the target. Aim toward confirming, supportive, and assertive communication.

As crucial as these types of acts are, they alone are insufficient for managing conflict. They need to be conducted within activities and episodes specifically designed for managing conflicts to maximize the possibility for productive and satisfying results.

Conflict Phases, Episodes, and Activities

As noted earlier, the second stage of the group development process is the conflict stage. In this stage the group sorts out and decides on tasks, role performance, and procedures. It is a stage particularly ripe for conflict. If groups do experience conflict, their ability to manage this stage will affect the quality of members' relationships. This largely depends on the group's success during orientation in establishing a positive communication climate and a satisfying distribution of roles.

Conflicts have patterns or phases that provide a foundation for identifying types of episodes and activities that contribute to collaborative conflict management.

Differentiation and Integration in Conflict Communication

Louise Pondy identified the stage of *manifest conflict* as one where a member of the group expresses a perceived or felt conflict.[13] Prior to this stage, conflict is felt by one or more of the involved parties but not overtly expressed. The conflict surfaces through communication acts. This critical juncture for the management of conflict may determine whether it is conducted constructively.

Joseph Folger and Marshall Scott Poole divide manifest conflict stage into two broad phases: differentiation and integration. In the *differentiation phase*, the differences between members' positions are expressed. The nature of the interaction during this phase largely determines whether the conflict escalates into a competitive fray, is avoided, or is resolved cooperatively. At this phase group members face the dilemma posed by the "simultaneous need for and

When to Avoid or Delay Conflict

Realistic assessment of significance of issues indicates unacceptable trade-offs or conditions:

Damage of important relationship is imminent.

Power is unequal.

No chance of acceptable resolution.

Minor issue(s) unrelated to immediate conflict.

Insufficient time or no appropriate place.

Inappropriate timing requiring acknowledged postponement:

Emotional tension and anger requiring cooling-off period to avoid radical escalation.

Controversy unrelated to immediate decision.

All relevant parties to conflict not present.

Group members discouraged and exhausted by efforts to resolve conflict.

Tension hinders clear and creative thinking.

Lack communication skills to manage conflict:

Inability to describe emotions and viewpoints.

Lack procedures to manage interaction or unwilling to follow them.

Third-party mediation unavailable.

Figure 7.3 In situations such as these, conflict should be avoided or postponed. You can find avoidance tactics in the following sources: Joseph P. Folger and Marshall Scott Poole, *Working Through Conflict* (Glenview, Ill.: Scott, Foresman, 1984), pp. 57–59; Joyce Hocker Frost and William Wilmot, *Interpersonal Conflict* (Dubuque, Iowa: Wm. C. Brown, 1978), pp. 114–122.

fear of differentiation."[14] Some conflicts should be avoided or postponed (see Figure 7.3). But when conflicts pose decisions critical to a group's success or relationships, they need to be addressed. A key to successful conflict management is to engage in constructive differentiation—interaction that clearly identifies issues, reasons, and the severity of difference between positions while maintaining positive relationships among members.

Successful differentiation prepares members for the *integration phase*, where an acceptable resolution is sought. This phase is characterized by interaction that draws on the information established in the differentiation phase to develop and evaluate solutions. During this phase, "parties appreciate their similarities, acknowledge their common goals, own up to positive aspects of their ambivalences, express warmth and respect and/or engage in other positive actions to manage the conflict."[15]

Symptoms of Escalation Cycles and Inappropriate Avoidance

Symptoms of Avoidance	Symptoms of Escalation
Marked decrease in group's commitment to solving the problem ("Why would we care?")	An issue takes much longer to deal with than was anticipated
Quick acceptance of a suggested solution	Members repeatedly offer the same argument in support of a position
Members stop themselves from raising controversial aspects of an issue	Members overinflate the consequences of not reaching agreement
People tune out of interaction	Threats are used to win arguments
Unresolved issues keep emerging in the same or different form	Mounting tension is felt in group
Discussion centers on safe aspect of broader and more explosive issue	Group gets nowhere but seems to be working feverishly
Little sharing of information	Name calling and personal arguments are used
Outspoken members are notably quiet	Immediate polarization on issues or the emergence of coalitions
No plans are made to implement a chosen solution	Hostile gazes or less-direct eye contact between members
Evidence offered in support of claims is unevaluated	Sarcastic laughter or humor as a form of tension release
	Heated disagreements that seem pointless or are about trivial issues

Figure 7.4 Group members need to recognize destructive communication practices such as those listed here to prevent escalation cycles and inappropriate avoidance. [From Joseph P. Folger and Marshall Scott Poole, *Working Through Conflict* (Glenview, Ill.: Scott, Foresman, 1984), p. 78. Used with permission of Joseph P. Folger.]

The constructive communication acts presented earlier provide initial guidance for achieving productive communication during differentiation and integration. The keys are to (1) recognize destructive communication practices that contribute to escalation cycles or inappropriate avoidance (see Figure 7.4) and (2) engage in communication practices that support constructive conflict management. Although we cannot review all the communication tactics associated with destructive and constructive conflict management, the practices for effective differentiation and integration provide procedural guidelines for collaborating in the management of group conflict.

Practices That Incapacitate Group Differentiation and Integration An ideal way to approach group conflict cooperatively is to solve a problem. You can adapt the problem-solving model described in Chapter 6 to manage conflict during the differentiation and integration phases by posing the conflict as a problem to be solved. Before elaborating the activities for conflict management, we will consider several disabling group problem-solving practices that need to be overcome. Identifying them will further your understanding of the difficulties of managing group conflict. Furthermore, it will provide a rationale for our suggestions later to counteract incapacitating practices during the differentiation and integration phases.

We have already looked at disabling communication acts. Several types of practices at the episode and activity levels of communication can directly undermine adequate differentiation and integration. Folger and Poole call these practices "trained incapacities."[16] They are inappropriate habits that work against adequate differentiation and integration. For example, most groups communicate through open discussion during meetings. However, brainstorming is a more appropriate way to generate lots of ideas. Yet even when groups are familiar with how to brainstorm, they still fall into the habitual pattern of open discussion. You need to be vigilant for when a habit is ineffective for conducting an episode activity.

Goal-centeredness is the tendency to focus on the outcome at the expense of the process for reaching it. Solutions, plans, and procedures are emphasized before accurately identifying the problem, its causes, and criteria for an acceptable solution. This situation is common in student groups. It is difficult to agree on the answer when we are not clear on the question.

Goal-centeredness contributes to conflict in part because group members have not shared in a careful analysis that leads to solutions. They do not understand the issues a solution addresses and thus are more resistant to it. Goal-centered thinking is not wrong; after all, goals direct group efforts. But the premature identification and discussion of goals or a solution to a problem can contribute to the emergence of conflicts and poor conflict management. Goal-centeredness becomes incapacitating when "(1) it prevents parties from conducting an adequate assessment of the problem underlying the conflict, . . . or (2) it becomes a way to quickly make a decision without a complete analysis of the chosen solution."[17]

Goal-centeredness also contributes to "positional thinking."[18] Roger Fisher and William Ury point out that conflict management should focus on interests, not positions. That is, arguing over preferences masks the issues and interests that make a choice reasonable to its advocate. The group does not clearly understand the position or identify shared interests. Fisher and Ury recommend a thorough discussion of the issues and interests that underlie positions in conflict. We believe that the analysis episode of the problem-solving process can discourage positional thinking and contribute to effective differentiation. This is especially important when the task is complex, unfamiliar, and addresses values, and when there are no obvious or expert solutions.

Destructive redefinition reflects a tendency to state a situation, problem, or goal with the objective of winning or beating an opponent. Redefinition is natural to decision making because discussion, circumstances, and information can alter a group's understanding of a situation. This is common in solving problems and setting goals when new information requires an alteration of the original problem or goal. Redefining a goal or problem can be used to conduct a preliminary analysis and help groups pinpoint the specific issue.

Destructive redefinition in conflict occurs when a member frames the conflict (problem) in a manner that emphasizes his or her own interest at the exclusion of others' interests or identifies others' interests as the problem. For example, if a conflict was over a company keeping costs down for a project, a destructive redefinition of the conflict would pose the cost as the problem: "How can we keep the company from being so cheap?" Notice how the company's interest in keeping costs down is cast in a negative light. A more constructive redefinition could be "Where could we find outside funding?" or "How can we reduce cost and maintain quality?" Constructive redefinition requires the inclusion and satisfaction of all members' interests. It tackles the problem of satisfying members' interests, not each other.

The *evaluative tendency*, discussed earlier in this chapter and in Chapter 6 under idea generating, instigates defensiveness and undermines the generation of creative solutions. We are evaluative creatures by nature and habit. Problem solving and differentiation are founded on evaluation. Even so, evaluation is destructive when it is misplaced.

Three situations require attention in avoiding destructive evaluation. First, when interaction gravitates toward defensive and emotional reactions, discussion should shift to descriptive statements emphasizing areas of agreement and commonality. Second, when a broad range of alternatives is needed, evaluation should be delayed. Fisher and Ury emphasize the importance of "inventing options for mutual gain."[19] Negotiants should look for all the possible solutions to resolve the conflict, but evaluation must be postponed to maximize the creativity and quantity of options to consider. Third, if groups lack sufficient or critical information about the conflict, they should suspend judgment until they have the needed information.

Using objective standards is appropriate in making decisions involving objective accuracy—those available for public inspection that you can see, hear, or touch. Using objective standards is appropriate when addressing conflicts over objective decisions such as the amount of money required to construct a building or the number of employees needed for a job. Conflicts over such decisions can be resolved by standards external to any person's preferences or prejudices. However, objective criteria can have destructive consequences if applied to decisions where such criteria do not exist. Individual preferences can masquerade as objective criteria. Most group decisions and therefore conflicts are based in social norms and preferences and thus lack truly objective criteria for determining the "correct" decision. Yet individuals will assume that a standard or preference is objective and argue inflexibly for a position. This contributes to thinking of a criterion or solution as the only or "right" one, which leads to inflexible and defensive communication behaviors.

Identifying and using criteria to make decisions is a major episode of critical problem solving. Groups should certainly identify both objective and preferential standards that underlie a decision in conflict. At the same time, it is important to recognize preferential criteria and not treat them as objective. The group also should establish criteria that include all relevant issues and members' interests to minimize conflicts over criteria selection. Finding solutions that satisfy all the criteria can be easier than arguing over whose preferences deserve inclusion.

Using procedures has its advantages and disadvantages in conflict management. Standardized methods such as parliamentary procedure provide a common process for participation and involvement. They establish rules for decision making (for example, voting, making motions, taking turns). Such procedures as the round-robin and nominal group technique can equalize power among members so powerful individuals or coalitions do not control interaction.[20] Procedures can ensure that specific task episodes are performed to maximize the quality of solutions. They can also become sources of conflict if they are incompatible with the situation or the decision-making style of members (tightly structured versus flexible and freewheeling).[21]

Some group procedures become part of a group's practices without formal acknowledgments but emerge and become institutionalized through routine use. The prevalent use of open discussion is a case in point. Regardless of how procedures are adopted, their use should fit the demands of the situation. Procedures and activities should minimize confrontation and escalation and should not suppress and avoid differentiation. However, the habitual use of procedures can be ineffective. For example, *Robert's Rules of Order* can ensure participation and involvement. At the same time, it encourages opposition through the use of motions to propose a solution to a problem before the problem has been agreed upon and its causes discerned. (Recall our discussion on goal-centeredness.) Other members face someone's solution, which has not considered all parties' views and concerns before being proposed. Add to that the use of the majority vote, which can polarize groups and alienate the losers, and you have a set of procedures that breed destructive conflict. Groups need to consider the appropriateness of practices for promoting collaborative efforts in the process of differentiation and integration.

Practices for Effective Group Differentiation and Integration

A group can employ several guidelines to manage conflict. We will present episodes for the differentiation and integration phases and suggest activities you can use to implement them. Before doing so, we offer a couple of reminders. First, if it is important that all members accept the group's procedures and decisions, be sure to involve everyone in the conflict management process. This can help depersonalize the conflict between coalitions or individuals and reinforce the group as the source of decisions. Second, remember to communicate in a confirming, supportive manner and assert your views. If the conflict has been personalized through attacks or evaluation, bring it to the group's attention. Establishing rules to manage destructive communication acts can help.

The goal of the differentiation phase is to establish a clear understanding of similarities and differences among positions and interests. Constructive differentiation can be divided into three episodes: position identification, position rationale, and position incompatibility.

Position identification is what it says: clearly stating the sides in conflict. Because most conflicts are over plans, procedures, or solutions, the positions should be concrete and specific. For example, in the opening scenario of this chapter, Susan's position regarding the dorm security problem was to use electronic dormitory keys. Joe's position advocated requiring the resident assistants to conduct a sign-in procedure using dorm ID cards.

Position rationale identifies the reasons for each position. The advocate for each position provides the reasons for his or her position; they should be related to the problem or goal. In the dorm security project, they would address why each solution would contribute to increasing security. However, reasons reflecting the personal interests or principles of the parties involved in the conflict are also legitimate. For example, Joe is also concerned with the role of the resident assistants. (He is the supervisor of RAs.) He believes that it is important to involve them because they are at the front desk; he also does not want to see the loss of student jobs through automation. Joe wants RAs used, not replaced. Although some may see this as self-serving, it is nonetheless a relevant factor involved in the security problem (or could be if ignored in the solution). Susan's position is also shaped by interests. She is particularly concerned that the solution does not inconvenience residents. Students should have easy and timely access to the dorm day or night. She also has a fascination with new technologies and their capacity to solve human problems efficiently.

Exposing all the interests underlying the positions will reveal hidden agendas. It is difficult to understand members' positions if they hide their reasons and motivations. This can lead to suspicion and defensive reactions. More importantly, you cannot find alternatives to satisfy interests that are not known.

The *position incompatibility* episode requires the group to discern the degree to which positions differ. This can be done at two levels: in terms of the differences between actual positions and in terms of reasons and interests. Susan wants the solution to be based on automation and Joe on a policy using existing resources. The group establishes where interests are shared and diverge. Common interests reduce the sense of difference—for example, both Susan and Joe think some form of identification is needed. Position-oriented discussions frequently hide the similarity of interests, thus creating an inflated perception of incompatibility; using electronic dorm keys does not mean replacing resident assistants. At the same time, an unclear view of the differences hinders resolution of the conflict.

This episode sets the course for the integration phase. The specific similarities and differences of reasons and interests prepare the group to search for a resolution, or re-solution, that maintains the shared interests and discovers a way to satisfy divergent interests.

The task of integration is to find a resolution to the conflict that integrates the issues, reasons, and interests of the involved parties—as well as keeping members integrated to this end. There are three episodes important to this phase: problem definition or redefinition, solution generation, and solution evaluation. Where differentiation analyzes the conflict, integration poses the differences as a problem for the group to solve. Chapter 6 discusses problem-solving steps. Here we will suggest some specific ways to use problem solving to manage the integration phase.

Problem redefinition is the most critical episode of integration because it could lead to destructive redefinition where the conflict poses the other's interests as the problem (how to reduce the need for resident assistants or how to use existing resources and not incur costs, for example). This places the group back into the conflict and may lead to re-escalation. The goal of constructive redefinition is to have the group work together in attacking the problem, not each other. You can do this by defining the problem in a way that encompasses the divergent interests identified in the position incompatibility episode. The group attempts to acknowledge all relevant interests in the conflict by searching for a solution to satisfy them. It is probably wise to generate several redefinitions to explore the variations of the problem and define the goals clearly. This might be accomplished with brainstorming or a round-robin. The trick is to phrase the problem in a way that recognizes the different interests. "What is the best way to support existing resources in the efficient management of dorm security?" might be an acceptable definition. (Notice how it acknowledges Susan's need for something efficient and helps Joe maintain the existing role of resident assistants.) The phrasing of problem statements should also be open, rather than limited by specific solutions ("How do we get RAs to use electronic ID cards?"). Although our example suggests that Joe's and Susan's original positions might be complementary, not mutually exclusive, they did not perceive them as such. Conflict management in group decision making is sometimes nothing more than getting members to slow down, think, and discover similarities that were blocked by misinterpretation and emotional reactions. Frequently positions can be combined to improve solutions.

Fisher and Ury encourage generating as many solutions as possible during the *solution generation* episode. The only requirement they pose is that the solutions address the interests of the involved parties. Brainstorming or idea-writing activities are very useful to this end. Be sure to separate the generation of solutions from their evaluation to increase the range and creativity of options.

Once the solution options have been reviewed, clarified, and perhaps reduced by ranking, the group is ready for the *solution selection* episode. This requires identifying criteria or standards for evaluating each solution. The group may already have established them prior to the conflict, or it can derive them from the list of reasons, interests, and issues developed in the position rationale episode. The group should formally develop the criteria for an acceptable solution. Of course, the initial interests that gave rise to the conflict should be included. Solutions that fit the criteria may be evident. The group may wish to use a weighting technique (see Chapter 6) to identify the degree to which solutions satisfy criteria. Do not overlook solutions that could satisfy criteria sufficiently through a minor change or addition to make them more acceptable. Problems with solutions can be fixed too. The following list outlines episodes and activities for collaboratively managing group conflict.

1. Identify clearly what the conflict is over. All members should agree on what is at issue.
2. Have members present their reasons for their positions on the conflict one at a time. (It is useful to place this information on a board or paper before the group.) What are the positions and interests and why?
   - Cover one position at a time, allowing all members who wish to contribute to the position to do so until all distinct ideas are on the table.
   - Follow presentations of positions with requests for clarification and further elaboration. *Do not evaluate* the positions or reasons.
   - Next have a member against a position summarize and paraphrase the position until the members holding that position agree that it reflects what they meant.
   - Repeat these three steps for each position to be considered.
3. Once all positions have been clearly identified, discuss and determine the degree of similarity and difference between positions and interests. Clearly define the incompatibilities.
4. Review the positions and incompatibilities. See if there are any readily available proposals to resolve the conflict. If so, evaluate them for acceptability. If not, develop a statement that poses the different positions and interests as a problem to solve. Be sure to state the problem in a manner that does not negate or exclude the various parties' interests.
5. As a group, generate as many ideas as possible on how to solve the problem. Review ideas for possible solutions. Evaluate the most promising ones using the itemized response. (See Chapter 6.) Look for ways to resolve concerns with an idea to make the solution workable.
6. If problem solving does not work or time is short, the group may have to resort to voting, compromising, or having the leader or another trusted member make the decision.

Once a group has settled on a solution, it should be cast in terms of implementation. The details of turning it into a plan for action need to be developed. See Box 7.1 for an example.

Box 7.1

Doing Your Fair Share: Conflict Management for Group Satisfaction

The Slumlords, a class project group investigating off-campus housing problems, started its fourth meeting. The usual chitchat and playful banter was replaced by disgruntled discussion over Tom's apparent lack of involvement with the group's project. This was the second meeting he had missed and his participation, when in attendance, was marginal at best. Sean felt that it was not fair that all of the other members attend meetings and do assignments while Tom got off the hook. "How can he make a contribution if he's not here?" asked Connie. Donna added, "Professor Bergren said we have to reach agreement on how we will distribute the points we earn on our project. We will have to deal with this problem eventually or give Tom points for work he may never do." Beth moaned, "Like always, the do-nothings get the rewards of other people's work. I'm sick of it! Why should he get the same grade as me?" Donna reminded the group that it might be premature to assume Tom would not come through. After all, it was only the fourth meeting. Sean quickly replied, "It's becoming a norm for him, and he never calls to explain his absences. We ought to nip this in the bud before the group becomes demoralized by it any further."

Donna asked the others what they thought should be done. Connie thought that they should bring their concerns to Tom's attention at the next meeting he attended. Beth suggested ignoring him if he did not wish to participate and take the points away from his final grade. "That might have to happen," Donna said, "but remember Professor Bergren will not accept our point distribution unless we all sign off on it. We will have to deal with Tom at some point or let it slide." The group agreed that the most sensible, although difficult, course of action was to communicate its concerns to Tom.

The group agreed it could get along without Tom's participation, but also knew that the planned survey of off-campus students was going to require everyone's help. Tom might fail the course if he received a poor grade on the project. The group speculated on what was motivating his behavior. Beth thought he was just an easy-going "low rider" who took advantage of others. Connie suggested he had a case of "senioritis" because this was his last semester. Donna thought it might be related to personal problems. No one knew for sure. The group moved on to its meeting agenda, having let off steam and given Donna the task of speaking with Tom in private to avoid the perception of ganging up on him.

Donna ran into Tom at the campus center the next day and let him know when the next meeting was scheduled. Tom apologized for missing the previous meeting and said he was not sure he would be able to fit the next meeting in his schedule. Donna felt irritated; she was also busy and found it difficult to schedule meetings. She restrained her exasperation and asked

Box 7.1 (continued)

Tom if they could meet so she could update him on the group's progress and discuss the scheduling problem. They both checked their calendars and agreed to meet after classes at 4:00 p.m. the following day in the library conference room. Donna wanted to have time and privacy for this difficult meeting.

Donna could not get to sleep that night. She imagined the various scenarios that might take place and rehearsed her reactions. Every time she imagined Tom getting angry and hostile, a shot of adrenaline sent a wave of anxiety through her body. She wanted a successful resolution to the problem so the group could get on with its project. While Donna contemplated her meeting with Tom, two phrases kept recurring in her thoughts: "conflict is an opportunity" and "invent options for mutual gain." The more she repeated them, the more she imagined scenarios that satisfied Tom and the group. She did not realize she was casting her role for the dreaded meeting.

Donna and Tom met and exchanged greetings, exclaiming how busy they were. Donna briefed Tom on the group's progress and its next meeting agenda and gave him a copy of the last meeting's minutes. Tom raised a couple of questions and shared a few ideas on the off-campus student survey. Donna then opened the scheduling problem with Tom and prefaced it by suggesting that they look for a way to satisfy both his and the group's needs in finding a way to resolve the scheduling problem. Tom quickly began listing the difficulties he was having making the meetings. Besides classes and work, he had a family and a one-hour commute to the campus. Because the group could not meet during the day, he had to return at night, which posed considerable hardship for him. Tom said he had considered dropping the class, but thought the information would be professionally useful, even if he did not receive his usual A or B grade for the course.

Donna proceeded to describe the group's feelings and perceptions of his participation. She emphasized that the other members wanted to be sure he got his fair share of the project points but did not know how he could if he did not perform. Donna also pointed out that even if he was satisfied with a lesser grade, it hurt the group to have one less member to depend on to perform group tasks. The group had selected and begun work on their project based on having five members. "What the hell do you expect me to do—leave my family and live on campus like the rest of you?" Tom felt cornered. Donna responded, "Tom, I can tell you're under pressure and don't expect to get something for nothing. Perhaps there is a way to reduce the strain on you and the group. Let's see if we can find a satisfying solution." Tom apologized for the outburst and agreed to explore some options.

Donna suggested that they identify both Tom's and the group's needs before looking for possible solutions. Tom agreed and asked what she thought the group's needs were. She said, "Ideally, attendance at all the

Box 7.1 (continued)

meetings and awarding points equal to participation in the project." Tom listed his needs as flexibility in attendance of evening meetings and enough points to ensure a C grade on the group's project. Donna explained that the group thought they could do without him at each meeting but did need support on the survey tasks. Tom said, "I need to be free from attending every evening meeting, but I'm willing to receive fewer points as long as I pass the project." Donna expressed concern with not attending most of the meetings because that is where a lot of work gets done and he would not become part of the group. Pointing out that he might not be able to do everything, Tom offered to help reduce the group's work load by doing tasks he could perform on his own time. Donna admitted this was possible, but was still concerned with coordinating tasks with the rest of the group.

They elaborated their interests and concerns until they had identified all the issues relevant to the problem. The key was finding a way to have Tom help the group in its work in a coordinated manner that would earn him a minimum of a C on the group project.

They listed possible tasks and ways of coordinating them with the group. Soon they had several ideas for both areas. They began to get energized at the prospect of finding a potential solution. Tom offered to use his computer skills in analyzing the survey data. He would provide a written report on the results and conclusions and would report on it at a group meeting. Donna added that he could coordinate this with the group through a survey subcommittee composed of members who would be free at the same time during the day. She pointed out that he would need to be involved in the survey instrument construction as well as its analysis but that the rest of the group would administer it. Tom squinted while he pondered the developing arrangement and said, "If I am guaranteed a minimum of a C for performing this task with the subcommittee, you've got a deal." Donna smiled, "I like it. It helps the group do a major task, it gets you your passing grade, the group is clear on your contribution and payoff, and we don't have to hassle the scheduling problem. I'll bring it back and see what they say. I think everyone can get their fair share!"

Summary

Constructive management of group conflict poses several general and specific communication requirements. First, it requires communication acts that enhance the relational dimension of the group. Second, it calls for episodes and activities that establish clear and productive communication during the differentiation and integration phases.

Conflict in groups is natural and desirable. Differences between members over ideas or relationship circumstances are a sign that deliberation is occurring. But members must communicate in a manner that acknowledges regard and respect for themselves and each other in general, especially during conflict interaction. That is, they need a confirming, supportive, and assertive manner rather than disconfirming, defensive, and aggressive ways.

When conflict is apparent or manifest, members need to engage in communication to differentiate—to identify the specific positions in conflict, establish the rationale for them and assess the degree of their incompatibility. This serves as a base from which to determine the severity of the conflict and to attempt the integration of differences toward an acceptable resolution. Ideally, when incompatibilities are real, the group can pose the conflict as a problem for the members to tackle cooperatively, using the problem-solving process.

When groups can practice what we have outlined here, conflict becomes an opportunity for resolution and discovery of otherwise hidden solutions. If groups are to maximize groupness, these considerations and practices are essential. Groups are unlikely to produce high-quality decisions if their members do not participate constructively in decision making and conflict management. Some circumstances and contingencies require competition and escalation. However, such situations do not promote effective group decision making and inherently undermine the value of groups for making decisions.

GroupQuests: Discussion Questions

1. Reflect on your experiences in groups and recall instances where you were either disconfirmed and responded to defensively or confirmed and supported. What did the person(s) say or do? What did you think and feel? How did you react? Did your (or other members') reactions make any difference to the group's task? How so?
2. Think back on the last group you participated in. Did it have a supportive, defensive, or mixed climate? What specific communication practices contributed to the climate? Did the climate affect the emergence of conflict? Explain.
3. Create two or three examples of each type of defensive communication act described in the chapter (see Table 7.2). Be sure to consider accompanying nonverbal cues. Attempt to rephrase each defensive statement in a supportive manner. Observe your effort to convert defensive to supportive statements. Was it difficult? What factors contributed to the difficulty or ease of converting the statements? What factors during group interaction would help or hinder the ability to speak in a supportive manner?

GroupWorks: Group Activities

1. Form groups of five to six members and prepare to role-play a conflict situation. Identify an issue and establish two positions that are clearly incompatible. Have one member advocate each position but do not assign or indicate the positions of the other members. Begin the role playing

by having each advocate state his or her position and reasons followed by other members' views on the positions. Conduct a discussion for a minimum of twenty minutes, using the guidelines for conflict management. Attempt to work toward a position that the group as a whole can accept. Treat the issue as if it really mattered to you. When time runs out, note what happened and discuss it among group members. Identify practices or perceptions that corresponded to or contradicted the material in this chapter.

2. Continue the role-playing situation and have each of the advocates for the incompatible positions take the opponent's position. Present the other's position as if it were your own, covering all aspects of it as you understand it. While this is going on, group members should observe the role takers in terms of their ability to present each other's position and their use of nonverbal cues, and types of communication. When the role players have completed stating their positions, reasons, and questions, have the group note its observations. Have the two opponents discuss whether their experience had any effect on understanding each other's position.

3. Obtain a videotape of *Twelve Angry Men* and view it. Explain whether or not the story portrayed a conflict, using the definition of *conflict* presented in this chapter. Provide justification for your views.

4. Watch *Twelve Angry Men* and see whether there was a differentiation and integration phase. What communication behaviors promoted or hindered adequate differentiation? What kinds of motivations or conditions of the jurors contributed to these behaviors? Did they need an integration phase?

5. Observe a campus student government meeting. Note signs or occurrences of manifest conflict. If conflicts were manifest, how were they managed and with what result? Did you notice any "trained incapacities" potentially or actually affecting the treatment and outcome of the conflict? Explain. What suggestions would you make to improve conflict management?

GroupActs: Practical Applications

If you have been assigned to a group project, have your group plan to discuss measures to prevent destructive conflict. Perhaps conflict has already been manifest in your group.

a. Have each member generate a list of specific communication practices that the group performs or does not perform that potentially or actually contribute to inadequate conflict management.
b. Have one member collect, compile, and report a master list, noting the frequency of items reported. Review the list to clarify each item.
c. As a group, rank the items in terms of those that are most problematic in managing conflict constructively. Review the ranking and explain the reasons for the top five items.
d. Devise ways or practices that can help the group prevent the top-ranked problems from occurring or continuing.

The group's goal is to arrive at consensus on how it will prevent destructive conflict and practice constructive conflict management.

Group Project Facilitator: A Guide for Group Meetings

Overview

The results of well over 100 group projects in "Small Group Communication" and other courses have shown us that many problems hinder projects' quality. Even in courses about group communication theory and practices, the majority of projects range from poor to marginal in quality. These are the most obvious problems:

- Students are typically unable to apply course and text concepts and practices while conducting the group project.
- Courses involving group projects do not *train* students in effective meeting, decision-making, or problem-solving practices.
- Complex task and relational considerations in group projects need guidance to improve efficiency and effectiveness.
- Frequently uneven and inconsistent participation of group members in decision making and other activities undermines the advantages of using groups.
- Uncritical and poor-quality decision making translates into ineffective project outcomes.

The group project facilitator (GPF) is designed to overcome these and other problems by providing *process facilitation*, which offers information on how to tackle meetings, project phases, decision making, and problem solving. The GPF is concerned only with providing process guidelines, not with the project's content. The project's content—its goal, ideas, decisions—and the selection and use of process guidelines in the GPF are the group's responsibility.

The GPF is a practical guide and a self-training approach to learning and applying effective project management and group communication practices. The tools and practices for decision-making meetings in the earlier skills chapters plus the GPF will help you become better at diagnosing problems and participating in group decision making.

The GPF is organized into four project phases: forming the group, project identification, analysis and information search, and project synthesis and delivery. Each phase contains an introduction, guidelines, pre-meeting activities, and standard phase agenda. To avoid information overload, we present the guideline segments as you proceed with each project phase.

The *introduction* of each phase establishes its purpose and orients you to the tasks that follow. The *guidelines* clarify steps and practices for use during each phase of the project. The *pre-meeting activities* require each group member to consider one or more aspects of a task in the given phase before the meetings. The activities are posed as questions each member can answer to prepare for decisions awaiting the group at a meeting. The *standard phase agenda* lists specific tasks typical of each phase of any group project. Each agenda list is arranged in a logical order, but circumstances may require following a different order, returning to an agenda item, or skipping some.

The phases of the GPF correspond to four major themes of group projects (see Figure 1). The first, *forming the group*, is concerned with organizing members, establishing roles and rules, setting the meeting time and place, and finding out how the group feels about using the GPF. The group must follow the recommended practices and agenda of this phase carefully because the process decisions made

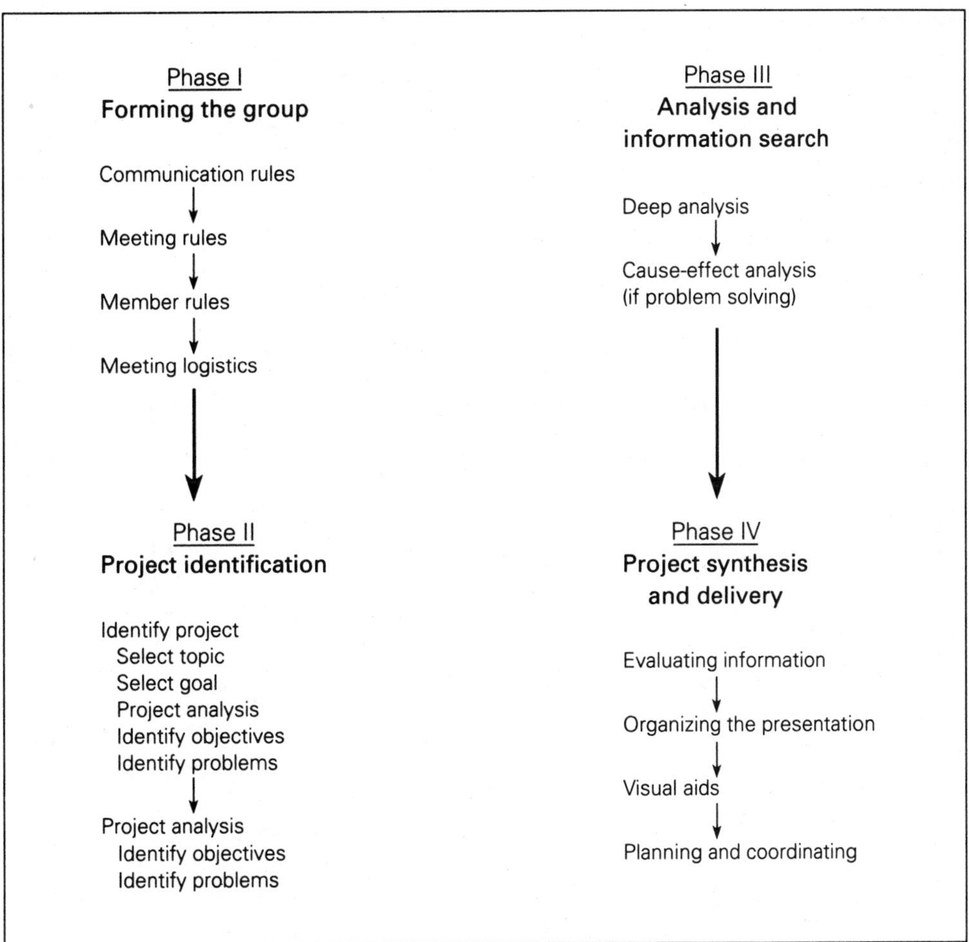

Figure 1 Map of the group process facilitator.

at this phase will serve or haunt the group throughout the project. Although the group can return to the phase to make changes if necessary, initially considering the issues of this phase carefully minimizes wasted efforts and frustration.

In the second phase, *project identification*, the group will be given a specific project or required to select one and will need to establish a clear and precise project goal and objectives. Then the group will assess the project's feasibility in view of constraints, resources, and commitment. Too often groups work on projects either without knowing what they are trying to accomplish or without assessing demands to determine whether they can successfully achieve their goal. Working without a clear project goal and assessing the group's ability to achieve the goal is casting the group's success to chance.

The third phase brings the group to the heart of the project, the *analysis and information search*. Here we recommend several basic tools for identifying questions related to the project and potential sources for answers to them. We also give attention to delegating research tasks, reporting information, and assessing it.

If the group has proceeded to this point with reasonable success, it is ready for the fourth and last phase, *project synthesis and delivery*. This phase deals with completing the project goal and preparing it for delivery or implementation. Guidelines and agenda items will address evaluating and organizing information and presenting the project. We offer suggestions for organizing the information, pointers on oral and written delivery, and the use of visual aids. Frequently, when groups feel that they have achieved their goal, they get careless about packaging it for presentation. But they really have two goals. The first involves the content of the project goal. The second is to communicate the achievement of that goal effectively.

The GPF guidelines address task and relationship dimensions of group communication for decision making. The task dimension is concerned with the project's content and goals. The relational dimension focuses on how people work together to accomplish their tasks. The GPF offers a map for communication that incorporates task and relational considerations.

The GPF is like a box of tools with instructions on how to use them. These tools are the product of years of development and evolution by theorists and practitioners. However, the tools are only as good as their users. It is the group's responsibility to select and implement practices to increase its effectiveness. The project will likely take more time and effort than group projects that do not use the practices advocated in the GPF. But the payoffs are potentially much greater. The conscientious use of the GPF will not only improve the possibility of a successful project but will also train you in practices you can use in task groups throughout your life.

Phase I: Forming the Group

If your task group is typical, it has been set up by your instructor, has no assigned leader or chairperson, and is composed of members who have not worked together before. Its assignment is to identify a project and present an oral or written report on its results.

It is natural for such groups to focus on the project, forgetting their other major task: producing an effective group. The quality of the group directly relates to the quality of the project, so we will first look at forming an effective task group.

B. W. Tuckman has identified four stages that newly formed groups go through in working together: forming, storming, norming, and performing.[1] The *forming stage* involves orienting the group to the project: what, why, and how. Getting members' names, phone numbers, and addresses; identifying meeting places and times; and developing ideas on project topics are typical tasks at this stage.

On the relational side, members begin to orient themselves to each other in terms of how dependent and independent they are together. Issues such as leadership, willingness to participate, ground rules, and establishing the general steps of the project shape the group's relational

1. B. W. Tuckman, "Developmental Sequence in Small Groups," *Psychological Bulletin*, 1965, *63*, 384–399.

characteristics. (Even if there is an assigned chairperson, the group's perceived leader may emerge as discussion proceeds.) The group may depend on one or more members to direct the project or it may develop cooperative and collaborative working relationships by consistently encouraging and soliciting participation among members. This cooperative climate is the most desirable for working in groups because it taps the most valuable resource of a group: its members.

In our experience, student groups address task issues in the forming stage, but seldom discuss relational issues. This lack of attention to how members want to work together contributes to the severity of the next stage: storming.

The *storming stage* results from different views on leadership, operating rules, topics, meeting times, and other matters. Here task issues frequently gravitate toward interpersonal conflict. To the extent that such issues are not discussed and resolved, the group will suffer from dissatisfying work relationships, which undermine its ability to effectively proceed with the project. If the group does not identify and overcome the sources of the storm, they will recur later in the form of apathy, lack of participation, and even open hostilities. To protect itself from damaging storms, the group should encourage different viewpoints and seek consensus on decisions.

The third stage of group development, *norming*, grows out of the development of norms, procedures, and particular member roles. Once the conflicts in the storming stage are resolved, operating norms emerge to structure the group. As norms become operational and acceptable to the group, a sense of cohesion emerges. Members begin to share ideas, seek opinions, explore options, take assignments, and generally feel good about the project and group. This outcome largely depends on the success of achieving norms that promote task effectiveness and that are acceptable to the group members.

The *performing stage* occurs as the group members individually, as subcommittees, or as a group conduct research, make decisions, and solve problems. There is a free flow of ideas and information.

These four stages of group development occur in a sequence, but can be repeated if a new forming issue arises (for example, a new member) or the useful but threatening "different idea" kicks up a storm. Tasks or problems that require the group to rethink or repeat work will likely recycle the group through the stages. If the group anticipates what will hinder its effectiveness and learns how to have productive storms, it can repeat stages painlessly.

The following information will raise issues and recommend procedures to consider for forming your group. The premeeting activity will help prepare you for the first meeting concerned with forming the group. Many of these procedures have been described in Chapters 5 and 6; some will be briefly reviewed here.

Communication Rules

Communication is the first process. When you speak you are addressing something, some content. At the same time, you indicate how you see yourself and how you see the other person. This relationship level of information is largely conveyed nonverbally. When human beings get together, they convey content and relationship information whether or not they intend to. Although the relational aspect of messages is typically implied and covert, it is nonetheless present. When, for example, a teacher talks to you with the voice of authority, he or she is posing a view of your relationship.

Groups use the resources of their members and develop a sense of "groupness" when all members have the opportunity to contribute information and opinions and participate in decisions. This does not mean that all members have to contribute the same amount or the same quality of information and ideas. If the GPF is to work effectively, the group must accept these three communication rules:

1. All members have the right and responsibility to communicate over matters concerning the project.
2. All members should listen to and acknowledge (not necessarily agree with) other members' statements. If a message is unclear, seek clarification.
3. There should be no personal attacks on any group members.

These ground rules mean that you have the responsibility to say what is on your mind and to ask others to share information and opinions. In addition, you must let others know that you heard and understood them before you give your information or point of view. Finally, avoid any remarks that put down another member's ideas or behavior. Differences of opinion or concerns over meeting behavior should be addressed directly. Focus on the issue, not the person. Should differences of opinion gravitate into a conflict, review the conflict management guidelines in Chapter 7.

These communication rules are fundamental, but will not by themselves ensure the group's success. There are further considerations regarding meeting procedures, logistics, and tools for group tasks. If communication is the first process, the second process is using procedures for conducting organized meetings and group tasks. For example, groups need to generate a list of possible solutions to a problem or evaluate the merits of various options. Certain procedures will increase the quality of the group's work.

The Meeting[2]

The first major activity of a task group is the meeting, the most complex group communication activity. Besides involving most of the different activities a group conducts, the meeting is a specific communication activity with particular characteristics and problems. The following information offers several guidelines for using the meeting rules that were discussed in Chapter 5.

The *focus rule* addresses the problem of discussion that wanders and moves in several directions. Unfocused discussion can discourage participation and reduce productivity. There are several task and relational problems associated with an unclear focus:

- Confusion due to disorganization
- Frustration over wasted time and energy
- Members feel ignored, rejected, and dissatisfied
- Uncritical discussion of a given issue
- Unsystematic work leading to poor-quality decisions
- Hindered group cohesion

Guidelines for implementing the fo-

2. This section is adapted from Michael Doyle and David Straus, *How to Make Meetings Work* (New York: Wyden Books, 1976).

Focus and Tool Rule Guidelines

1. Develop an *agenda*, a list of tasks to be covered at the scheduled meeting. (See Appendix A, Tips on Agenda Setting.) Watch for agenda items that have two or more specific focuses (subtasks). Note: An agenda item is not necessarily a focus. Some agenda items may have two or more focuses within them. For example, the agenda item "to develop a survey" has several parts: purpose, questions, format, sample population, administration, and data analysis. These issues are related but need to be treated separately. Each agenda item should clearly state what it is to achieve.

2. Use the meeting agenda as a starting point and ask the group what the first focus should be and what it should accomplish. Allow all possible focus options to be identified before selecting the first focus. If it is not clear which options should be first, discuss the best order of the focuses.

3. Once agreement on the first focus is established, discuss the best tool for conducting it based on the type of task activity and the relational situation of the group (low participation or high cohesion, for example). Discuss tool options and select one. Both focus and tool decisions should be acceptable to all members.

4. Proceed using the selected tool until the focus is completed. The focus or tool can be changed or tabled for later treatment. Sometimes a focus requires more than one tool.

5. Repeat the process and select another focus and tool until the meeting is over.

cus rule are combined with guidelines for the next meeting rule.

The *tool rule* overcomes an often overlooked problem of task group communication: matching the procedure or practice with the selected focus. When the group has decided on a focus, it then decides on the best tool for conducting it. There are two considerations to make when selecting the best procedure for a given focus: the task and the relational situation. When a group does not choose the most appropriate practice for managing discussion of a focus, it risks:

- Inefficient use of time
- Lower quantity and quality of information and decisions
- Loss of member input and participation
- Hindering relational satisfaction and group cohesion

The guidelines above outline the procedure for using the focus and tool rule during meetings. If your group adopts these rules, it will need to consider how it will ensure their implementation. We address this in the discussion on members' roles.

Meeting Activity Tools

A meeting focus emphasizes one of several types of tasks: information sharing, idea generating, decision making, or the more complex task of problem solving. The types of tools and their guidelines for these tasks are outlined in Chapter 6.

The following sketch of the meeting process shows the relationship of four factors involved in using the focus and tool rules.

Focus	Type of Task	Tools	Relational Issues
Focus A	Information sharing	Open discussion Round-robin Reports	Tension?
			Participation?
Focus B	Idea generating	Brainstorming Idea writing Idea-spurring questions	Too cohesive?
			Dominating member?
Focus C	Decision making	Consensus Voting Itemized response Ranking Weighting	Commitment?

Two additional issues require consideration in forming the group: member roles and meeting logistics involving time, place, and evaluation.

Meeting Roles

Members' roles are a major consideration in forming the group for your project. Recall that a role is a specialized job with specific behaviors that fulfill some aspect of the meeting process. Such roles occur informally or can be established formally. As noted in Chapter 4, members' roles will emerge as groups go through the development process. Some members will be seen and informally recognized as performing certain meeting functions (coordinator, devil's advocate, content expert).

Your group may decide to adopt several process rules, formats, and procedures after having reviewed the information in the GPF and other issues related to your project. But how will the group make sure they are followed? The members could share this responsibility, but their involvement in the project makes it difficult to remember to watch for rule or procedure compliance. The more jobs you have to perform at a given time, the more likely someone will get slighted or overlooked. Ideally, a neutral third party could guide the meeting to remove that burden from members who already have other responsibilities. An impartial person can also help the group maintain the rules and procedures it chooses to follow.

Once a group has decided on how to conduct meetings, it should decide on how to implement its rules and procedures. This requires a clear sense of each procedure or rule, when it is to be applied, and who will monitor its correct application.

We recommend that each group cover three roles: the facilitator, recorder, and

Facilitation Guidelines

1. By mutual consent identify all rules and procedures to be used during project meetings.
2. Establish a specific discussion focus, with a clear outcome.
3. Determine a procedure or tool for each focus; review the rules or steps if the group has not had sufficient experience using it.
4. Keep an eye on what is happening to determine if a rule or procedure is being followed. If not, bring it to the group's attention.
5. Suspend, change, or modify rules or procedures if the group finds reason and agrees to do so.

coordinator. At the same time, a group can create any rules and roles to implement that it thinks will be useful. If no one is assigned to an important job, it is less likely to get done.

The Facilitator The GPF is your facilitator—a project guide for group communication. Unfortunately, we cannot be present to help you use the rules, tools, and procedures outlined here. It is up to the group to perform the facilitation role. All members are responsible for implementing and monitoring all adopted rules and procedures. The guidelines above can help your group do this collectively.

The group should complete the following pre-meeting activity to prepare for establishing facilitation guidelines.

Pre-Meeting Activity

Identifying Meeting Problems

1. List all the specific meeting practices and behaviors you have experienced in group projects and meetings that interfere with effective performance. Think of what hindered decision making, cooperative working relationships, and effective meeting communication. List the problematic practices and behaviors below, and provide a specific reason why each impedes efficient meetings.

Problems	*Why*

Pre-Meeting Activity (continued)

Identifying Meeting Problems

2. Review your list of problems and select those you believe to be the most critical. List the solutions of these problems below and determine when the group will know if the solution (rule or procedure) is needed. Then consider how it should be implemented: What will be done? By whom? Be specific.

Solutions	*When/How*

Recording Guidelines

1. Develop a format for organizing the display of meeting information (see Appendix B).
2. Write legibly and clearly, use various colored markers to create distinctions or codes.
3. Record the main ideas using the words of the speaker.
4. Avoid editorializing or adding ideas.
5. Check with members if ideas are unclear by using questions, paraphrasing, and summarizing.
6. Keep pace with the meeting to avoid slowing it down. Use abbreviations for common and repeated terms or phrases.

Beware that the group does not get careless about following rules and procedures. When practices are inconsistently applied, questions emerge regarding the motives of those who try to enforce them. If the group adopts certain rules or procedures, it should follow through or agree to change or drop them. Even though your group does not have a single dedicated process facilitator, all members can and should serve as facilitators because they select the rules and procedures for your meetings.

Recorder[3] This role creates the *group memory*, a record of the meeting that is displayed before the members as the meeting progresses. This provides easy access of the meeting's content to all members, freeing them to concentrate on the business at hand. The ideal way to create this display is to hang large sheets of easel paper (or discarded computer paper) with masking tape on the walls: use felt-tip pens so all can read the writing. Writing boards are usually too small to accommodate the information of a whole meeting. Writing on paper can be saved—an advantage if the group draws up meeting minutes to distribute to its members or instructor.

This role is relatively easy to perform once a recording format is selected. (See Appendix B for guidelines.) Someone not in the group could be the recorder, or the group could assign the role to a group member or rotate it.

Coordinator The main job here is to organize the logistics, tasks, and members of the project. Like the chairperson of a committee, the coordinator makes sure things get done. It is frustrating to come to a meeting to find key people absent, equipment missing, or members with incomplete assignments. It is frequently better to cancel meetings and save members' time than conduct an unproductive meeting.

The following list provides suggestions for shaping this role, but individual projects tend to create unique coordination needs.

1. Serve as contact person for group members and with outside groups and individuals.
2. Arrange for meeting room, equip-

3. Doyle and Straus, *How to Make Meetings Work*, pp. 38–44.

ment, or special tasks (for example, guest speaker, refreshments, computer services, duplication, visual aids).

3. Check with members to be sure meeting assignments are ready.
4. Act as liaison with the instructor or project director.

The coordinator should not be overloaded with other group tasks if he or she is to be effective.

Meeting Logistics

The most obvious but frequently trivialized decisions in forming the group have to do with the time, place, and evaluation of meetings. Students often hold meetings in the most uncomfortable and noisy locations with members missing because of schedule conflicts. Some groups repeat unproductive practices meeting after meeting because they fail to evaluate meeting effectiveness. The following pointers will help your group make its meetings more effective.

1. An average group project meeting ranges between forty-five minutes to an hour. Shorter meetings are usually not worth holding. Be sure there is sufficient work to be conducted at the meeting, members are prepared for the agenda activities, and sufficient time is allotted.
2. Identify the optimal times when members can meet. Schedule meetings when members are fresh, alert, and fed.
3. Make sure members are clear on how long a meeting will last. If extra meeting time is needed, ask if members are able and willing to stay.
4. Meet frequently at the beginning of the project to avoid surprises from unanticipated events or tasks.
5. Start meetings on time. Do not let tardiness become a meeting norm.
6. Hold meetings in a room that is private and free of distraction such as traffic, TV, or phones.
7. The room should have wall space for hanging large sheets of paper or a chalkboard for display of meeting information.
8. The room should provide seating that permits easy visual access to all members' faces; a semicircle is best.
9. Meeting rooms should have adequate lighting, ventilation, heat, and enough space so members can sit comfortably together.

Meeting Feedback

Ninety-nine percent of all groups ignore evaluating meeting effectiveness. Yet if the group does not evaluate how it is operating, it is difficult to know how well it is working and what needs fixing.

Actually, when groups are not working well most members know it (except the person causing problems), but choose to avoid dealing with it. Evaluating meetings may lead to spending time on resolving operational dysfunctions, but this effort produces more efficient and effective meetings.

Feedback aims to prevent and eliminate ineffective practices. Obtaining feedback on meetings involves two questions: When should meeting practices and members' behavior be evaluated? Should such evaluations be handled publicly or anonymously?

In terms of prevention, the group could conduct an evaluation at the end of meetings to monitor practices and behaviors. This would allow the group to fix problems before they become disabling. As the project comes along and the group appears to be operating smoothly, it may not need to schedule meeting evaluations at the end of each meeting.

A less formal approach to evaluation addresses a problem when it occurs. If a member perceives that something seriously wrong is taking place, he or she should bring it to the group's attention and seek agreement to focus on it. This manner of evaluation can be valuable during early project meetings when the group is attempting to implement the rules, procedures, and roles it has adopted.

Feedback can be conducted during the meeting publicly or after the meeting anonymously. Public feedback (see Itemized Response Evaluation Procedure, Chapter 6) at the end of a meeting requires that the members express what they like, and what they would like changed, about practices and behaviors. Anonymous feedback requires the group to adopt a format (see Appendix C) for the members to privately record their perceptions of the meeting. This is followed by a scheduled review and discussion of the feedback during the next meeting. Obtaining feedback this way is most appropriate when members feel inhibited about expressing themselves candidly before other group members. Either way, members need to talk with each other about their meetings.

We advocate public feedback sessions at the end of each meeting. Five minutes should suffice. Then the group can choose to discuss problems or place a specific problem on the next meeting's agenda for deliberation. The following pre-meeting activity will give you practice conducting a post-meeting evaluation.

Pre-Meeting Activity

Evaluating Meetings

Review the Itemized Response in Chapter 6. Once you understand how it works, reflect on your experience in your group's last meeting. (If your group has not held any meetings, think of the most recent group you belonged to.) List all the most notable positive practices, events, or outcomes of that meeting in the column headed "Positive." Next think of those things that you perceived to be problematic and unproductive. Phrase unproductive meeting practices in a constructive manner under the column headed "Needs Improvement." Do not state what is wrong but what would be helpful.

Meeting Evaluation

Positive	*Needs Improvement*

Now you have the means for forming an effective working team. It will take some effort to make your group good at communicating, processing information, and making decisions. Yet once you identify the rules, roles, and logistics for your project meetings and apply them, they will soon become easy and natural. Designing your meeting format is like learning a new game: you have to play it a few times before it becomes fun.

We now turn your attention to preparing for your first meeting of the group formation phase. The list of standard agenda items related to forming the group (page 195) will help you plan and prepare for your meetings.

Standard Agenda Items for Meetings on Forming the Group

The agenda items listed in the left-hand column are typical issues for meetings concerned with forming the group. Review them and add any others you believe should be considered. You can add other items or focuses under a given agenda item. Then rank order the list by numbering each agenda item. If an item has several focuses within it, order them, using *a*, *b*, *c*. Next consider what tool options should be used to tackle the agenda item during the meeting. Finally, list the desired outcome for each individual agenda item or focus in the right-hand column. We provide an example with the first agenda item.

Agenda/Focus	*Tool*	*Outcome*
Meet group members		
name, phone number, address	round-robin	written list
Establish meeting time		
open time slots		
common open slots		
best meeting time available		
Meeting place		
possible meeting places		
best meeting place		
Identify practices for effective group meetings		
potential problems		
rules or procedures to manage problems		
selection of members to perform roles		
Set agenda for next meeting		

Phase II: Project Identification— "The Big Picture"

Now that your group has formed and established some operating procedures, it is time to identify the project, establish its goal, and determine what is needed to achieve the project goal. The objective of this phase is to get a clear picture of the project's demands—a map of the territory.

Regardless of whether a group or the instructor selects a project, it requires some analysis to know where you are going, how to get there, and what is needed before committing to make the trip. Too often groups shortchange this phase. They take on a project without a clear goal. Thus discussion tends to wander; because there is no set goal, any direction is possible. Another common problem is not knowing what the project requires to achieve the goal successfully. A specific goal is not enough. The following guidelines for identifying the project goal and analyzing the project describe specific practices to help you develop a realistic project.

Establishing the Project Goal

If your group is selecting its own project, it can consider a two-step process for identifying the project topic and goal: selecting a general topic and then narrowing its focus to a specific goal. In other words, if the group wishes to work on the topic of "sex on campus," it still needs to figure out what it wishes to accomplish with the topic. Does the group wish to simply assess and describe the prevalence of sex on campus or wish to make a case for the virtues of sex education on campus or . . . ? As you can see, the topic is only the beginning. Identifying the project can be done quickly or carefully to ensure that the project fits the intended audience, instructor's specifications, and group's interests.

Selecting the Topic Topics are general themes or subjects—for example, teen pregnancy, nuclear disarmament, or student loans. If the group gets to choose its project, it should generate possible topics for selection unless a specific topic is already acceptable to the group. If the group does not have a topic, developing a list of topics can help the group explore

---

Topic Selection Guidelines

1. Generate a list of topics. Brainstorming or idea writing are useful tools for this.
2. Reduce the list of topic options by ranking the top three to five topics (see ranking procedure in Chapter 6).
3. Identify all constraints or requirements that the group must fulfill with the project topic such as relevance to audience and access to information.
4. Review ranked topics and consider each one in terms of fitting constraints and requirements. Sometimes a modification in focus or emphasis can make a topic more acceptable. Select a topic by mutual agreement.

Goal Selection Guidelines

1. Place the selected topic at the top of a page. State the goal if it has already been identified. Generate a list of alternative goals underneath the topic or goal by developing both narrow and broad goal statements; explore them. Consider modifying the emphasis of statements already identified.
2. Review the list of possible goal statements and narrow it to three to five options unless there is a clear project goal that members agree on.
3. Review the goal options in terms of the project requirements identified earlier. If these requirements have not been developed, do so now. if the goal statement does not fit all project requirements, attempt to modify it to fit.
4. Select a project goal that fits the requirements and the members' interests.

options that generate interest among members and select a topic that fits the requirements of the assignment, audience, and situation.

Selecting the Project Goal The next step in defining the project is to determine its specific direction and product. What does the group want to accomplish? A project goal statement includes a topic and specific purpose.

The exploration of goal options is a form of project topic analysis that helps the group better understand the topic. Even if your group has an assigned project goal, it should still explore other possible directions for the selected goal statement before moving on to analyzing the project goal for acceptance by the group.

Example: Alternative Goal Statements

Topic: Teen Pregnancy

Narrow Goal Statements:

- Identify the causes of teen pregnancy.
- Determine the role of sex education in reducing teen pregnancies.
- Identify programs to help prevent teen pregnancy.

Broad Goal Statements:

- Identify the impact of teen pregnancy on society.
- Establish ways to prevent teen pregnancy in America.
- Evaluate the success of teen pregnancy prevention programs.

Modifications of the goal "Identify the impact of teen pregnancy on society" could be:

- Determine ways to reduce the cost of teen pregnancy to society.
- Identify the impact of unwed teen mothers on society.

Note in the example above that broad goal statements usually include narrow goals within them. For example, "evaluate the success of teen pregnancy prevention" requires fulfilling the narrower goal "identify programs to help prevent teen pregnancy." You need to identify existing programs before evaluating them.

Terms like *identify*, *determine*, and *evaluate* indicate what is to be accomplished with the topic (teen pregnancy) and its focus (impact on society, causes of, prevention of). If the project is delegated to the group, it should have a clear goal indicated. If not, the group should seek such information from the delegator. Although the goal statement may be modified after more thorough analysis, it provides a direction for continued exploration.

Before moving on to analyze the goal statement, we provide a pre-meeting activity (page 199) so you can practice generating alternative goal statements of a topic. If your group has already identified a topic or goal statement, use it as your starting point for generating alternatives.

Pre-Meeting Activity

Selecting a Goal Statement

Write a topic or goal statement in the space provided below. Then list all the possible alternative goal statements. Determine which are narrow and broad and place an *N* or *B* next to the statement. Try to modify goal statements that are too broad and attempt to make them more manageable.

Topic: ____

List alternative goal statements:

1.

2.

3.

4.

5.

6.

7.

8.

9.

10.

11.

12.

Goal Objectives Guidelines

1. Generate a list of information objectives vertically along the left side of a sheet of paper.
2. Review the information objectives and list them in the approximate order in which they need to be completed.
3. Create a parallel procedures column alongside the information objectives, and identify procedures needed to fulfill the objectives.
4. Develop specific objective statements from the list of objectives.

Project Goal Analysis

This step of project development is concerned with determining the demands of the project to assess whether they are acceptable. Too frequently groups select a project only to find out later that they bit off more than they could chew. Analyzing the project can make the goal statement more manageable.

The main issue is whether the group can achieve its goal with the time and resources available. A useful way to determine this is to identify the goal objectives and project problems. The more complex and unfamiliar the project, the more difficult it is to achieve. At this stage of project identification, the group works on getting the "big picture." What is involved in reaching its goal? This analysis is the most critical step in maximizing successful completion of the project.

Identifying Goal Objectives A *goal* is an overall outcome or desired end result. An *objective* is a subgoal related to the main goal; it is one of several specific tasks that needs to be accomplished to reach the goal. The group needs to determine how to achieve the goal before committing itself to it. You may find that the necessary objectives to fulfill the goal are more than the group can or wishes to handle.

Objectives emphasize the need for obtaining information and a procedure for obtaining it. For instance, "identifying the causes of teen pregnancy" would be an information objective. The procedural aspect of the objective would emphasize the *method* of doing something—review literature or conduct interviews, for example. Objective statements should identify the type of information needed and the method of obtaining it.

Identifying objectives of a project goal serves several purposes:

1. It provides an overview of what needs to be done to adequately fulfill the goal.
2. It allows the group to determine whether it can fulfill the objectives.
3. It supplies information that could lead to modifying the original goal or objectives in view of new insights about the goal or more efficient ways to accomplish objectives.
4. It provides an overall view of the project for planning and coordinating group tasks.

To avoid overlooking the goal's needs in terms of information and procedure, think about them separately and then in relationship to each other. The following example will illustrate.

Example: Types of Objectives

Project Goal: Identify the ways of reducing the incidence of teen pregnancy in the community.

Information Objectives	*Procedural Objectives*
Incidence of pregnancy	Literature
Causes of teen pregnancy	Literature and interviews
Prevention	Literature and interviews
Prevention methods used by local teens	Survey

Project Goal Objective Statements:

1. Use current literature to obtain statistics on the occurrence of teen pregnancy in the United States.
2. Determine the causes of teen pregnancy based on readings and interviews with experts.
3. Identify the most effective ways for preventing teen pregnancy based on research reports and interviews.
4. Survey teens on pregnancy prevention practice and compare your findings to effective prevention practices to assess effectiveness of local teen pregnancy prevention practices.

If the group lacks the time or skill to conduct interviews, it would have to determine whether a review of the literature on the subject would be sufficient to achieve the goal. If so, the group could achieve its goal without interviews. However, interviews with local experts probably would be essential because there might be little or no published information on the community.

If your group has identified a goal statement, use it for the following premeeting activity on identifying and developing objectives. If not, create your own goal statement.

Pre-Meeting Activity

Identifying Goal Objectives

Write the project goal in the space provided. List the information objectives in the appropriate column and number them in terms of logical priority. Then identify the procedural objectives for each information objective. When you complete the list, develop statements of objectives.

Project goal: ______________________________

Information Objectives	*Procedural Objectives*

List statements of objectives

Identifying Project Problems At this point your group should have a general picture of its project. However, one last step will prevent difficulties later. This requires identifying the problem or obstacles the project goal poses to the group. There are two types of project problems: the goal itself and how to achieve the goal or an objective. Your goal statement may be a problem to be solved in itself (how to eliminate teen pregnancies?) or the problem may be how to proceed (how to find out about preventing teen pregnancy).

By now, whether your goal statement indicates a problem to be solved or not, you have already established the solution. The identified objectives are a solution in that they are the way to reach the goal. Thus *how* to tackle the project goal is not likely a problem. Even if the project goal is a problem, the objectives you have identified provide a basis for solving it. If the group's project goal states a problem, the analysis guidelines in Phase III will be useful for the analysis step of problem solving.

If your group has been unable to identify objectives needed to fulfill the project goal adequately, then it has a problem. If you have an objective but do not know how to accomplish it, you have another problem. Although most problems are easily solved through consulting books or experts, they may place unacceptable demands on the group. Too often, student groups lack the skills and time needed to complete the objective well.

Use the following guidelines to review your project for problems. We do not intend to have you solve the problems at this time, although solutions will be apparent. The important thing is to identify them so your group can assess the problems before committing itself to the project goal.

Project Problem Assessment Guidelines

1. Review and discuss the project objectives and determine whether they will provide the types of information needed to fulfill the goal. If there is any doubt, tag the goal statement for further analysis.
2. Review and discuss each objective statement and consider *how* it will be accomplished. If there is any doubt, tag the objective statement for further analysis.
3. Convert each tagged statement into a *problem statement*. Identify the difficulty or doubt and turn it into a problem question (for example, who are the expert sources on teen pregnancy in the community?). Consider alternative problem statements until the group feels it has identified the difficulty.
4. Use the following questions to analyze difficulties unresolved during the discussion. List the answers for each problem statement.
   - What is the desired outcome to the problem?
   - What are the disciplines of knowledge involved with the problem's subject?
   - What do members know about the subject?
   - Where can you find information on the subject?
   - What are the causes of the problem?
   - Will access to resources and services to solve the problem be readily available?
   - Is there sufficient time to solve the problem?
   - Will solving the problem take a lot of members' time and energy? How so?
   - Is solving the problem important to achieving the goal? How so?
5. Review the answers to the above questions for each problem reviewed. Determine if the problems are feasible to solve based on the analysis. If not, consider modifications of the objective or goal.

A pre-meeting activity to aid your problem assessment follows. The information obtained from this pre-meeting activity will provide insight into the project's demands. Unacceptable demands can be addressed by modifying the project goal or objectives or using the problem-solving model in Phase III.

The identification of the project's goal objectives, problems, and potential solutions provides a general analysis, giving the group an overview of the project's demands. This is when the group makes its commitment to accept the project goal. Phase III, Analysis and Information Search, will review procedures for identifying specific information needs and solving stubborn problems.

Pre-Meeting Activity

Project Problem Assessment

Review the project goal and objectives to determine if you perceive any problems. Identify specific problems and determine their causes. Divide two sheets of paper horizontally into five columns—two on the first sheet, three on the second. Label them (1) Difficult Goal/Objectives, (2) Problem Questions, (3) Problem Exploration, (4) Problem Restatement, and (5) Possible Solutions. The following steps correspond to the column numbers.

1. List those goal or objective statements that you think might pose a problem to you or your group.
2. Develop a problem question for each of the potential problems listed in the first column. (For example, should we interview teen mothers to understand prevention problems?) Attempt to develop alternative problem questions, especially if the first question does not seem to pinpoint the problem.
3. Examine each problem question using the questions in step 4 of the Project Problem Assessment Guidelines. Note the answers for each problem question.
4. Reexamine each problem question and restate it if information derived from the previous step suggests refocusing or adding additional details to the problem.
5. Note any obvious solutions (answers) for each of the problem questions. Evaluate these answers for effectiveness. (Use the Itemized Response in Chapter 6.) Consider the implications of each problem and solution in terms of the project's completion and quality and working relationships.

Standard Agenda Items for Meetings on Project Identification

The agenda items listed in the left-hand column are typical issues for meetings concerned with project identification. Review them and add any others you believe should be considered. You can add other items or focuses under a given agenda item. Then rank order the list by numbering each agenda item. If an item has several focuses within it, order them, using *a*, *b*, *c*. Next consider what tool options should be used to tackle the agenda item during the meeting. Finally, list the desired outcome for each individual agenda item or focus in the right-hand column. We provide an example with the first agenda item.

This phase may take two or three meetings, depending on how the group approaches the task. Members can prepare for the meetings by generating topics or goal statements at home and having them collected by a member to compile and present to the group for review and discussion. Such assignments reduce meeting time and enable members to focus on issues needing discussion.

This list of agenda items and focuses is not necessarily complete and detailed. There may be other focuses.

Agenda/Focus	Tool	Outcome
Project identification:		
project selection criteria	Idea writing (list at home and compile for meeting)	Determine criteria
project topics		
topic goal		
Project goal assessment:		
project objectives		
project problem(s)		
project modification or acceptance		
Meeting evaluation:		
Other agenda:		
Agenda for next meeting:		

Phase III: Analysis and Information Search—Questions, Answers, and Solutions

Your group should now be ready to thoroughly investigate the topic and its issues. Phase III covers critical analysis of the project's goal and objectives. The objectives identified in Phase II have established general information needs; the analysis you are about to conduct will help you identify the specific questions inherent in each objective.

Analysis for Information Search

Analysis involves taking something apart to examine how its parts function and what their relationship to each other is. The goal of analysis is to understand something. Whether your group's goal is simply to identify and describe (the requirements and procedures for becoming a resident assistant, for example) or to solve a problem (how to be an effective resident assistant), it should identify the information needed to fulfill the goal objectives.

The most powerful tool for analysis is the question. All unfulfilled goals indicate a question. Selecting its project goal and analyzing the project has given your group some idea of what needs to be examined. However, the goal and objectives are likely to pose a web of related questions that need to be identified and answered if the group is to fulfill its goal effectively.

Several basic and specific questions will help your group identify the critical issues of your project and set up your information search tasks. The basic questions are those of definition, fact, value, and policy discussed in Chapter 6. Here we introduce a specialized question, the cause-and-effect question, which is particularly useful for problem solving. The following guidelines, examples, and premeeting assignments will help you identify questions needing answers for each project goal objective.

Deep Analysis This activity requires identifying all the questions related to the goal and objectives concerning the subject and task procedures. Although your group raised numerous questions regarding these matters in Phase II, it has not systematically identified all relevant questions needing answers to fulfill the project goal.

Your group's project will involve questions of definition and fact. If the group's goal involves making a judgment about something, it could involve questions of value or policy. Every project goal is ultimately establishing either the definition, fact, value, or policy of something. Guidelines for writing questions of definition, an example, and a premeeting activity follow.

Question of Definition Guidelines

1. Review your goal and objectives statements. Identify all terms or phrases that need to be defined to establish the group's specific meaning for them. Beware of terms that are common or might be interpreted differently by audiences of your project.
2. List the terms along the left-hand margin of a sheet of paper. Identify possible sources for defining the terms in a parallel column next to each term.
3. Check the most appropriate sources for their definitions and select or compose a workable definition for each term.

Example: Questions of Definition

Project Goal	*Terms to Define*
Identify all sources of funding for student organizations and their proposal procedures.	Student organization
Objectives	
1. Identify campus funding sources, types of organizations, and purposes of funding.	Funding source
2. Determine the procedures and standards of each source's funding proposal.	Proposal

The three terms to be defined in this example could be phrased as questions of definition—for example, "What is a student organization?" The answer, or definition, could be determined by the group. However, because the group is dealing with campus agencies that provide funding, it would be wise to find out how they define a student organization. Different funding agencies may have different criteria for defining a student organization. This would lead the group to a question of fact, "What are the definitions of student organizations used by funding sources?"

Pre-Meeting Activity

Identifying Questions of Definition

Review the Question of Definition Guidelines. Identify all terms to be defined, their definition, and sources of the definitions. Place this information in the columns provided below.

Terms	*Source*	*Definition*

Question of Fact Guidelines

1. Review the project goal and objective statements. Focus on the subject and procedures indicated in the statements to identify the information needed. Try to anticipate the types of information needed that are related to the subject or procedures.
2. Phrase all identified information needs as questions of fact. Cluster questions together that are related to the same subject or procedure.
3. Examine all the questions of fact and determine which need answers first in order to answer other questions.
4. Review each question of fact and identify the sources or methods for seeking an answer. (See Appendix F.)

Questions of fact are the most prevalent type of question in most projects. They not only address the content or subject of the project but can also focus on procedures or methods. For example, if the group used interviews to fulfill an objective, a fact question seeking information on interviewing practices—"How do you conduct data-gathering interviews?"—would be in order. Procedural fact questions are frequently overlooked, and this leads to practices that are typically inadequate to achieve what was desired. We have seen numerous student surveys that were virtually useless because of their inappropriate surveying practices. Guidelines for writing questions of fact appear at the top of the page, and an example follows. (See Appendices D and E for interview and survey guidelines.)

Example: Questions of Fact

Objective

Identify campus funding sources, types of organizations funded, and purposes of funding.

Questions of Fact	*Source/Method*
What campus agencies offer funding to student organizations?	College catalogue, interviews: dean of students and student body president
What types of student organizations are funded by each agency?	Interview with each identified agency
What will each campus agency fund?	Interview with each identified agency
How do you conduct an information-gathering interview?	Library resources Consult Professor Dokes Group members
When will we need the information on agencies, fundable organizations, and purposes of funding?	Group members

Notice how the preceding questions of fact begin with substantive issues and then focus on procedural matters. Can you think of other questions of fact related to these? How about a specific question on the criteria for qualifying as a student organization?

Also note that these questions have a logical order of priority and will provide the foundation for interview questions. To be sure you get all the information you need, questions of fact, value, or policy related to other objectives should be identified before conducting interviews or surveys. A pre-meeting activity follows.

Pre-Meeting Activity

Identifying Questions of Fact

Review the Question of Fact Guidelines. List each objective one at a time and identify the substantive and procedural questions of fact. List possible sources and methods for obtaining answers to each question.

First Objective:

Questions of Fact *Sources/Methods*

Second Objective:

Questions of Fact *Sources/Methods*

Third Objective:

Questions of Fact *Sources/Methods*

(continue on another sheet of paper)

Question of Value Guidelines

1. Review the objectives statements and identify all the issues involving evaluation or a decision. Look for phrases or terms indicating the judgment of a substantive issue.
2. Phrase the value issues as questions of value.
3. Identify whether the answer should be sought through expert opinion, examples, or both. If through expert opinion, identify possible sources.

Example: Questions of Value

Objective: Identify the characteristics of successful proposals.

Questions of Value	*Sources*
What is a good proposal?	Literature
What are the characteristics of successful proposals?	Interview funding agencies Review examples of successful proposals

Questions of value involve evaluation and are typically based on questions of fact, which provide a major basis for making judgments about an issue.

To answer the questions of value in the example (above), the group must explore general principles of writing good proposals and discover specific standards set by the funding agencies. Answers to both questions would provide comprehensive information on what is needed for an effective proposal. A pre-meeting activity follows.

Pre-Meeting Activity

Identifying Questions of Value

Review the project goal and objectives identifying issues requiring evaluation or judgment. Examine objectives for possible issues of evaluation even though the objective may not be directly concerned with the issue. Phrase all possible value issues indicated in the objectives as value questions and identify possible sources for answers.

Objective:

Questions of Value *Sources*

Objective:

Questions of Value *Sources*

Objective:

Questions of Value *Sources*

(continue on another sheet of paper)

Example: Questions of Policy

What standards should be used to award funding to student organizations?

What types of requests from student organizations should be funded?

Should there be any priority regarding the types of funding requests?

Unless the goal of your group project is to investigate or develop a policy, it is not likely you will need to answer any policy questions. Issues of policy may be lurking in the project, but the project's purpose does not involve answering matters of policy. Policy questions are complex projects unto themselves.

Notice how the first policy question in the example above is broken down into two specific policy issues in the following questions. The policy question is usually determined by the circumstances in the "real world" that give rise to it. If there was a perceived problem with the types of events funded, then the issue of types of funding priorities is relevant (for example, social versus educational events).

If your group project is a policy matter, you have already conducted the deep analysis on it by identifying the questions of definition, fact, and value.

Conducting a deep analysis using questions is easy, but be careful that the first few questions you identify do not lull you into thinking that you have found all the relevant questions. Some questions give rise to others; research for answers frequently reveals more. The goal is to generate a broad range of questions to prepare and plan for information searches. The following guidelines will help your group conduct the deep analysis together:

1. List all the questions of definition, fact, and value relevant to the project goal (members can prepare by completing related pre-meeting activities). Organize them in relation to the objectives. (If the group *did not* identify goal objectives, it could organize the questions based on topics.)
2. Review the questions as a group and arrange them by type and order of answer needed.
3. Identify the sources for answering each question (see Appendix F). Determine which questions need to be answered first. For example, questions of definition may take priority over questions of fact.
4. Make information search assignments. Be sure to establish the specific questions to be answered, preferred sources, format of reporting answers to the group, and date of report. (Statistical information may be best presented graphically.) If the group is to conduct interviews or surveys, it should create a specific agenda, perhaps for a subcommittee to do and report on.

With this analysis of its project goal and a clear direction for its information search tasks, the group may wish to modify the goal in view of new information about the project's demands.

If the group's goal is a problem to be solved or a policy question, it should consider an additional analytic activity: cause-and-effect analysis. This analysis

Cause-and-Effect Analysis Guidelines

1. Place the clearly defined problem statement at the top of a sheet of paper or board.
2. Develop a list of cause categories—general types of causes—to help reveal potential relationships among categories of causes. Examine each cause category to determine if it has subcategories.
3. Generate a separate list of possible causes of the problem. Once the list is completed, assign the potential causes to one of the categories or subcategories. If the list reveals new categories, add them.
4. Develop a cause-and-effect analysis, using a fish bone diagram (see page 218) so all members can see it. Place the problem statement above a vertical line. Draw lines diagonally like fish bones equaling the number of categories. Place one cause category at the end of each diagonal line and any secondary causes (more specific causes related to a cause category) along that line.
5. Review the cause-and-effect diagram and identify questions needing answers and causes needing verification. Causes will vary in terms of difficulty of verification. Do not assume that a possible cause is an actual cause.
6. Keep the diagram and add information as the verification search progresses. After you complete this search, review the diagram and reduce the list to the verified cause(s) of the problem.

can be conducted without a deep analysis if the group is *very* familiar with the problem domain. If the group knows little about the problem, it needs to gather information on it first.

Cause-and-Effect Analysis A problem can be viewed as a general effect caused by some prior situation or condition(s). A problem is known by its symptoms. However, the symptoms are not the problem, the causes are. Thus, the symptoms of a cold are the undesirable effects; the virus and its action on your physical system cause the discomfort. Critical problem analysis requires identifying the cause(s) of the problem symptoms.

The value of cause-and-effect analysis is its focus on causes instead of symptoms.[4] Although symptoms indicate the presence of a problem, identifying causes focuses on eliminating the sources of symptoms in order to eliminate the symptoms themselves. The guidelines above provide a step-by-step procedure for conducting a cause-and-effect analysis in a group. It is important that the group have some background knowledge (answers to questions of fact) before attempting such an analysis.

A cause-and-effect analysis has the

---

4. Roger G. James and Aaron J. Elkins, "Cause-and-Effect Analysis," *How to Train and Lead a Quality Circle* (San Diego: University Associates, 1983), pp. 57–66.

Example: Cause-and-Effect Analysis

Problem: High rate of funding proposals rejected

Categories	*Subcategories*
Events for funding	Types, Participation, Location
Proposal guidelines	Funding Agencies, Eligibility, Literature
Preparing proposal	Skills, Information
Presenting proposals	Method, Timing, Style

List of potential causes for Events for funding category

Subcategories	*Potential Causes*
Types of events	Academic, athletic, social, professional
Participation	Public, private by invitation or membership
Location	On campus, off campus

group develop an understanding of the problem by identifying and conceptualizing the various phenomena related to it. The examples above illustrate this point. See Figure 2 (page 218) for further examples of subcategories and potential causes in the form of a fish bone diagram.

Now that your group has completed the first two steps—problem identification and problem analysis—it is ready to generate possible solutions to resolve the causes of the problem. Perhaps some brainstorming is in order for the idea-generating step of problem solving.

Steps of Problems Solving

Cause-and-effect analysis can lead to a redefinition of the problem. In the preceding example, the problem was initially conceived of as a "high rate of proposal rejection." After the cause-and-effect analysis, the problem could change to "incomplete proposals" and be refocused to "how to have campus organizations present complete proposals." The group's research would have verified this problem and likely have identified specific things that were not complete in most proposals.

Chapter 6 described the complete steps of the problem-solving process. If the group's goal was a problem to solve that has already been analyzed, it may begin at the solution-generation step. If your group has identified a problem within your project goal as a result of its deep analysis, it should start from the beginning of the process.

Analysis and information search activities are the detective work of the project. As Sherlock Holmes has illustrated time and again, good detective work starts with the right questions. Plan to spend a lot of time in this phase of the project; it is the most work intensive. Do not let the volume of work fool you into thinking that it ensures a high-quality project. The information needs to be assessed for its relevance and quality and then packaged for presentation. We will look at these issues in the last project phase. Review Phase IV soon.

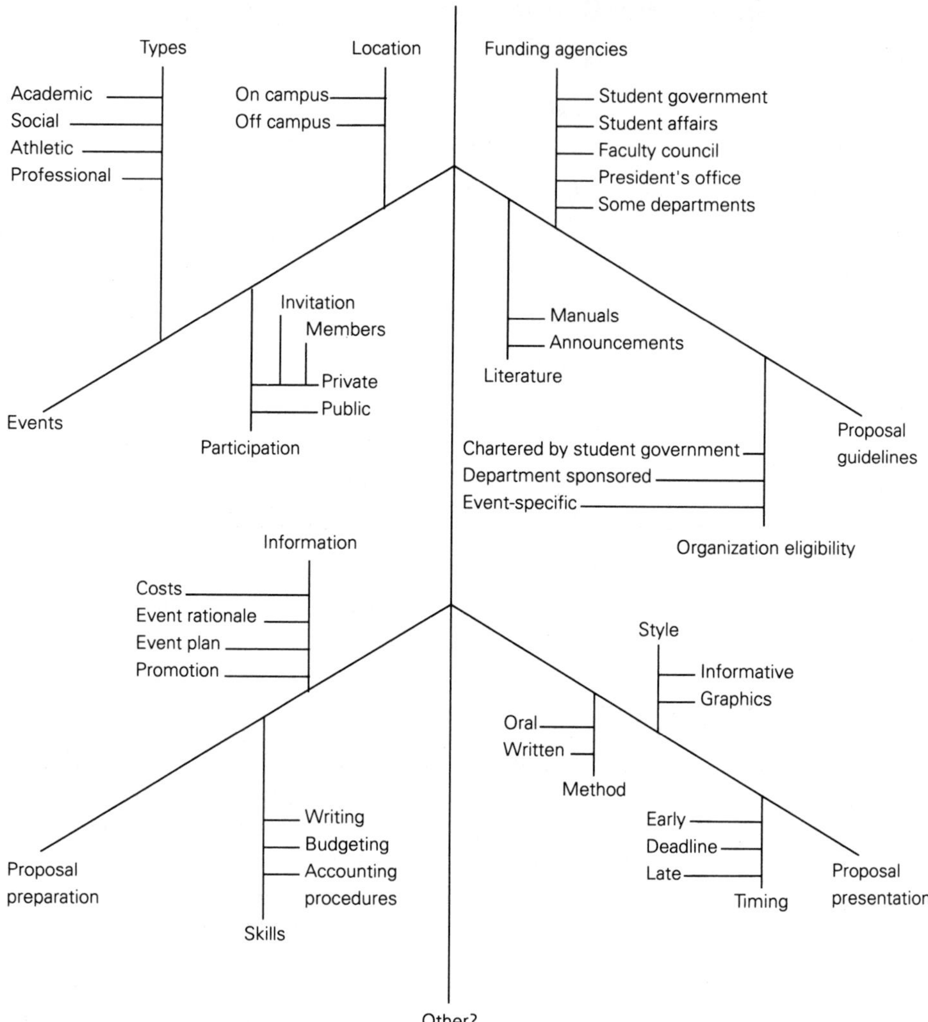

Figure 2 Fish Bone Diagram for Cause-and-Effect Analysis

Standard Agenda Items for Meetings on Goal Analysis and Information Search

The agenda items listed in the left-hand column are typical issues for meetings on analysis and information search. Review them and add any others you believe should be considered. Keep in mind that this phase of the project has the largest number of tasks, especially if a survey or interviews are to be conducted. You can add other items or focuses under a given agenda item. Then rank order the list by numbering each agenda item. If an item has several focuses within it, order them, using *a*, *b*, *c*. Next consider what tool options should be used to tackle the agenda item during or outside the meeting. Give special attention to items or focuses that members can do outside of meeting time. Finally, list the desired outcome for each individual agenda item in the right-hand column.

This phase of the project will likely have the most tasks and therefore more meetings. You can estimate the number of meetings needed for this phase of the project by identifying the specific agendas or focuses that would be reasonable to complete in a typical meeting. (Label agenda items for meeting 1, 2, and so on.) Consider longer meetings for some tasks or reduce meeting time through take-home assignments.

Agenda/Focus	Tool	Outcome
Deep analysis		
identify relevant questions and resources		
group and prioritize questions		
delegate information search tasks		
report on research tasks		
other?		
Cause-and-effect analysis (if applicable)		
identify cause categories and relationships		
identify potential causes per category		
develop cause-and-effect diagram		
select perceived causes		
identify and assign cause verification tasks		
Problem solving (if applicable)		
generate list of possible solutions		
identify criteria for solution selection		
select solution(s)		
develop plan for solution implementation		
Meeting evaluation		
Agenda for next meeting(s)		

Phase IV: Project Synthesis and Delivery

The bulk of your information search tasks are probably completed and beginning to show a clear path toward the project goal. Do not relax. This phase can make or break a quality group project. Even well-researched information, arguments, and solutions lose their impact when poorly presented. The common belief that style wins over content is true. Style is not more important than content, but if oral or written delivery is flawed to the point of being distracting, it detracts from the content. In the same vein, a great presentation can camouflage deficiencies in the project's content, at least for the untrained audience.

One cause of poor completion of a project is the tendency to hand off synthesis and delivery tasks to one or two people without the group's input or evaluation. Sometimes this is done so a member can make up for previous absences or lack of input. For whatever reason, it is a bad idea. There is a strong impulse to be done with the project. There is nothing wrong with delegating tasks to members with the time and skill to perform a task. But it is careless to let one person make decisions that require the breadth of all members' understanding and insight.

The group's remaining tasks fall into two areas: project synthesis and project delivery. Synthesis involves evaluating the adequacy of the collected information and organizing it for presentation. Delivery involves decisions on packaging the project for presentation.

Project Synthesis

The group needs to evaluate the information it has collected over the past weeks to determine whether it needs to continue searching for information. It may need answers to new or unanswered questions or more current information. After all, answering the questions identified in Phase III is the foundation for fulfilling the project goal. By reviewing the collected information, the group can check for completion and quality.

Evaluating Information Evaluation helps the group identify missing but needed information and assess the quality of the collected data. Although evaluation can be postponed until the bulk of information search tasks is completed, it is probably less tedious if the group or a member evaluates information as it becomes available. This will also indicate earlier what questions remain to be answered or need further information.

Assessing the completion of gathering information requires a systematic review of the questions used to establish the research tasks and their answers. (The questions were established from the deep analysis in Phase III.) If your group's goal is to solve a problem, this activity should be conducted prior to the solution-generation step of the problem-solving process. You have to know the causes of a problem to develop realistic solutions.

Two types of answers are facts and opinions. Facts are declarative statements—examples, illustrations, or statistics—that refer to an observation of something that can be directly or indirectly verified as either true or false. For example, "Alaska is the largest state" or "There are 1,760 yards in a mile." The quality of a fact is based on the credibility of the methods used to arrive at it, its verifiability, and the degree of qualification. Additionally, statistical facts are judged by the appropriateness of the research methods used to obtain them. The variety of issues for evaluating statistical facts is beyond the scope of our

Information Evaluation Guidelines

1. Write all questions that are related to each other on a sheet of paper. Use one set of questions per sheet to leave space for later assessment of information quality. (This evaluation could be assigned as part of an information search task and reported to the group.)
2. Identify the answer to each question, capturing the essential information.
3. Establish the data's source (author and publication or other origin of information) and date. Determine whether the answer is a fact or opinion.
4. Review each answer and evaluate the quality of the facts and inferences using the Information Evaluation Checklist in Appendix G. Note any quality problems next to each answer.
5. After evaluating the information, determine whether the group needs to continue researching a given question. Identify the specific search tasks (more varied sources of information or updated data, for example) and possible places to find answers.

discussion here, but the Information Evaluation Guidelines above offer some fundamental considerations for evaluating facts.

Opinions and inferences are statements of preference, value, or taste. They are neither true nor false, but are judgments usually based on facts, experiences, and intuitions. For example, "Alaska has the most beautiful wilderness areas of any state," or "Running a mile is easy on level ground." The quality of an opinion depends on internal and external factors. Internal factors are those associated with the statement of opinion, the quality of information and reasoning that supports it. External factors address the relationship of the opinion to its sources, other facts and opinions, and logical or practical consequences.

Organizing the Presentation The group's goal is to describe, report, evaluate, or propose something. Concluding the project requires the group to organize its information to fulfill one or more of these purposes. This organization has a general format—an introduction, body, and conclusion—and a content specific format. Content specific organization considers the specific content and goal.

The following instructions will review the process of organizing the information while guiding your group through the task of setting up an outline. Outlining is invaluable for consolidating information for delivery. It provides the road map to guide the group (as well as any audiences) through the project report. The key to effective presentation is to be thoroughly versed in the topic, which includes knowing how the information fits together. A well-developed outline also prepares the presenters for confident delivery.

The group should work together and agree on the outline. Using the whole group increases the likelihood of includ-

Introduction Outline Guidelines

1. Identify the general purpose (to inform or persuade) and specific purpose of the presentation. Develop a succinct and clear statement of purpose.
2. Consider introducing the group and the presenters if the presentation is to be delivered orally. Emphasize any information about members that contributes to the group's credibility. For example, a member's expertise relevant to the project could be cited ("Joe's three years on the campus funding committee was valuable in obtaining an inside view of the funding process").
3. Develop a rationale for the project goal as stated in the specific purpose. Why did the group select the project? Why is it worth the audience's attention? If the project was assigned to the group, review the delegator's purpose for assigning the project.
4. Preview what will be covered to fulfill the specific presentation purpose. This overview will be clear once the group completes organizing the body of the presentation.
5. If the presentation is orally delivered, the spokesperson should greet the audience and consider using an attention-getting statement related to the topic and audience. Keep the introduction brief.

ing all relevant information and identifying all relevant relationships. Keep in mind that the outline is not an essay. Use a sentence or phrase to represent each major point and subpoint, not a paragraph. Major points are the basic themes or claims of presentation. Subpoints are specific and distinct issues, supporting evidence, or types of examples that expand upon a major point.

The introduction should be easy for the group to develop because it covers familiar project issues. Its aim is to gain attention, establish the presentation's purpose, and orient the audience to what will follow. It should also introduce the presenters and any information that might establish the group's credibility to report on the topic. To establish the relationship of the presentation to the audience, identify the needs or interests of the audience that the presentation will address; anecdotes, leading questions, and humor can help you engage the audience. But keep the introduction succinct. (See the guidelines above and the example on page 223; a pre-meeting activity follows on page 224.)

Example: Introduction Outline

I. Introduction: The process of student organization activity funding at Smith University

   A. Story on how student organization folded due to lack of funds to support its mission

   B. Why knowing the funding process is important

      1. organizations always in need of funding to support their operation and activities

         a. operating costs such as . . .

         b. special events and activities such as . . .

      2. organizations miss opportunities to obtain funds

         a. unaware of funding sources

         b. miss deadlines

         c. incorrect proposal format

   C. Orient to presentation and speakers on the funding process

      1. Sandy Kent, student representative to the Office of Student Affairs, on the variety of funding sources, what they fund, and organization eligibility

      2. Joe Dennison, treasurer of Alpha Theta Kappa, on the steps of the funding process

      3. Dora Basso, group project coordinator, on most common funding proposal problems and proposal tips

      4. Raphael Montoya, president of Latin Student Union, on presenting proposals to funding agencies

Pre-Meeting Activity

The Introduction Outline

Review the Introduction Outline Guidelines and determine the presentation's purpose and its major introductory points and subpoints. Consider speakers for each major section of the presentation and any qualifications they may have that would enhance the credibility of their presentations.

Presentation Purpose:

Major Points	*Subpoints*	*Speaker*

Body Outline Guidelines

1. Review the project goal and objectives and identify the major points or themes to be covered in the presentation.
2. Review the organizing schemes (see Appendix H) and decide which are suited for the presentation purpose. Provide the reasons for your choice. If there is more than one choice, point out the advantages and disadvantages for each in supporting the purpose.
3. Organize the major presentation points based on the selected scheme. Then, identify the secondary points to be covered under each major point. Use a sentence or phrase for each major point and subpoint. Clearly separate main points and subpoints. There should be a minimum of two distinct subpoints for any major point that has parts to it. If there is only one subpoint, combine it in phrasing the major point.

The body of the outline is the heart of the presentation. It determines what will be introduced, so develop it before you finalize the introduction. The project's goal, objectives, and information should point to a logical organizational scheme. In some instances there may be more than one approach or a combination of organizational schemes to consider (see Appendix H).

When selecting an organizational scheme, consider your overall purpose and information. The project's objectives and categories of information will suggest a particular organizational pattern. Some schemes are more appropriate for descriptive or informative purposes; others are better for evaluating, persuading, and proposing. For example, if the group wished to tell the audience about campus funding, it would likely use a chronological or process pattern of organization, which lends itself to describing the steps over time for soliciting funding. This pattern reinforces the group's goal. The group might be tempted to use a topical pattern of organization based on the types of funding agencies. However, this scheme does not directly serve the presentation's overall purpose: to describe the funding process. (But the topic pattern may be useful for reporting on types of funding.)

The challenge of organizing the body of the presentation is to establish logical and clear relationships between the major points and subpoints of the presentation. Make it easy for the audience to follow along.

Outlining the body of the presentation requires the group to identify and determine the relationship of its major points and subpoints. Keep in mind that the first conception of the body outline may not be the best one. Consider alternative ways to organize the material. Look for logical and practical arrangements that will help the audience understand the relationship of the parts and follow the presentation. (Guidelines appear at the top of the page, an example appears on page 226, and a pre-meeting activity follows on page 227.)

Example: Body Outline

II. The Funding Process for Student Organizations
   A. Funding Sources on Campus
      1. Student Governing Board
         a. Funding for organizational operation and events
         b. Organizational eligibility and funding
            1. Chartered organizations
            2. Constituted organizations
         c. Funding deadlines
            1. Spring application for operating costs and annual activities funds
            2. Open funding application for special events
      2. Student Affairs Office
         a. Funding for educational and professional events
         b. Eligibility based on activity need and service, not organizational status
         c. Funding on first come, first serve basis
   B. Steps of Funding Process
      1. Obtain funding guidelines from agency
      2. Develop funding proposal
         a. Type of funding: organizational operation and/or events
            1. What: operation needs or planned events
            2. Why: value of funding operations or events
            3. Who: officers, project coordinators, advisors
            4. Where: on or off campus, buildings
            5. When: date, time, and conflicts with other campus events
         b. Financial information and budgets
            1. Budget for organizational operations based on previous years' financial records
            2. Itemized budget of proposed event
         c. Detailed implementation plan of proposed event

Pre-Meeting Activity

Outlining the Body of the Presentation

Review the guidelines for outlining the body of the presentation. List the major and subpoints in the columns below. List minor points to subpoints under them.

Major Points	*Subpoints*

Conclusion Outline Guidelines

1. Review the purpose and body of the presentation.
2. Summarize the body of the presentation and how it fulfilled the purpose. If the purpose was to persuade the audience, briefly review the arguments leading to the conclusion.
3. Conclude with a comment, quote, or clever way to reinforce the presentation's purpose and establish its value to the audience. If the purpose was to pursuade, indicate what action you want the audience to perform.

Example: Conclusion Outline

III. Numerous Opportunities for Funding Student Organizations
   A. Proposal process is easy but requires attention to details
      1. Steps of process
      2. Tips for successful proposals
   B. Value of the funding process to students
      1. Supports mission and interests of student organizations
      2. Provides experience in political process
      3. Enriches educational experience

The conclusion, usually the shortest part of the outline and presentation, can restate the purpose of the presentation, what was reported that fulfilled it, and reasons why the information or proposal is important to the audience. If action is advocated, the conclusion needs to specify what it wants the audience to do (write letters or vote, for example). The arguments in the body of the presentation should clearly support and legitimize the requested action.

Once the outline is completed, the group should review it. Does it follow a clear, organized pattern? Does it cover the project topic and goal? Does it fulfill the general and specific purpose?

Use your outline in making your oral or written report. A written report of the project will require more detailed information. For example, while the outline may indicate the conclusions of a survey, the written report would likely include the results and conclusions. The group should have two outlines if both an oral and written report are required. The oral presentation outline will be the basis for the more detailed written report outline.

Project Delivery

The group has concluded the project's initial goal once it has outlined its findings for delivery. The last major task is preparing the project for written or oral presentation. We will focus on the oral presentation because the outline for it will provide the basics of what is needed for a written report.[5]

Group oral reports typically use several speakers. Whether your group involves all its members or a select few, make sure that the flow of the presentations is smooth and easy to follow. The audience needs to clearly know what is happening as the presentation unfolds. Reading from a written report will not do. The oral report must be designed for listening.

Two issues regarding group oral presentations are usually overlooked and managed poorly: multiple speakers and visual aids. It is easy for presentations involving several speakers to sound fragmented and become distracting. Presentations can easily appear disjointed and hard to follow if the audience does not clearly understand the relationship of each speaker's report to the others. The outline should certainly fulfill this need, but remember, the audience cannot review, stop, or study the ideas as in written reports. Therefore, help the audience follow and connect each speaker's part of the presentation into a coherent whole.

The other problem with multiple speakers is the distractions due to movement of speakers and use of visual aids equipment. The more speakers, visual aids, and media, the more the presentation has to be coordinated to create flawless movement and flow.

Visual aids are one tool to help overcome presentation fragmentation; they can be used to emphasize, illustrate, gain attention, stimulate interest, and map the presentation flow. They can also be distracting. The problems most groups have with visual aids, if they use them at all, are in determining what is suitable to visualize, selecting an appropriate form and design for visualization, and incorporating them during the presentation.

Visual Aids

Visual aids can enhance a presentation or detract from it, depending on what is visualized, how it is visualized, and how it is delivered. Avoid using visual material if the group is not committed to effective development and use of it. The creation of quality visual materials takes time, so plan in advance, especially if slides, videocassettes, or overhead projector transparencies are going to be used.

The first question the group needs to ask itself is what should be visualized? Key information, conclusions, data, examples, or illustrations are likely candidates for visualization. The group may also wish to use visuals to heighten interest and create variety as well as cues for the speaker. There are two important considerations for determining the use of visual aids:

1. They must directly support important content in an efficient and effective manner.
2. They must be designed and used to enhance communication.

Visual aids should not waste time or be difficult to interpret. Use them to present and reinforce detailed information or complex relationships, dramatize important issues, and illustrate visual content referred to in the presentation.

The three main *forms of visualization* in group projects are charts, graphs, and

5. See Thomas Pearsall and Donald Cunningham, *How to Write for the World of Work* (New York: Holt, Rinehart and Winston, 1978), or check your library or writing center for similar books.

Flip Chart Guidelines

1. Print boldly (letters should be at least two inches high); do not use cursive lettering.
2. Use black or blue markers predominately because they are the easiest to see. Use red for highlighting.
3. Markers bleed through the paper, so leave a blank sheet between pages you write on.
4. Check that all visuals are in the proper order.
5. Maintain eye contact with the audience; do not talk to the flip chart.
6. Make sure that the visual is accessible to all members of the audience and that you do not block the view.
7. Display a page when you are ready to discuss it, not before.
8. Secure the flip chart to the easel to avoid embarrassing accidents.
9. Do not crowd information on a single page. Provide spacing between items. Put summaries or conclusions on a separate page.

---

images. There are several common applications for each, depending on the content to be visualized.

1. Charts represent conceptual relationships such as chronologies, hierarchies, processes, and quantities. The more common types are organizational charts, classification charts, time lines, flow charts, and tables (see Appendix I).
2. Graphs present numerical data, relationships between data, or data trends in the form of bar, pictorial, pie, and line graphs (see Appendix J).
3. Images display or illustrate material that cannot be adequately delivered or dramatized using language alone. Visual displays are typically photos, drawings, sketches, and objects.

Visualization media most often used for presenting visual information are the flip chart, overhead projector, and slides.[6] A fourth medium gaining popularity is the videocassette. Regardless of which type of media is used, they all need to be prepared in advance and controlled by the speaker, so he or she can maintain eye contact with the audience.

Flip charts are usually large pads of paper or poster board mounted on an easel. The speaker can write on them during a presentation or they can be prepared with verbal/visual information in advance and shown one page at a time. Different colored markers can direct the audience to important information or distinctions. The most common use of this medium in group presentations is to outline the parts of the presentation with key words. They can also be used to

6. Derived from Robert Heinich, Michael Molenda, and James Russell, *Instructional Media*, 2nd ed. (New York: John Wiley, 1985).

Transparency Guidelines

1. Control the audience's attention by turning the projector off between transparencies.

2. Add information to transparencies to add an element of spontaneity. Use a blank transparency as an overlay if you need to save the original.

3. Direct the audience's attention to parts of the transparency by using the following techniques:

   a. Point to the specific information on the transparency by laying a pencil on it. Any elevation of the pencil will put it out of focus and hand movements will be projected on the screen. Do not point at the screen.
   b. Reveal information a line or section at a time to control the pace by placing a sheet of paper on the transparency and moving it down as needed.
   c. Mask unwanted information by covering it with a sheet of paper, or use a cardboard "window" to reveal the desired portion.
   d. Add information by superimposing transparencies one at a time to present complex ideas. Up to four transparencies can be overlaid effectively.

display sketches, charts, and graphs if they are drawn neatly.

Overhead projectors use acetate transparencies that can be prepared with special pens or photocopied from a typed sheet of paper. Your school may have a visual design specialist who may be able to help you produce slick verbal or visual transparencies. As with the flip chart, you can write on transparencies during the presentation. (Only pens labeled for overhead marking are sure to project in color and not rub off.) They can be used to display outlines, graphs, and line drawings. Graphic software for personal computers has added a way to generate visual materials for transparencies.

Slide Use Guidelines

1. Make sure your slides are in the right sequence and will be right side up when projected.
2. Consider using verbal title slides between pictures to create visual variety and introduce segments.
3. Use a remote-control device so you can stand to the side of the room to keep eye contact with the audience while also keeping an eye on the slide.
4. Use a penlight or flashlight so you can see your notes when the room is darkened.
5. If there is a long section of speaking between slides, use a black or gray slide. (It lets enough light through so the speaker can be seen; you can buy one from photo shops.) Do not display an irrelevant slide through a long discussion.
6. Begin and end the slide presentation with a black slide to avoid the irritation of the projector's bright light on the screen.

Slides are the best medium for displaying photographic visuals. If your presentation covers issues that require visualization for dramatic impact (for example, a disaster or military action) or illustration (a product, architectural design, natural phenomenon), slides are effective. The main disadvantage is the advance time and skill needed for preparation. They must also be presented in a darkened room, so you need a suitable room.

As access to video cameras and recorders increases, videocassettes provide the most effective way to display moving images. Still images can also be recorded on videotape instead of using slides if visual detail is not important. Videorecording of broadcast TV programs is an easy way to obtain dramatic displays and illustrations. Those familiar with video cameras can take to the streets to record events, interviews, or staged material. But do not get carried away. Groups can become enamored with the medium, presenting all the material they have recorded. This wastes time and displays unimportant information. For example, we have observed groups use videocassettes to present interviews with experts, taking several minutes to deliver information that could have been easily and quickly summarized. Recording the interviews took a lot of effort to produce, but showing segments during the presentation added little in supporting the project goal. Avoid showing unimportant material by editing or using fast-forward features. Also, be sure that there are sufficient monitors for the size of the audience and that screens are large enough.

The effective design and use of visual aids can make the difference between a dynamic, professional presentation and a lackluster, amateurish one. Too often the impact of group presentations is diminished by the lack or poor quality of visuals. Keep in mind that the group is presenting not only information but also itself. A pre-meeting activity follows.

Pre-Meeting Activity

Selecting Visual Aids

Identify presentation content—issues, data, orientation, summaries—that need to be illustrated, reinforced, exemplified, or displayed. Establish your reasoning for visualizing the content. Select the most appropriate visual form and media. Consider available time and access to materials and equipment.

Content	*Why Visualize?*	*Form/Media*

Planning and Coordinating Speakers

The following pointers can help you plan the presentation and coordinate multiple speakers.

- Review the outline and decide on the most natural and efficient breakdown of the presentation's parts.
- Mention the major segments or areas to be covered at the end of the introduction of the presentation.
- Speak for listening! Do this by using the *internal summary* and *transition statement.* The internal summary briefly repeats the speaker's main points. For example, "We have just reviewed the three major sources of funding on campus: the administration, faculty groups, and student government." The transition statement follows the internal summary and establishes the link between the previous speaker's information and the next report. It can follow or be part of the internal summary. Most importantly, it must orient the audience to the next speaker's presentation and establish the relationship between the two presentations. For instance, "Now that we know the three main sources for funding activities on campus, Joan will review the types of activities these sources fund. They fall into four categories: athletic, academic, professional, and social."
- The previous speaker or the next one can deliver the summary and transition statements or split between them. Or a moderator can perform this duty. Be sure that these summaries and transitions are ready for delivery along with each speaker's presentation notes. Visual aids can reinforce the introduction of each speaker's topic.
- When several speakers have short presentations, their frequent up and down movement (from sitting to standing) draws attention away from the content. Use fewer speakers, longer presentations, or delivery from the seated position to avoid this problem.
- Establish the time limits for the presentation, which usually takes twenty to forty minutes. Make sure you can cover the material in the allotted time. Allow time for audience questions.

Once the group has its presentation packaged for delivery, it should conduct a full dress rehearsal. Coordinating speakers, visual aids, and media takes planning and practice to pull off a flawless delivery. If possible, rehearse in the room where the group will be delivering the final presentation.

Be sure to check the presentation room to plan seating, visual display placement, electrical outlets, lighting, and the need for extension cords. Test all equipment before the presentation. Have extra projector bulbs and markers on hand. Be fully prepared: planning prevents poor performance.[7]

---

7. For additional information on planning the oral presentation or the use of visuals, see Jo Sprague and Douglas Stuart, *The Speaker's Handbook*, 2nd ed. (San Diego: Harcourt Brace Jovanovich, 1988).

Standard Agenda Items for Meetings on Project Delivery and Synthesis

The agenda items listed in the left-hand column are typical issues for meetings on synthesizing information for delivery. Review them and add any others you believe should be considered. (For example, we have not included agenda items on preparing a written report.) You can add other items or focuses under a given agenda item. Then rank order the list by placing a number next to each agenda item. If an item has several focuses within it, order them, using *a*, *b*, *c*. Next consider what tool options should be used to tackle each agenda item or focus during or outside of the meeting. Finally, list the desired outcome for each individual agenda item or focus in the right-hand column. The time available to complete this phase of the project may be tight, so identify the number of meetings that should be held and specific agendas or focuses for each meeting. (Label agenda items for meeting 1, 2, and so on).

Agenda/Focus	Tool	Outcome
Evaluate collected information		
Outline collected information		
Identify information for visual aids		
specific information		
format and media		
Prepare delivery		
segments		
speakers		
equipment		
rehearsal		
Other agenda		
Next meeting agenda		
Meeting evaluation		

Appendix A
Tips on Agenda Setting

The meeting agenda is a guide to planned meeting activities. Set the next meeting agenda at the end of each meeting so all members will know it well in advance.

An effective agenda states what is going to be covered and the specific action and outcome for each item. Follow these tips for agenda setting to plan and coordinate meeting activities.

1. State agenda items in the form of an outcome and indicate any relevant details of the item (e.g., develop list of survey questions, evaluate and select a solution, obtain report from Tom on campus recycling plan).

2. Consider if the agenda item has subparts or focuses within it. Note them and their specific outcomes as well. The group may not be aware of subtasks for an unfamiliar activity such as designing a survey.

3. Place agenda items and focuses in logical order so items leading to later items come earlier in the agenda.

4. Be sure agenda items establish important details or responsibilities of members.

5. Clarify whether an agenda item or focus requires pre-meeting activity such as members providing ideas to the chairperson before the meeting.

6. Estimate or establish the time allotted to each item. Schedule the least important and shortest items at the start and end of meetings. (Members who arrive late or leave early can miss them without losing touch with the project.) Avoid spending excessive time on these minor items so you can devote the bulk of the meeting time to important items.

7. Present information needed for later activities before decision-making tasks that require the information. It is a good idea to separate report tasks from decision tasks in the agenda.

8. Be prepared to review activity procedures, techniques, or methods if they need attention. Schedule time to learn procedures and techniques or solve meeting problems when needed.

9. The evaluation of the meeting should be the last agenda item. This should be a standard agenda item, especially during the early stages of the group's formation and project.

For those interested in more detailed information on meetings and agenda setting, the following references will be helpful.

L. P. Bradford, *Making Meetings Work: A Guide for Leaders and Group Members* (San Diego: University Associates, 1976).

Michael Doyle and David Straus, *How to*

Make Meetings Work (New York: Wyden Press, 1976).

Eva Schindler-Rainman and Ronald Lippitt, *Taking Your Meetings Out of the Doldrums* (San Diego: University Associates, 1975).

John E. Tropman, *Effective Meetings: Improving Group Decision-Making* (Newburg Park, Calif.: Sage, 1980).

Appendix B
Group Memory and Meeting Minutes Format

The *group memory*, a record tracking the meeting's progress, is written on large newsprint suspended before the group. It takes the place of secretarial meeting notes. *Meeting minutes* are a written record of the meeting that is made available to the members and the instructor or supervisor. They are typically drawn up and distributed before the next meeting.

Use the following list to design the format of the group memory and serve as the basis for developing meeting minutes. It basically identifies the types of information that you should include in a group memory and meeting minutes.

1. Date of meeting and time started and ended.

2. Members in attendance or members absent (easier to identify those absent).

3. Agenda or focus stated in specific outcome form. Some groups will list general agenda items (for example, develop survey instrument) that have several specific subtasks by identifying the focuses (generate list of survey questions, identify target population). Modify the planned agenda when necessary. If your group discovers that an agenda item has several focuses within it, identify and work on them one at a time.

4. The "tool rule" requires the group to identify how it will work on an agenda/focus. Record the tool used on a group memory to remind the members of the procedure selected for managing the discussion. It is not important to put such information in meeting minutes unless it is requested by the instructor.

5. The outcome identifies what actually happened after the item was discussed. Was it tabled for the next meeting? Was a specific list generated? Did the group decide to have Tom interview the head of campus security? Identify what was accomplished or planned and what an assignment requires.

6. Develop the next meeting agenda so all members know what to expect. It can be general; you can identify specific focuses at the next meeting.

7. In the meeting evaluation the group identifies what it liked about the meeting and what it would like to see in future meetings. (See Itemized Response in Chapter 6.) If this evaluation raises a problem that needs attention, the group can put it on the agenda for the next meeting.

8. The final information is the name of the recorder or secretary of the minutes.

Example: Format of Group Memory and Minutes

Group: Campus Funding Project
Date: 9/21/89 Time Started: 11:45 a.m. Adjourned: 1 p.m.
Members Absent: J. Wilson

Agenda/focus: Identify project questions of fact
Tool: Brainstorming
Outcome: Developed tentative list (attached); review and finalize at next meeting

Agenda/focus: Assess the value of interviewing student organization presidents on funding experiences
Tool: Open discussion
Outcome: Established interviews would help identify problems with funding process; need to determine interview questions

Agenda/focus: Review tentative list of questions of fact for interview questions and develop others
Tool: Review list/open discussion, brainstorm additional items
Outcome: Developed list of questions for interviews (attached)

Agenda for next meeting: 9/31/89, North Hall Lounge, 7 p.m.

- Review list of questions of fact to finalize and assign information search tasks
- Identify list of campus student organization presidents to interview (Sam will obtain list of campus organizations)
- Plan interview format and analysis

Meeting Evaluation:

Positive	Needs Improvement
members listened to each other	more ideas from all members
brainstorming was productive	quieter meeting room
recorder kept up with meeting	have meetings start on time
project appears to be on track	remember to stick to the discussion focus
joking around did not stop meeting progress	

Submitted by: P. Printz

As you can see, this format provides a useful and careful way of tracking a meeting by noting brief but specific details. If the group uses a group memory, it can easily translate it into meeting minutes. If the group does not keep meeting minutes, it can always refer to the group memory. Past meeting memories should be accessible at every meeting for reference. Minutes are easier to carry around and all members can have a copy, while a group memory provides a common visual reference as the meeting progresses. It keeps everything fresh in the members' minds and frees them from note taking to listen and contribute. We recommend using both a group memory and meeting minutes to maximize effective communication.

Appendix C
Post-Meeting Evaluation Form

Circle the number that best reflects your evaluation of the most recent meeting you attended. Include comments beneath each question.

---

1. There was regular and consistent participation by most members.

   yes 1 2 3 4 5 6 7 no

   Comments:

2. Members showed signs of listening (paraphrasing, responding to points made, summarizing others' points, nodding).

   always 1 2 3 4 5 6 7 never

   Comments:

3. Members appeared to be prepared for the meeting.

   prepared 1 2 3 4 5 6 7 unprepared

   Comments:

4. Discussion was focused and stayed on the topic or task.

   always 1 2 3 4 5 6 7 never

   Comments:

5. Members' statements were clear, brief, and easy to follow.

   always 1 2 3 4 5 6 7 never

   Comments:

6. Group appears able to use the best technique or procedure for managing meeting agenda or focuses.

   always 1 2 3 4 5 6 7 never

   Comments:

7. Members' evaluations and criticism were phrased constructively.
   always 1 2 3 4 5 6 7 never
   Comments:

8. Members appeared to work in a cooperative manner.
   always 1 2 3 4 5 6 7 never
   Comments:

9. Members were willing to offer opinions, ask questions, and contribute to discussion.
   always 1 2 3 4 5 6 7 never
   Comments:

10. Evaluation of opinions, ideas, proposals, and information was thorough and carefully done.
    always 1 2 3 4 5 6 7 never
    Comments:

11. Relationships among members appeared to be friendly and pleasant.
    always 1 2 3 4 5 6 7 never
    Comments:

12. Members volunteered to perform group tasks.
    always 1 2 3 4 5 6 7 never
    Comments:

13. The meeting room's environment was conducive to conducting business.
    yes 1 2 3 4 5 6 7 no
    Comments:

14. The meeting was productive; the group made progress.
    yes 1 2 3 4 5 6 7 no
    Comments:

Each group member should fill out the preceding form. (You may wish to copy it to use again.) The group can decide if it wishes to have the evaluations anonymous. One member can compile the results and report back to the group.

Appendix D
Information Interviewing Tips

Information-seeking interviews are a way to collect information when there is no other means of obtaining it, especially when you need an expert's opinion or knowledge. The key to effective and efficient information interviewing is planning. Use the tips here to plan your interviews.[1]

Conduct initial research to obtain background on the topic, issues, and potential persons to interview. If your group has conducted an analysis, the research questions for the project have been identified. Look for answers before you select interview questions and people to interview. Next select and design appropriate interview questions by identifying the purpose of the interview, the information needed, and questions to solicit the needed information. Use these three types of questions, depending on what information you need:

1. *Bipolar questions* request specific information that is characterized by two opposite choices, typically *yes* and *no*. Others ask people to choose between such opposite terms as *good/bad*, *fair/unfair*, and *best/worst*. Avoid using this type of question if there are clearly more than two choices.
2. *Closed questions* offer more choices than bipolar questions do. This "multiple-choice question" is useful when there are several clear options or when items need to be ranked. Provide an "other" category to anticipate choices you may not be aware of.
3. *Open questions* request information on a topic or issue but do not restrict how the interviewee can respond. These questions can elicit a lot of information. They are especially useful when you know little about the interview topic. Unlike bipolar and closed questions, open questions are difficult to analyze when used in surveys because of the possible range of answers and difficulties in interpreting them.

Your interview should have three parts: introduction, body, and conclusion. First introduce yourself and explain the purpose of the interview. State how the information will be used and why you are interviewing a specific person, and review the topics you will cover and their order. The questions are the *body* of the interview. You should cue the interviewee to each topic before asking the questions in that area. Then conclude with a brief summary of the main information you obtained. Ask if there is other information the interviewee thinks you should have or other people you should

---

1. Derived from Eric W. Skopec, *Situational Interviewing* (New York: Harper & Row, 1986), pp. 17–42.

interview. Be sure to thank the interviewee.

Manage the interview so that you keep it on track and get the information you are seeking. Be prepared to respond to the interviewee when he or she misses the point of a question, digresses, or provides insufficient or short answers. If you do not manage the interview, the interviewee may manage you. You can use direct and nondirect probes to manage the interview. *Directive probes* are questions to pinpoint specific information. They typically reduce the choices available to the interviewee and provide a greater control than nondirect probes do. There are four basic types of direct probes for following up an initial question:

1. *Elaboration questions* request more information when an interviewee provides insufficient information. Identify the specific area you wish to be elaborated.

2. *Clarification questions* are asked to make sure you understand unfamiliar terms and phrases or a complex issue or idea.

3. *Repeated questions* are useful when the response to your question is not appropriate because it was not heard or understood or because the interviewee was being evasive.

4. *Confrontation questions* may emphasize a potential conflict in the interview if sensitive or threatening issues are addressed. Use them to point out inconsistencies, expose misrepresentations, and clarify misunderstandings or errors in the interviewee's information.

Nondirective probes are more subtle ways to encourage the interviewee to talk and should be your first choice when possible. With the right nonverbal emphasis, sometimes a nondirect technique can accomplish the same thing as direct probes. Try these four methods:

1. *Silence* promotes talk. The interviewer's job is to listen. When combined with nonverbal signs of interest such as eye contact and nodding, silence signals the interviewee to continue.

2. *Mirror statements* paraphrase what you understood the interviewee to say and show that you are listening and interested. They also check the accuracy of your understanding. A questioning tone of voice can make this technique work like a clarification probe. An incredulous tone of voice can serve as a confrontation.

3. *Neutral phrases* demonstrate attention to the speaker and interest. Phrases such as "I see," "I didn't know that," and "I understand," can encourage the interviewee to continue. Vary the use of such phrases so you appear sincere and truly involved.

4. *Internal summaries* can be used at junctures in the interview to be sure you recall what was said about a topic. They invite interviewees to add to or correct what they have said.

Prepare to record your interview by writing your interview questions in a notebook with spaces between them for answers and follow-up questions. It is desirable to tape record the interview so you can devote attention to the answers and the interview process. However, you must seek permission to do so from the interviewee. Forgo such requests if the subject matter is sensitive and you believe tape recording would inhibit candid responses.

For more detailed suggestions about conducting an information-seeking interview, consult these books:

Charles J. Stewart and William B. Cash, *Interviewing: Principles and Practices*, 3rd ed. (Dubuque, Iowa: Wm. Brown, 1984).

Michael Z. Sincoff and Robert S. Goyer, *Interviewing* (New York: Macmillan, 1984).

Appendix E
Survey Development and Administration Guide

Developing, administering, and analyzing a survey is a labor-intensive task that takes a minimum of four weeks. Use a survey only if the information you need cannot be obtained through other means. Frequently, direct or indirect information is available to answer research questions, but insufficient detective work leads groups to use surveys. When there is no answer to a key question about a population's perceptions of a specific issue—for example, how members of a certain campus community perceive campus parking—use a survey, following these guidelines:[1]

Survey Development

1. Unanswered research questions that are central to your project goal should be evident before you develop a survey instrument. Identify the specific population(s) and issues of the research.

2. Establish the purpose of the survey and the questions needing answers. Place the questions in a logical order.

3. Design the survey instrument by first developing an introduction stating its purpose, confidentiality, topic and issues, and time needed to administer. This information can be given in a cover letter if the survey is not conducted in person or by phone. Next include demographic questions to tell you what you need to know about respondents—for example, their gender, age, or title.

4. If no standardized survey instruments or questions are available, develop your own. Select the types of questions that fit the type of information you are seeking. (See Appendix D for types of questions.) Also consider the task of analyzing survey data. Bipolar or closed questions can be easily quantified and administered using computer optical scan forms; this allows for quick processing through computer tabulation. Open-ended questions provide a lot of information and allow subjects to define what is relevant, but they are harder to quantify for analysis because the answers are typically in the form of statements. A combination of types may be useful.

5. Phrase questions from the perspective of the respondent. Do not use jargon or unfamiliar terms. Provide answer options that allow the respondent to indicate a lack of knowledge or information on an issue ("don't

---

1. Derived from John H. Maher, Jr., and C. Edward Kur, "Constructing Good Questionnaires," *Training and Development Journal*, June, 1983, pp. 107–110.

know" or "have not thought about it"). Consider the biases of the survey population and word questions in a neutral manner.

6. Write the survey questions. Be sure that the response options are specific and match the question. See the following checklist for question development.
7. Put the survey instrument together and test it before administering it to the target population.

Question Development Checklist

1. Do the questions contribute to the survey's purpose?
2. Are the questions grouped together according to format?
3. Are the questions organized in a logical content order?
4. Are the questions free of bias?
5. Have threatening introductory questions been avoided?
6. Have questions asking essentially the same thing been deleted?
7. Does each question address only one main issue or idea?
8. Are the questions grammatically correct?
9. Are the questions specific and clear?
10. Are terms and abbreviations familiar or defined?
11. Is wording at the subjects' language level?
12. Do closed-ended questions provide all relevant response options?
13. Are response options mutually exclusive and distinct?
14. Are response scales (if used) biased toward particular options?
15. Is the response format for similarly structured questions the same?
16. Is there sufficient space for open-ended response?
17. Have the survey questions been designed anticipating the analysis of the answers?

Survey Administration

There are two fundamental issues in planning a survey: the population size and method of administration. The first issue involves obtaining information from members of the population in question in an adequate number and a manner of selection that permits generalizing to the whole population. Administration involves efficiency in obtaining a sufficient quantity of completed surveys representative of the population being studied.

First identify the population (students at State University) and any relevant demographic subgroups (freshmen, students with athletic scholarships). Identify the number of subjects in the population and subgroups. If the whole population is not going to be surveyed, you must randomly draw a *survey sample* from it. This means that everyone must have an equal chance of being selected from the population for the survey. You can do this by methods as simple as picking every tenth person (if you are sampling 10 percent of total population) on a master list or using a table of random numbers (see a survey or statistics text) to select the sample. If the sample is not randomly selected, you cannot assume that the survey data represent the population surveyed. For example, if you survey all the seniors in a dorm about parking problems, your results indicate only perceptions by seniors who live on campus, not all seniors and certainly not all students. If distinct types of subjects in the target population are relevant to the survey, be sure that they are proportionately selected. (For example, if the population has 60 percent females and 40 percent males, the sample should have the same proportion.)

Closely related to sample selection is *sample size*. The size of the sample in relation to the total population is a second critical factor in being able to generalize the data of the sample to the population. If you randomly select 10 subjects out of a population of 10,000 (one thousandth of 1 percent of the total), such a small sample probably would not represent the possible responses among population members. Sufficient sample size is necessary for a representative sample. The general rule of thumb is that the larger the population, the smaller the random sample needed; the smaller the population, the larger the sample needed. A 1 percent random sample is used in national surveys. In survey populations of less than 100, select a sample of 20 to 30 percent to ensure it is representative. Sampling the whole population in such cases is best.

In the method of administration, the key issues are ease of administration, timing, and the number of completed returns. Experience suggests that the most efficient approach is either to administer the survey face to face (visit at home) or by phone. These two approaches guarantee a completed sample in a timely fashion. Mailed surveys are notorious for poor returns and incomplete surveys, spoiling the sample representation.

Survey Analysis

Once you have the completed surveys, analyzing the results begins. Consider these points in preparing the survey for analysis.

1. Determine how you will analyze the data. You will likely want tabulations of response options per question. If a question has five choices or degrees of intensity, you will want to know the percentage of subjects who made each type of response. Consider demographic breakdowns that might be important in the analysis such as male and female response frequencies.

2. Consider whether the survey responses can be computerized using optical scan forms. Most computer centers can help you conduct a basic tabulation of the data, which can save considerable time compared to tabulation by hand, especially if you have a large number of surveys.

3. If the research questions involve comparing items or subgroup responses, you can use computer software for statistical computations such as correlations (the relationship between two responses) and measures of statistical difference (for example, Z-test or T-test). These computations can be pursued if the group has the time to do so or has a member who is versed in statistics.

Books on Surveying

Paul J. Lavrakas, *Telephone Survey Methods* (Newbury Park, Calif.: Sage, 1987).

Floyd J. Fowler, *Survey Research Methods* (Newbury Park, Calif.: Sage, 1984).

Appendix F
Information Search Resources

If your group is not aware of specific books, journals, magazines, newspapers, and other printed material related to its project topic, it will have to begin by identifying relevant material through the numerous reference indexes available in libraries. Even if the group is familiar with useful publications, it still has to identify specific titles and articles related to the project's themes and research questions.

Knowing what questions need answers and what themes need to be explored and understood will enable you to identify key terms to search the reference books for specific subjects. Most indexes can also be searched by authors and title. Basically, a reference book can answer three questions: What articles have been published on a given subject? What articles has a given author written? Where are the articles?

The following list covers the most common reference indexes.[1] They cover various types of printed material and range from general to specific in focus. A thorough investigation would require the group to review at least all the reference books over the past five to ten years that might index material related to the project's topic. If the project involved a historical matter, the search would go back to the date of the event, or earlier, if prior events had an influence.

1. Derived from Alden Todd, *Finding Facts Fast*, 2nd ed. (Berkeley, Calif.: Ten Speed Press, 1979), pp. 24–35.

A Reference on References

The reference librarian is a consummate reference resource, trained in the art of finding what is available on a subject.

Reference Books: A Brief Guide is an index of reference books. If you are uncertain about what reference books would be useful, consult this handy guide for indexes by subject.

Book References

The library card catalogue is probably the first convenient source to find books on the project's subject. Some libraries have computers that will conduct book searches of a library network to identify titles available through interlibrary loan.

Books in Print indexes all books published and available (in print) by year according to subject, author, and title.

Popular Periodical Resources

The *Reader's Guide to Periodical Literature* covers popular and some specialized magazines. This is a great source for finding articles in newsmagazines.

The *New York Times Index* provides information on news and feature stories covering major and popular issues and events.

The *Wall Street Journal Index* is a good source for its coverage of and commentary on financial and economic news.

Specialized Periodical Resources

Applied Science and Technology Index
Art Index
Biological and Agricultural Index
Business Periodical Index
Communication Abstracts
Education Index
General Science Index
Humanities Index
Index to Legal Periodicals
Psychological Abstracts
Social Science Index

Government Document References

The *Congressional Directory* indexes resources of the federal government, focusing on Congress, its committees, lists of federal courts and judges, and agencies and offices of the executive branch. It also provides the addresses, phone numbers, and names of agencies' public information officers.

The *United States Government Organization Manual* provides detail on each agency of the executive branch of the federal government.

The *Statistical Abstract of the United States* is an annual publication covering data from both government and nongovernment agencies and associations. It has all kinds of demographic information and economic, social, financial, and population statistics.

Appendix G
Information Evaluation Checklist

When evaluating the quality of information or answers to research questions, you should apply several fundamental criteria. Use the following lists to help you determine what to look for when assessing information.

1. Review the answers to each research question. Be sure that you have the exact information. If there is only one answer per question, ask yourself why.

2. Determine whether the information is a statement of fact or opinion. If it is an opinion, is it founded on any facts? Is the reasoning from the facts to the opinion sound? If it is a fact, how was it determined? Was the method valid? Could any limitations in the method undermine the reliability of the fact?

3. Note the authors of the information. Are they known experts in the subject? (If unknown, ask reference librarian for professional and general biographical references such as *Who's Who in America*. Establishing authors' credibility can be important for persuasive presentations.) Could the authors' membership in any prestigious association bias their opinions?

4. Note the publisher of the information. Ask the same questions as with the author. Does the publishing company specialize in any discipline or topics? Is it associated with any organization or ideology? Might it be biased toward a particular view?

5. Check the date of the publication and of in-text citations. The authors could be using dated information even if their publication is recent. Has the passage of time undermined the believability of the information, whether fact or opinion? Have changes in social trends, values, and events affected the reliability of the information? Today's fact may be tomorrow's myth—facts are not absolute.

6. Review the answers to the preceding questions and assess the strengths and weaknesses of the information evaluated. Based on this assessment, determine if you should do anything to improve the quality of the information. Should the group look for more sources of information, seek corroborating evidence, or find more recent data or less biased authors?

Appendix H
Presentation Organizing Schemes

The information and goal of your presentation will largely determine how you will organize the body of oral and written outlines. Some schemes are more suited to descriptive presentations, others to persuasive efforts.[1]

Organizing by Time

Projects that document events over time (for example, the evolution of the automobile) can use a chronological organization format. If a part of the presentation describes events over time, you can incorporate this format into a larger organizational scheme.

Organizing by Space

This scheme organizes information along geographical or spatial lines. Information that describes direction or location can use this format effectively. North to south, up and down, left to right, and near to far are ways to organize spatial information that are easily visualized by the audience or through visual aids.

Problem-to-Solution Format

When you are establishing a problem and proposing a solution, clearly identify and describe the problem and relate it to the interests and needs of the audience. Then describe how the solution will eliminate the problem and fulfill the listeners' (or readers') needs. Be sure to consider *how* you will implement the solution. If it is not clearly workable, a solution can be easily dismissed.

Cause-and-Effect Approach

This is a prevalent motif in people's thinking and thus lends itself to organizing presentations that propose action. Like the problem-to-solution format, it focuses on problems. It differs in that it focuses on the causes of the problem. If the presentation's purpose is to propose a solution, be sure to establish how it will eliminate the causes. Make sure that the causes are really the source of the problem. Look at a cause over time and the web of related causes for a more realistic depiction of what created the problem. (You might use a time scheme to organize this part of the presentation of causes.)

Topical Organization

This is the most common organizational scheme for informative presentations. The natural segments of the information determine the organization. For example, a presentation on sources of funding campus activities could naturally fall into the categories of sources of funding: faculty, administrative, and student government. Sometimes the topic may be organized

1. Derived from Michael S. Hanna and Gerald L. Wilson, *Communicating in Business and Professional Settings*, 2nd ed. (New York: Random House, 1988), pp. 369–385.

around the group's concerns with it. If the type of activities funded was the main concern, the outline could be organized around the function of funding: promoting social, athletic, professional, and academic development.

The Motivated Sequence

Alan H. Monroe developed this powerful scheme for persuasive presentations,[2] which uses a common pattern of thinking familiar to our culture. (If the purpose of the presentation is to inform, the visualization step is not needed.) These guidelines indicate the kind of information needed to fulfill each part of this versatile organization format.

- *Attention:* In the introduction of the presentation you want to get the audience eager to continue listening or reading. You can do this by establishing a common ground, honestly complimenting the audience, raising issues of special interest to the audience, using tasteful humor, establishing the subject's significance to the audience, and leading the audience to your purpose with a story or illustration. These attention-getting devices are useful for any introduction regardless of the scheme used.

- *Need:* Establish the problem or need to know. Consider the audience's needs and how the situation leaves the need unfulfilled and wanting. The audience should feel that something needs to be done, felt, or known.

- *Satisfaction:* This step fulfills the need established in the previous step. Make the link between the need and manner of fulfilling clear. The audience ought to believe that the proposed action, belief, or delivered knowledge takes care of their earlier aroused need.

- *Visualization:* This step creates concrete, easy-to-follow images of what will happen if the action or belief is adopted or not adopted. Here you establish the consequences and review the advantages or disadvantages.

- *Action:* The action step seeks audience follow-through depending on what is requested: belief or action. Clarify the desired outcome of the presentation, especially when action is requested (for example, write to your senators telling them you oppose certain legislation).

There are other organizational schemes that you may devise or that may emerge in the collection of information. When selecting a scheme, make sure it serves the purpose of your presentation and accommodates the necessary information available to fulfill that purpose.

The outline you develop using these schemes will set up an oral presentation that should focus only on major points and supporting information. A written report can use the same outline but should include details.

Do not outline using paragraphs. Use sentences, phrases, key terms, and figures. For an oral presentation, transfer the outline to note cards. They are easy to handle and are not as distracting as sheets of paper. Do not read a written report for the oral presentation. Its details are not useful in an oral report, and reading reduces the eye contact needed to establish a connection with people.

2. Alan H. Monroe, *Principles and Types of Speech* (Glenview, Ill.: Scott Foresman, 1935).

Appendix I
Types of Charts[1]

Organization charts (see Figure 3) show the relationship or chain of command in an organization such as a company, corporation, civic group, or government department. Usually they deal with the interrelationship of personnel or departments.[1]

Classification charts (Figure 4) are similar to organization charts but are used chiefly to classify or categorize objects, events, or species. A common type of classification chart shows the taxonomy of animals and plants according to natural characteristics.

Time lines (Figure 5) illustrate chronological relationships between events. They are most often used to show time relationships of historical events or the relationship of famous people and these events. Pictures or drawings can be added to the time line to illustrate important concepts. Time lines are very helpful for summarizing the time sequence of a series of events.

Flowcharts (or process charts) (Figure 6) show a sequence, a procedure, or, as the name implies, the flow of a process. Flowcharts show how different activities, ingredients, or procedures merge into a whole.

Tabular charts (or tables) (see Figure 7) contain numerical information, or data. They are also convenient for showing time information when the data are presented in columns, as in timetables for railroads and airlines.

1. Derived from Heinich, Molenda, and Russell, *Instructional Media*, 2nd ed. (New York: John Wiley, 1985).

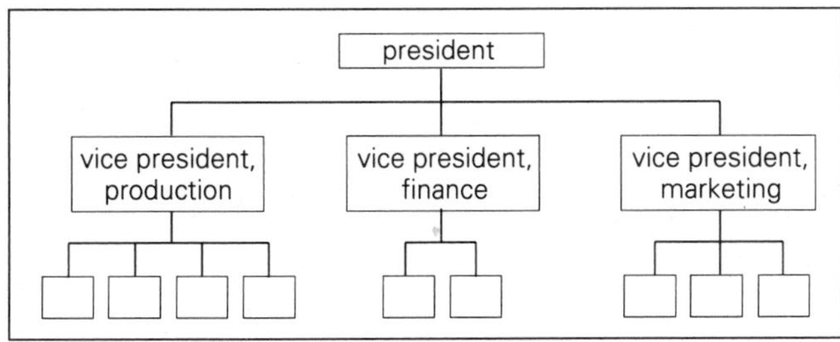

Figure 3 Organization chart.

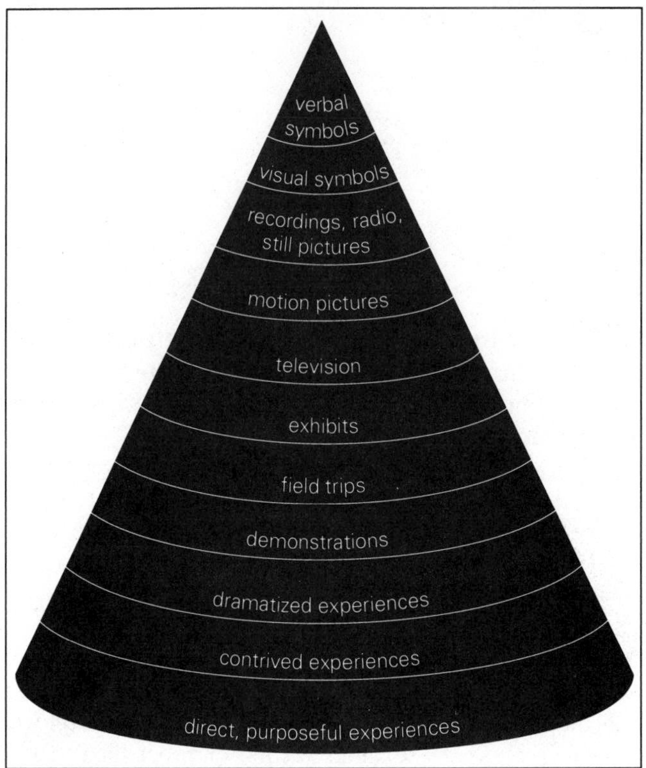

Figure 4 Classification chart.

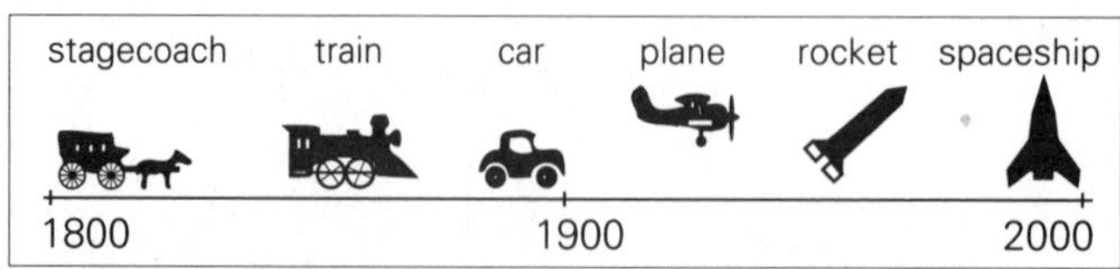

Figure 5 Time line.

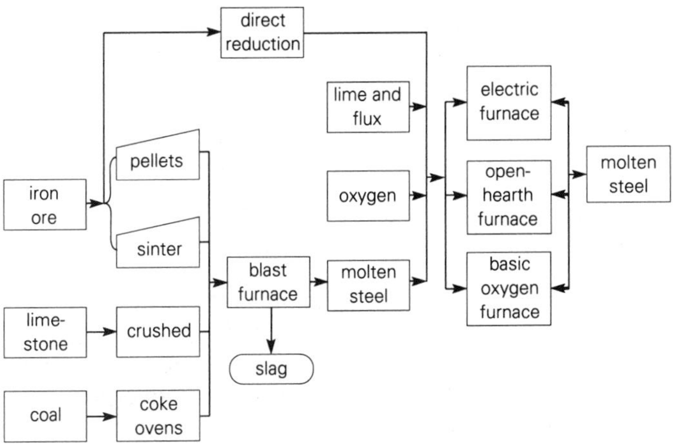

Figure 6 Flowchart.

Import Percentages				
	Wheat	Cotton	Steel	Oil
USA	—%	—%	20%	35%
England	65	95	35	10
France	15	95	30	90
Japan	85	15	—	95
Brazil	—	—	20	70

Figure 7 Tabular chart.

Appendix J
Types of Graphs

Bar graphs (Figure 8) show variation in only one dimension. The height of the bar is the measure of the quantity being represented. The width of all bars should be the same to avoid confusion. A single bar can be divided to show parts of a whole. It is best to limit the quantities being compared to eight or less; otherwise the graph becomes cluttered and confusing. This one-scale graph is particularly appropriate for comparing similar items at different times or different items at the same time—for example, the height of one plant over time or the heights of several students at any given time.[1]

Pictorial graphs (Figure 9), an alternate form of the bar graph, use a series of simple drawings to represent the value. Pictorial graphs are visually interesting and appeal to a wide audience, especially young students. However, they are slightly more difficult to read than bar graphs. Because pictorial symbols represent a specific quantity, partial symbols depict fractional quantities. To help avoid confusion in such cases, print values below or to the right of each line of figures.

Circle (or pie) graphs (Figure 10) are relatively easy to interpret. In this type of graph, a circle is divided into segments, each representing a part or percentage of the whole. One typical use of the circle graph is to depict tax-dollar allocations. The combined segments of a circle graph should equal 100 percent. Areas of special interest may be shown separately from the others, just as a piece of pie can be illustrated separately from a whole pie.

Line graphs (Figure 11), the most precise and complex, are based on two scales at right angles. Each point has a value on the vertical scale and a value on the horizontal scale. Lines (or curves) connect the points. Line graphs show variations in two dimensions—how two or more groups of quantities changed over time. For example, a graph can show the relation between pressure and temperature when the volume of a gas is held constant. Because line graphs are precise, they are very useful in plotting trends. They can also help simplify a mass of complex information.

---

1. Adopted from *Instructional Media*, 2nd ed. (New York: John Wiley, 1985).

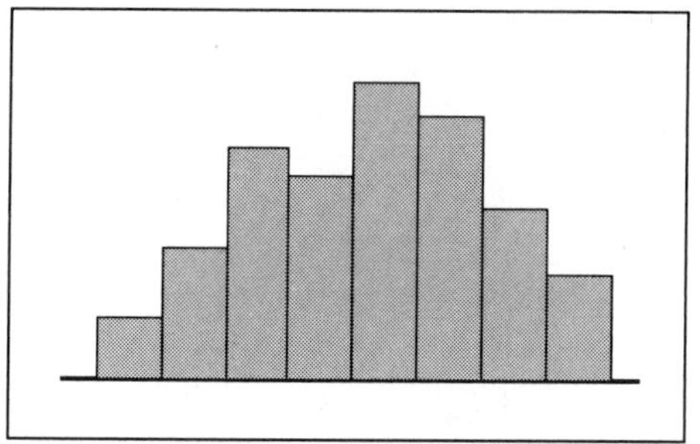

Figure 8 Bar graph.

Figure 9 Pictorial graph.

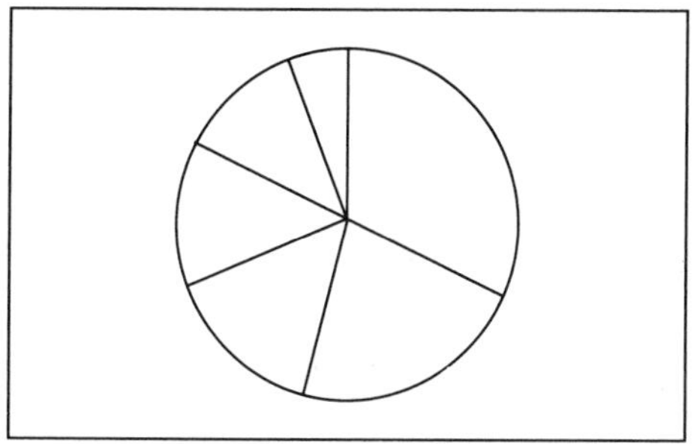

Figure 10 Circle (or pie) graph.

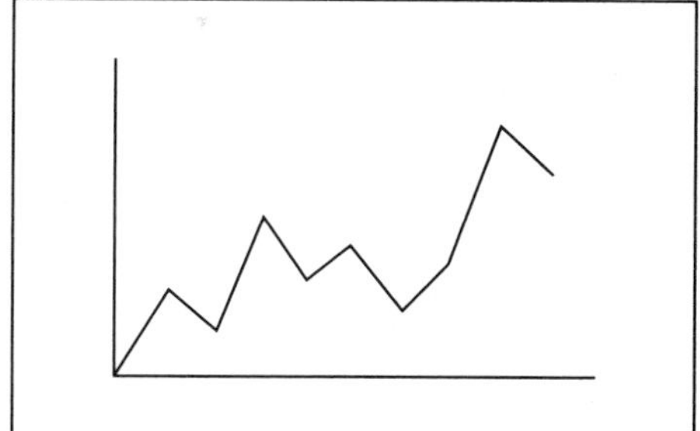

Figure 11 Line graph.

Part III

Analyzing Group Process from a Descriptive Perspective

CHAPTER 8

The Individual Level: Managing Personalities in the Group

A frequent complaint we hear about working in groups is how hard it is to get along with the other members. The problem is usually defined in terms of "personality clashes." As a result, everyone curses the person responsible for assigning him or her to that particular group of people. On the other hand, members seem almost ecstatic when personalities and skills mesh. They cannot show enough gratitude to the genius who recruited the group. Because of such reactions, we feel it is important to address the issue of how the individual fits in the group.

Our culture attaches a lot of importance to the individual. We tend to believe that the success of any group depends on the quality of the individuals who make up the group. It is easy to typecast individuals and decide which types you would or would not like to have in your group. We often think of personality as a fixed set of attributes that "cause" people to behave in inflexible ways. Social scientists, however, are beginning to question this view of personality. Many researchers now believe that individuals have multiple self-concepts and that displaying a particular "image" of self is influenced by perceptions of the situation and of other group members, as well as by the type of interaction, or feedback, within the group.

Imagine, for instance, that Sam sees himself as an extroverted guy who has no trouble talking with people one-on-one but clams up in more formal situations with more people—like classrooms and committee meetings. As a result, he puts on his more introverted "face" when he walks into his first evening class at the local community college. He glances around and realizes that he has met more than half the members of the class through his business associations. The instructor begins the class by engaging the students in a very informal dialogue, and the people who know Sam from numerous conversations with him treat him as the "extrovert" they "know" him to be. Before long, he has shifted gears and is operating from his more extroverted self-concept.

Such transformations of personality are not uncommon. We may fail to recognize them as such because they do not feel like transformations—we usually adapt to changing circumstances slowly and more naturally. As an example, think of the kind of person you are at home as opposed to at work or at school. The time it takes to change settings (by driving or walking) is usually enough time for us to adapt our sense of self and act accordingly without recognizing how much of a change has occurred. What if you did not have the time to make those adjustments gradually? What if you had to move instantly from a kitchen conversation with your mother to a business meeting with your boss to a discussion with friends in your dorm room? Chances are that you could not adjust as smoothly. You would probably be more keenly aware of your different "selves" or personalities.

At this point you may be wondering if knowledge of group members' personalities will help you understand or predict their behavior in groups. This has been the subject of considerable debate among researchers. Some believe that personality is essentially a myth that leads people to view each other in stereotypical ways and prevents them from communicating more effectively. Proponents of this perspective point out that personality is a concept created by researchers that has had only limited success in predicting how individuals behave. Furthermore, they argue that thinking of others as "having a personality" makes it easier to blame them when they behave in ways we do not like. Instead of trying to work out differences of opinion or behavior, we are likely to give up and attribute the differences to unchangeable personality factors.

On the other hand, some researchers believe that behavior is the result of the complex interplay of personality, situation, communication, and other factors. Rather than write off personality as a useless concept, they suggest that we recognize it as one of several influences and strive to better understand how all of these factors work together. We think group members should avoid using personality as a scapegoat for group problems, but a balanced view of the role of personality can help us render group situations more understandable. We will develop this balanced view more fully in the next section of this chapter.

Knowledge of personality factors coupled with an understanding of situations and other influences can help us manage three different purposes related to working in groups:

- *Motivational purposes.* If you can figure out what makes a person "tick" in a particular situation, you may be able to discover how to maximize his or her productivity and contributions to the group.

- *Persuasive purposes.* You also need to understand personalities if you hope to be persuasive on issues that are important to you. Your persuasive appeals will be more likely to hit their target if you know how the person will respond to them.
- *Compatibility purposes.* Perhaps the most important reason for assessing personality is to help you determine how to create and maintain compatibility among the group's members. If you are responsible for choosing members to join the group, a careful assessment can help you identify people who are likely to work well together. When the group is already intact, you can use your knowledge of personality issues to recognize when and how to manage personal differences that might threaten or even enhance the group's compatibility.

As a group member, you should also be concerned about how to modify your own self-presentations to fit changing circumstances. Our goal in this chapter is to help people manage all of these concerns. This is no small agenda, but any headway we can make in building stronger groups is worthwhile.

A Perspective on Personality

At the outset, we need to differentiate two terms that we have been using rather freely up to this point: personality and self-concept.

Personality and Self-Concept

Personality involves the regularities and consistencies in the behavior of a given person across situations.[1] It is generally conceded that personality is a researcher's construct—something that has been measured by paper-and-pencil tests that reflect behaviors researchers are interested in and believe to be related in some way. When an individual completes a personality inventory, that person does not usually get to offer a private or subjective view of what he or she thinks of himself or herself. Personality is thus a relatively objective view of how a person differs from others on a standard set of questions or self-reports of behaviors. The term *self-concept*, on the other hand, refers to an individual's subjective view or image of himself or herself.[2] Thus self-concept is really a more appropriate term for many of our concerns about how people behave in groups. We are interested in how a person sees himself or herself and how that image alters the way he or she communicates with other group members.

Unfortunately, most of the research conducted in groups has involved only measures of personality, not measures of self-concept. Thus while a person may score high on a given personality trait (say, aggressiveness), that particular trait might not figure prominently in the self-concept that he or she adopts in a given situation. This means that we have to interpret and use the results of studies of personality and group behavior very carefully. In applying the research findings described throughout this chapter, try to look at the situation

Members who have a low tolerance for ambiguity are uncomfortable making decisions in situations where opinions and information conflict.

from the perspective of the other rather than trying to use personality labels too freely. How do you take the perspective of another?

1. Listen carefully to the information the member discloses about himself or herself. Try to develop a sense of his or her own subjective view of self and especially any circumstances that seems to alter his or her self-confidence or demeanor.
2. Try to identify how he or she sees the situation at the moment, asking yourself how your perspective would change if you were in the same position.

Overestimating Personality

Using the strategy just outlined, you should be able to minimize the very human tendency to attribute more blame to others than to ourselves. We all tend to explain the behavior of others (especially negative behavior) as a reflection of their personality, while viewing our own similar behavior as being influenced by the nature of the situation. Psychologists call this tendency the *fundamental attribution error*.[3] In addition to judging others more harshly, we also tend to credit ourselves more when we succeed, and we seem to discover situational factors to account for our failures. We rarely give others the same credit and often blame their failures on their personality, not on the situation.

Finally, researchers have noted that we tend to overestimate the amount of effort we put into group projects, while typically underestimating the effort of others. When we commit the fundamental attribution error, we simplify our understanding of the people we are working with and their relationship to the group. In essence, we use personality as an explanation of behavior only when it is convenient for us to do so.

Underestimating Situations

A more complex view of personality requires that we understand how situations affect the role of personality on group behavior. Until recently, about all social scientists could tell us was that the influence of personality on behavior "depends on the situation." Now, however, we are beginning to understand how situations limit or encourage us to express our personalities. Mark Snyder and William Ickes have proposed that situations be termed *weak* or *strong* to show the extent to which the situation (or personality) is more likely to influence a person's behavior.[4]

Strong Situations A *strong situation* is one that is highly scripted—we know what behaviors to expect. For example, brainstorming (see Chapter 6) involves clear-cut rules of behavior to be followed. Such a situation usually limits the influence of personality. A person who is predisposed to be contentious or argumentative would be acting inappropriately if he or she criticized an idea during brainstorming. If, however, the definition of a situation happened to fit a member's personality, it would probably increase the chances of that person moving to the forefront of group discussion. For instance, the same contentious person whose personality was inhibited by a brainstorming situation would no doubt show his or her "true colors" during an episode of evaluating solutions. In this way, strong situations can activate the display of some personality traits and discourage the display of others. We would speculate that when a group follows a highly prescriptive process such as that of the group project facilitator (see insert), the expression of members' personalities would be more restricted than the same group interacting in a less prescriptive manner.

Weak Situations *Weak situations* almost always encourage people to engage in behavior that exhibits the most prominent aspects of their personality or self-concept. Weak situations are not well defined in terms of the specific behaviors or communication style expected of participants. A group that consistently uses open discussion and does not enforce a focus rule gives its members a lot of room to maneuver. When a wider range of behavior is allowed by the situation, personal predispositions are more likely to influence a member's behavior. Snyder and Ickes have demonstrated how people often actively manage the fit between their personality and the situations they encounter. One strategy is to seek and interact more frequently in situations that match one's personal dispositions. A person who believes that he or she is a "natural leader" may join many more groups than will someone whose personality is more reticent. Another strategy is to try to redefine the situation during interaction so that one can more easily behave in accordance with a preferred self-concept. For instance, a person who prefers to dominate might suggest that the group not set too many ground rules, knowing that such rules might limit his or her opportunities to control the flow of discussion.

Activating Group Identity Another situational factor that can affect the prominence of personality displays is the salience of group identity. A number of social scientists have noted that individuals not only have several different self-identities but they also have numerous social identities. John Turner defines *social identity* as "those aspects of an individual's self-concept based on his or her social group membership."[5] He points out three levels of self-categorization that influence how one behaves:

1. *"Human identity"—self as human being.* When we conceive of the self in this way, we identify and emphasize common features shared with other members of the human species.
2. *"Social identity"—self as group members.* Here we identify the self in terms of *similarities* with members of a particular grouping (males, steel workers, yuppies) and *differences* from other groups (females, management, working class).
3. *"Personal identity"—self as unique individual.* At this level, we view our self in terms of how we differ from other group members. Personality differences are only prominent when this level of self-concept is activated.

Research has shown that when one of these levels is "activated" (or becomes prominent in our thinking), the other levels of identity seem to be "switched off." When people are encouraged to think in terms of group identity, for instance, they tend to view people not in the group in terms of stereotypes rather than as unique individuals. Activating the group identity also creates more intragroup cohesion and cooperation as members overlook each other's unique differences.[6] This suggests that situational factors such as competing against other groups will also limit the influence of personality and the tendency to evaluate each other in terms of personality differences. We do not know, however, how long members can sustain such a group identity without some internal communication (such as a conflict) triggering a return to the personal identity level.

So far, we have shown how personality can but does not always influence group members' behavior. Take the complex interplay of personality and situation into account as you read the following descriptions of research results. We believe that personality does influence group behavior but only under circumstances that do not constrain it. In the next section, you will learn how different personality characteristics predispose members to behave during group deliberations. If you couple this knowledge with an understanding of the situational factors described earlier, you will be in a much better position to know what to expect from the members of your group.

Personality and Typical Behavior in Groups

How might a given personality characteristic influence a person's behavior in a group decision-making setting? Researchers have studied so many different personality traits that a list of them would only confuse you. We limit our discussion here to those traits studied in a group context and focus on three primary dimensions of personality: dominance-submissiveness, friendly-unfriendly, and instrumental-emotional orientation.[7]

As you read, keep in mind our warning that some characteristics are likely to recede and others to emerge in different situations. When the situation calls for behavior relevant to a given dimension of personality, we can expect people who differ on that dimension to interact in quite different ways. For example, if a situation calls for dominant take-charge leadership and one member of the group has a more dominant personality than the others, we might expect that person to engage in more leadership behaviors. The success of those behaviors depends on whether or not the group interprets the behaviors as appropriate to its definition of the situation. Let us look at the perceptual and behavioral tendencies of people who differ on the three major dimensions of personality.

The Dominance Dimension: Dealing with Control

People differ greatly in the degree to which they try to control their circumstances or allow others to establish that control. This has obvious implications for groups. Individuals who know how and like to take charge of situations can help groups organize their tasks and provide leadership. And leaders cannot function without followers. The traits we will discuss along the dominance-submissiveness dimension include locus of control, need for control, authoritarianism, Machiavellianism, and self-monitoring.

Locus of Control Individuals generally believe that events in their lives are internally or externally controlled.[8] They think either their own behavior shapes events or forces outside of them determine what happens. *Internalizers* tend to believe that they are more in control—that whatever happens is the result of their own hard work and motivation or their own mistakes and lack of dedication. *Externalizers* tend to think that they have little control over the events that occur in their lives. They are more likely to find fate or big government or a cruel world responsible for the way things go. Some research suggests that the differences between internalizers and externalizers are more pronounced when negative things happen.[9] Both types may accept responsibility for successful outcomes, whereas the externalizers may give up more easily when things take a turn for the worse. In group efforts, externalizers may have trouble maintaining their commitment to a group that seems to be floundering; they may prematurely write the group off if they believe the odds are stacked against it.

Box 8.1

High Anxiety: Personal Tendencies That Inhibit Groups

One of the most consistent findings in the research on personality and group interaction is the negative impact of members who have what might be termed one of a family of anxious personalities. Different types of anxiety (manifest, achievement, and test anxiety), self-consciousness, communication apprehension, paranoia, sensitivity to rejection, depressive tendencies, and emotional instability are some of the personality types that belong to this "family." Their effects on group cohesion and decision making are varied but almost invariably negative.

Individuals who feel anxious in small groups have trouble establishing positive relations with their fellow members. They tend to talk less, take longer to respond when asked to participate, produce more tension and awkward silences, and bring up more irrelevant topics than other members do. In addition, they have difficulty producing positive nonverbal behaviors, such as smiling, eye contact, casual touching, relaxed body and gestures, and vocal expressiveness. These are all communication behaviors that enhance the development of cohesion. Self-conscious members are more likely to take criticism of their ideas personally and feel rejected by the group. As a result, they sulk and put a damper on the group's morale. A depressed person has the same negative effect on cohesiveness, morale, and group motivation.

In terms of the task dimension, highly anxious people conform more to group opinion, perhaps in the hope that they will be more accepted (and thus reduce some of their anxiety) or at least so they will not have to voice their objections. To make matters worse, anxious members tend to have very low aspirations. They do not expect their group to accomplish much and are easily satisfied with whatever outcomes the group does produce. Because they do not appear capable or interested in helping the group achieve its goals, apprehensive members are rarely consulted by the group. In effect, they become excess baggage that weighs the group down and saps much of its positive energy. (For a review of research on the influence of anxiety on group process, see Shaw, 1981.)

What can groups do to minimize these typical problems of the anxious group member? Perhaps the first step is for both anxious and nonanxious members to realize the negative effects of this behavioral pattern. Of course, an anxious person does not want to feel tense and does not really desire to see the group do poorly. But we suspect that such a person feels that he or she will do as little damage as possible by going along with the group and staying out of the way. This only makes the problem worse, however, because other group members sense the uneasiness but do not know why or how to deal with it. The anxious member would probably be better off admitting that he or she is shy and gets nervous when called on, but does

Box 8.1 (continued)

want to help the group do well. In turn, this admission should lead other members to be more understanding and more aware of their own role in improving a potentially negative group atmosphere. One of the premises of this text is that interaction patterns are produced not by single acts alone (the anxious person's hesitant delivery, for example) but by the combination of the act and the group's response (awkward silence or active listening and empathic understanding).

In short, the influence of almost any negative personal tendency on the group process can be managed if the group is alert to what is happening and wants to minimize its effects.

Additional reading:
Marvin Shaw, *Group Dynamics*, 3rd ed. (New York: McGraw-Hill, 1981), pp. 199–209.

An internal or external locus of control can also affect the judgments group members make of one another. Several researchers have discovered that internalizers are more likely to attribute deviant behavior to internal causes and then discourage or punish that behavior more severely. One common group norm is for members to prepare and bring relevant information and materials to meetings. If a member comes unprepared, an internalizer is more likely to be upset, believing that the individual chose not to prepare. Externalizers tend to perceive deviance more as the result of circumstances and are less likely to punish group members who deviate.[10] Suppose that one or more influential group members are externalizers. The preceding discussion suggests that they may hinder the group's efforts to make high-quality decisions. Can you think of positive contributions an externalizer might make? In what way could an internalizer have a negative impact on group interaction?

Need for Control Several decades ago William Schutz proposed a theory of interpersonal behavior: fundamental interpersonal relations orientation (FIRO).[11] He argued that individuals orient themselves toward others on the basis of three different needs: inclusion, affection, and control. (The needs for inclusion and affection will be discussed later in this chapter.) In terms of control, Schutz identified two types of people. He called the person who has a strong need to be in control an *autocrat*. Such a person likes to run the show and must feel that the group needs his or her guidance. He or she is likely to engage in many of the dominating behaviors mentioned in Chapter 4. It is hard for such a person to give up authority to anyone else. He or she may delegate responsibility to other group members, but typically reserves the right to evaluate that work. The autocrat usually pushes for his or her ideas and standards to become the group's ideas and standards. The *abdicrat*, on the other hand, has a strong need to be controlled. He or she looks to others for approval and tends to support group norms or the ideas of more powerful members.

Imagine how difficult it would be for a group of five or six autocrats to get along. The communication among group members would feature constant interruptions and conflict. No one would be able to dominate the others for very long. But a group composed of all abdicrats would be just as difficult, if not more so. When no one wants to take control, the group flounders about without direction. A typical group meeting might be filled with awkward attempts to seek information from each other, long silences, and few attempts to critique ideas or propose solutions.

Authoritarianism As its name suggests, the authoritarian personality has great respect for positions of authority or power. Such a person tends to be highly prejudiced, rigidly endorses conventional values, condemns those who disagree, submits to authority, and opposes subjective viewpoints.[12] When such people are in power, they demand respect and tend to be autocratic in their leadership style.[13] They expect other group members to follow their leadership without questioning it.

An authoritarian not assigned a position of authority takes on a highly subordinate role in relation to the group leader. He or she expects the formal leader to give orders and to make demands of the group and readily conforms to the ideas and opinions of high-status sources.[14] In terms of evaluating proposals and information, the authoritarian would judge their value based on the credibility of their sources. If a source represents a legitimate authority, the authoritarian would rarely question the information. Although credibility of sources is important, it is not the only criterion. The information may be out of date or irrelevant to the question the group has to address. But the authoritarian is often blinded by the light of the source itself. In terms of interaction with group members, a highly authoritarian person is likely to conform to the views of the group's leader, while showing little tolerance for those who disagree. For more information on this trait, see the classic *Authoritarian Personality* by Theodore Adorno and his colleagues or Milton Rokeach's *The Open and Closed Mind*.[15]

Machiavellianism The Machiavellian person thrives on manipulating other people in order to achieve his or her own goals. The term comes from Niccolò Machiavelli (1469–1527), author of *The Prince.* Machiavelli, distraught by the moral corruption of his fellow citizens and the weakness of the Italian states, felt that the only way to save his beloved Italy was for a "new prince" to carefully manipulate the people into submission. He described the necessary strategies in his admonitions to the Prince. Taken out of context, these strategies imply a ruthless approach to power, which is what the psychological construct of Machiavellianism is all about. Someone who is highly Machiavellian maintains a cool and detached exterior and does not get emotionally involved with either people or their causes.[16] Such a person is capable of single-mindedly pursuing his or her own strategy at the expense of and through the unwitting compliance of others.

High Machs seem to assume that people are fools waiting for someone to take advantage of them. How does such a person interact in a small group? First of all, high Machs tend to emerge as leaders.[17] They are adept at reading people and appearing to provide what the group wants. As a leader, the high Mach will serve the group well only if his or her goal and the group's goal coincide. If they diverge, the group will suffer. One problem is that the typical high Mach is so good at manipulating others that the group seldom catches on until it is too late. If a member does identify the high Mach and tries to alert the rest of the group, that member is in for a rough time. A high Mach can be ruthless and extremely unpleasant and seems to find ways to outfox an opponent. A high Mach can usually manipulate the group until it sees the opponent in a negative light.

How likely are you to encounter a high Mach in the groups you participate in? Evidence suggests that our culture is becoming more Machiavellian. The mean scores on the tests used to measure Machiavellianism have increased over the years since the scale was first administered.[18]

Self-Monitoring Another way that people establish control is by monitoring their presentations of themselves. A person who tries to adapt his or her self-image to fit the situation is called a high *self-monitor*.[19] Such an individual approaches a situation asking, "What kind of person does this situation call for and how can I be that person?" A low self-monitor tries to maintain a consistency in self-image across situations. He or she asks a different question: "What kind of situation is this and how can I be *me* in this situation?" Low self-monitors, more than other people, try to alter the situation to fit their own personal dispositions.

In group decision making, high self-monitors offer particular strengths and weaknesses. They are more flexible group members because sensitivity to changing circumstances enables them to be the kind of persons the group needs at the moment. In addition, high self-monitors tend to change "personas" against a backdrop of friendly behavior.[20] This suggests that group members are unlikely to be put off by the chameleonlike identity of the high self-monitor. The "changes" in personality are probably not even noticed because the behavior usually fits the situation. On the downside, high self-monitors are more susceptible to group pressure than low self-monitors are.[21] Driven to behave in accordance with their self-image, low self-monitors are predisposed to be more independent thinkers in a group context.

The Friendly Dimension: Dealing with Approach and Avoidance

While the control dimension of personality refers to how assertive one tends to be, the friendly dimension characterizes how positive or negative one is toward other people. At one end of the continuum are those people who like to be with others and are friendly and easily approachable. You might say these people "move toward" others. At the other extreme we find two types of people: those who "move against" others by being hostile or disagreeable and those who "move away" from others by being shy, anxious, or otherwise avoiding interaction. Several personality traits fall along this continuum, including the needs for inclusion and affection, self-esteem, sensitivity to rejection, and communication apprehension.

Need for Inclusion People have varying degrees of need for social contact and bonding.[22] William Schutz used the term *oversocials* for people with a very strong need for togetherness. They like to be with others and will often go out of their way to make friends and to be sure they are invited to parties. This need can be demonstrated in two ways: (1) in efforts to include others in one's own activities and (2) in more passive behavior designed to solicit invitations for inclusion from others. A group setting is a natural way for people to meet their needs for inclusion. *Undersocials* lack strong inclusion needs; being in a group is not as rewarding to them. They may not be as active or as concerned as others are about building a cohesive bond in the group.

Need for Affection The *overfriendly* person has a high need for emotionally close and personal relations with others. Such people offer and seek self-disclosures from other group members. They are uncomfortable until they know a lot about each group member. Overfriendly people may also be more immediate in group interaction by engaging in more eye contact, smiling, and casual touching. You would expect more direct expressions of affection ("I really like you guys") from such a person and also a greater need to be liked by everyone else. At the opposite extreme is the *underfriendly* individual, who values privacy over self-disclosure and expressions of affection. Such a person may like having a lot of casual friends (high inclusion) but not many close friends (low affection). He or she may also have a hard time praising members for their efforts in the group.

Some people may be easily identified as having strong or weak needs for control, affection, or inclusion, but most of us probably are moderates. One need may be greater at one time, only to give way to a different need later. Be aware of this mutability when interpreting the behavior of your fellow group members. Their behavior may often be the result of fluctuating interpersonal needs. Those underlying needs may have to be fulfilled in order for that member to more fully concentrate on the task at hand.

Members whose needs remain relatively constant and incompatible with others may have a more substantial impact on the group. Research by Schutz and others has demonstrated the importance of need compatibility among group members.[23] For instance, a group in which three members have very high needs for affection and two other members have very low needs is likely to splinter into subgroups. Establishing norms for how members should relate to one another socially would be very difficult. Unless the group recognizes that their subgroup interaction indicates members' differing orientations and not personal dislike, it may never find a way to work together successfully. Need orientations may also help explain why different groups can be successful without spending the same amount of time socializing (inclusion), becoming friends (affection), or fighting for the floor (control). If members do not have strong needs in these areas, they may be able to concentrate more on the task.

Most of us want to be liked and included in the activities of our groups. But many of our interpersonal needs are shaped by feelings we have about ourselves. If we like ourselves, it is much easier to be positive toward others. This makes self-esteem a significant trait among those on the friendly dimension.

Self-Esteem People who feel good about themselves and have a positive self-image approach communication situations quite differently from those who see themselves in a less positive light. In a recent summary of research, Howard Giles and Richard Street demonstrate how self-esteem affects the range of personality characteristics one exhibits. They show how high self-esteem is directly related to a person's willingness to attempt to influence others.[24] If a group member feels good about himself or herself, he or she is more likely to adopt one of several *assertive* self-presentations (being dominant, outgoing, or friendly), which is likely to influence the direction of the group. When self-esteem is low, a person enacts a more *defensive* self-presentation (being ingratiating, apprehensive, or submissive), thereby reducing his or her potential for influence. From a group perspective, the individual self-esteem of every member is very important. Members with high esteem are more likely to be fully functioning in terms of creativity, confidence, and willingness to test ideas critically. Members with low self-esteem may not trust their own ideas enough to express them to the group and will not likely test the ideas of others.

Sensitivity to Rejection When a person does not feel positive or confident, he or she needs a lot of positive feedback from others to bolster the weak ego. This produces even stronger needs for inclusion and affection, but also prompts the fear that others may not like you any more than you like yourself. Albert Mehrabian identifies the sensitive person as one who fears being slighted or disliked.[25] As a result of this fear, the person constantly looks for signs that other people are disinterested or do not like him or her. Such a person *expects* the outcome of interactions to be negative. Preoccupied with other people's reactions, the sensitive individual forgets to be sociable and friendly—the very behaviors that other people are most likely to respond to favorably.

People who are sensitive to rejection need to be handled carefully if they are to be productive group members. The group must demonstrate a clear acceptance of each member, while encouraging the sensitive person to verbalize his or her disagreements with the opinions of others. If this encouragement is not forthcoming, the sensitive person is likely to agree with everyone and create a false sense of consensus.

Communication Apprehension Fear or anxiety about communicating can also result from low self-esteem. *Communication apprehension* is the term used to describe people who experience anxiety across a wide range of situations, including group discussions. And according to the research of James McCroskey, nearly 15 to 20 percent of the U.S. population qualify as highly apprehensive.[26] What kind of communication behavior does this anxiety produce? As you might expect, it leads many people to become quiet nonparticipants in the group. When they do talk, the level of anxiety felt often translates into a lack of verbal fluency and a tense nonverbal delivery.[27] Some evidence indicates that highly apprehensive people may interject more tangential or off-target comments, presumably so that others will not expect much from them.[28] Many apprehensive people are also sensitive to rejection and may fear group criticism of their ideas as much as talking about them.[29] Many apprehensive people take the active listener role, providing nonverbal support for the ideas of others. When researchers have studied entire groups made up of either highly reticent or highly talkative members, the reticent groups tend to have lower levels of participation, fewer attempts to give or seek information, less coordination of activity, more task and less socially oriented discussions, lower satisfaction, and less attraction to their group.[30]

The verbal free-for-all inherent in such tools as brainstorming and open discussion inhibit the highly apprehensive members of a group. Recent research has shown that groups with apprehensive members may be better off if they use methods such as idea writing that require members to generate ideas on paper rather than voicing them aloud (see Chapter 6). Apprehensive members produce more ideas and are more satisfied when given the opportunity to help the group without having to talk a lot.[31]

The Instrumental Dimension: Dealing with Tasks and Emotions

The third dimension of personality is concerned with an individual's general tendency to be emotional (expressive) versus analytical and task oriented (instrumental). Emotional people tend to be more spontaneous, more dramatic, and more open about how they feel. They are also more likely to take an intuitive approach to problem solving. Instrumental people are often highly task oriented and sticklers for detail and organization; they also use logical analysis to solve most problems. Researchers have found, on average, that males in our culture have more instrumental personalities and females more expressive personalities.[32] Two particular personality traits that fall along this continuum are relevant to group interaction: tolerance for ambiguity and communicator style.

Tolerance for Ambiguity Some people need or prefer things to be spelled out very clearly. They have a low *tolerance for ambiguity*. Others seem to enjoy the mystery inherent in an ambiguous message or the challenge imposed by a difficult situation. For people who tolerate ambiguity differently, group decision making itself can often present a problem. First of all, some problems or tasks are more ambiguous. Complex problems cannot always be easily defined. The group may have to grapple with the problem for a while before it can clearly specify goals.

In addition, people show markedly different preferences for the way group interaction is managed. Members with a low tolerance for ambiguity prefer a highly structured and orderly set of task procedures. They are likely to ask for procedural clarification, make goal-related statements, summarize frequently, and announce when the group changes topics. In contrast, groups of people with high tolerances for ambiguity interrupt each other more, engage in more side conversations, and switch back and forth between task-related and socially oriented issues.[33] For the person with a low tolerance for ambiguity; the preference for procedural order is accompanied by a dislike of tasks involving a large amount of conflicting information or complex and unstructured tasks. This type of person wants the facts to speak clearly. In contrast, the individual who tolerates ambiguity well seems to thrive when confronted with conflicting information.[34] You can imagine how these two types might respond to the question of whether or not certain information is relevant to their project.

In one recent study, researchers assigned people to groups based on their "preference for procedural order," a concept closely linked with tolerance for ambiguity. Groups were thus composed exclusively of people with a high preference for order or a low preference. Each group was then given a problem to solve using either a highly or a loosely structured discussion format. The results indicated that members with a high preference for order worked best with the highly structured format and did not work well at all with the loose format. Groups with a low preference for order worked effectively using both types of formats, although they did perform better with a loosely structured one.[35] This suggests the importance of keeping members' tolerance for ambiguity and procedural order in mind when choosing discussion procedures.

Both types of people can be useful (as well as harmful) to a group. The person who does not tolerate ambiguity will encourage procedural clarity, goal identification, and other forms of organization. This person may also be anxious, worrisome, and negative in the face of complex, unstructured tasks. The individual with high tolerance will remain undaunted by such tasks and will present and permit multiple points of view. At the same time, this person may contribute to ambiguity and conflict by interrupting others, changing the focus, or introducing too many ideas at one time. Ideally, the group will allow each type of person to function in ways that help it.

Communicator Style One traitlike characteristic that is especially relevant to group interaction is *communicator style*, which is the way one verbally and nonverbally interacts to indicate how a message should be understood.[36]

Robert Norton has identified nine different styles. (See Figure 8.1 for definitions and examples of each style.) You will notice that some styles, such as the relaxed, attentive, and contentious styles, fall closer to the instrumental end of the continuum. The open, animated, dramatic, and impression-leaving styles are more representative of the expressive personality. Most people do not adopt one style exclusively but tend to develop a style profile—a combination of several styles. For instance, say that Mark and Mary Lou have very similar styles. Both tend to be dramatic, animated, and impression leaving. Mark is also contentious, while Mary Lou is very attentive. The group probably knows exactly where Mark stands on the issues and why he takes those positions. But Mary Lou may be helpful in a different way. She can help the group understand and remember the significant points of agreement because her attentive style enables her to mark the consensus of the group. Try to identify your own style profile and think of ways that it might be advantageous (or disadvantageous) in group decision making.

Relating the Three Dimensions of Personality

With so many personality traits having been studied, it is difficult to know how to evaluate any given individual in terms of personality. Keeping in mind our earlier warnings about typecasting a person as having a single, fixed personality, we suggest that you try to determine how a given person usually behaves on each of the three dimensions we have investigated. Is the member primarily predisposed to be dominant or submissive, more or less friendly, and more instrumental or expressive? You might pay particular attention to how this person behaves in situations that we earlier defined as weak ones that allow greater room for personality influences. Note the particular combination of traits that would define his or her most prominent self-concept. Then over time, note how he or she alters the presentation of self as situations change so you have a general sense of the individual's various self-concepts or personal identities that he or she may call on in different situations. As your observations improve, you will begin to recognize when members are responding on the basis of their self-identities, the group identity, their perception of the situation, or some combination of these factors.

Consider an example of how we might view a particular group member in terms of these factors. Suppose you note that Sally rarely initiates any communication and never challenges anyone else's ideas. She would be categorized as more submissive on the first dimension. You also notice that she seems motivated by a high need for inclusion, tempered somewhat by her sensitivity to rejection and moderately high level of communication apprehension. She is not unfriendly, but does fall closer to the negative end of the friendly dimension. Finally, Sally will do anything the group asks of her. She is highly task oriented.

What kind of communication can we expect from Sally, and what kind of meaning should we attach to what she says? And how can we help Sally be a more successful group member? In terms of the social dimension, her combined

Nine Communicator Styles

Communicator Style	Verbal and Nonverbal Manifestations
Dominant	Tendency to come on strong, take charge of social situations, speak frequently, and otherwise control conversations.
Dramatic	Likes to act out the point physically and vocally. Tells jokes, stories, and often exaggerates to make the point. Speech tends to be picturesque.
Contentious	Loves to argue, quick to challenge others, precise about defining things, and often insists that others show proof to back up their arguments. Once wound up, hard to stop.
Animated	Very expressive nonverbally: constantly gesturing, using a wide variety of facial expressions; face and eyes usually reveal emotions and feelings.
Impression-leaving	What this person says, and the way he or she says it, is almost always memorable. People usually don't forget such a person easily.
Relaxed	Comes across as calm and collected during interaction, especially under pressure. The rhythm and flow of speech is rarely affected by feelings of nervousness.
Attentive	Listens to others very carefully and lets them know it by giving nonverbal feedback such as eye contact and nodding. Shows empathy and can usually repeat back exactly what the other said.
Open	Readily reveals personal information. Openly expresses emotions.
Friendly	Gives positive feedback to recognize, encourage, and reinforce other people.

Figure 8.1 Because a group member's style as a communicator has a strong influence on the group's interaction, it is advantageous to identify your own style and analyze the ways your style could help or hinder the group decision-making process. [Derived from Robert Norton, *Communicator Style: Theory, Application, and Measures* (Beverly Hills, Calif.: Sage, 1983), pp. 64–72.]

traits suggest that Sally is more likely to behave in subtle ways to achieve inclusion. For instance, she might ask, "Are we doing anything before the next meeting?" in hopes that someone will suggest and include her in some activity. Or whenever she overhears other members making plans to get together socially, she may try to catch their eye or hang around after the meeting in hopes of being included. In other words, her unique combination of traits means that she is less direct in trying to achieve inclusion than someone who is always asking others to join them. In the task and procedural dimensions, we might expect to see Sally contribute more once she really feels accepted as a part of the group. But other group members will probably have to draw out her contributions.

We might also discover that there are specific strong situations in which Sally is much friendlier than normal. For instance, when group discussion breaks down into several one-on-one side conversations, Sally may view those episodes as requiring a friendlier face. She may be considerably more animated and less task oriented in such situations.

You also need to recognize how the flow of communication among group members contributes to each member's behavior. We have known for some time that interaction on the dominant-submissive dimension operates differently from interaction on the friendly-unfriendly dimension.[37] Behavior along the dominance-submission dimension usually provokes its opposite: Dominance elicits obedience; submissive behavior prompts leadership by someone else. But behavior along the friendly-unfriendly dimension tends to be reciprocated. Being critical often provokes an equal amount of hostility, while showing affection generally gets a positive response. No specific research has addressed how interaction on the instrumental-expressive dimension operates, but we suspect that it works in a reciprocal fashion as well.

Summary

The influences on how we communicate in groups are many. Personality is only one of them, and it interacts with many other factors. In this chapter, we have seen that the concept of personality itself is complex. Most people have several different conceptions of themselves and use these varying self-concepts in different situations. We also noted that most of us overestimate the influence of personality when observing the behavior of others, especially if that behavior is negative in some way. We saw how the definition of the situation influences the behavior of group members and how some situations encourage or discourage behaviors that members might be predisposed to perform due to personality.

In addition, we explored the types of communication behaviors we can expect from group members when particular self-concepts are activated. We organized the various self-concepts along three major dimensions or aspects of personality: dominance, friendliness, and an instrumental versus expressive orientation. Dominant personalities are more likely to exert greater influence on task and procedural matters of importance to the group, especially when there are no formal procedures to constrain or equalize participation among group members. Those who exhibit friendly personalities can have a dramatic impact on the development of a group's social dimension. Instrumental types tend to be very task oriented and analytical and are often annoyed by the overly sentimental and emotional concerns of more expressive persons. Differences in all three of these dimensions can make it very difficult for members to behave in compatible ways that will foster goal achievement and cohesiveness.

For now, we hope you have developed an appreciation for the diversity of personal dispositions that individuals bring to the group setting. Effective decision-making groups are made from these raw materials. And while it is not easy to manage all of these individual elements, the group that dedicates itself to doing so will benefit the most.

GroupQuests: Discussion Questions

1. Why do you think most people fall prey to the fundamental attribution error? In group interaction, does this error make personality more of an issue than it should be?
2. Discuss how activating one of the three levels of self-identity can influence group interaction. As a group leader, under what conditions would you want to try to get group members to think of themselves as human beings, group members, or unique persons? How could you activate the self-concepts of members at each of these levels?
3. Compatibility among personalities is stressed in this chapter. Given the various personality dimensions and types discussed, what composition of types do you think would create an ideal group of five to seven members? Keep in mind the various skills and attitudes necessary for effective decision making. Would the personality mix you have created be likely to have all of these skills? Finally, how might group communication overcome potential personality differences?

GroupWorks: Group Activities

1. Each member of the group should complete Discussion Question 3 prior to meeting as a group. Each one should make a chart or model describing the personality types he or she thinks would be most compatible and effective. In addition, all should list the reasons why they think the group would be both compatible and effective. Using a round-robin, have each person present his or her model to the group and explain the reasoning. The group should respond with questions or try to point out potential incompatibilities or problems that might limit group effectiveness. Once each member's model has been discussed, try to reach consensus on a group version of this model. Present the results to the rest of the class.
2. As a group, discuss an appropriate set of ground rules for managing "personality clashes" among group members. First make a list of five to seven common types of clashes—for example, always disagreeing with other members' ideas. Then identify ground rules to minimize such clashes before they get started. Make sure the ground rules are realistic and specific enough that a group would really follow them.
3. Read *The Brethren: Inside the Supreme Court* by Bob Woodward and Scott Armstrong, (New York: Simon & Schuster, 1979) or the play *Twelve Angry Men* by Reginald Rose (in "Twelve Angry Men and Other Plays," *American Scholastic Scope Magazine*,

1971). Write a brief description of the key group members, their personal dispositions, and any clashes with other members that seem to be based on personality differences. Suggest several ways that these problems could have been minimized or used in a more constructive manner.

4. If you are involved in an ongoing observation of a real decision-making group, analyze the individuals who make up that group—their knowledge, skills, attitudes, and personal dispositions. Try to determine how compatible the group is and what its membership needs are. Write a job description for recruiting a new member for the group. Make sure this new recruit will help fill in some of the group's missing ingredients. (You may want to review the skills and attitudes described in Chapter 3 before doing this observation.)

GroupActs: Practical Applications

Now that each member of the group has read this chapter, it is time to take stock of your group's skills, attitudes, knowledge, and personal dispositions. Each person should conduct his or her own self-analysis by making a chart listing:

a. Any individual skills or expertise that he or she believes to be relevant to the group's tasks. (See Chapter 3.)
b. Any prevalent attitudes toward working in groups in general and this group in particular. (See Chapter 3.)
c. Perceptions of his or her most prominent personality traits.

Once the self-analysis is completed, do similar (anonymous) portraits of each member in the group. Write down your impressions of the others' skills and personalities. These portraits should be typed to preserve anonymity. Your instructor will collect these perceptions and give each group member a packet containing the other anonymous portraits. Each member then writes a brief comparison of his or her own self-analysis with the group's perception of himself or herself. Such a comparison should help you determine how well you are communicating your skills and dispositions to the group. It may also be useful in setting personal goals for improvement during the rest of the term.

CHAPTER 9

The Relationship Level: Leaders and Followers

Our culture attaches a great deal of importance to leaders. This is true in large and small groups alike. Many people believe that having a good leader is the single most important aspect of an effective decision-making group. If you are one of those people, you may have expected to see the leadership chapter among the first three or four chapters in this text. But we chose to discuss leadership at this point in your reading for a very specific reason. We believe that the best preparation for group leadership is a thorough understanding of communication and group processes, and the best formula for leadership is a willingness to put that knowledge to work. Although there are almost as many approaches to leadership as there are experts who have studied it, you will not be able to effectively apply any approach unless you understand how groups work. Because you have already been exposed to many different aspects of the group process, you are now in a position to think about leadership as an opportunity to integrate and apply what you have learned and will learn in the remaining chapters. To help you do that, we will discuss a number of traditional (and some untraditional) approaches to understanding leadership. As you review what others have said about leadership, we hope you will form your own ideas of what leadership is. And we think you will come to the same conclusion that we have: Effective leadership is always possible when group members understand group process.

Leaders and Leadership

The failure to distinguish between leaders and leadership can cause some confusion. A leader is a person whom other members view as having a legitimate position of influence in the group. He or she is an individual that others expect to provide them with leadership. A leader sometimes emerges from the pack and at other times is assigned a formal role from the outset. The confusion arises when we think of leadership as the sole province of a single person. We view leadership as a process of influencing the group's task, social, and procedural efforts. As a process, leadership always involves more than one person; it implies a relationship between leader and followers. A significant part of that relationship is the followers' willingness to be led. Furthermore, the process involves a set of leadership behaviors, any one of which could be performed by any member of the group. With these distinctions in mind, several different forms of group leadership are possible:

- A single formal leader may be assigned responsibility for and actually perform all or most of the leadership behaviors in the group.
- A single formal leader may be assigned, but other group members may actually perform many leadership behaviors.
- A single emergent leader may take responsibility for and perform most of the leadership behaviors.
- A single emergent leader may assume responsibility for leadership, while still encouraging or permitting others to perform some leadership behaviors.
- A pattern of shared leadership may develop in which no one person emerges as *the* leader, but leadership functions are still performed in a timely fashion.
- Little or no leadership is provided by any member of the group.

No matter what form group leadership takes, there is always the issue of the *quality* of leadership provided. A single leader can be effective or ineffective, as can a system of shared leadership. A common lament in groups that fail is the claim, "We didn't have a leader. We just couldn't get going." Some people, on the other hand, are uncomfortable about giving any one person a lot of power and responsibility: "The job is too big for one person." "Give a guy a little power and it goes to his head. He tries to run everything." So while people often want leadership provided, they are also concerned that it not be too dictatorial.

A leader can emerge or be chosen. Either way, a group runs some risk that the leader may turn out to be a tyrant. If a leader is appointed, he or she may believe the group has provided a license to run the show as the leader sees fit. In groups where a leader emerges from the ranks, there is a tendency for more dominant personalities to outlast other bids. So what is a group to do? Should you appoint a leader, allow one to emerge, or bank on a system of shared leadership?

An individual with expert knowledge or skill relevant to the group's task may be perceived as a leader.

The Case for a Single Leader

Conventional wisdom suggests that a group should have a single leader. Studies show that membership satisfaction is usually higher when members can identify and agree about who is in the leadership role.[1] Perhaps members feel more comfortable when someone bears the burden of responsibility. But should this issue be decided early on or be allowed to emerge as part of the natural group process? Julia Wood, Gerald Phillips, and Douglas Pederson have been among the most outspoken advocates for appointed leadership.[2] They argue that the leadership position is so important that it needs to be dealt with at the outset. They cite several reasons for appointing a leader:

- Most groups have designated leaders. This simple "fact of life" should prompt any training group to prepare itself for the way of the world.
- Shared leadership is an unnecessary gamble. There is no guarantee that all members will be sufficiently capable and motivated to provide leadership when they do not have to.
- Counting on a leader to emerge wastes valuable time and also risks the chance that no leadership will surface.
- An appointed leader has the legitimate authority to settle disputes when the group cannot reach consensus.

- The group has someone ultimately responsible for its products and procedures and the maintenance of a productive climate.

You may recognize other advantages that accrue when a leader is selected. For instance, an appointed leader is the group's natural representative for maintaining contact with other groups.

The emergence of a single leader, while a risk in some ways, also has some advantages over appointing a leader. As we saw in Chapter 2, a group is likely to settle on its leader during the "emergence phase" of decision development. From a more descriptive perspective, this timing offers several advantages:

- The group (or whoever assigns the leader) always runs the risk of not appointing the best person for the job. Letting a leader emerge gives the group time to observe and assess the capabilities of the various contenders for the title.
- By the time a leader emerges, he or she will have a much better sense of group expectations and norms, which should enable the leader to be a more effective organizer and motivator. An appointed leader would have had to impose structure without knowing how well it would fit the group.
- There is less likelihood of resentment toward the leader who is not appointed because the group has had time to make more of an informed choice in its selection of a leader.

The claim that emergent leadership wastes valuable time can be countered somewhat by the knowledge that the group and the leader-to-be are making very important judgments during the initial phases of development such as determining what kind of leadership is appropriate for the group. The emergent process also minimizes the chances of one person dominating the early stages in which the group defines the nature of the problem and possible solutions. In the absence of a defined leader, the group is less likely to conform to the opinions of the person in such a high-status position. Organizations traditionally assign leadership roles, but that does not prevent leadership from emerging. Groups commonly have both a formal structure (with a designated leader) and an informal one (with an emergent leader who really motivates and organizes the group). Past practice in organizations is not necessarily good practice. Why not assign formal titles to people *after* they have discovered the role they perform best in their work group?

The Case for Shared Leadership

Whether a leader emerges or is assigned, the focus is still on the *person* who performs leadership functions most of the time. The shared leadership perspective places a greater emphasis on the *process* of leadership. The assumption is that if leadership is any behavior that moves a group closer to its goal or helps improve social relations, then it is not the prerogative of any one individual. In action, shared leadership means that any member who recognizes what kind of behavior needs to occur— whether task, procedural, or relational— can ask for or perform that behavior. Here are some advantages of such an approach:

- Members develop overlapping specializations. If more than one member becomes proficient at summarizing and integrating information, or identifying appropriate procedures, or any other leadership behavior, then the group can always function, even when some members are absent or have a bad day.
- Members can still develop unique roles, but one's personal role in the group is likely to include specializing in one or more aspects of leadership. Because the leadership role is complex and demanding, a single person is unlikely to be equally skilled at all of its facets.
- Shared leadership promotes a greater degree of responsibility and participation among group members. If everyone is responsible for providing leadership, no one can sit back and "let someone else do it."

Shared leadership is not a panacea. Members are still likely to compete with one another in specific areas of leadership and confusion will occasionally occur. It is not always possible to establish a climate for shared leadership in groups that have already built traditions, routines, and expectations around the standard idea of a single leader. As we will see later, some task and situational factors affect the type of leadership the group needs. But when circumstances call for it, and members want to make it work, the advantages of shared leadership outweigh the difficulties.

There is no shortage of theories about what leadership is and how it works. Not surprisingly, most theories assume that leadership resides in a particular person. We will now explore several of these approaches and then talk about how they can help us steer our groups in a productive direction.

Alternative Approaches to Group Leadership

Think for a moment about questions you have heard others ask about leaders or leadership. What kind of person makes a good leader? Are leaders born or made? Why, for instance, did a leader like Winston Churchill get dumped after leading England through World War II? In what ways was Adolph Hitler a good leader? What were John F. Kennedy's weaknesses as a leader? What leadership qualities did Harriet Tubman have? The questions that we ask dictate the answers we seek. This is a powerful truth. It suggests that there are many different angles on the leadership issue, some of which have not been explored because we have not yet asked the right questions. Let us look at some of the questions researchers and theorists have asked about leadership. You may be surprised at some of the answers.

Personality and Leadership: The Trait Approach

Two questions dominated the thinking and research about leadership during the first half of this century. Researchers sought to answer two questions: "How are leaders different from nonleaders?" and "What personality characteristics are associated with leadership?" The assumption behind this research was that leaders have specific innate qualities that set them apart from the crowd. Perhaps you can identify personal qualities that you think made Martin Luther King, Jr., Margaret Thatcher, or Lee Iacocca effective as leaders. Researchers felt that if they could only identify the right personality traits, then the best people could be selected to lead groups.

The early research showed some promise; several studies reported apparently similar results. Summarizing this research, Ralph Stogdill noted consistent findings regarding fourteen different personality traits associated with leadership.[3] Later, L. F. Carter grouped these traits into three categories:[4]

- *Group goal facilitation.* Skills that enable a leader to help a group reach its goals, for example, intelligence, insight, knowing how to get things done, scholarship ability, and adaptability.
- *Group sociability.* Traits necessary for building and maintaining cohesion and good working relationships, such as sociability, responsibility, cooperativeness, and popularity.
- *Individual prominence.* Traits that produce a desire to be recognized by the group—initiative, self-confidence, persistence, socioeconomic status, and participation in the group process.

But a closer look at these studies revealed several weaknesses with the trait approach. A laundry list of traits is fine in the abstract, but it does not predict who will become the leader in specific instances. Fisher criticized this approach on the grounds that it does not explain why (1) a person may emerge as the leader in one group but not in other groups; (2) someone may achieve a leadership position but fail to maintain it; or (3) some leaders are better than others.[5] Good leaders do not, for instance, have more of these traits than bad leaders have. Fisher and many others have declared the trait approach to be a dead end. Personality may be too elusive to measure precisely and the group process too complex to be explained this easily. One sign that these recommendations have been heeded is the lack of research on leadership traits over the past twenty-five years.

A Consistent Demeanor: The Style Approach

In response to the lack of success of the trait approach, researchers began rephrasing their questions. Instead of asking "What type of *person* . . . ?" researchers turned the question to "What type of *leader* is more effective?" The attention is less on how a leader emerges and more on how he or she leads. More specifically, the researcher looks at the kind of overall relationship the leader develops with his or her followers. This approach reduces the issue of complexity, because it is much easier to typecast leaders than to try to typecast everyone else. In fact, only three types of leaders have consistently emerged in this research:

- *Autocratic.* This kind of leader generally supervises and directs the group effort. He or she assumes ultimate authority and largely expects things to be done "his way" or "her way." The leader-member relationship is clearly one of following the leader. Members are expected to be passive when generating procedures and big ideas, but active in carrying out the leader's initiatives.
- *Democratic.* In contrast to the autocrat, the democratic leader tries to involve members in discussion and decision making. He or she tries to maximize input from members and seeks to identify the consensus or majority view on most issues. The relationship with members is participatory. He or she leads by example and by trying to stimulate members to do their best work.
- *Laissez-faire.* This is a hands-off approach to leadership. The leader assumes that members are both able and willing to function in their respective roles. He or she develops a relationship of trust and an expectation that the leader will only be called on when members run into problems they cannot handle or work out among themselves. The leader is, for the most part, just another member of the group, although he or she may still assume responsibility for the ultimate group product.

Research comparing the different leadership styles has produced some interesting results.[6] In general, both autocratic and democratic styles spur greater productivity than does the laissez-faire style, but in different ways. Autocratic groups tend to be more efficient, making fewer errors in structured tasks and working better under stressful conditions. Democratic groups, while taking more time, tend to produce decisions of higher quality than the other groups, especially when time and stress are not serious factors.[7] Most studies also reveal that the greatest levels of membership satisfaction are attained under democratically led groups. One study demonstrated the difficulty in establishing an effective democratic style. Both the most and least effective groups were headed by democratic leaders.[8] The laissez-faire style has been given the roughest treatment in the research literature. It has seldom been reported as an effective way to lead, but we will see later that this style does have some merit in the situational approach to leadership.

One of the assumptions behind the styles approach is that leaders maintain a single style throughout the life of the group. This may not always be the case. In most of the laboratory studies on leadership style, leaders have been trained to behave according to a consistent style over a relatively brief time span. In more natural settings, group members have usually been asked to report their *perceptions* of the leader's style. This can be a problem because members may summarize how the leader behaves most of the time, thus ignoring how the leader actually alters his or her style on occasion.

Another difficulty with this approach is that perceptions of the autocratic style may be so negative that it is not given a fair trial. Our culture preaches democracy at every turn, yet there are clearly situations in which an autocratic style works best. Military situations offer a good example. If the leader of a combat group caught under cross fire consults the rest of the group before barking out "orders" based on group consensus, the group probably will not survive long enough to tell of its "success." In some situations, a "benevolent dictator" may be a group's best hope. We know of one faculty group ruled with an iron hand by a person who knew where all the administration's skeletons were hidden. As a result, this person protected the group from an administration that would have preferred to do away with its department.

Fisher argued that the so-called preference for democratic leadership reflected in research studies was an artificial one. He believed that members probably respond better to a democratic style initially, but that this was likely to dissipate over time. Viewing the task and social dimensions to be interrelated, he claimed that the early success of an autocratic style on the task dimension (efficiency) would eventually lead to an increase in satisfaction as members took pride in their accomplishments.[9] We cannot point to any research that validates Fisher's theory, but it cannot be easily refuted either.

Much of the research on leadership style indicates that situational factors make a particular style more or less appropriate. This finding has led researchers to develop more complex models of the leadership process, which can be summarized as situational approaches.

Adapting to Changing Circumstances: The Situational Approach

This perspective tries to identify the relevant aspects of a group's situation and then determine the kind of leadership that would be most effective under those circumstances. The most common situational variables that have been studied include:

- *Task dimensions.* Any aspect of the task itself—the type of task, its clarity, degree of structure, novelty, difficulty,
- *Social structure.* Any variables that affect how group members work together—group history and norms, work habits, decision schemes, level of cohesiveness.
- *Physical environment.* Any aspect of the physical setting in which group meetings take place—room size and design, comfort level, seating patterns.
- *Environmental constraints.* Any external demands placed on the group by other groups, the organizational culture, or the task delegator—deadlines, demands for quality, competition with other groups, organization-wide norms.

- *Leader characteristics.* Any qualities typical of the person in the leadership position—personality, skills, preferred leadership style, motivations.
- *Member characteristics.* Any traits of the individual group members—skills, personalities, expectations.

Given the large number of situational factors identified, you can imagine how difficult it is to get a good reading of a situation and then modify one's leadership approach to create a better fit. Most of the models developed to explain leadership in situational terms focus on only a few of these characteristics. It may not be possible to summarize all of these influences into a simple prescription for an appropriate leadership style to govern every situation. Before we give up on the situational perspective, however, let us look at two of the theories that researchers have developed.

Fiedler's Contingency Model of Leadership Effectiveness For his model of the fit between leadership style and situation, Fred Fiedler studied over 1,600 group leaders and measured the leader's task-oriented or relationship-oriented style of leadership.[10] Note the similarities here with autocratic (task-oriented) and democratic (relationship-oriented) leadership styles. Fiedler felt that three major situational factors were crucial: (1) how much power the leader's position granted him or her, (2) the degree to which a group's task could be structured or programmed, and (3) the nature of the leader's personal relationships with group members. Fiedler concluded that task-oriented leaders were more successful in either high-control or low-control situations. In a *high-control situation*, leader-member relations are good and the task is highly structured. In a *low-control situation*, leader-member relations are poor, the group is uncooperative, and the task is highly unstructured.

The power afforded by a leader's position did not seem to make as much difference as the nature of the task and the leader's relations with the group. In both situations a task-oriented leader is likely to focus energy on task productivity. In the high-control situation, the task-oriented leader will be relaxed due to group acceptance and can concentrate on moving the group through the task step by step. In the low-control situation, the task-oriented leader essentially defines the task for the group and must maintain a firm hand to ensure that the group does its work.

The relationship-oriented leader, who places a higher priority on group relations, will not fare well under either of these extreme conditions. In the high-control situation with its structured task, the more democratic leader seems to have difficulty leading a group through an already-defined sequence of steps. The tendency will be to ask for group input when it is not really needed. In the low-control situation, the leader may be too concerned about the poor relations and not enough about the yet-to-be-defined task. The relationship-oriented leader will be most effective in *moderate-control situations*. There are two types of moderate-control situations: (1) In the moderately favorable situation, leader-member relations are good and the task is unstructured; (2) in the moderately unfavorable situation, leader-member relations are poor and the task is highly structured. Perhaps you can see why the relationship-oriented leader would perform well under these circumstances. When relations among members are already good, the leader can focus on making sense of the task. In the moderately unfavorable condition, the leader can afford to seek improvement in group relations because the task is relatively simple and does not require as much attention. The task-oriented leader, on the other hand, may push too hard for the quick fix when the task is ambiguous and may be seen as overbearing when the task is relatively simple.

In summary, Fiedler's model suggests that task structure and member relations are more important than other situational factors. It also offers some specific guidelines for determining the type of leadership style that will work best under each set of conditions.

Hersey and Blanchard's Situational Theory of Leadership Paul Hersey and Kenneth Blanchard developed another situational perspective.[11] As with Fiedler, Hersey and Blanchard believed that different leadership styles would be more effective under certain circumstances. They focused on only two situational factors: the maturity level of the group and the type of power base the leader has developed. We will look at these two factors momentarily, but first we need to examine Hersey and Blanchard's conception of leadership styles.

They identified four distinct leadership styles, based on the degree to which the leader emphasizes concern for the task or concern for people and group relations. Figure 9.1 shows how the following four styles reflect these concerns:

- *Telling style.* In this task-oriented approach, the leader makes decisions and tells the group what to do and how to carry out assignments.
- *Selling style.* This leader presents a preferred approach and then tries to convince the group to follow his or her lead, selling the group his or her ideas. This style reflects a high concern for both task and people; the leader still directs what the task will be, but respects the members' right to disagree.
- *Participating style.* Encouraging the group's involvement by seeking the full range of its ideas and possible solutions, the leader either makes a decision or asks for the group's help in deciding. In this people-oriented approach, the assumption is that if you get members involved, the task will get done.
- *Delegating style.* The leader essentially assigns the decision-making process to the group as a whole. He or she may participate in that process, but does not exert any more influence than any other member. There is little concern for either the task or the people involved; the leader feels certain that effort on both dimensions will continue without any prodding.

Although the styles have different names, they are similar to previously mentioned styles. (See Figure 9.2 for a comparison of labels.) According to

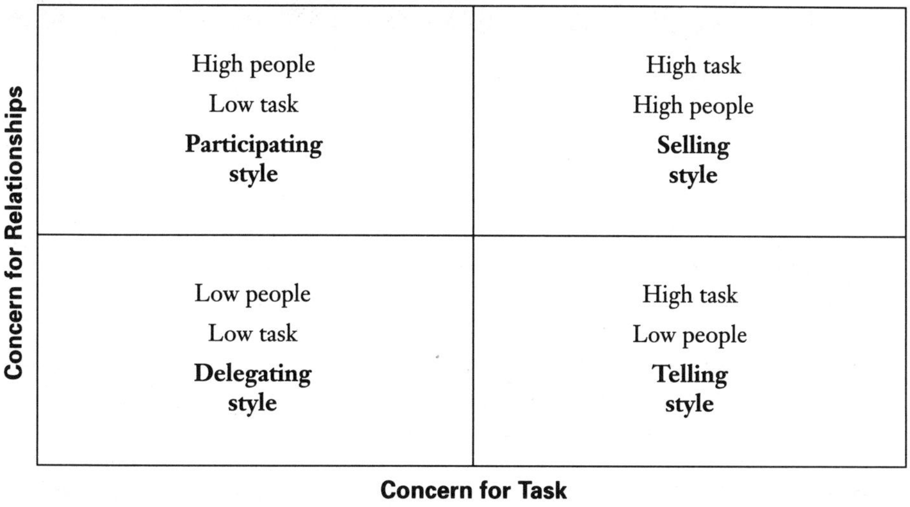

Concern for Relationships	High people Low task **Participating style**	High task High people **Selling style**
	Low people Low task **Delegating style**	High task Low people **Telling style**
	Concern for Task	

Figure 9.1 Emphasis on task and relationships in Hersey and Blanchard's leadership styles.

Hersey and Blanchard, the effectiveness of a given style depends a great deal on the maturity of the followers.

For any leader or would-be leader, the starting point should be an analysis of the people he or she hopes to lead. For Hersey and Blanchard, this analysis starts with an assessment of members' maturity. They discuss several components of maturity, but the two that are deemed most important are the members' ability and willingness to do the job. Ability to do the job includes the technical knowledge each member possesses and other related skills that might be needed to complete the task competently. Willingness to do the job is more of a motivational question: Are members favorably disposed to being responsible for managing the task at hand? An analysis of maturity might also include the group's track record in setting high but obtainable goals. If the group consistently underachieves or sets goals it cannot reach, you might question the overall wisdom of its members. You might also consider the psychological maturity of group members—their feelings of self-confidence and self-respect. If members have uniformly low opinions of themselves, they may not be willing to take the necessary risks to do a good job.

In Hersey and Blanchard's view, the maturity level of a group is likely to change over time, and an effective leader will adapt his or her style as the group matures. Figure 9.3 depicts the relationship between group maturity and leader style. The lowest level of maturity exists when most group members are inexperienced with the task and not very motivated to improve their knowledge or skills—they are unable and unwilling. Imagine a group of computer-phobic clerical workers being asked to recommend which of several

Autocratic	Task oriented	Telling
Democratic	Relationship oriented	Selling Participating
Laissez-faire		Delegating

Figure 9.2 A comparison of leadership style terminology.

computer systems and word-processing packages the company should buy. With very little knowledge of computer systems and a negative attitude toward their use, could this group make a good decision on its own? The most appropriate leadership style for such a group would be an autocratic telling style. The leader's emphasis on the task is crucial for much the same reasons that Fiedler suggested. It is not very helpful to focus on improving relationships (or motivation) until members know how to perform the task.

However, some groups start out with high hopes and lots of energy, even though they have little collective experience with the task. Such groups start as unable but willing. As a result, the leader must pay attention to both the task and social dimensions simultaneously. Suppose that in spite of its inexperience with computers, the clerical group was intrigued with the potential of a computerized office system. The leader's style would have to be task oriented because the members do not know what they are doing. The necessity of a social orientation (concern for people) may not be so obvious. Hersey and Blanchard see it as necessary to *sustain* motivation because members are not yet able to derive any intrinsic motivation from their task performance. The "selling" approach combines task instruction with a greater degree of involvement by group members. Because of its interest in computerizing, the clerical group would probably appreciate being shown the advantages of different systems and being allowed to voice concerns on the issue.

Once members develop an understanding of the task, they move to one of the higher maturity levels. If the group has yet to muster the desire to work hard, it is considered to be able but unwilling. Groups often lack motivation at this point because they now know what to do and resent what appears to be unnecessary direction from the leader. Consider the clerical group at the lowest maturity level. Suppose that over time its members were trained to use several different word-processing packages. Their skills improved but not their attitude. For the leader to be effective, he or she would need to shift styles and attend primarily to the social dimension. The participating style accomplishes this by giving members more responsibility for the task and a little more warmth and positive feedback from the leader. The leader might have to tell the group that it has no choice in the decision to computerize the office, but will be given a chance to influence which software to purchase.

If and when a group reaches the highest level of maturity—able and

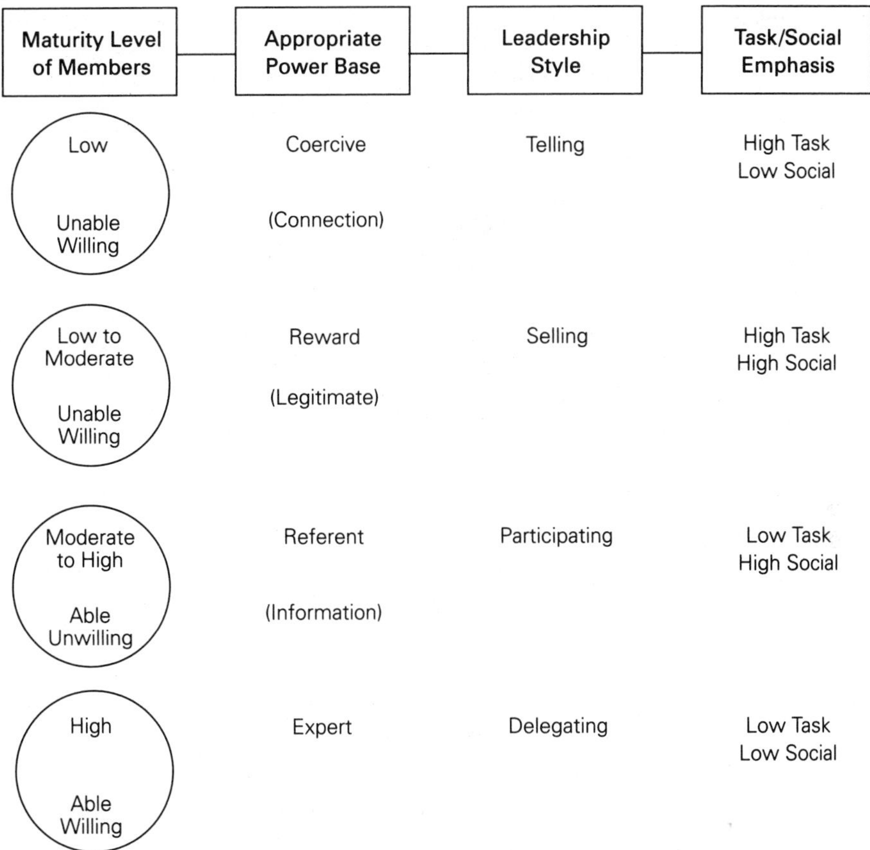

Figure 9.3 Hersey and Blanchard's model of situational leadership.

willing—the leader can allow the group to virtually run itself. The delegating style is basically a laissez-faire approach to leading. Members do not need strong leadership at this point, although they need to know the leader is there if a change in the task alters their ability to perform or if an unforeseen crisis occurs. Suppose we looked in on the clerical group two or three years later to find that the members had not only become convinced about the need for computers but several also had asked for additional training, purchased home computers of their own, and were avid readers of computer books and magazines. At this point, the leader could easily delegate to the group many decisions regarding purchases of new equipment and software.

Although the maturity level essentially dictates the style a leader should use, other factors will influence the leader's ability to pull off a particular style. For example, leaders must be able to assert themselves in order to establish a telling style and must be capable of integrating the ideas of different members to successfully manage a participatory style. Hersey and Blanchard include a second situational factor, the leader's access to different power bases, which support different styles and enable the leader to use that style more effectively. A leader has power when she or he is able to influence other group members. A power base refers to the source of that power, which can range from one's position in an organization to relationships built on friendship or mutual respect. Note in Figure 9.3 how each of the following power bases is related to a given leadership style:

- *Coercive power.* The ability to mete out punishments to group members that will lead to their compliance—for example, physical strength, use of threats, assigning unwanted tasks, embarrassing others.
- *Reward power.* The ability to reward group members for their compliance or performance through praise, special privileges, promise of a good recommendation.
- *Connection power.* An indirect ability to reward or coerce because of the perception that the leader "has the ear" of someone who can dish out punishments and rewards such as the president's son-in-law, a manager's right-hand man, a teacher's pet.
- *Legitimate power.* When group members accept another's right to prescribe their behavior by virtue of his or her position or title—administrator, manager, instructor, consultant.
- *Referent power.* The degree to which others allow a person to influence them because they admire, respect, or like him or her; examples include doing a favor for a friend, emulating another's behavior, anticipating what the leader wants.
- *Information power.* Having access to information that others do not have but want or need—hoarding research, keeping detailed notes, interviewing experts.
- *Expert power.* Granting influence to a person perceived as having more knowledge or skill in a certain area such as technical expertise or knowledge of group process.

A leader is advised to develop as many of these power bases as possible and to treat them as scarce resources to be protected and used wisely. If a single power base is relied on too often, its effectiveness typically erodes. Some power bases erode more quickly than others. For instance, the use of coercive power is always risky because members rarely like it and frequently resent it. Nonetheless, if used sparingly, it can be an effective tool. The important point about power bases is that *it is difficult to establish and maintain a given leadership style in the absence of an appropriate power base to support it.*

Hersey and Blanchard's theory is very practical. It suggests that a leader's first consideration should be an assessment of the group's maturity level. Based on that analysis, the leader should have a good idea of the leadership style that will be most successful. If care has been taken to develop the appropriate power bases, the appropriate style can be enacted easily. All that remains is for the leader to remain aware of changes in the group's ability and willingness to perform, and adapt his or her style to fit the changing situation.

At first glance, the situational approach to leadership may seem too complex and too messy to be of much value. None of the theories to date take into account more than a few of the potentially relevant factors. And even if they did, it may well be impossible for us to focus our attention (at least at a conscious level) on all of the factors at one time. But we may not need to do this. Making ourselves aware of some of the major factors may be enough to help us make good choices. We probably do not give our brain's powerful information-processing capabilities enough credit in this regard. The more we acknowledge the various facets of the group situation, the more intuitive we may become in realizing what needs to be done to move the group in a positive direction.

Framing Group Reality: The Rhetorical Approach

While situational approaches suggest that a leader should attend and adapt to the nature of the task, the environment, and the people in the group, the rhetorical approach goes much further. From this point of view, leaders do not simply respond to objective characteristics of the situation: leaders and followers engage in a process of *creating* those characteristics through communication. This view of leadership is relatively new, but it is consistent with the definition of communication as "a process of creating social reality." Several analyses have emphasized the rhetorical nature of leadership as a process of persuasion.[12]

Linda Smircich and Gareth Morgan have advanced one of the most intriguing rhetorical perspectives. They refer to leadership as "the management of meaning."[13] In other words, leaders frame or define situations in ways that consolidate or change the group's perception of its problem, task, goals, or the nature of the group itself. When a person offers and the group accepts a new definition of its situation, the group's effort takes on new meaning. The revised definition of the situation then serves as a fresh basis for group action. For instance, a university task force was investigating the functional and financial stability of one of its departments. The committee had been told that its sole purpose was to evaluate the viability of the unit and recommend the program remain open or be closed. Early on in the group's deliberations, one member attempted to frame the group's situation in a different way:

> I think we all realize what's going on here. We've got a renegade unit that is not very well respected across the university, and the administration knows that. The program is in financial trouble, and the administration would like to dump it. We're supposed to add legitimacy to the process by interviewing a whole lot of people, look at the ledger sheets, and come to the same conclusion as the administration. But I'm telling you that if we do what they want, we're sounding our own death knell. If we agree that this program can be closed because its enrollment is down, we set the precedent that the university can use any time one of our programs reaches a low ebb.

If the group accepts this rendition of what its work means, it will likely take a very different course of action. The problem will be much bigger than initially imagined. If someone else offers a competing definition of the situation, then a struggle for leadership will probably ensue.

From this view, leadership takes place when members buy the vision of reality that one of its members offers. Managing meaning can be just as important as using a coercive or reward power base. If a leader manages the way a group thinks, he or she can easily move its members to action. Leadership emergence is not only being in the right situation at the right time but framing the group experience in a way that makes sense to the members. The tools for managing group meaning include inventing images, making use of metaphors and images the group already accepts, establishing ritual, creating drama, using stories to illustrate a vision, and making myths work for you. Leaders can often invent images that capture concretely what had been previously understood in a largely implicit way. The problem is that members often give up their rights to define situations and come to expect leaders to always do so for them. Smircich and Morgan demonstrate that even weak leadership defines the situation in ways that lead to inaction or unwise actions (see Box 9.1).

Leadership: The Functional Approach

As you may have noticed, most of the previous approaches—traits, styles, and situational perspectives—assume that leadership is embodied in a single person. The exceptions are the rhetorical and the functional perspectives. Both stress the communicative acts of group members, but the functional perspective is the more specific of the two. Aubrey Fisher, perhaps the leading spokesperson for the functional approach, conceived of leadership functions as specific communication behaviors that move a group closer to its goal.[14] We described many of these behaviors in Chapter 4 and repeat them here to remind us of the specific acts that constitute leadership:

- Setting goals or establishing an agenda
- Providing orientation or framing the situation
- Encouraging a focus or suggesting procedures
- Regulating interaction
- Summarizing and integrating information
- Verbalizing consensus
- Modifying group process
- Seeking, contributing, and clarifying ideas and information
- Evaluating the quality of work and ideas
- Listening to, supporting, and encouraging members
- Reducing tension and mediating disagreements

The list could no doubt go on. But the key to recognizing leadership functions is that the acts are performed in a competent manner at the appropriate time and are accepted as such by the membership.[15] Any one of these acts could be performed when the situation does not call for it or the group does not respond positively to it. When this happens, the behavior is not functional and it is not leadership. Leadership also can exert a negative force in the group. If members positively reinforce a series of inappropriate acts, the group will be led in a less productive or even counterproductive direction.

Furthermore, these behaviors need not be performed by any one member. The functional approach assumes that in most groups leadership will be shared to some extent. Even when a leader has emerged or has been designated, other members still perform a number of leadership tasks.

The appeal of the functional approach is that it can explain how leadership takes place in groups with or without a specific person serving as "the leader." Effective leadership always occurs when one or more persons recognize the need for a specific communication act and either does it well or convinces someone else to do it. Still there are critics of the functional perspective. Julia Wood and her colleagues question the assumption that most group members are sufficiently skilled to produce leadership behavior in a timely fashion.[16] And Fisher himself later claimed that the search for a comprehensive list of functions unique to leadership was doomed to failure.[17] Instead he began to advocate a perspective on leadership that embraces group interaction in all its complexity.

Managing It All: The Complexity Approach

As the various contingency theories point out, leadership is a complex phenomenon involving literally hundreds of variables. Our understanding of leadership has been limited because theorists have tried to explain it in terms that are too simplistic. First, leadership was thought to be an aspect of personality, then a matter of style or rhetoric, now a set of functions. Only the situational perspective acknowledged the infinite complexity of leadership, but as we have seen, the theories themselves took into account only a handful of the many relevant factors. The most recent approach has been to view leadership as managing complexity. Two prominent theorists, Karl Weick and Aubrey Fisher, have pursued this perspective.[18] Weick's contribution has been to conceptualize the leader as "a medium" capable of handling the group's complexities, task, and environmental constraints. Weick does not mean that leaders are fortune tellers or spiritualists but that they tend to absorb and interpret more information than other group members. Fisher augmented Weick's approach by describing how the medium communicates in order to lead.

Leader as Medium When a group faces a complex decision, leaders have two choices to make. They can simplify the information-processing load or they can meet complexity with complexity, according to Weick. The first approach is taken when members selectively attend to certain information,

Box 9.1

Operation June 30th: Leadership as Managing Meaning

Mr. Hall, president of an insurance company with about 200 employees, had been hearing frequent complaints from district sales managers that their field agents were not getting prompt service from the home office. A backlog of insurance claims, renewals, and other requests was causing delays. To stem the tide, Mr. Hall initiated "Operation June 30th," a plan to bring all paperwork up to date by the end of June. At the same time that this operation began, researchers Linda Smircich and Gareth Morgan were conducting a field study of communication within this particular company. Operation June 30th (OJ30) provided them with a good opportunity to study the rhetorical aspects of a leader's attempt to manage meaning in the field.

As part of OJ30, employees in each department with a backlog were asked to work overtime while other members were asked to "volunteer" any extra time they had to help out. Status reports were made each week until all operations were made current. The plan was declared a success at the first staff meeting after the June deadline. However, OJ30 was not viewed as a success company-wide. Many group members felt that the operation failed to address the company's real problems.

Smircich and Morgan analyzed as much of the communication that took place during this period as they could—memos, written statements of progress, and overheard conversations. They discovered that the rhetorical choices made by the leader, President Hall, framed the situation in a particular way that directed attention away from the larger problems in the company and focused it intently on one narrowly focused goal. First of all, the decision to identify the solution as OJ30 focused all eyes on a future date, not on the past circumstances that led to the problem. It dramatized the situation as a fairly simple problem with a concrete end point: June 30th. In his interactions with the home office group, Hall used such phrases as "special program," "highest priority," "concerted effort," and "sprinting to the finish," which made the problem look like a one-time difficulty that could be solved by united teamwork with no need for any conflicting viewpoints.

Interviews with staff members revealed quite different impressions of the whole situation. Most of them viewed the problem as stemming from a group that was far from being a team. They pointed to prominent people who did not help out in the operation and noted the president's "not wanting to hear if things are bad" as part of the problem. They characterized the organization as a fragmented, uncooperative group in which conflict was hidden because the president refused to deal with their real problems. Many felt that operations would soon be backlogged again.

On the surface, many would say that Hall was simply an ineffective leader. But Smircich and Morgan would not accept the simple answer. They

Box 9.1 (continued)

argued on the contrary, that "weak" leadership is just as effective at defining situations as is strong or effective leadership. Several executives said they knew what the real problems were, but felt powerless to do anything about them. They felt that confrontation was needed, but could not bring themselves to confront the president's definition of their situation. Hall, in fact, had a very powerful influence on the whole group.

What can be done in situations like this one? Smircich and Morgan argue that until we can get beyond the traditional ideas of leadership as stemming only from a single person in a particular position, we are unlikely to find satisfactory options. The traditional conception of leadership has the unintended consequence of creating passive, powerless group members who are afraid to offer what might be better definitions of the situation.

Source: Linda Smircich and Gareth Morgan, "Leadership: The Management of Meaning," *Journal of Applied Behavioral Science*, 1982, *18*, 257–273.

ignore other data, form quick judgments, and reduce alternatives to a manageable few. Leaders in such situations often develop a plan and then persuade the group to follow. The second approach is what Weick and Fisher advocate. In Fisher's words:

> Leaders are not necessarily leaders because they perform functions unique to leadership. They are more likely to be leaders because they are themselves complex and perform functions which exhibit complexity. They behave differently with different people; they behave differently at different stages of group development; and they behave differently when the task situation differs.[19]

The leader is a medium in that he or she has the ability to take a variety of inputs from group members, consider a number of possible ways to interpret and integrate them, and reach a tentative conclusion—all without becoming too confused to move on. He or she may later reshuffle the pieces in light of some new information and offer the group a new tentative conclusion. In short, a good leader is more complex than nonleaders are and will exhibit a wider range of communication behavior than other group members do.

Research on Leadership Complexity Among the studies supporting the complexity perspective, an early one found that effective leaders often develop unique and different relationships with each group member. Other group members do not seem to do this to the same extent.[20] Many effective leaders adapt their leadership style to each member and motivate members in different ways. In other words, leaders have more complex relationships with followers than those followers have with each other. Leaders also adapt to situations. Two studies have shown that effective leaders change their behavior when the group encounters a crisis or when it becomes obvious that the group's approach to its task is failing. They lose status with the group when they do not adapt.[21] As further proof, G. Lloyd Drecksel observed and coded the interaction of every single member of eighteen different decision-making groups that met once a week for eight weeks.[22] This enabled her to compare the types and range of communication behaviors displayed by leaders versus those of other group members. Expecting to find that leaders performed a specific set of leadership functions, she did not observe any consistency by leaders from group to group. Expecting to find that individual leaders were somewhat consistent in the functions they performed from meeting to meeting, she found no consistency. The only similarities among the leaders she observed was that they engaged in (1) a wider range of communication behaviors than did nonleaders, (2) more atypical kinds of interaction, and (3) different communication styles with each group member. She concluded that leaders attend to and process more information than nonleaders. They also adapt their messages to fit the interests and concerns of each group member.

How Then Do We Lead?

What do all of these perspectives on leadership tell us? How can we translate them into practical advice for managing group decision making? Which questions do we ask ourselves to determine if the leadership of our group is effective? Our conclusion is that each perspective offers us a different vantage point for seeing the whole. Just as multiple perspectives on the issues of discussion increase our chances of finding a good solution, so multiple points of view on leadership can help us understand what it is. Here are some suggestions that we have derived from these differing viewpoints:

- Assign a single leader only when one member is clearly more capable than other members and the group or organization demands or prefers it.
- Avoid the "leader-does-it-all" syndrome. As a follower, do not become passive and dependent on the leader. All group members are responsible for group outcomes.
- Welcome an emergent leader when one comes forward who exhibits the complexity, rhetorical skill, or strong desire to lead.
- Push for shared leadership when group members have a high level of maturity and you want to promote greater involvement, responsibility, and independence of all group members.
- Develop the ability to enact each leadership style competently and be

sensitive to the situational contingencies in which each style is most appropriate.

- Encourage the group to take frequent stock of its situational contingencies and how they may be influencing the group's decision-making process. Increase your own ability to "be complex" by acknowledging the complexity of situations, and gradually learn to take more factors into account.
- Be alert to both the possibilities and the limitations of the way members define the group by framing the nature of its goals, problems, and solutions.
- Learn to perform adequately each of the leadership functions, and develop a sense of when each function is needed.
- Reflect on the effective and ineffective examples of leadership you observe. Try to improve the metaphors that are used to describe leadership.

From the six different perspectives on leadership, we have drawn our own conclusions and suggestions. Ultimately, your own conclusions and actions will help you and the groups in which you participate.

Summary

Decision-making groups need strong leadership to be successful. However, we have questioned the conventional wisdom that leadership is necessarily embodied in a single person. In addition, we examined a variety of perspectives on leadership. Some of these perspectives assume that leadership resides in the individual. The trait perspective sees personality as the primary reason for a leader's success. Some individual traits do seem more characteristic of leaders, but researchers have been unable to identify any particular type of person who consistently emerges as a leader. The styles approach, initially searching for an ideal leadership style, assumes that a variety of group and situational factors often make one style more appropriate than another.

The rhetorical and functional approaches are more communication oriented and stress that any member of the group can provide leadership. The rhetorical approach recognizes leadership as the creation of a vision or framework that enriches the group's understanding of its own goals, motivations, or identity. The functional approach, perhaps the most concrete of all the perspectives, identifies very specific task, procedural, and relational behaviors that help groups progress toward their goals. Finally, the complexity perspective assumes a single leader, but one whose understanding of people and of group process enables him or her to develop unique relationships with each member of the group. Such a leader may use a different style of leadership with each member and may alter that style under different circumstances.

We have not endorsed any one of these perspectives as the correct one. But the choices you make as leader or as member will be more effective ones because you now have a richer sense of the concept of leadership.

GroupQuests: Discussion Questions

1. We have identified several advantages and disadvantages of designated, emergent, and shared leadership approaches. Which of these approaches do you favor? Why? What additional reasons can you give in support of your choice?
2. Surveys of Americans consistently reveal that most people believe that leaders are born (the trait approach), not made. Why do you think people feel this way? Do you think the trait perspective deserves more attention or should researchers abandon it? Why? What arguments can you advance in favor of a trait approach?
3. How is leadership in a small group different from leadership of larger groups (say, twenty or more people), of corporations, and of nations? Do any of the different perspectives explored in this chapter explain leadership of large groups better than they explain it in small groups?

GroupWorks: Group Activities

1. Have two or three members prepare a list of positive and negative group tendencies. (See Figures 1.2 and 1.3 and add other concepts.) As a group, work through each tendency and discuss whether designated, emergent, or shared leadership would help or hinder the group's ability to manage the negative tendencies and encourage the positive ones.
2. Secure several different textbooks on small group communication from your instructor. Assign one to each member of the group and have each person summarize:
   a. The author's preferred approach to leadership. Which perspective does the author endorse? What advice is given about single or shared leadership?
   b. The author's general guidelines or advice for improving leadership in small groups.
   c. Any specific communication behaviors associated with leadership and advice on how or when to perform them.

   From all this input, select an approach (or integrate various advice) that reflects the most practical way to approach leadership in a small group.
3. Identify someone that you think of as an effective leader and observe his or her behavior in groups over two or three meetings. Note which leadership functions this person performs and try to describe the situation in the group *prior* to the leader's behavior. What does this tell you about when particular leadership functions are most appropriate?
4. For this long-term project to be conducted over several weeks or months, observe as many different decision-making groups as you can and summarize each group's approach to leadership. To the extent that you can determine, why has each group chosen the type of leadership that it has? Can you identify relevant contingencies that account for the leadership of the various groups? Do you see any consistencies in the approach taken by more successful groups versus less successful groups?

GroupActs: Practical Applications

As a group, review the conclusions at the end of this chapter and add any of your own. Work through each suggestion and evaluate how leadership in your group is consistent with or in contrast to our "advice." What conclusions can you reach about the leadership of your group? (Note that we did not say "the leader.") Do they suggest any changes that might be needed?

CHAPTER 10

The Group Level: How Groups and Their Members Socialize Each Other

Lewis F. Powell was appointed to the Supreme Court by Richard Nixon in 1971. On his first day at the Court, he was hailed by fellow Justice Thurgood Marshall:

> "Do you have your capital punishment opinion written yet?" Marshall asked jovially, slapping Powell lightly on the back. Powell smiled tentatively. Was it possible that he was expected to have mastered such a difficult and consequential area of the law so rapidly? Had the others completed their opinions, even before the Court had considered the cases or heard oral argument?
>
> "No, I haven't had time to consider that yet," he replied. "Well, I wish you luck," Marshall said. "My wife Cissy is after me, and thinks we should string them all up. But," he added, patting a wad of papers in the inside pocket of his coat, "you'll see what I've written."
>
> He slipped out the door with a chuckle.[1]

When new members join a group, even such a prestigious and select group as the Supreme Court, the uncertainty about expectations and appropriate behavior is not easily managed. There is so much to learn. Like Justice Powell, we have to judge when we are being told the truth and when someone is spoofing us. We must discover the rules that other group members take for granted. And we must decide which rites and rituals we are allowed to participate in and which ones we are expected to watch from the sidelines. In short, we have to master a whole subculture and learn what it takes to achieve full membership in that culture. This chapter focuses on how groups develop a productive social dimension by creating cohesiveness and group identification and by learning to manage group norms and deviance from those norms. In addition, the chapter demonstrates how an already-established group socializes new members and how they adapt to and influence the group culture.

Developing Group Culture

As a group of people work together, it develops its own unique ways of doing things. These patterns of behavior become the values, ideals, rituals, and time-honored traditions of the group's culture. Ernest Bormann defines *group culture* as "the sum total of ways of living, organizing, and communing built up in a group of human beings and transmitted to newcomers by means of verbal and nonverbal communication."[2] In essence, the group creates its own miniculture that heightens expectations and reduces uncertainty for members. This culture is built up as members exchange stories and information that reinforce similarities among themselves, make the group an attractive place to be, and create ways for members to identify with one another. Although every group culture will have its own unique earmarks, the *process* of creating a group culture is similar from group to group. We refer to the ingredients in this process as "the makings of group culture." Our starting point is the first meeting of a new group.

Forming the Group

As you recall from Chapter 1, a collection of people does not become a group overnight. It takes time to create a structured network of interdependent members who see themselves as having common goals, shared norms, and a group identity. Group culture develops as part of the group process. And while a group's culture is always changing, it is fascinating to watch the groundwork for that culture being laid in the initial meetings of a new group. Two very different instances of the formation of group culture occur, depending on whether the group is new or intact.

The Zero-History Group In the *zero-history group*, members have had little contact with one another before and have never worked as a group before. Groups formed in the classroom are often a good example of this type. To join such a group gives us the chance to see the whole culture develop before our own eyes. It is a culture built from scratch and one in which the entire historical record of the group is available to us. If you observe this type of group carefully, you should have little difficulty identifying how its communication patterns evolve and what aspects of its culture hold the group together or drive it apart. Surprisingly, the first meeting or two of a new group is not as crucial as you might think. Such groups are usually tentative because members are unsure of what they are doing. Members may form initial impressions of the group, but they seldom establish any pattern or routine immediately. Members probably do have preconceptions of what a good group ought to be like, but they seem to take a wait-and-see approach, hoping things will move in the direction of those preconceptions. Even so, the culture starts to build act by act. By the third or fourth meeting, patterns of interaction begin to emerge.

The Intact Group Outside the classroom, we are more likely to encounter an *intact group*, one that already has a history and culture that we must learn and adapt to. Not being privy to that history, a new member has to discern which group behaviors have more symbolic importance, which ones represent the group culture. The process of socializing new members into an existing group culture forces the group culture to adapt as well. As we shall see later, the new member does most of the adapting at first. Nonetheless, new members start a process of cultural change and we see the re-forming of a slightly (and sometimes radically) different group.

Over the years, a group may change a lot. But the evolution in traditions and values is so slow that members adjust to the changing image. Sports teams provide good examples of this because of high member turnover each year from trades, retirement, and frequent changes in coaches and owners. From the 1920s through the mid-1960s, the New York Yankees were the most feared team in professional baseball. They played in the World Series thirty-three times, winning twenty-two times. Their players included Babe Ruth, Lou Gehrig, Joe DiMaggio, Yogi Berra, and Mickey Mantle. The Yankee tradition (its group culture) survives today in spite of the fact that the current crop of Yankees have little in common with the great teams of the past. They have failed to win as much as a divisional championship in the past seven years. Over the past twenty-five years, the team has won its division only five times. Among players and fans alike, there is widespread dislike for the team's owner, George Steinbrenner. He is seen as the villain who disrupts the players' concentration by talking about them to the press and overruling or firing managers when they do not agree with him. One thing that has not changed is the amount of press coverage the team receives from residing in New York City. Yet the rich history of the franchise gives it a continuity in the minds of players and fans alike. A true fan or player might see the behavior of the current owner as "out of character" for a Yankee, as a deviation from the group norm that will only deserve a footnote in the group's long-running history.

As our discussion proceeds, we will focus on the makings of the group culture with the zero-history group in mind. We will look at how such a group can develop a strong culture that exhibits cohesiveness and productivity. These cultural processes will ebb and flow during the life of a group and will still be in effect when an intact group experiences membership changes. We will deal with the intact group from the perspective of how it socializes new members into its existing cultural framework. For now, we want to consider how that cultural framework gets built in the first place.

The Makings of Group Culture

Group culture refers to the total package of thought and behavior that defines the group's values and its customs. As such, group culture encompasses all three of the major dimensions of group interaction: task, social, and procedural. In this chapter, we focus largely on how group culture develops along the social dimension. In the following chapter, we will look more closely at the task and procedural dimensions.

Cohesiveness The social dimension of group culture is perhaps best judged by the level of *cohesiveness* that exists among members, what Leon Festinger called "all the forces acting upon the members to remain in the group."[3] We also say a group is cohesive when its members enjoy being together, can coordinate their efforts smoothly, and value the group's perspective on most issues. A productive group culture depends on cohesiveness.

Cohesiveness is easier to accomplish if group members like each other and like the group as a whole. There are two different bases for attraction in small groups: interpersonal and group attraction. When a person is attracted to a group because of particular individuals in that group, we say the bond is based on *interpersonal attraction*. Many people join groups because they already know and like some of its members. In a zero-history group, however, mutual liking often takes time to develop. Knowing some of the factors that relate to interpersonal attraction can help you encourage its development. Generally, people are attracted to one another for some combination of physical, task, or social reasons.[4] (You cannot make members more physically attracted to each other, and no evidence indicates that physically attractive people make better group members.)

You can enhance *task attraction* by encouraging members to share their previous experience and expertise with topics related to group goals. In task groups, the perceived and demonstrated ability of other members strongly influences our desire to work with them. Marvin Shaw and J. C. Gilchrist investigated attraction between people who had been either successful or unsuccessful in previous problem-solving situations. They found that initially the successful problem solver was more likely to be chosen as a task partner. However, over time the unsuccessful individuals gravitated toward other unsuccessful persons.[5] This suggests the importance of involving and rewarding all group members in the task effort. You do not want a coalition of nonparticipants to sap energy from the group.

Researchers have also identified factors that encourage *social attraction*. To some extent, proximity (the physical distance between members) can affect interpersonal attraction. Group members who live near each other or work in the same office have a greater opportunity to interact and become friends. In their classic study of university housing, Leon Festinger and his associates found proximity to be the best predictor of friendship. People who lived next door to each other became friends more often and people who lived at the end of the complex showed a marked tendency to become social isolates.[6] Perhaps the best predictor of social attraction is the degree of similarity in members' attitudes, personalities, gender, and ethnic background. A multitude of research studies have demonstrated the relationship of similarity to attraction.[7] But, such similarities must be perceived. Group members must communicate their similarities if they are to foster cohesion through mutual attraction. Note that too much similarity among members can be detrimental to a decision-making group that relies on differences of opinion and perspective to encourage thorough analysis. For a group to be effective, it must encourage expressions of similarity as long as they do not compromise critical inquiry. This balancing act is a constant problem for groups.

Group attraction takes place when members find the group itself desirable, regardless of its individual members. A person may want to join a group because of the group's goals or activities. For instance, one woman may join Greenpeace because she agrees with its goals to protect the environment and the rights of all living creatures. She approves of its cause. Another may join the group because of the dangerous and exciting protest activities Greenpeace engages in (for example, using motorboats to interfere with whaling ships). Finally, the *prestige* attached to group membership may be another reason for being attracted to a group. Some groups have established reputations on campus, in a city, or across the country. Membership in the group can itself be a measure of success, especially if that membership was difficult to obtain. Some students see acceptance into a particular fraternity or sorority as a status symbol. Joining the local chamber of commerce is desirable if an entrepreneur wants to become influential in the business community. Many people join professional groups to pad their résumé and secure future employment. Some reasons for being attracted to a group are legitimate; others may lead you to question the motivation of a prospective member.

Although cohesion can exist simply because group members like each other, it can be further solidified by several aspects of the communication among members: the clarity of goal paths, the nature and timing of feedback, the nature of conflict, and perceived freedom to participate during discussions.

The *clarity of the path to a goal* simply means that group members have discussed and understand a shared goal and the specific steps they will take to reach it. Note the difference between a group that ends its first meeting with the assignment for everyone to "go find all the information you can on topic X" versus a group that decides it will first conduct a computer search for library materials on the topic, then select appropriate articles to review and identify themes, prepare questions about each theme, and finally conduct a survey to see how students on campus view those themes. Remember that clarity does not mean the same thing to every person. Recall our discussion in Chapter 9 about people who differ in the ability to tolerate ambiguity. Depending on the members' personalities, some groups may need more clarity than others.

The *nature of the feedback* that group members exchange also influences cohesion. Generally, a group will be more cohesive when members balance the amount of positive and negative feedback they give to others' ideas and efforts. In addition, timing counts: Cohesiveness is usually higher when positive

Dress norms are a common way to symbolize and reinforce group identification, unity, and cohesion.

feedback is consistently provided first; groups are less cohesive if negative feedback is given first.[8] Be careful that the positive feedback does not become perfunctory or insincere. We have seen group members provide positive feedback as if they were only filling time before the "yes, but . . . " part of the message.

If managed carefully, *conflict* can produce cohesion. Conflict episodes give a group the strength to tackle bigger and more complex problems (see Chapter 7). Recall that willingness to engage in conflict is one of the most important attitudes group members need to bring to meetings (Chapter 4). But the nature of conflict matters. When a conflict involves disagreement in values or basic principles, it can damage the fragile bonds of cohesion because it implies that group members are not similar in their basic outlook. When members agree on the values and goals they want to pursue, their conflict is usually concerned with the best way to achieve those goals. This type of conflict creates rather than destroys cohesion.

When group members communicate in such a way that everyone *feels free to participate* in the group discussion, cohesion is enhanced even further. All members do not have to participate equally, but no member should feel inhibited from speaking. How can you create such an atmosphere? Listen. If members do not sense that you are really listening to what they are saying, they will begin to talk less and lose interest in the discussion. Being too quick with negative feedback can be inhibiting, and status differences in the group tend to inhibit quieter members especially. You may have to ask for their participation (without demanding it) more frequently. Try using discussion formats that promote frequent participation by all members such as the round-robin.

While cohesion can be the result of group dynamics such as attraction and quality communication, it can also be a by-product of productivity. Groups that have successfully solved problems tend to be more cohesive.[9] This may be the result of pride in accomplishments as well as respect shown to members by colleagues or peers outside the group. Success obviously makes it easier to recruit new members and acquire additional resources that can be rewarding to the group. Being productive can also inspire confidence in each other and make members more attractive to one another in terms of the tasks they perform.

In an extensive review of the research on membership satisfaction, Richard Heslin and Dexter Dunphy identified *perceived progress toward the group's goals* as a factor that led to greater satisfaction with one's group.[10] For progress or success to be perceived, it has to be pointed out. The group that keeps tabs on its accomplishments, rewards itself with a verbal pat on the back, and builds on its successes is establishing an enriching culture. Small acts of praise and homegrown methods of recognition are often the best reward a group member can ask for. One classroom group established its own weekly awards ceremony in which the most productive member was honored as the "Sweat Hog of the Week" along with the "Vice President for Crisis Management," the person who helped the group survive any tight squeezes or ruffled feathers.

Group cohesiveness is a very desirable attribute in any group. But there is one major drawback associated with too much cohesion. When a group is close knit, members want to retain the feelings of satisfaction and enjoyment that they have experienced. As a result, they create a subtle but strong pressure toward uniformity. Because members value the group and its goals, they adopt many of the norms without questioning them. They often become reluctant to disagree with each other in any substantial way. Even groups that know better will often disagree only at a superficial level. Obviously, this can damage the group's commitment to making high-quality decisions.

The group may avoid discussion about problems or bad habits it is developing. The full range of solutions to acknowledged problems may not be considered because members do not want to risk damaging their social dimension. When members do raise objections, others quickly squelch them, saying things like, "Oh, we can handle that. No problem," or by diverting attention to other topics or issues. In Chapter 12, we will pursue the full effect of this pressure when we investigate the phenomenon of groupthink, the tendency to achieve consensus at virtually any cost.

The consequences of cohesion can vary depending on the basis for that cohesion. In an early study of the effects of cohesion, K. W. Back discovered several patterns of interaction associated with different kinds of cohesion. He found that groups that were highly cohesive because of interpersonal attraction tried to prolong their discussions and socialized a great deal. Groups that became cohesive due to task attractiveness were much more efficient, finishing their tasks as quickly as they could. Finally, when cohesion was based on group prestige, members were overly cautious. They did not want to do anything that might hurt their image as a group.[11]

Group Identification While attraction to group members and group goals helps a group become cohesive, another dynamic in groups enhances the bond among members. *Group identification* refers to a shared consciousness among group members, a feeling that they have transcended their own individual identities and have become a part of something larger than themselves. The distinction between group identification and cohesion is an important one. A group can be cohesive without members identifying themselves closely with the group. To identify with means "to see oneself as one with."[12] When members begin to see their group as having special or unique qualities, almost like a "group personality," they may feel "at one with" the group because together they have shaped the group's identity. You can recognize the presence of group identification in several ways, including changes in language use, the adoption of group rituals, the creation of group heroes and villains, participation in group fantasies, and the expression of group values.

When members begin to think of themselves as a group, you will probably see a subtle shift in their language use. Collective pronouns such as *we*, *us*, and *ours* replace *I*, *you*, *me*, *yours*, and *mine*. The group may give itself a name that captures its spirit: "the dirty half-dozen" or "the henchmen." In Tracy Kidder's chronicle of the development of a new minicomputer at Data General Corporation, he notes how the group that created the computer called themselves "the kids." The subgroup that developed the hardware were known as the "Hardy Boys," while the software group called itself the "Microkids."[13] These group names are more than just cute attempts to forge group identification. They symbolize the essence of the group's uniqueness and the members' commitment to one another. In the case of the Hardy Boys and the Microkids, the group became a kind of surrogate self. Members thought nothing of working the entire weekend to help the group achieve its goals.

In conversation, group members echo one another, using the same catchphrases and slogans. One of your authors joined a group of colleagues who envisioned themselves as creating a graduate-level liberal arts program, trying to restore an emphasis most undergraduate programs had abandoned. I knew I had started to identify with the group when one member said to me, "You'd better be careful. You're starting to sound like one of us." As identification grows, members are likely to personify the group, as if it had a separate existence: "the group thinks," "the group feels." In addition, private symbols such as inside jokes or terms understood only by group members develop. Members indicate the degree to which they think of themselves as a group by the language they use to describe their individual and collective actions.

The emerging group consciousness also is reflected in group behavior. Some rituals are as simple as a particular way of greeting or shaking hands. Others may be complex. One student group created its own vocabulary with such terms as *conflict check* (to make sure no one's feelings were hurt). During almost every meeting, members took some time to coin a new term to add to their growing lexicon. Many groups engage in a ritualistic Monday morning talk about their weekend or their upcoming social plans, if only to break up the routine of task work. Kidder reports that the Data General group had a rite of "signing up," a simple verbal agreement ("Yeah, I'll do that") that was actually a commitment to long hours and lost weekends to work on a project related to the overall goal.

One way that groups raise their shared consciousness is by creating and exaggerating the accomplishments of heroes. These heroes are often former (or even current) group members whose behavior serves as a standard for others to emulate. The hero can also be a fictitious character or even an inanimate object as long as it is something the group can identify with. The whiz kids at Data General named the computer they were trying to invent "Gollum" (after a *Lord of the Rings* character). The computer became one of their significant heroes and a key source of their identification as a group.

Groups also love to hate a good villain. They often manufacture a "common enemy" when one is not readily available. Any kind of outside threat will prompt group members to identify more closely as they try to ward off the threat. Other groups are the most common type of enemy. Imagine the Moral Majority trying to arouse its members to action without reference to those "secular humanists," or Ronald Reagan getting funding for his "Star Wars" defense plan without an "evil empire" to defend against. Sometimes the villain is one of the group members whose deviant behavior makes him an easy target for group wrath. Without a clear-cut enemy, it is often hard to muster the troops.

Another strong indication of group identification is the occurrence of what Ernest Bormann calls group *fantasy themes*. Bormann defines *fantasy* as "the creative and imaginative shared interpretation of events that fulfills a group psychological or rhetorical need."[14] In other words, a group fantasy is a story members elaborate upon that makes them feel unique and helps them deal with some current group problem. For instance, a group began having a problem with one of its senior members who complained frequently in a whiney voice and also picked on the only freshman in the group. Without realizing the connection, one member mentioned seeing an old episode of "Leave it to Beaver," and the others chimed in about their favorite episodes. Most of their comments centered on the character of Eddie Haskell, who whined a lot and always picked on the Beaver, who was younger than Eddie. The senior complainer was very vocal in his dislike for Eddie's tactics. Although nothing was said (or even consciously recognized) about the group having a similar problem, the whining and teasing began to decrease and eventually disappeared.

Bormann argues that group members identify with one another when they share a group fantasy because they become caught up in the story and its characters. Each member responds in a chain reaction to the developing storyline and adds elements to it. Members experience an emotional identification with the story and the heroes or villains included in it. Later, a single code word is all that is needed to remind the group of the story and re-create instant identification. While the process of a group energized by such a story is called a fantasy, its content is referred to as a *fantasy theme*. The theme of the fantasy might address any number of issues in a group: fear of the unknown, achievement motivation, or personality clashes.

In the long run, fantasy themes enable members to experience the feeling of group identification in a dramatic and unique way. A group of graduate students, no doubt fearful that they might not survive the rigors of their program, engaged in an extended series of group fantasies that helped bring them together. One late-night study session turned into a fantasy regarding which members of the group would become most famous in their field. As the unfolding storyline emerged, it became clear that they were all destined for greatness and that some day a major motion picture would chronicle this special group. So they decided which famous actors would be cast in each of their roles. As a result of this one fantasy session, some members referred to each other for weeks by the name of the actor chosen to play them in "the movie." One member continued the fantasy by keeping a somewhat fictitious journal of the group's exploits and shared it with the others. "The journal" remained a prominent theme for the group throughout their year together.

One consequence of all the story telling, hero making, and villain bashing in groups is the elevation of group standards or values. The themes that run through the various rituals and fantasies often represent values that the group comes to identify as its own. An achievement theme in group talk can easily convince members that they can do their best work. As a result, they begin to internalize values such as excellence and motivation. Of course, the group can also exalt values that are contrary to effective decision making. Some or even all of a group's members may identify more with the villain than the hero.

You may be wondering if these heroes, villains, and values are the product of your authors' own fantasizing. The groups you have participated in may seem tame in comparison to these examples. Many groups do not experience this kind of dramatic interaction and emotional identification. Ernest Bormann and his colleagues have been observing group fantasies since the early 1960s at the University of Minnesota. In the following paragraphs, we will look at his explanation of why some groups develop strong cultures and others do not.

Symbolic Convergence: A Theory to Explain Group Culture

In response to observations of group fantasy themes and other communication patterns in classroom groups, Bormann has developed his *symbolic convergence theory*. The term *convergence* refers to the way in which the private symbolic worlds of two or more people begin to come together or overlap.[15] As group members adopt a shared set of symbols, communication becomes easier and more efficient. They can assume a common pool of meanings, which allows for greater understanding of one another, less effort in decision making, and a greater emotional commitment to the group and its decisions. Bormann identifies three different elements in symbolic convergence theory:

- Evidence that a group consciousness exists
- Dynamic tendencies in the group's communication that give rise to that shared consciousness
- Reasons why some groups engage in the process and others do not

We have already explained the first two elements, so we can turn our attention to the third: why these communication patterns occur. While research continues, Bormann offers three tentative explanations: group members' predispositions, common group concerns, and the rhetorical skill of members.

Group members do not leave their personal lives at the door when they participate in group discussions. They may bring a number of psychodynamic problems with them to meetings. Such personal concerns might include apprehensions about being in a new group, unresolved emotional needs, low self-esteem, and loneliness. A common predisposition for many people is a dislike for working on group projects. Such concerns may either inhibit or facilitate an individual's attraction to or identification with the group. They may also affect one's participation in a fantasy theme or inside joke. A person who has repressed certain needs might shy away from participating in a fantasy theme that hits too close to home. On the other hand, an individual who has recently worked through a problem is more likely to initiate conversation on that theme. In other words, some group members are more likely than others to initiate and participate in episodes that foster group identification. Others are likely to cut off such discussions before they get started.

As the group begins its work, other problems or opportunities are likely to emerge that become concerns for the whole group. These will be issues that did not exist before the group was formed. They are concerns of the group's own making: struggles for leadership, personality clashes, and deviation from norms, for example. Many groups tend to avoid dealing with such potentially devisive issues and never work through them. But directly or indirectly working through such problems can create strong group identification.

Bormann also notes that the dramatic story-telling skills of particular individuals can affect the quality of group narratives. The person who can tell a good tale can help drive the imagination of the whole group. When a group has no such person, it is hard for the dramatic story telling to get started. You need someone to energize the group and get it going.

The example of the graduate students told earlier can illustrate each of the three explanations Bormann advocates. In terms of individual predispositions, eleven of the twelve students were from out of state. Because they were all adjusting to a new place, were no doubt lonely, and were unfamiliar with local customs, they had plenty of initiative to identify with other group members. The list of common group concerns soon developed. All graduate students participated in a three-day workshop that prepared them to assume teaching responsibilities the following week. None of them had ever taught a class before. All twelve students attended the same classes and had the same assignments and the common concern of how to spend what little free time they had. Those who were more skilled in oral communication became the principal storytellers. The one member who kept the journal elaborated on those stories.

The creation of group culture is a fascinating process to observe and participate in. A significant part of group culture is the development of social norms that define what kind of behavior is expected of group members. Let us look at how group norms develop and change as a result of group communication.

Norms and Deviance: A Creative Tension

In Chapter 1 we advised you to beware of the tendency for group members to conform to social pressures. The emergence of group norms is an inherent part of the group process. But creating and following norms has a very positive side as well. Without norms, a collection of people would find it very difficult to work together. *Norms* are established patterns and standards of group behavior that reduce uncertainty and establish expectations. In contrast to roles, which establish different expectations for each member, norms usually apply to all members of the group. Thus, norms are rules for "what must, or must not, be done" in different situations.[16] They are the behaviors that members consider proper (or typical) for their group.

No one follows all of the rules all of the time. Deviation from norms is as natural as norms themselves. So no study of group norms would be complete without taking into account deviant behavior. In this section, we examine how groups establish and enforce norms as well as how individual members respond by conforming to or deviating from those norms.

The Nature of Group Norms

When asked to describe the norms at work in their group, most people have a hard time identifying many of them. Members say things like, "Everybody is expected to attend meetings and be on time" or "We expect each other to be prepared for meetings." Norms are often hard to "see" because once they become accepted, we follow them without much thought. We might recognize norms that we do not like. If you are the only member in your group who smokes, for instance, and the others grimace every time you light up, you may feel pressure to refrain from smoking during meetings. Other norms are more positive, but nonetheless exert pressure on members to comply. We observed a faculty group that had a "laughter norm." Members who did not regularly participate in telling jokes, brief slapstick performances, or the banter of friendly insults were treated as less than full members. They found themselves on the outside looking in.

To help you identify group norms, we will look at some of their properties—aspects that make some norms stronger than others. Jackson's model of group norms describes these properties.[17]

Jackson's Return-Potential Model of Norms Since the 1940s, a body of research on conformity consistently demonstrated how difficult it was for individuals to withstand the pressure of group norms. But J. A. Jackson was not satisfied with general explanations such as "a pressure to conform." He wanted to know the specific aspects of norm-governed group behavior. From his research, Jackson developed a model that explains why members follow some norms but not others. His model suggests that members learn how to behave in the group by evaluating the potential "return" (approval or disapproval) their behavior is likely to elicit from others. If a specific behavior such as "being friendly" seems to get very high approval no matter who does it, that behavior will become a group norm, especially if members respond to alternative behaviors such as "being hostile" or "remaining neutral" with high disapproval. Jackson's model specifies several properties that indicate the strength of various group norms. These properties include ideal behavior, the range of tolerable behavior, the intensity of reactions to the behavior, and the degree of norm crystallization. Each of these properties is described here and depicted in Figure 10.1.

Behaviors that most or all group members consistently and strongly approve represent the ideal that other members should follow. These are the expectations for what members *ought* to do to maintain and enhance their membership. Sometimes ideal behavior is identified in group talk: "It would be great if, for the first time in the history of this company, no one missed a single meeting for the duration of the entire project." But often ideal behavior is implied by the positive feedback members give each other when they engage in that behavior. Imagine that you videotaped a meeting and recorded the length of each speaking turn during periods of open discussion. In addition, you charted the verbal and nonverbal feedback of members to each speaker. Suppose you discovered that the group gave mostly positive feedback for the first thirty seconds of a speaker's turn and that after forty-five to fifty seconds most group members were either looking away, yawning, or trying to interrupt the speaker. What would this tell you about the ideal speaking turn? Group norms are often established by repeated behavior that simply comes to be thought of as "normal."

The ideal behavior gets the highest approval, but most members do not live up to the highest standards. Yet they get by and are accepted as members because they follow the norm, if only to a lesser degree. Their behavior falls within the range of what is considered acceptable behavior. Note in Figure 10.1 that our hypothetical norm for length of speaking turns includes a range of tolerable behavior. Members who took anywhere from ten to fifty seconds to speak were responded to in generally favorable terms. Those who spoke beyond fifty seconds were probably seen as dominating, or repeating themselves needlessly, or rambling on. Those who spoke for fewer than ten seconds might have gotten looks of puzzlement because they did not explain what they meant or made irrelevant comments. To fit in, members need to identify the range of tolerable behavior.

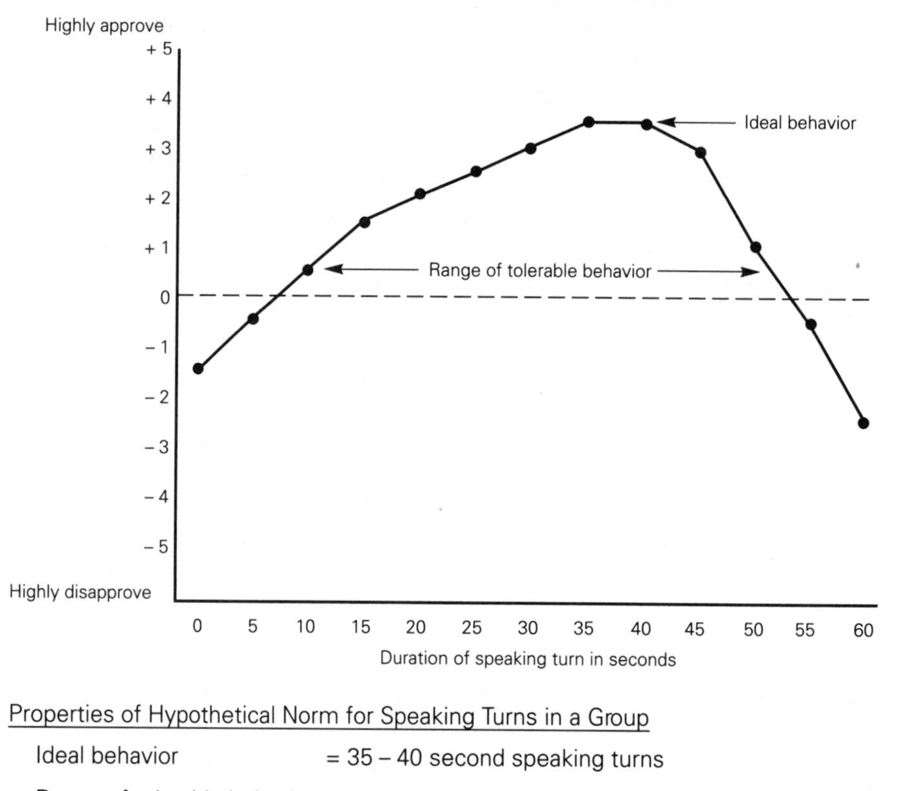

Figure 10.1 Jackson's return-potential model of group norms.

Some norms are more important to the welfare of the group than are others. In one group, it might be considered ideal if members were always polite to each other, but the group would be willing to sacrifice politeness if it meant a better quality decision. Thus norms that relate to productivity would be more important to the group than those that regulate the social dimension. Another group might feel just the opposite. It might believe that civility in human relations is more important than any given task outcome. More important group norms are usually recognized because of the intensity of members' reactions to behaviors that either conform to or violate the norm. A norm that is held intensely is very highly approved when a member conforms and very strongly disapproved when one deviates. Note in Figure 10.1 that the norm for speaking turns is not intensely held by the group. Reactions to violations are only moderately disapproving (for example, disinterest or boredom). No one tells the deviant speaker to shut up or to leave the meeting. The strongest reaction is that another member interrupts or starts a side conversation. A norm for attendance at meetings, on the other hand, might be intensely held by the group. Members may even establish sanctions such as undesirable assignments to discourage missing more than two meetings.

The crystallization of a norm means that there is nearly complete agreement among group members about the ideal, range, and importance of a particular dimension of behavior. For example, say you polled members separately and asked them about their group's norms regarding amount and type of conflict. Suppose most members agreed that certain types of conflict behavior were ideal (questioning the validity of an idea) and that others were not acceptable (questioning the integrity of another member). Furthermore, they all agreed that each member was responsible for verbally reprimanding anyone who tried to make a conflict personal. Because group members agreed on most of these issues, we would say that the norms concerning conflict were crystallized. Obviously, group interaction would be much easier to conduct if most members agreed on what kind of conflict behavior was appropriate. This is the main reason we suggest that groups talk about the norms that they would like to see governing them.

Types of Group Norms Although groups can develop norms for almost any conceivable behavior, the manner in which the norm emerges will be either explicit or implicit. Norms that are orally discussed or written down as a code of expected behavior are called *explicit norms*. Many groups establish a formal set of bylaws or regulations that serve to make membership criteria, forms of interaction, and administration of sanctions easier to manage. When a group agrees to follow Robert's *Rules of Order*, it is making explicit some of the norms that will govern its interaction and decision making. If a group takes our advice, discussing and then agreeing upon a set of ground rules, it is doing the same thing.

Most group norms are not as obvious as those just mentioned. They are expectations that develop during routine interaction and come to be taken for granted. Some of these are *unconscious norms*. Group members are not even aware that some aspects of their behavior have become uniform. For instance, norms about speaking turns such as the one we described earlier could be operating in a group without members realizing it. Other informal norms are *implicitly recognized norms*. Some group members may be aware of them but do not articulate them. A group may observe the norm that "members should not lose their temper when arguing" even though members have never discussed it. They just seem to recognize that if anyone did so, it would be frowned upon. Implicitly recognized patterns can become explicit norms if members comment on them.

The Emergence of Norms As with roles, norms emerge as part of the communication process. The positive and negative feedback of members to specific behaviors is central to the evolution of group norms. In contrast to role emergence, where members selectively reinforce the behavior of a single individual, norms evolve because members reinforce a particular set of behaviors regardless of who performs them. But as with role behavior, development of the most important norms may take several episodes in which ideal behaviors are strongly reinforced, tolerable deviations are mildly approved or reacted to indifferently, and unacceptable deviations are intensely rejected. Other less significant norms may emerge by repetition of communication patterns until they are seen as normal.

The emergence of some norms is assisted by a very general social norm, the *norm of reciprocity*. This is the "do as I do" norm. People often respond to each other's behavior in kind. If you approach someone in a friendly manner, he or she is likely to react in a similar way. If you scowl at someone, he or she probably will scowl in return. Thus group members often mimic each other's behavior, which starts the cycle of positive feedback that results in the formation of a norm.

Several other factors can aid in the creation of normative behavior. Conversation among members often results in symbolic convergence as members indirectly tap into a shared value system. A group conversation about the movie *Rocky* might be enough to trigger a "can do" attitude that eventually makes acceptance of a norm to work hard easier. When members are already cohesive, norms have a better chance to develop and endure. Cohesion adds a subtle atmosphere of conformity to a group. Members begin to change behaviors and beliefs because of a real or imagined group pressure.[18] A third factor is the existence and acceptance of authority in the group. If a group accepts and values the authority of its leaders, the leadership can often dictate the norms. Finally, the status of the group can increase the likelihood that norms will emerge and be followed. People who really want to belong to a group may accept behavioral restrictions that they would not otherwise follow. As a result of his desire to be "a good soldier," Lieutenant Colonel Oliver North helped arrange the unlawful sale of U.S. weapons to Iran and then diverted the profits from those sales to support the Contras in Nicaragua. His defense was that he believed he was doing what his superiors (his group) wanted him to do.

When group members adopt explicit norms, they short-circuit the process of emergence. Even so, the process is not complete. Once norms are agreed upon orally, it still remains to be seen how well the group actually follows its rules. Any member of a group that may have spent hours developing explicit bylaws can tell you how quickly those bylaws are forgotten once the group starts working.

The major point we want to make about norms, whether explicit or implicit, is the extent to which they are the product of a collective process. Each member of the group plays a part in establishing, assessing, and enforcing norms. Members contribute to the emergence of a norm every time they initiate or reinforce ideal behavior; ignore, rebuke, or reinforce deviant behavior; and talk or refuse to talk about the norm. *Norms can emerge, be sustained, or be changed only through members' actions.*

The Power of Norms Much of what we have already said about norms indicates how weak or powerful they can be. The degree of crystallization, the intensity of sanctions, and how important the group is to the individual members all affect willingness to abide by the group's norms. Research also indicates that some personality types are more prone to conformity than are others (see Chapter 8). Authoritarians tend to follow the rules and go along with those in command. Group norms have greater salience for members who are sensitive to rejection or have low self-esteem.

Although most Americans think of themselves as highly individualistic, normative influence is an extremely powerful force. Teenagers do not reject the normative influence of their parents' generation as much as they shift their allegiance to a new one, their peer group. On the whole, people comply with norms much more often than they deviate from them. Groups typically reward compliance and punish deviance, especially when the norm reflects the group's ideology and values. Norms make life in groups stable and less anxious. Members will frequently resist change in order to preserve what they are familiar with. The city council of a medium-sized town (it could have been Anywhere, U.S.A.) had a small fountain in the town square painted a more historically appropriate dark shade of green. (It had been silver for over fifty years.) The community uproar was surprising, but should not have been. The city had recently become a "boom town," and all the changes threatened to destroy life as most citizens knew it. The "normal" rate of change in groups is so incremental that members do not even realize the norms have been altered. People who leave and then return to a group are often appalled at the changes they witness. "It's just not the same anymore. What's happened to those people?" Keeping things familiar is a powerful reason to comply with normative pressure.

The normative influence of external primary groups can make it more difficult for a new group to establish effective norms. Primary groups—such as our family, religion, or friends—are those from which we derive much of our self-concept. As long as members have strong allegiances to their primary groups, they may not feel as compelled to go along with the emerging norms of the newer group. Herbert Kelman distinguishes between two types of conformity that may emerge in such circumstances: public compliance and private acceptance.[19] *Public compliance* occurs when a member expresses attitudes and behaviors that conform to group norms, but privately believes otherwise. He or she may be trying to avoid the pressure of the moment, without changing beliefs that may be highly valued by a primary group. *Private acceptance*, on the other hand, takes place when a member internalizes the norm and behaves in accordance with it even when other members are not present. When this happens, it suggests that the new group is becoming very important to the individual. There may be a third option. Individuals often *compartmentalize* their views, which means that they can accept a set of standards as appropriate for one group without internalizing those standards or applying them to other groups or other situations. Thus conforming to group norms does not always mean that you compromise your principles.

Group norms preserve the status quo, which is not always the best approach to solving problems. As with other practices, norms usually outlive their usefulness and need to be changed. But change does not come easily. Members of the group typically do not perceive the need for change simultaneously. As a result, the first person to deviate and push for change can expect a difficult time.

The Role of Deviance

From a group perspective, deviant behavior usually seems like a slap in the face. Deviants are seen as troublemakers who flout the rules and seldom have the group's goals and interests in mind. And sometimes people do deviate to see what they can get away with or because they are not really committed to the group. Any member whom the group needs more than that member needs the group is in a position to deviate more frequently from group norms. The group allows the deviations because it might be difficult to proceed without that member. So people in power occasionally take advantage of that fact and do not work as hard as the rest of us.

But there are also some good reasons for deviant behavior in groups. At a simple level, deviance helps articulate group norms by demonstrating very clearly the range of tolerable behavior in the group. It also tests the group's willingness to punish deviant behaviors in order to protect those norms. Many groups seem to need a deviant member or scapegoat so they can have someone to blame when things go wrong. Finally, excessive deviance by members may be a warning that the group's leadership is failing its members. To further delineate some of the positive and negative aspects of deviance, we will define several types of deviance that occur in groups.

Types of Deviance Robert K. Merton has identified four different ways that members deviate from society: ritualism, retreatism, rebellion, and innovative deviance.[20] Although Merton did not specifically address deviance in small groups, his four types apply at the group level as well.

Ritualism refers to blind conformity to social norms. How can conformity be deviance? Merton saw ritualism to be deviance from the social norm that one should think for oneself. If a group member conforms to or agrees with the majority simply because they are the majority, he or she is violating every principle of effective group discussion. Members should be informed, take a stand, and be ready to provide reasons for their vote on any issue. This kind of deviance is deplorable, yet members get away with it all the time.

Retreatism is also debilitating to a group. A member who retreats withdraws from the group and deviates by not participating at all. The ritualist at least pretends to participate by supporting group decisions and following the norms.

The retreatist does neither. He drops out in mind and spirit, leaving the group with a dead weight.

The rebel also rejects the group's norms and values, but tries to have an impact on the group. The rebel usually wants to see a change in the group norms to reflect his or her own views, but is rarely satisfied when a change is made. *Rebellion* always demands more change. No plan is ever good enough. Some analysts have called this type of behavior "role deviance" to describe the member who disagrees with the group on so many issues that he or she is always expected to deviate. As a result, the role sometimes becomes more important than the cause. Realizing that the type of group they desire is unlikely to develop, rebels try to make the rest of the group as unhappy as they are. The most typical group reaction to role deviants is to ignore them.

Merton found one form of deviance that has the potential to improve the quality of group decision making. *Innovative deviance* occurs when a member is committed to the group and its goals, but deviates on matters of opinion or the method of achieving one of those goals. Other analysts refer to this as "opinion deviance." Members who disagree with the emerging consensus in a group are engaging in innovative deviance. So are members who try to convince the group that a particular norm has outlived its usefulness. The goal of such deviance is to effect a positive change that will benefit the group.

Group leaders are often innovative deviants. They can and do deviate from group norms without being rebuked as severely as other group members. Edwin Hollander describes a process in which group leaders are initially the strongest conformists but eventually become less so.[21] Typically, leaders are the role models for ideal behavior. In early group meetings, they build up "idiosyncracy credits" as they perform more tasks to help the group than other members do. As norms stabilize, leaders may also be the first to recognize that some norms are no longer functional and need to be changed. Thus the leader is often the first to deviate from established norms. Take the acknowledged leader of a musical group as an example. Having strongly influenced the type of music the group is known for, he or she realizes that its style is in danger of becoming outdated. So the leader deviates by pushing the group to experiment with and evolve a new sound. According to Hollander, the group is more lenient with a leader who deviates because he or she has previously established a large bankroll of "credit" with the group. The leader is merely spending a few of those credits.

Group Reactions to Deviance Group members have a range of options for responding to deviant behavior. Cheryl Tromley has identified three general strategies that groups use in dealing with deviance: social quivering, influence attempts, and incorporation or rejection of the deviant.[22]

A typical reaction to deviance is a kind of hesitant, halting nonresponse by group members that Tromley calls "social quivering." This response is often due to lack of agreement about how important the norm is to the group. It is also the standard response of unassertive group members and is more likely to occur when high-status members violate norms. Others may be reluctant to challenge more powerful members.

If a norm is important to members, they will likely initiate attempts to influence the deviant member back into alignment with the group norm. They may use a variety of compliance-gaining strategies to convince the deviant. For disagreements about ideas, initial attempts are usually based on logic and efforts to prove that the group's point of view is superior to that of the deviant. For behavioral violations, group members may shower the deviant with positive incentives, promise favors, make a moral appeal, or even beg, "Oh, come on, just do it for us." If matters get worse, members may try threats or other negative forms of group pressure. If influence attempts are successful, the deviant behavior is abandoned and the status quo is maintained.

If direct influence fails, group members may have to try other, more complex strategies. Tromley views the group as having a continuum of options, ranging in severity from incorporation of the deviant behavior as an approved group behavior to outright rejection of the deviant. Figure 10.2 depicts the continuum; its options are described here:

- *Incorporation* occurs when the group is swayed by the deviant's arguments. This may happen most frequently in cases involving innovative deviance. The outcome: A new group norm replaces the old one that had been violated.
- *Acceptance* means that the group allows the deviant behavior to continue. The group does not adopt the behavior as its own norm, but it does not see the deviance as significant enough to erode the group standard.
- *Discommendation* takes place when group members verbally disapprove of the deviant behavior, but then continue as if nothing had happened. It is as if members hope for a return to the group standard, but do not want to invest the energy to make sure it happens.
- *Ignoring* the deviant's actions is another possible response. Here members do not acknowledge the deviance in spite of a widespread feeling of disapproval. This may be appropriate when the deviant behavior is not likely to recur or when the deviant simply wants attention. It differs from acceptance and social quivering in that it is an attempt to not reinforce the deviant's behavior. The strategy seems to be "ignore it and it will go away," much as a parent hopes to extinguish a child's negative behavior by not drawing attention to it.
- *Institutionalization* occurs when the group defines the deviant behavior or the deviant person as a special case, as an exception to the rule. As mentioned earlier, groups often need scapegoats or someone who is a little different to be the butt of their jokes.
- *Rejection* of the deviant is usually the last straw. When deviance begins to threaten the very fabric of the group, it may be necessary to strip the person of his or her membership.

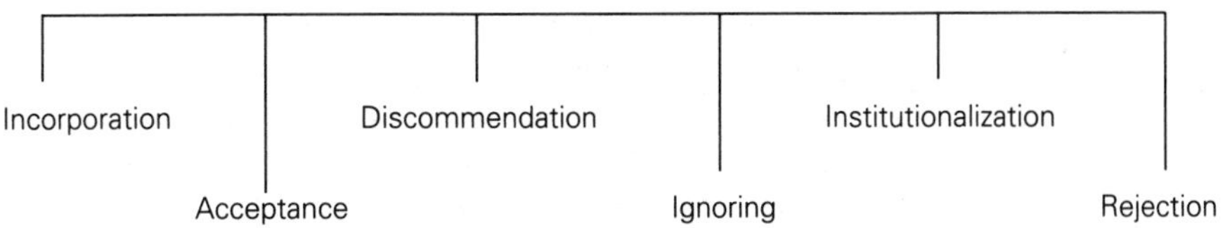

Figure 10.2 Group responses to deviance: the incorporation-rejection continuum. [Adapted from Cheryl Tromley, "The Strategies Groups Use to Deal with Deviant Members," Ph.D. dissertation, Yale University, 1984.]

Tromley argues that groups seldom consider all the options for responding to deviance and so fail to use the creative tensions that deviance brings on.

Guidelines for Managing Tension

Groups norms that are too strict or outdated can stifle creativity or produce a prisonlike atmosphere in the group. Deviance, if not managed properly, can threaten cohesion and consume precious time and energy. To help manage the inherent tension between these two group dynamics, we suggest the following guidelines:

- Spend some time assessing the explicit and implicit norms operating in the group. Bring to the group's attention those norms that you believe are dysfunctional or potentially negative.
- Use Jackson's model to identify specific problems with norms or their enforcement. Perhaps the range of tolerable behavior is too strict and needs to be relaxed. Or maybe the norm itself is fine, but sanctions need to be more uniform.
- Always consider the possible unintended consequences of changing a norm. Does the norm capture some central feature of the group's identity? To what degree will change threaten cohesion? Will a change prompt other, more serious problems?
- Use Tromley's model to deal more constructively with acts of deviance in your group. Many groups wait too long to react to the three dysfunctional forms of deviance (ritualism, retreatism, and rebellion) and then feel that rejection is their only option. Earlier use of the other options can help keep these types of deviance in check.
- Remember the potential value of institutionalizing some deviant behaviors, if only to remind the group of the boundaries. If the group is initially annoyed by one member's constant clock watching, members might occasionally ask, "What time is it, Joey?" to signal their displeasure and to remind themselves not to be ruled by the clock.

- Allow room for a little deviance on occasion so members can blow off steam and retain their sense of individuality.
- Consider innovative deviance and its potential useful suggestions and new behavioral norms that may initially seem out of line. You will not discover creative solutions unless you are willing to try a fresh approach from time to time.

Group culture can be either productive or unproductive. The level of cohesion and group identification that emerges can give rise to norms that enable a group to work well or poorly at decision-making tasks. The group can thwart deviant behavior or it can consider the appropriateness of change. Every new episode of interaction can reinforce the existing culture or move in the direction of change. One of the most telling and challenging episodes for a group to handle is the addition of new members or the loss of old ones.

The Socialization of Members

Intact groups do not always remain so. Members come and go, making it necessary for the group to recruit and socialize new members. *Socialization* is the process of individuals acquiring the behaviors considered appropriate by the group and influencing the group to modify its standards of appropriateness.[23] Richard Moreland and John Levine developed an interesting model of how groups and individuals adapt to each other over time.[24] We will explain their model next.

Key Processes in Socialization

Moreland and Levine offer us a model of group socialization that is both dynamic and reciprocal. The model is dynamic in its recognition that the relationship between the group and any single member changes over time. It is reciprocal in that it views the process from both the perspective of the individual and that of the group. From the individual's perspective, the model describes the process by which a person surveys the group before joining, tries to fit in, and looks for ways to expand his or her role and influence group norms. From the group perspective, the model outlines how groups recruit new members, socialize them, change in response to them, and excommunicate them when they stray too far from group norms. Moreland and Levine stress three basic processes that characterize group socialization: evaluation, commitment, and role transitions.

Evaluation When a group assesses the potential or actual value of a particular member, that group is engaging in evaluation. Similarly, when an individual tries to determine what rewards the group has to offer, evaluation takes place. Both groups and individuals use criteria to assess the other. Groups sometimes specify their criteria in job descriptions, but more often they are implicit rather than explicit. Task groups often evaluate members in terms of how well they help the group achieve its goals and enforce and conform to group norms and whether or not they are fun to be around. An individual may judge the group in terms of how much time the group demands, how much he or she enjoys meetings, and the extent to which the group can satisfy his or her interests and needs. Each of us is evaluated by members of the various groups we work in and socialize with every day.

Commitment When evaluation results in a positive outcome, greater commitment is likely. If the group is a rewarding experience for the individual, he or she becomes more committed to the group's goals and its decisions. Such a member is more likely to promote activities that enhance cohesion, sacrifice personal gain for the good of the group, desire that membership in the group continue, and strive for consensus instead of trying to win arguments.[25]

From the perspective of the group, commitment means something different. The more an individual is evaluated positively by the group, the more the group is willing to expend energy to help that member during a crisis or cover for his or her absence. The group will be more accepting of the individual's needs and values, maintain friendly ties, be more likely to accommodate deviant behavior, and want him or her to remain as a member.[26] Normally, the commitment levels of the group and the individual are evenly matched. When they are not, Moreland and Levine suggest that the "principle of least interest" applies:

> The party that feels less committed has greater power in the relationship. If the group's level of commitment greatly exceeds that of the individual, then he or she may come to occupy a position of status and authority within the group. In contrast, if an individual's level of commitment is greater than that of the group, then he or she will tend to have low power and may be derogated and devalued by other group members.[27]

This principle may seem odd. Why would someone with less commitment have more power? But if you have ever worked with a group in which one member truly did not care about the group or the consequences of a poor group performance, then you understand this principle well. With nothing at stake, the group member is free to do as he or she pleases. The group is powerless to control the deviant's behavior because nothing it can do will matter to him or her. On the other hand, the group may take advantage of the member who is too committed. The group will let him or her do all the work for little of the credit. Perhaps you have witnessed groups in which commitment levels were not equal. Sadly, many group members avoid demonstrating a commitment because they fear that the commitment will not be returned.

Stages of Membership and Role Transitions

Moreland and Levine identify five stages of the group socialization process: investigation, socialization, maintenance, resocialization, and remembrance. The movement from one stage to another is marked by a change in the role of

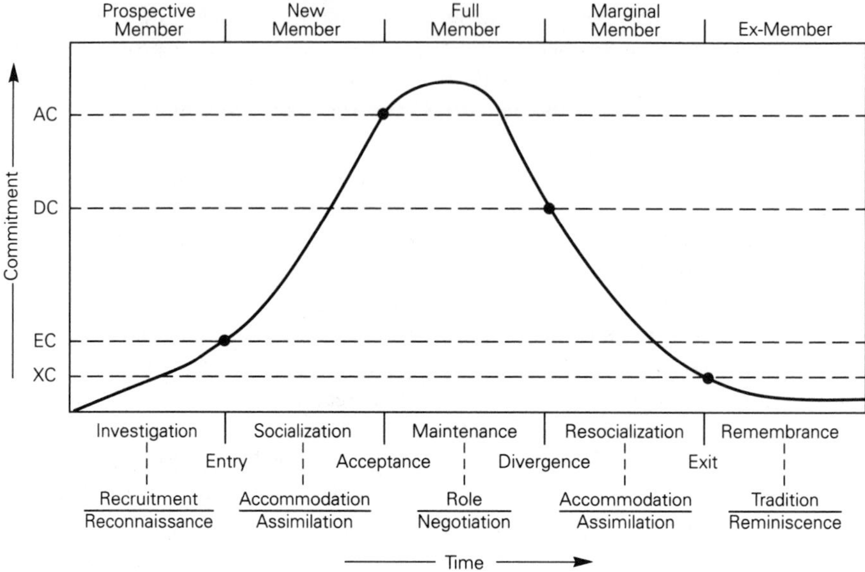

Figure 10.3 Moreland and Levine's model of group socialization. [From Richard Moreland and John Levine, "Socialization in Small Groups: Temporal Changes in Individual-Group Relations," in *Advances in Experimental Social Psychology, vol. 15*, edited by Leonard Berkowitz (New York: Academic Press, 1982), p. 153. Used with permission of Academic Press.]

the new member in relation to the rest of the group. Thus, there are four role transitions:

- *Entry* marks the movement from the investigation into the socialization stage.
- *Acceptance* signals the move from socialization to maintenance.
- *Divergence* characterizes the shift to resocialization.
- *Exit* delineates the transition to the remembrance stage.

The relationships among these five stages and four role transitions are diagrammed in Figure 10.3. We begin with a description of the first stage.

Stage 1: Investigation When a group needs new blood or an individual scouts prospective groups to join, both are involved in investigation. For the group's part, this means *recruitment*. Members size up the potential fitness of those who indicate a willingness to join them. The classified ads in daily and specialized newspapers often include descriptions of the kind of person who will fit in with the group or organization looking to hire. The individual engages in *reconnaissance*, trying to find the right group to satisfy his or her needs and ambitions. The rush period sponsored by fraternities and sororities is perhaps the most obvious example of this stage. Groups often demand that prospective members engage in unpleasant initiation activities. Such unpleasantries often force the individual to justify membership worth the effort. The group wants the member to think: "I wouldn't be doing this if I didn't value the group." See Box 10.1 for examples of initiation.

The *entry* role transition involves the movement of an individual from the category of nonmember or prospective member to new member. It is the rookie season in which the new member learns the ropes and the group keeps an eye on the new member's moves. Members work overtime on evaluation during this period. Longtime group members usually know precisely what they want to see and hear from new members, but refuse to divulge their criteria. They like to see if the new member can figure it out for himself or herself.

Stage 2: Socialization Once the new member is on board, the group attempts to teach him or her the behaviors, thoughts, and feelings appropriate for a member of the group. The individual must undergo a process of *assimilation*, adopting new behaviors and identifying with the group as a whole. Few people want to be seen as complete conformists, so most new members try to make at least a small mark on the group. You might try to get the group to adopt or modify the way it does certain activities. Convincing the group to alter the way it records its minutes would be a concession, for instance. When the group changes its behavior, it shows *accommodation*. Once the initial give-and-take of socialization takes place, both the group and the new member can rest. Full membership has been granted and the *acceptance* transition is complete.

If the new member gets high marks, in time the transition to full member takes place. It is often difficult to tell exactly when this transition takes place, but one sure sign of its occurrence is that the new member starts receiving the same treatment as everyone else. All the rights and responsibilities of group membership are accorded to the new member. No one watches you carefully anymore.

Stage 3: Maintenance During the next period of socialization, the group and the individual experience *role negotiation*. The group tries to cast the new member in one or more roles that will most help the group to achieve its goals. A group that has been lacking a good "idea person" may push the member to come up with new ideas. The individual, on the other hand, may have designs of his or her own. The new member may try to create a role that will satisfy personal needs or ambitions or wrestle a role from another group member. If they are successful in negotiating a good compromise, the maintenance phase may last for months or even years. If not, or if after some time of wedded bliss, the group or individual wants a new role performed, the process of *divergence* signals a shift to the next stage.

Divergence marks the process of falling from grace. The once full member slides toward marginal membership status. Often this is a conscious move by the member who decides that other groups are more important. He or she

Box 10.1

Socialize Me: Experiences of New Group Members

When people really want to belong to a group, they will do almost anything to prove they belong. The tradition of hazing, or harassment, lives on in so many different forms that we often forget its significance. Groups seldom accept new members without some level of testing to see if the rookie is made of "the right stuff." Some groups advertise the criteria by which they will judge you; others prefer to make things mysterious.

The Marines are always "looking for a few good men." But to prove you are one, you know you will have to show the strength and stamina to survive boot camp and demonstrate spit-shine cleanliness, an unwavering loyalty to authority, and the spirit of "semper fi." The requirements are strict but straightforward. You will be pushed to your physical limit and possibly stripped of your self-importance, but at least you know what is likely to happen from the outset.

In many other groups, newcomers do not quite know what unusual behavior the "veterans" will demand of them. A rookie at a pro football summer training camp may be told to stand on a dining table and sing his school song or repeat some embarrassingly silly cheer to an unappreciative audience—no applause, no laughter, no indication that his cracking voice was even heard. In *Paper Lion*, writer George Plimpton revealed what it was like to be an unheralded rookie with the Detroit Lions football team during their 1963 summer training camp. He tells of rookies eating their meals in the woods for fear of being called upon to perform if they ate in the dining hall.

On occasion, new members are seen as potential threats to the status quo or to the pecking order already established in an organization. A friend of ours, an executive secretary to a financial analyst, moved with her boss to a new company. She arrived at her new office a few days before her boss was scheduled to start working. He had told her to go ahead, meet her new coworkers, and become familiar with their office routine. Afraid that she would upset their standing in the office hierarchy, employees gave her the cold shoulder. No one spoke to her, no one gave her a tour of the facilities, and no one returned her requests for information. For nearly a week she was ostracized. Only after members realized that she was not a threat did they begin to show signs of acceptance. By then, it was almost too late.

In *Corporate Cultures*, Terrance Deal and Alan Kennedy tell the story of Henry Kissinger, when he was Secretary of State, welcoming a new member to his staff by giving him an "urgent" report to write. Wanting to please his new boss, the employee stayed up nights to finish the report on time. The next day the report was returned with a note that it was "unacceptable" and would have to be rewritten. It was rewritten, not once but two or three times. At last, Kissinger responded positively: "Good, now I'll read the

Box 10.1 (continued)

report." The message of this rite of initiation was harsh but clear—do not hand in anything but your best work.

Sometimes group members themselves are not sure how far they will go in hazing a new member. Over the past few years a number of incidents have been reported of college fraternity and sorority members going too far, often resulting in violence, injury, and even the death of would-be group members. Many colleges have banned hazing activities as a result of these incidents.

The most natural aspect of this socialization is that established groups do not want to see their group identity (and the "normal" pattern of activities that supports that identity) dissolve as a result of changes in membership. So new members are not made to feel too comfortable until they have shown some respect for the group's authority. But another dynamic often takes over. When groups do test a new member and find him or her willing to be submissive, it seems to unleash a kind of unbridled power trip. Group leaders and members get caught up in the frenzy to see how far the rookie will submit. This is one of the dark sides of group interaction that we must remain aware of and caution ourselves against.

References: Terrance Deal and Alan Kennedy, *Corporate Cultures: The Rites and Rituals of Corporate Life* (Reading, Mass.: Addison-Wesley, 1982); George Plimpton, *Paper Lion* (New York: Harper & Row, 1966).

begins to create more distance from the group and fails to put in a full effort or observe the group's norms. Sometimes the group decides to initiate the divorce. The group may not keep the member fully informed or may pay less and less attention to that member's contributions.

Stage 4: Resocialization When the fit between the individual and the group begins to diverge, attempts are often made to resocialize one another. *Assimilation* and *accommodation* begin anew and sometimes result in a new role for the member and a return to the maintenance stage. If resocialization efforts do not succeed, both parties begin to assess the option of an *exit* transition.

The final transition is from marginal to ex-member. When there is a clear-cut divorce from the group, the transition is easy to see. But frequently the exit is ambiguous. A member may not show up for several meetings with little or no account for such behavior. The group may remain in limbo for weeks, not sure if it will ever see the member again. Eventually, it writes him or her off.

Stage 5: Remembrance When a member leaves the group, his or her physical presence is replaced by the memory of membership. For the group, the individual becomes part of the group *tradition* and may be referred to on occasion as an example of "what not to do" if you want to be a member in good standing. For the individual, *reminiscence* ensures that the group will not be forgotten. An assessment of what went wrong can always be helpful in the future. No one wants to make the same mistakes twice.

Moreland and Levine's model can be a valuable tool for judging your experience in almost any kind of group. Most of us will enter and exit many groups before we find ones that we can commit ourselves to for an extended time. Knowing how the process of socialization works should enable you to anticipate some of the things that will happen during your tenure in a small group. In the final section of this chapter, we consider ways you can make practical use of this knowledge.

Managing the Socialization Process

A number of risks and pitfalls can occur during the socialization process. Consider some of the following implications that we have drawn from Moreland and Levine's model.

New members can destabilize the group. This suggests that you should proceed cautiously when entering a new group. Be careful about expressing opinions or asking questions that might be unsettling to the old guard. We recommend several tactics, including:

- Progressively increasing your level of participation: Do not come on too strong during the early meetings.
- Become a member unobtrusively: Take on the role of the anthropologist who attends to everything (listens and observes) and says precious little.
- Attach yourself to a full member in good standing: Seek his or her advice about what is going on. Others will start to see your potential if they think one member has already accepted you.

If new members join a group in which you are already a member, try to remember what it was like for you and help ease the transition for them.

Be on the lookout for implicit entry criteria. Listen carefully to what full members say to you. They are probably trying to tell you what expectations they have of you without being too blunt about it. But do not simply parrot what you hear members say. One new professor overheard colleagues complaining about their students and joined in, offering his own complaints. The response he received was a lukewarm, "You haven't been here long enough to complain." As a full-fledged member, you can try to make entry criteria as explicit as possible to new members without overwhelming them.

Entry can be demeaning. So do not overreact when you are the object of the old-timers' remarks or when you are given the worst of assignments. Pass these little tests and you will get the chance to make your mark later. One typical problem is that most of us enter a new job or group with inflated, optimistic expectations that make the demeaning entry phase even more difficult to handle. But do not worry, it will pass. When others join the group, be kind and remind them that they will not always feel like a second-class member.

Take advantage of role transitions. Once you sense that the group is becoming comfortable with you, take that as a sign to start shifting gears, slowly. When the group accepts you, it is time to express your views and begin the process of role negotiation.

Keep these suggestions in mind and remember the stages and role transitions that mark your passage through the group. If you do, you can make group life a little easier for yourself.

Summary

We have focused on three major aspects of group interaction in this chapter: the development of a cohesive group culture, managing conformity to and deviance from group norms, and the socialization of new members into the group. We saw how physical proximity, perceived similarities among members, the group's cause, the quality of group communication, and group successes can foster cohesion in the group.

In addition, we noted the importance of developing group identification through speech patterns, rites and rituals, and fantasy themes. We examined several types of group norms and how they emerge, noting the significance of ideal behaviors, the range of tolerable behavior, how intensely members endorse the norms, and how much they agree about what the norms should be. The positive and negative role of deviance was discussed, with an emphasis on the alternative responses a group can make when deviance does occur.

Finally, we explored the stages of socialization that groups and new members typically go through. Again, we recommended ways to make such transitions easier to manage. Knowledge and practical application of the factors outlined in this chapter will help you build a strong social dimension in your group. And as you already know, a strong social dimension complements and enhances the group's ability to achieve its task. It can also make the work much more enjoyable.

GroupQuests: Discussion Questions

1. In this chapter, we present several factors (attraction to the group, quality of group communication, and successes of the group) that produce cohesion and several other factors (language use, heroes, villains, values, and fantasy themes) that lead to group identification. What other ingredients help create a strong social dimension?
2. Why do you think the principle of least

interest occurs when some group members are more committed or less committed to the group than the group is committed to them? How can a group or individual minimize this problem? If you were a devalued member, what would you do?

3. Can you think of any additional suggestions (beside those presented just before the Summary) to help new group members manage the socialization process? Use Moreland and Levine's model to derive implications as well as your own experiences as a newcomer to a group.

GroupWorks: Group Activities

1. Discuss Moreland and Levine's model of group socialization. As a group, try to identify some of the more common criteria used to evaluate members for entry, acceptance, divergence, or exit. Think of groups on campus (sororities, fraternities, student government groups) and try to list the criteria you think they probably use. Be sure to distinguish between implicit and explicit criteria.

2. From the perspective of a college freshman who has not yet joined any groups on campus, engage in a reconnaissance mission, scouting the various social and task groups to which you might belong. First make a list of prospective groups and then identify the reasons why a freshman would or would not want to join each group. Try to be objective in listing the pros and cons of each group.

3. Interview several members of a social or task group and try to discover what their group culture is like. Formulate questions based on the section of this chapter pertaining to group culture. Ask them to tell you what attracted them to the group, and have them describe its rites and rituals and the kinds of stories or fantasy themes that group members share. Prepare a brief written sketch of the group's culture for presentation to the class.

4. Contact several groups on campus or in the community that are inviting or accepting new members. Ask for permission to sit in on the first couple of group meetings in which new members are allowed to attend. Record examples of verbal and nonverbal messages that transpire between new members and the group. Interpret these messages in light of the concepts presented in this chapter. Note especially those behaviors that the model of socialization does *not* help you understand. Perhaps you can think of ways to modify the model to explain what is happening in the group.

GroupActs: Practical Applications

For a period of one week (or two or three group sessions), your instructor will assign a member of another group to join your group. (One member of your group may be assigned to observe another group as well.) You should continue work on your project but at the same time, you must integrate and socialize the new member *as if* he or she were going to remain in the group indefinitely. At the end of the week, reserve at least thirty minutes for this person to describe what he or she has found out about your group culture and what it was like to be socialized into your group (both the positive and negative aspects). Based on this person's report, talk about which aspects of your group culture or socialization process you might want to alter.

CHAPTER 11

The Group Level: Decision Development

Jim Jenkins could not understand why the Task Force on Better Relations had to meet so frequently and took so long to get anything accomplished. Three meetings in three weeks had produced only a rough outline of the group's goals and objectives. Jim had expected the group to be halfway through the project by now. To him, the problem seemed simple. Several recent incidents caused by racial tension had erupted on the work floor in the manufacturing plant. Jim was sure he knew who the troublemakers were and thought they should be disciplined before things got worse. He could not understand why other members of the Task Force did not see the problem in the same way he did. Instead, several members wanted to gather information on each incident, and one person was pushing for access to the company's disciplinary files over the past three years. How long, Jim wondered, would the group keep spinning its wheels?

Perhaps you have found yourself in situations similar to that of Jim Jenkins. It can be an extremely frustrating experience when the "simple problem" you agreed to work on seems to be defined differently by each member of the group. It is frustrating but not uncommon. Most groups go through an initial phase of high anxiety simply because they are operating on the basis of five or seven individual opinions on every issue. It takes time to carve a group perspective out of the differing information and viewpoints that each member brings to the discussion. In Chapter 10, we noted how much time and effort it takes to develop the full potential of a group's social dimension. Group characteristics such as cohesiveness and group identification cannot be manufactured in one or two meetings. In the same way, a group cannot be expected to produce decisions quickly. Developing a strong task dimension requires that we learn to allow decisions to evolve slowly and carefully. This process is known as decision development.

How Do Group Decisions Develop?

A consistent theme in group research has been the search for the pattern by which decisions emerge over time in a group. Researchers have speculated that group members focus their energies on different aspects of task and social relations at different times. The goal of this research has been to identify predictable phases of group decision making. If phases can be identified, group members can take advantage of such knowledge in several ways. They can learn to:

- Anticipate the next phase and judge what is happening in their group in light of the overall phase model
- Better manage their contributions, timing them to fit the nature of the current phase of interaction
- Be more patient with slow progress, as long as decisions seem to be developing according to the expected phases
- Take corrective action if the group appears to be off the track—that is, not following a typical path

Researchers have proposed several different models of the phases of decision development. We will describe three different types: the traditional unitary phase model, the contingency model, and the punctuated equilibrium model.

Traditional Unitary Phase Models

For nearly forty years, unitary models have been the dominant view of how groups develop and change over time. A unitary phase model predicts that decisions develop through a single, fixed set of phases. In other words, effective groups are believed to proceed in a very similar manner: first through Phase A, then through Phase B, and so on. This pattern is expected to occur even in groups of different sizes, with different types of tasks, different styles of leadership, and with different levels of cohesion. Although researchers have carved up the sequence into three, four, and sometimes five phases, there has been a remarkable similarity in the behavioral content of those phases. We will review three traditional models and show you the similarity among the models by Bales and Strodtbeck, Tuckman, and Fisher. You have already encountered (in Chapter 2) Fisher's model of the natural group process, which includes the four phases of orientation, conflict, emergence, and reinforcement.

Bales and Strodtbeck's Model In the early 1950s, Robert Bales and Fred Strodtbeck proposed that groups with full-fledged problems to solve followed a three-phase course of action involving orientation, evaluation, and control.[1] In the orientation phase, groups spent most of their time trying to decide the nature of the problem, giving and asking for information, repeating and clarifying information, and confirming what they already knew about the problem. The next phase was characterized by members giving and asking for opinion, analysis, and evaluation of ideas. Members were more likely to express their own feelings and desires about a given proposal during this evaluation period. Finally, in the control phase, members got down to business by giving and asking for suggestions, a direction to take, or a specific course of action to be followed. They decided what needed to be done about the problem.

As for the relational communication among members, Bales and Strodtbeck noted that positive reactions such as agreeing with one another, joking and laughing, showing satisfaction, and rewarding and helping each other increased over time from the first phase to the second. At the same time, negative reactions such as disagreeing, passive rejection, withholding help, showing tension, and withdrawing from the group also increased. In fact, the negative reactions continued to increase into the first half of the control phase, but dissipated toward the end of that phase. The latter half of the control phase was almost exclusively positive in tone. This three-phase pattern also repeated itself when groups finalized one decision and took on a new task.

Tuckman's Model In the mid-1960s, Bruce Tuckman synthesized the research on group development and proposed a five-phase model that he believed captured the essence of the emergence of decisions. For Tuckman, groups faced consecutive periods of forming, storming, norming, performing, and adjourning.[2] Each phase reveals a change in group behavior along both its task and social dimensions.

For the task dimension, the group's problem during the forming stage is how to identify the task. Effort is devoted to determining exactly what the group is supposed to do and drafting a plan of attack. In terms of the social dimension, this is a period of awkward relations, with members cautiously trying to build an appropriate level of dependency and trust in each other.

Once members understand their task, they begin to focus on their own individual (and often emotional) reactions to that task. In this storming phase, as members become more comfortable with each other, they feel freer to question authority, disagree with each other's ideas, and assert an interest in particular roles such as leadership of the group.

Out of the tempest of intragroup conflict, members begin to develop shared interpretations and perspectives on the task at hand. This norming phase usually results in major breakthroughs on the task dimension. The many small decisions the group has already made begin to add up to one major plan of attack. Socially, members begin to resolve many of the differences that have emerged and threatened their existence as a group. In this period, group standards about roles and norms emerge. Cohesive feelings become strong during this time.

In the fourth phase, performing, groups seem to get the most work accomplished. The group now is busy working on its overall plan. With group relationships in a positive vein, the cohesive group can focus its energy on work.

As the completion of its project nears an end, group members make another shift in their pattern of behavior. During the adjourning phase, talk begins to focus on tying up loose ends and otherwise creating a sense of closure about the task. If the group is to disband, members may reflect on their time together or talk about their individual futures. If the group expects to remain together, it may anticipate the next assignment and what adjustments it may need to make in the future.

Fisher's Model In the early 1970s, Aubrey Fisher departed somewhat from earlier models by focusing specifically on the pattern of interacts that characterized group communication over time.[3] An *interact*, you will recall from Chapter 4, consists of the behavior of one group member and the immediate response (feedback) of the next speaker. By focusing on interacts, Fisher was able to determine which types of communication behavior were most likely to be reinforced or squelched during a specific phase of interaction. Fisher's four-phase model was described in Chapter 2, so our comments here will be brief.

As with earlier researchers, Fisher observed that group interaction is initially awkward and cautious. The first phase, orientation, is typified by small talk and a reluctance to allow any one member or idea to dominate the direction of discussion. More specifically, members are most likely to give each other mildly positive or ambiguous feedback about their ideas. Members appear to need time to orient themselves to one another (by socializing) and to the task (by proposing ideas tentatively).

Tentativeness and ambiguity give way to heated discussion during the conflict phase. Members express much stronger opinions and will not accept ambiguous feedback. They want to know where each person stands on the issues and proposals being discussed. This level of disagreement is necessary if groups are to clearly understand the nature of the problem and the options available to them. Also typical of this phase is interpersonal role conflict as members try to establish their place in the group's role structure.

A third shift in the group's communication pattern indicates an emergence out of conflict as well as the emergence of several specific group products, such as a major decision, a stable role structure, and a clearer sense of group norms. The emergence from conflict is noted by the return of ambiguous feedback to proposals. Fisher believed that ambiguity at this point was a face-saving device. It allowed group members who were initially against the emerging consensus to back down gracefully. For instance, a member who first opposed the idea of conducting a survey might say, "I am still afraid that we will spend an inordinate amount of time waiting for the survey results, but if we spend that time wisely—I can see some benefit to doing a survey." If we look at the statement closely, we'll see that the first part of it contains a mildly negative reaction (wasting time), the second part presents a conditional reaction (if we spend time wisely), while the last part is more positive (some benefit). Taken together, the statement qualifies as ambiguous because members could focus on any one of the three parts, ignoring the others; be confused about what the member really thinks; or recognize it as a reconciliation. If the group is striving for consensus, this is the phase in which the shape of a final decision starts to become apparent to members. Roles and norms are also more easily identified at this point because members now have enough experience with each other to recognize these habitual routines.

In the final phase of interaction, reinforcement, Fisher observed almost exclusively positive feedback among group members. Reaching consensus eliminates the need for negative or ambiguous feedback. Even groups whose final product may not have been all they hoped it would be seem happy to have produced a finished product on time.

The similarities among these traditional unitary models are readily apparent. Although researchers have used different terminology to label each phase, little in their descriptions of the sequence of group activity contradicts any of the other models. In their critique of these models, Marshall Scott Poole and Jonelle Roth argued that unitary models tend to be similar because researchers were looking for consistent changes over time.[4] They assumed that some pattern of phases did exist, and this very assumption made it easier to observe similarities and ignore differences in the paths that groups follow toward a decision. In the next section, we explore Poole's alternative explanation of decision development.

Poole's Contingency Model

Since the early 1980s, Marshall Scott Poole and his associates have tried to show that there is a coordinated sequence to most group activity, but the sequence is likely to be more complicated than most unitary sequence models allow.[5] Poole views the unitary model as a kind of "ideal sequence," one that may reside among the cognitive schema of most competent members of society. But he also believes that groups depart from the ideal when certain contingencies arise. Four aspects of his contingency theory of group development deserve our attention: activity tracks, breakpoints, contingency factors, and multiple decision sequences.

Tracks of Group Activity Poole argues, as other researchers have, that groups must manage at least three primary dimensions or "activity tracks" while making decisions:

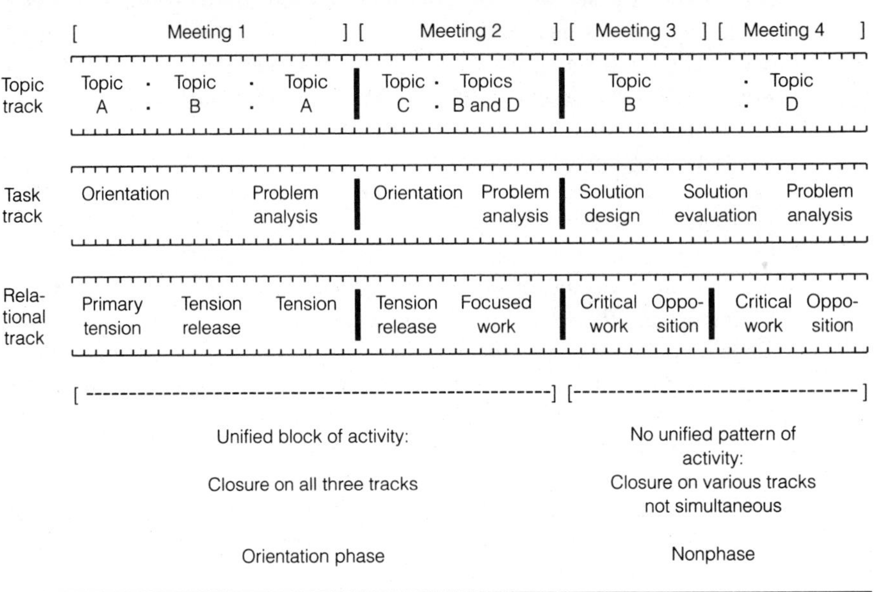

Figure 11.1 A comparison of unified and nonunified activity tracks.

1. *Task process behavior.* Activities related to the management of a group's task—for example, problem analysis and evaluation of solutions.
2. *Working relations.* Behaviors reflecting the working arrangements in the group—primary tension, conflict, focused work, integration.
3. *Topical focus.* Substantive issues under discussion at any time.

Unlike other researchers, Poole sees decision development as "a series of intertwining threads of activity that evolve simultaneously and interlock in different patterns over time."[6] If a group happens to reach consensus on all three tracks at one time, then a unified phase may indeed take place.

Take the hypothetical example of group development in Figure 11.1, for instance. Note that in the first two group meetings, the group repeatedly returns to two primary topics (Topics A and B in the topical track). The group's task track is characterized as mostly orientation behavior and some problem analysis. All the while, the group experiences an alternating sequence of primary tension and tension release in its relational track. Note especially how activity along all three tracks is resolved near the end of the second meeting. When activities interlock in such a coordinated fashion, the group's development would look very much like the orientation phase predicted by the unitary sequence models.

But look at the group's interaction during the third meeting. Even though only one topic is the focus of the group's attention, activity on the task track has moved abruptly from problem analysis to solution design, elaboration, and evaluation. At the relational level, members shift back and forth among periods of focused work (members concentrate on their task and do not disagree with one another), critical work (members' disagreements are centered on ideas), and opposition (disagreements are more personal). Resolution of the various activities does not occur at the same time; some issues are carried over into the next meeting. There is no solid block of activity that can be neatly described as a conflict phase. Indeed, the task track seems more characteristic of Fisher's emergence phase. This pattern may work well for the group, but it does not fit the simple, straightforward unitary sequence model.

Poole argues that the three activity tracks may interlock in one of three ways: (1) in "unified blocks of activity," producing unitary sequences; (2) in a "coordinated, but complicated" manner, producing one of several alternative decision paths; or (3) in a "disorganized" manner, so that some periods of group life are best described as nonphases. Changes in activity tracks are likely to occur at major breakpoints in the group process.

Breakpoints *Breakpoints* are events that disrupt the normal flow of productive discussion or work and may indicate that the group is moving on to another phase of development.[7] Three types of breakpoints are described by Poole: normal breakpoints, delays, and disruptions. *Normal breakpoints* create a break without disrupting group activities—for example, shifts in the topic or adjournments. *Delays* cause the group to repeat or rework previous efforts such as redefining the problem in light of new information. *Disruptions* halt group progress for a significant time; a major conflict or failure to find any satisfactory solutions can disrupt progress. Breakpoints are natural places to evaluate group development. They are most often viewed as negative because they slow the group down. But breakpoints can also help a group if they prevent wasted effort and dead-end pursuits.

Contingency Factors Why do some groups move in an orderly progression of phases while others appear disorganized or take a roundabout decision path? Poole has proposed and tested several factors that seem to make a difference. He has categorized the factors as three sets of contingencies that structure group interaction and result in a particular decision path: objective task characteristics, group task characteristics, and group structural characteristics. Figure 11.2 shows how these factors are related to group interaction and decision paths.

Objective task characteristics are aspects of the task itself, regardless of a given group's level of knowledge or experience working on such a task in the past. Poole describes six different objective characteristics:

- *Openness.* If the group receives a predefined set of solutions to evaluate or decision options to consider, its task is closed; if the group has the freedom to generate options, the task is open.
- *Goal clarity.* If the group gets a clearly defined goal at the outset of its

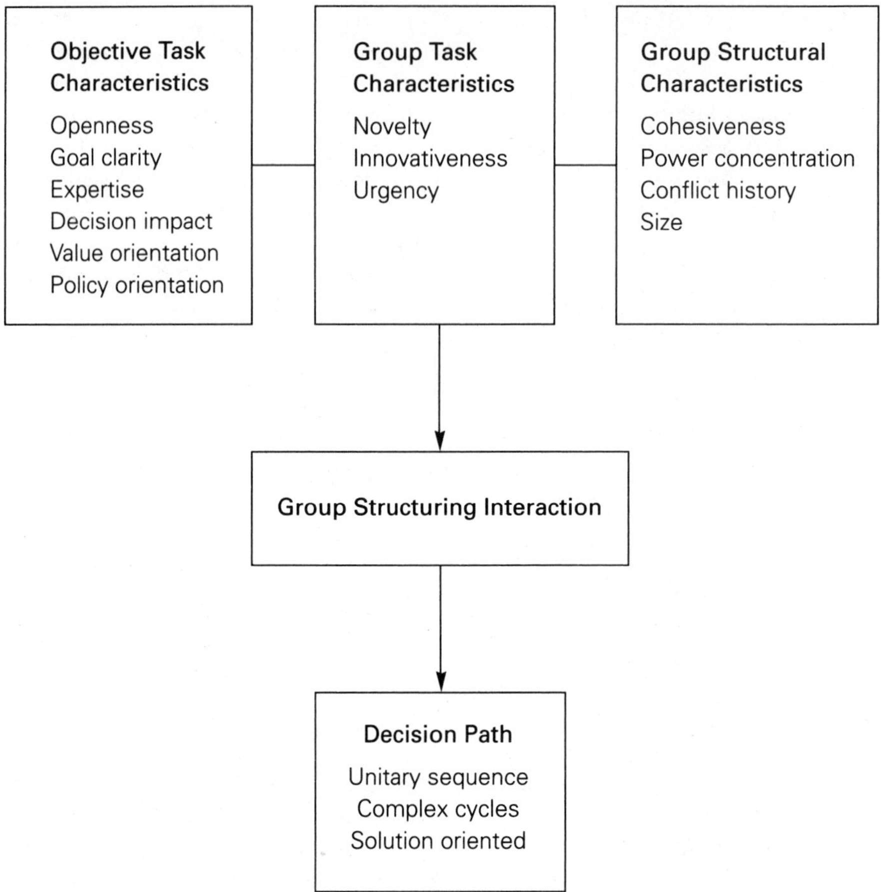

Figure 11.2 Poole's contingency model of decision development. [Adapted from Marshall Scott Poole and Jonelle Roth, "Decision Development in Small Groups V: Test of a Contingency Model," *Human Communication Research*, 1989, *15*, 552. © 1989 by Sage Publications. Reprinted by permission of Sage Publications, Inc.]

project, goal clarity is high; if no goals are articulated (or if they are stated ambiguously), goal clarity is low.

- *Required expertise.* The degree to which specialized knowledge is necessary for a satisfactory decision.
- *Impact of the decision.* If the decision affects a diverse audience outside the group, impact is high; if it affects only people inside the group, impact is low.
- *Value orientation.* If the decision involves mostly factual issues, orientation is low; if it involves many value-laden issues, orientation is high.

- *Policy orientation.* If the decision focuses on specific actions, orientation is low; if issues are to be generalized beyond the specific case, orientation is high.

Group task characteristics relate to the group's knowledge and experience with the type of task it must tackle. Poole identifies three such characteristics, although there may be many more:

- *Task novelty.* The degree to which the group is familiar with the issues to be decided.
- *Innovativeness.* The degree to which the group must create a new solution, as opposed to adopting or adapting a model decision made by itself or another group on some similar problem.
- *Urgency.* The time pressure under which a group must make a decision.

Group structural characteristics are aspects of the group that affect the way its members work together. Poole cites four factors, but again, there are no doubt others that could be included:

- *Cohesiveness.* The degree to which members perceive themselves to be a unified group and are attracted to it.
- *Power concentration.* The degree to which power is concentrated in the hands of a few members or is shared by most members.
- *Conflict history.* The extent to which group members have disagreed openly in the past.
- *Group size.* The number of members in the group.

Each of these three sets of contingency factors are thought to have a potential impact on the decision path a group follows. We turn our attention now to the final aspect of Poole's model, the multiple sequences of group development in making a decision.

Multiple Decision Sequences What are the different paths that groups follow in reaching decisions? How many are there? How do the various contingency factors influence which decision path a group will take? Poole and his colleagues have attempted to answer these questions. In a recent study, twenty-nine groups were observed making a total of forty-seven different decisions.[8] The groups ranged from a medical school teaching team and a city energy conservation committee to several managerial groups and student project groups. In that study, three major decision paths were discovered, with each one having several variations or subtypes. The major types are reviewed here; Figure 11.3 lists the subtypes.

The first major type of decision path was the traditional one predicted by unitary models. However, groups followed a strict unitary sequence in only eleven of the forty-seven decisions observed, just 23 percent. Thus this path was not the most frequent, let alone the only decision path. In a follow-up

A Typology of Decision Paths

Main Type	Subtype	Description
1. Unitary sequence	1a. Simple unitary sequence	Unified periods of activity: orientation/problem analysis and solution analysis/reinforcement
	1b. Overlapping unitary sequence	Limited overlap of problem analysis and solution analysis phases
	1c. Solution-unitary sequence	Group had short false start solution phase, then went into sequence 1a or 1b
2. Complex cyclic	2a. Focused cycles	Two to seven cycles of unitary sequences and problem/solution phases coupled with a working relationship of focused or critical work
	2b. Conflict cycles	Same task cycle as 2a but working relationship of opposition and open conflict
	2c. Solution-complex cycles	Began solution phase, then went into sequence 2a or 2b
3. Solution oriented	3a. Focused solution-oriented	Solution behavior interspersed with orientation, integration, and disorganization periods; relational climate of focused work or critical work
	3b. Conflictive solution-oriented	Same task cycle as 3a but working climate of opposition and conflict
	3c. Focused solution-confirmation cycles	Steady stream of solution work regularly broken up by decision confirmation activity; focused or critical work typical of relational climate
	3d. Conflictive solution-confirmation cycles	Same task cycle as 3c but a relational climate of conflict and opposition exists

Figure 11.3 Poole and Roth have identified three main types of decision paths that groups follow to reach decisions, along with a number of subtypes. [Adapted from Marshall Scott Poole and Jonelle Roth, "Decision Development in Small Groups IV: A Typology of Group Decision Paths," *Human Communication Research*, 1989, *15*, 323–356. © 1989 by Sage Publications. Reprinted by permission of Sage Publications, Inc.]

study, Poole and Roth tested the influence of the various contingency factors on the decision path chosen. They found that a unitary sequence was most likely when the following factors were in place:

- A larger group with shared power and low cohesiveness; also likely in large, cohesive groups.
- A factual problem with unclear goals and no preliminary solution proposals.

Groups taking this approach, however, were unlikely to engage in conflict, suggesting that the conflict phase in unitary models may be overrated. But this research does give us a picture of the type of group that is most likely to make decisions by the book.

Complex cyclic paths, a second type of decision path, consisted of groups that engaged in repeated problem/solution cycles over time. Twenty-two of the forty-seven decisions (47 percent) followed one of two complex cyclic paths. In about half of these cases, the problem/solution cycles also involved enough orientation and reinforcement that they could be considered as small unitary sequences in their own right. In the other half of the cases, groups simply displayed a problem focus followed by discussion of solutions, followed by another problem focus, and so on. The groups did not reorient themselves or reinforce their decisions. Differences in relational activity accounted for the subtypes within this path. In about half of the decisions, group members engaged each other in open disagreement and conflict. The other half avoided conflict, as was the case with the unitary sequences.

When are groups most likely to follow a more complicated path such as this? According to Poole and Roth, this type of path will occur when:

- Goals are unclear and associated with value-laden issues.
- A group lacks previous experience with the issue but feels a sense of urgency.

We may also expect a complicated path when a group faces a value-oriented, familiar task with clear goals and urgent time constraints.

In *solution-oriented paths*, the third major decision route, groups were observed to move almost instantaneously to a discussion of solutions. There was very little task activity related to problem definition or analysis. In fourteen of the forty-seven decisions (30 percent), groups displayed this pattern. In all, over half of the groups studied showed a marked propensity to begin deliberations with a solution-oriented focus. Some groups overcame this tendency and redirected their efforts down one of the other paths, but many did not. These data reinforce our comment in Chapter 1 regarding the tendency of groups to become solution oriented too quickly. However, the contingency model shows that there may be a good reason why *some* groups remain focused on a solution. Under the following conditions, groups chose a solution-oriented path:

- A small, cohesive group with concentrated power and little previous history of conflict

- Clearly defined goals, prespecified solutions, and a task requiring little innovation

In most cases, Poole notes that contingency factors do not necessarily determine which path a group will take because group members may not always interpret a particular factor to be relevant to their situation. But a few contingencies do seem to operate in highly predictable ways. For instance, value-laden issues (versus factual ones) almost always produce a more complex path. Urgency also seems to prompt more complicated paths. In its haste to get everything done, the group may jump from topic to topic and exhibit more disorganization. And groups with highly concentrated power tend to follow a solution-oriented course, perhaps because the dominant member has preconceived solutions in mind.

Poole and Roth summarize their findings by specifying two general rules that seem to guide groups toward particular decision paths.

1. *Process economy rule.* Direct group activity to satisfy only those decision requisites not already met when discussion begins.
2. *Coordination rule.* Concentrate on organizing the decision path when group conditions suggest organization will be difficult; otherwise focus on the content of the decision.

These two rules may help you account for your own experiences in groups. Perhaps you have participated in group discussions where the task problem was clearly defined at the outset and group members did not perceive a need to spend time on orientation and problem analysis.

We find Poole's contingency model extremely helpful. It explains some of the more complicated aspects of group interaction by referring to a relatively small handful of task and social contingencies. The only major criticism we have of the model is that studies have not yet determined if some decision paths do or do not lead to higher quality decisions. Presumably, a group will select the path best suited to the contingencies it faces. But as you know, groups do not always do what they should. Many groups struggle to reach their potential. If your group seems to be struggling, do not give up hope. Box 11.1 demonstrates that even struggling groups eventually get their second wind. If your group wants to get an efficient start, take the time to look closely at the situational factors the group faces. The contingency model can help you decide how to respond to those circumstances. It certainly can help you understand why your group makes decisions in a particular manner.

Managing Decision Development

What do these models of decision development tell us? How can we make use of these theories to improve our own group experience? There are several conclusions to draw from this work. Knowledge about alternative decision paths enables you to:

- Assess the various group contingencies and help your group decide if it should try to organize the group process. The process economy and coordination rules are especially helpful in this regard.
- Be patient with the group process if it seems to be on an appropriate track. (You now know which contingencies to look at to determine if the group is on an appropriate track.) Have patience if the group does not follow the standard sequence of phases.
- Take corrective action when the group really is off the track. For example, if the group focuses on solutions when contingencies do not suggest it, you can ask the group to start over by defining the problem.
- Judge progress on the basis of whether the group seems to understand its problem well enough by the transition period to organize its effort for phase two of Gersick's model (see Box 11.1).
- Take advantage of the natural midpoint on the group's calendar to reassess group progress and make contact with important external forces.

If you occasionally remind yourself of what you now know about decision development, your ability to turn that knowledge to practical advantage may surprise you.

Summary

In focusing on how group decisions emerge over time, this chapter demonstrates the variety of ways that groups can sequence task-oriented episodes and activities to achieve high-quality decisions. One simple alternative, especially appropriate for beginning groups, is to sequence activities according to one of the traditional unitary models: to anticipate periods of orientation, conflict, emergence, and reinforcement, for instance. We also reviewed Marshall Poole's situational contingency model, which describes several situational factors that signal when an alternative decision-making path might be more feasible. For instance, on-going groups may need very little time to orient themselves to a new task. Groups that have inherited a precisely defined problem can probably forego problem analysis and take a more solution-oriented path.

We also explored the optimism of Connie Gersick's punctuated equilibrium model (see Box 11.1), which demonstrates that groups can survive and even prosper despite a seemingly disorganized first half of their project. Finally, we described some ways to use these models to analyze and better manage your own group's decision-making process. Altogether, this chapter should provide you with the comfort that while the road to high-quality decisions is not always straight, it can be more predictable if you know which signposts to follow.

Box 11.1

Mid-Life Crisis in the Small Group

If you have ever participated in a decision-making group that seemed to be in utter disarray and had trouble getting started, you may wonder if there is any hope for such groups. Some recent research suggests that getting organized early is important, but a chaotic pattern of group development is not necessarily fatal. It seems that groups, just like humans, often experience a mid-life crisis that gets them back on track.

Connie Gersick conducted an intensive study of eight task groups from the beginning of a major project to its conclusion. None of the groups she observed followed a unitary sequence. Neither did she find any consistent sequence of discussion themes across groups. (Poole would probably suggest that each group followed a different decision path.) But seven of the eight groups did display a consistent two-phase process. And she found a remarkable similarity in the timing of each group's transition from phase one to phase two. A diagram of these phases appears in Figure 11.4.

Phase One

One striking feature of the groups Gersick observed was the significance of their first meeting. Each group started out by establishing a distinctive framework (not always intentionally), often within the first few minutes of the meeting. The framework (a particular set of behaviors, procedures, or content themes) then served as a constraint that dominated the first half of the group's life. As an example, note the framework established by this group of four bank executives during the first twenty-five seconds of their first meeting:

Don: What do you think we ought to do to start this, Rick? Just go through each of these? [referring to a list of topics]

Rick: Well, I want to explain to Gil and Porter—we had a little rump session the other day just to say "What the hell is this thing? What does it *say*, and what are the things that we have to decide?" And what we did was run through a group of 'em. . . . These are not necessarily in order of importance—they're in order of the way we thought of 'em, really.[1]

Gersick notes that this group followed Rick's lead in several ways for the rest of phase one. Its approach to problem solving was to continually ask questions such as "What is this thing?" and to make lists of "the things we have to decide." Furthermore, every group meeting was preceded by a "rump

Box 11.1 (continued)

Phase 1			Phase 2	
First meeting	Initial period of inertia	Transition episode	Second period of inertia	Final meeting
Interaction establishes framework for subsequent meetings	Work	Group pauses to reflect and assess progress; establishes new direction	Work	Marked acceleration of activity to finish project

Figure 11.4 Gersick's model of decision development. [Based on Connie Gersick, "Time and Transition in Work Teams: Toward a New Model of Group Development," *Academy of Management Journal*, 1988, *31*, 9–41.]

session" between the leader and one other member where the agenda for the meeting was planned. The other groups she studied also developed their own distinctive approaches during the first meeting and stuck with that approach throughout phase one.

The importance of the first meeting contrasts somewhat with the descriptions of the orientation phase found in unitary models. In the traditional models, groups approach matters more cautiously and seem to be more concerned with the social rather than the task dimension. Gersick studied groups in both work organizations and university settings and found that the first meeting set the tone for all that was to follow. Perhaps earlier researchers did not look carefully enough for the influence of such patterns.

After the first meeting, groups seemed to fall into a period of inertia. If the first meeting was a stalled effort, the group remained stalled for some time. If the group's distinctive approach got it going right from the start, it kept moving on the same course of action. If the team started out in harmony, it remained so through phase one. If conflict was experienced in the first meeting, it occurred throughout the first phase.

The Transition Episode

The halfway point between the group's first meeting and its official deadline marked a significant turning point for each group. This "mid-life crisis" occurred regardless of the differences in project length. Some groups met for as few as seven days; others for as long as six months. *In each case, a major transition took place just about midway through the project.* At this time, the group experienced a "concentrated burst of changes" resulting in a new outlook and dramatic progress toward its goal.

Box 11.1 (continued)

In addition to the predictable timing of transitions, each was typically associated with several "empirical earmarks":

- A low point before the transition
- The completion or abandonment of the agenda of phase one
- Expressions of urgency about deadlines
- Renewed contact between the group and the person who assigned the task or some other superior in the organizational hierarchy
- Group agreement on specific new directions its work should take
- A change in group routines as a result of the new direction pursued

For groups that had already been productive, transitions offered the chance to slow down, identify aspects of the problem that had been overlooked, and fill in the missing ingredients. For groups that had been struggling, transitions were "exhilarating periods of structuring, making choices, and pulling together."[2] An important conclusion Gersick reaches is that groups do not necessarily need to show "visible progress" by making many decisions during phase one. She demonstrates that the group could simply generate the raw materials (information, ideas) that will enable a successful transition to take place. The group may only need to understand the problem and various alternatives well enough to start organizing at the midpoint.

One unusual aspect of the midpoint transition was that groups focused exclusively on task goals. They did not spend any time discussing their internal group process, even though Gersick reported that some groups needed to address internal problems.

Phase Two

All seven groups set out in phase two with renewed hope. (One group was disbanded and its task reassigned.) And all seven accomplished the basic task goals they had revised at their midpoint. Gersick describes phase two as resembling the performance phase of Tuckman's model of group development. She quotes one member describing phase two: "We decided what we were going to do [at the midpoint meeting] . . . and the rest was just mechanics."[3]

The detailed nature of Gersick's observations enabled her to see a number of small but potentially significant patterns that other approaches to group development tend to overlook. Her study is a good example of the benefits of close attention to detail, something that you can strive for in your own observations of groups.

Box 11.1 (continued)

Source: Connie Gersick, "Time and Transition in Work Teams: Toward a New Model of Group Development," *Academy of Management Journal*, 1988, *31*, 9–41.

Notes:

1. Gersick, "Time and Transition," p. 19.
2. Ibid., p. 28.
3. Ibid., p. 30.

GroupQuests: Discussion Questions

1. According to Poole's research on phases of decision development, fewer than one-quarter of the groups observed followed a simple unitary sequence (for example, orientation, conflict, emergence, reinforcement). Why do you think group development is so complicated? Are groups naturally disorganized and therefore in need of structure? Or, as Poole suggests, are groups responding to different situational contingencies?
2. What advantages or disadvantages do you see with the notion of a group assessing and refocusing its efforts during a mid-point transition period? (See Gersick's model in Box 11.1.)
3. Why do you think most experts view the unitary phase model as an ideal model? Would you advise a group to follow it if it is unsure how to proceed? Why or why not?

GroupWorks: Group Activities

1. Divide your group into three subgroups. Have each subgroup review one of the three major decision paths that Poole identifies (unitary, complex, or solution-oriented sequences). The subgroup should discuss the following issues:
   a. Why would a group follow such a path? (Identify as many contingencies as you can that make the path appropriate.)
   b. What should a group do to maintain the highest level of quality possible when following such a path? (Identify any negative tendencies a group is likely to fall prey to and how they can be overcome.)

   When the whole group reconvenes, subgroups should share their thoughts on each decision path. Focus specifically on the issue of maintaining quality control.
2. Conduct a brief debate on the value of the decision development models presented in this chapter. Divide the class into four groups and give the first three groups a few minutes to prepare a list of reasons why its assigned model (see below) is a better guide to decision development than the other two models.

   Group 1: Fisher's unitary sequence model

   Group 2: Poole's contingency model

   Group 3: Gersick's punctuated equilibrium model

   Your instructor will monitor the debate,

while Group 4 will determine which group wins the debate. Conclude by discussing some guidelines that groups should use in determining which decision path to follow.

3. This project requires a trio, and each person must have a watch with a second hand. It may be presented in class. Observe a live or (preferably) videotaped meeting of a decision-making group. Each member of the observation team will be responsible for recording the sequence of events for one of the three tracks of group activity. Synchronize watches at the beginning of the session:
   a. *Topic changes.* One person records each topic change as it occurs and notes the time in minutes and seconds (for example, 9:35:15).
   b. *Task activities.* One person records changes in task process (for example, orientation, problem analysis, and solution design). You may want to use the decision functions coding scheme (see Poole and Roth, "Decision Development in Small Groups IV," *Human Communication Research*, 1989, *15*, 334). Again, record the time at which changes in activity occur.
   c. *Group relationship activities.* One person records shifts in the nature of working relations (focused work, critical work, and opposition, for example). You can use the group working relationships coding scheme (see Poole and Roth, 1989, p. 335). Remember to record the time at which you first notice a change in relational activity.

   When observations have been completed, create a time line comparing all three tracks (like the one in Figure 11.1). From this you should be able to decipher the type of decision path the group is following (see Figure 11.3). Write a brief report summarizing your findings and assessing the fit between the group's decision path and the nature of its task and structural characteristics (from Figure 11.2).

4. Research how trial juries (in your particular state) are instructed by the court to reach a verdict. Review these instructions in light of the information in this chapter on decision development. Write a brief paper indicating what changes (if any) should be made in the guidelines given to a jury. Is there a need to make the process more organized or less?

GroupActs: Practical Applications

Videotape or audiotape one session of your own group. Assign a subgroup (three members) to study the tape and identify the sequence of topic shifts and task and relational activities (as in Group Activity 3). Have the subgroup report its findings to the rest of the group as soon as its analysis is complete. The group should discuss the report and any changes in activity that seem to be appropriate.

CHAPTER 12

The Group Level: Explaining Decision Shifts

In this chapter, we want to look more closely at some of the factors that lead group members to make unusual shifts of opinion related to alternative decision proposals. A *decision shift* occurs when group discussion creates a consensus or majority view significantly more extreme from the private views that members held initially. When a shift in a decision or choice occurs because members have been convinced by credible information or reasonable arguments, the group will most likely make a high-quality decision. If a group, however, is unaware of the process underlying the shift of opinion, it may be in trouble.

Two extreme kinds of decision shifts in groups are the tendencies to engage in polarization and groupthink. We will describe each of these tendencies in turn and in the process learn how to increase the chances of making good decision shifts.

Polarization: The Extreme Decision Shift

Imagine taking a bus tour with several of your friends to Atlantic City or Las Vegas. For $25, you each purchase a bus ticket and $20 worth of quarters to play the slot machines. Being a little curious, you ask each friend privately how much money he or she is willing to risk in the casino. Tallying their responses, you find that the average person plans to spend about $35, quite a bit more than the $20 voucher from the casino. On the way, a group discussion takes place about this very issue—each person reveals his or her plan to the others. Shortly after this discussion, Laura informs you that she had decided to increase her risk by $10. Later, Clarence says he's spending another $20. You cannot believe what you are hearing, so you ask the others. Each one now seems willing to risk considerably more money. What has happened? Why are you now thinking you can afford to spend another $15 yourself?

Your group has just experienced a phenomenon known as *group polarization*, which is the tendency for individuals to make decisions that are more extreme, but in the same direction as the average response before discussion.[1] For some reason, members do not always gravitate toward the norm or average position, but seem to push the norm in a more extreme direction. Why does this happen? To fully understand it, we need to look at the history of research on this phenomenon. That history reads like a detective story in which you are unsure what crime has been committed.

Historically, the prevailing wisdom about groups was that they are conservative. Pressures to conform were believed to make each of us think twice before wearing a skinny tie or a miniskirt when it was out of fashion. The group was seen as an inhibiting force that restricted the behavior of its members. In 1961, James Stoner tested the conservative assumption against the hypothesis that groups might actually take greater risks than individuals.[2] When Stoner found that groups often produced a risky shift, other researchers became interested. For several years, a series of studies demonstrated that shifts to risky decisions take place in a wide variety of groups and on a wide variety of topics. Theories were developed and tested to explain why groups took such risks.

But the old prevailing wisdom did not disappear. Eventually researchers were able to show that on some issues, cautious shifts take place after group discussion. Usually these were discussions about topics on which individuals already held conservative views. By the time Roger Brown offered the possibility of a generosity shift, researchers realized that the phenomenon was more general than a shift to greater risk or more caution.[3] Finally, the term *group polarization* was selected because it emphasizes that groups tend to push decisions toward the polar extreme. In other words, if more members leaned toward a risky (or cautious or generous) position before discussion, they are likely to emerge from that discussion holding a similar but more extreme viewpoint. But why?

Why Polarization Happens

One of our graduate students, also the mother of a fourteen-year-old, was explaining the concept of risky shift to a group of her son's teenage friends. She asked them why they thought people behaved this way in groups. Without realizing that they were doing so, each one offered an explanation from the four dominant theories about group polarization tendencies:

Tim:	Sure, it makes sense because if you were gonna rob a bank, you'd want about four people. If the police came, you could scatter and have more chance not to get caught. If you did get caught, it wouldn't be just your fault like it would if you were alone. I'd never rob a bank alone. (diffusion-of-responsibility theory)
Stephen:	No, that's not it. You take more chances in a group than alone because you don't want to look like a nerd if you don't [go along]. (social comparison and cultural value theories)
Jeff:	If you're with your friends and you don't want to see a movie, but your friends tell you about some good parts, you'll spend the money and go. (persuasive arguments theory)[4]

Although our adolescent theorists were right on track with their theories, we need to explore these theories in more depth. First, we will look at the diffusion-of-responsibility theory.

Diffusion-of-Responsibility Theory This theory posits that groups take more extreme positions because members do not feel personally responsible for the decision. If a member views himself or herself as acting alone, he or she has to bear the responsibility of any choices. But if the decision is seen as belonging to the group, the individual is at least partially absolved from responsibility. According to the theory, this diffusion of responsibility among all the members of the group may lead members to take more extreme, especially riskier positions. On the other hand, when a member is singled out and held responsible for the group's decision, a cautious shift is more likely.[5] Rebecca and Timothy Cline demonstrated how members negotiate responsibility in the way they communicate. They coded the types of pronouns that group members used (for example, *I*, *we*, *you*, *they*, *it*) and speculated that members accepted more responsibility when they used "I" statements and rejected responsibility by using more "we" and "you" statements. Sure enough, discussions by groups that made cautious shifts were marked by more "I" statements, while there was a preponderance of "we" and "you" statements in groups that made risky shifts.[6]

Cultural Values Theory At the height of research on the risky shift, Roger Brown proposed the idea that risk is a highly placed value in our culture and that most people want to *appear* like risk takers when in groups.[7] The American Way has always involved taking risks (trying a new form of government, exploring frontiers, investing in a new business, sending astronauts to the moon). Studies have shown that risky shifts occur more often in American groups while cautious shifts take place more frequently in Chinese groups.[8]

But cultural norms change. Witness the freewheeling 1960s as opposed to the more conservative 1980s. As these larger cultural values shift, we would expect a corresponding shift in the likely direction of group choices. More recent versions of this theory have also taken into account that even a culture that values risk does not value it equally in every situation. Caution may be more highly valued on some issues or in some situations.

Social Comparison Theory Groups may also take extreme positions because of complications in the way members use each other to evaluate their own worth and self-identity. Social comparison theory suggests that people measure and adjust their own opinions in light of what others in their group think. According to the theory, most people like to think of themselves as not average, but a cut above the average. A person may, for example, rate himself as more ethical than most people, but not as ethical as the cultural ideal. The problem is that most of the time we do not know what the average is. So we venture a guess and take a position on an issue that is just a little more extreme than (a cut above) the assumed average. If the health trend in the neighborhood is to walk two miles early in the morning, we will get up earlier and walk just a little further than that. But we often find out in group discussions that we have underestimated the group average. This may in fact be true, or it may be that everyone else is trying to espouse an opinion that is slightly above the norm. (They want to "look good," too.) This touches off an escalating cycle of members taking more extreme positions as each revises his or her opinion upward to remain a bit better than average.

D. Myers and M. Kaplan found that simply providing information about group norms was enough to prompt a shift to a more extreme position. Before church members completed an attitude survey, the researchers divided them into three groups. They showed one group the average results from a sample survey of fellow church members. Another group saw not only the average but also a complete distribution of the results, including extreme positions. A third group was not given any information. As expected, the third group's attitudes were about average. The group shown the average reported its own attitudes to be higher than average on most issues. But the group exposed to the extremes showed the greatest degree of polarization.[9] Thus the social comparison can stimulate more extreme choices.

Persuasive Arguments Theory But social comparison is not a complete explanation. Some studies have shown that giving people information about norms is not enough to produce a major shift.[10] Proponents of the persuasive arguments theory suggest that when discussion reveals differences of opinion, members begin to speculate about the reasons (arguments) that must have led others to their opinions. Even if arguments are not advanced in the discussion, members will infer reasons and evaluate them. Eugene Burnstein and Amiram Vinokur propose three characteristics of arguments that tend to make them more convincing: their number, reasonableness, and novelty.[11] You can probably see how members would support an alternative if they could

Overestimation of the group and pressure toward conformity were two groupthink symptoms apparent from Oliver North's Iran-Contra testimony.

think of many reasonable arguments in favor of it and few against it and if some of the arguments favoring the idea were novel. But why would persuasive arguments lead the group to take more extreme positions? This appears to happen because the alternative with the most arguments favoring it is usually the choice of most of the members before the discussion. Because discussion tends to produce even greater confidence in the preference members are predisposed toward, they may push the idea even further. Presumably, polarization would be minimized if the most persuasive arguments did not reflect the preferences of members prior to group interaction.

Most researchers believe that elements of all four theories are true and that no one theory best explains the polarization effect. Determining which theory best explains the shifts in choices you observe in your own group can help you decide how to counteract or take advantage of this tendency.

Managing Group Polarization

What can you and your group do to better manage the polarizing tendency? We have several suggestions that hinge on the group's ability and willingness to observe and talk about its decision process. Polarization is one of those hidden group tendencies. Researchers have been able to identify it because they gather a lot of information about members prior to and after discussion. A typical group is unlikely to realize that polarization is taking place unless the membership also gathers and makes use of the relevant information. Thus our suggestions:

- Consider making it a regular practice for members to reveal where they stand on the issues at the outset of discussion on major issues. This allows you to see what their predispositions are. However, this can be dangerous. Some members might become wedded to these initial and very public positions, so they need to be expressed as tentative views ("until all the evidence is in").
- As arguments for different alternatives are advanced, double-check your responses. If you catch yourself revising an opinion simply so you can reinforce your own social standing in the group, think about it again. Advise other members to do likewise.
- As decision choices are made, check them against the group's preferences prior to discussion. If you see that a risky or cautious shift has taken place, discuss the appropriateness of the shift. Are you dealing with a situation that calls for greater risk (or caution)? Is the group's willingness an advantage because members think the plan is a good idea but are hesitant to accept individual responsibility for it? What is the worst-case scenario if the group's decision is too risky or too cautious?

Your group may be able to identify other ground rules or ways to manage polarization. At a minimum, you need to recognize that groups are prone to this tendency, which can work for or against them.

Groupthink: The Cohesive Decision Shift

One of the most devastating choice shifts that can occur in a group is a tendency to engage in groupthink. Irving Janis coined the term *groupthink* to refer to "a mode of thinking that people engage in when they are deeply involved in a cohesive in-group, when the members' strivings for unanimity override their motivation to realistically appraise alternative courses of action."[12] We refer to groupthink as a decision shift because group members seldom start out with the same preferences before discussion. But they rather quickly shift their opinions to coincide with the dominant view that emerges in the group's discussion. Members often make the shift without giving it much thought or they stifle their own criticisms because of the pressure to join the group consensus.

Janis discovered the groupthink problem while studying the decision-making fiascoes produced by several groups of high-ranking presidential advisers. Among the fiascoes Janis investigated were the failure to adequately secure Pearl Harbor (1941), the decision to invade the Bay of Pigs (1962), decisions to escalate the war in Korea (1950) and in Vietnam (1964–1967), and the Watergate cover-up (1972).[13] He noted a number of conditions that encouraged groupthink and several symptoms that indicated its presence. A

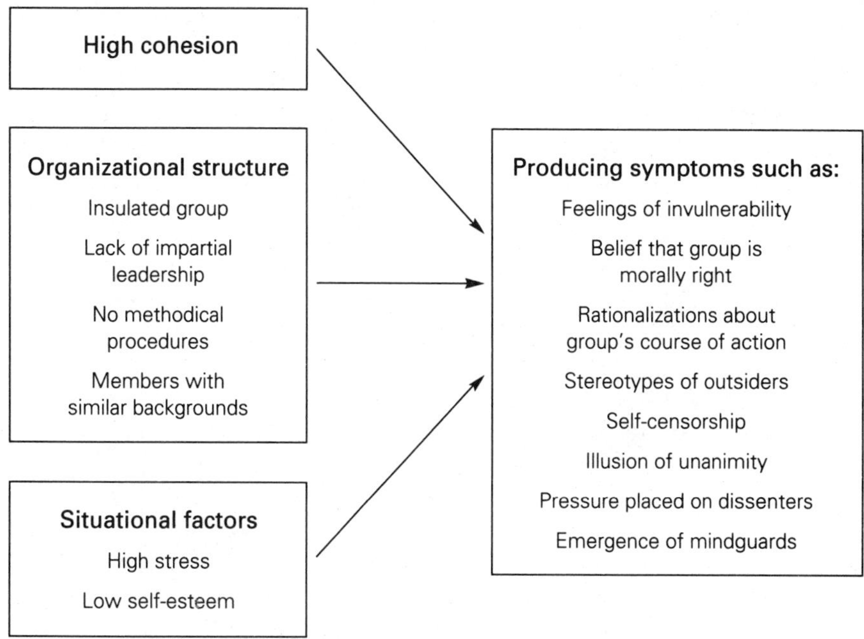

Figure 12.1 Factors that encourage groupthink.

diagram of these factors appears in Figure 12.1. Let us look first at some of the conditions that make it easier for groups to suspend critical thinking.

Conditions That Produce Groupthink

Janis has described several possible conditions that facilitate the occurrence of groupthink. Among these are the cohesive nature of the group, particular structural features of the organization of which the group is a part, and certain situational constraints.

Janis emphasizes repeatedly that without a high level of group cohesiveness, groups would not display many of the symptoms of groupthink. Although a group lacking cohesion might also show signs of defective decision making, groupthink would not be the cause of it. Only when a group is highly cohesive should you be very concerned about the other conditions that lead to groupthink.

Sometimes the way an organization sets up and administers its decision-making groups can facilitate the development of groupthink. Four structural faults are insulation of the group, lack of a tradition of impartial leadership, lack of norms requiring methodical procedures, and member homogeneity. Policy groups are often *insulated* so that they have little opportunity to contact outside experts or seek critical evaluation from others within the organization. When *no tradition of impartial leadership* exists, leaders are likely to exert too much influence. Unless members are encouraged to be openly critical of ideas, they will not likely go against the recommendations of those who lead them. A third factor is the *lack of norms requiring methodical procedures for decision making*. If groups are not held accountable for how they reach decisions, they are not likely to be very thorough in their information search or analysis. Procedures such as writing position papers or listing the pros and cons of various alternatives are examples of being methodical. Finally, *when the social backgrounds of group members are too similar*, the group loses the benefit of having different perspectives on issues. Members may think too much alike and decrease the chances of generating enough alternatives for consideration.

According to Janis, groupthink tendencies are likely to increase as a result of two situational contingencies. One of these conditions arises when the group faces both *high stress* from external forces and *low hopes* of finding a solution better than the one the leader prefers. Stress from outside the group, such as antiwar protests during the Vietnam War, often has a different effect than that intended. Rather than forcing the group to reconsider its decisions, external stress tends to make group members rely even more on each other for social support. They then insulate themselves from outside influence and frequently turn to their leader for a way to reduce the stress. Finally, group members may be subject to internal sources of stress that result in *a temporary lowering of self-esteem*. For example, the failure to solve a previous problem may make group members feel inadequate and subsequently affect their current deliberations. Baseball players experience this feeling when in the midst of a long losing streak.

Combine a poor organizational structure, a highly cohesive group, and a situation that provokes high stress and low self-esteem and you have all the ingredients for groupthink. These conditions produce groupthink, but they do not tell us how to recognize what groupthink looks or feels like.

Symptoms of Groupthink

You can recognize groupthink by the twin symptoms of group members' attitudes and behaviors. Janis identified eight different symptoms in the case studies he observed. He grouped them into three main types: overestimations of the group, closed-mindedness, and pressures toward uniformity.

In cohesive groups, members often develop such a high opinion of themselves that they develop two traits. One is the *illusion of invulnerability*. Group members develop an overly optimistic view of their capabilities and begin taking excessive risks. "No one can touch us," and "We can't be beat" are the theme songs of such a group. Here the group's risky shifts are dangerous because they are not founded on any realistic view of the situation. A second trait is an *unquestioned belief in the group's inherent morality*. Ethical issues and moral consequences of action are not discussed because the group assumes it will do what is right. Or more likely, it will support unethical means as long as they are directed toward the "right" ends.

Box 12.1

The Shuttle *Challenger* Tragedy: Was It Groupthink?

On January 28, 1986, the space shuttle *Challenger* exploded seventy-two seconds after takeoff. The tragedy shocked a nation that had come to expect spaceflights to be as routine as daily flights in and out of major airports everywhere. But it also caught the management at NASA off guard. No one was prepared for a failure of this magnitude. But should they have been?

Within the week, a special group, the Rogers Commission, was assigned by President Reagan to investigate the disaster. The U.S. House of Representatives also sought a report from its Committee on Science and Technology. The results of those investigations revealed a number of serious flaws in the decision-making process at NASA as well as at Morton Thiokol, the contractor that had built the solid rocket booster, which was ultimately identified as the physical cause of the accident.

As it turned out, information on the flaws in design of the solid rocket booster was widely known at almost every level of the space shuttle management. Long-term plans were being made to phase-in a new type of joint design for the solid rocket booster, but there was no sense of urgency to do anything soon. On the evening before the launch, some engineers at Thiokol objected to a launch because of the potential effects of low temperature on the O-ring joint seals. Morton Thiokol management initially recommended against the launch as well, but reversed that decision over the protests of its own engineers. Some senior-level NASA officials later claimed to be unaware of these objections. Crucial information had not been passed on to them. The various flaws in the decision-making process read like a veritable laundry list of groupthink symptoms:

1. Erosion of the joint seals on previous flights was not reported in the flight-readiness review for the January 28th flight (adverse information rationalized away).
2. Thiokol engineers raised objections only to their immediate supervisors, not wanting to override the chain of command (a form of self-censorship by the engineers and mind guarding by their superiors).
3. Thiokol management reversed its initial decision to postpone the launch at the urging of managers at the Marshall Space Flight Center. Thiokol then put pressure on its own engineers to "prove" that the solid rocket boosters would not work at the temperature projected for launch time (external pressure by Marshall; direct pressure on dissenters at Thiokol).
4. NASA's twenty-five-year history of success and incredibly good luck led management on a course that increasingly underestimated risks and overestimated the likelihood of further success (illusion of invulnerability).

Box 12.1 (continued)

5. NASA management was so convinced of its own safety record that it viewed the shuttle program to be fully operational—the testing phase was viewed as complete. NASA management actually held some discussions with various airlines about taking over the space shuttle program. Airline officials were astounded. Most experts said the system was still in a research and development phase. (Collective rationalization created a mindset that the system was fully operational.)
6. In a speech at Edwards Air Force Base in 1982, President Reagan reinforced this mindset in public: "The test flights are over, the groundwork has been laid, now we will move forward to capitalize on the tremendous potential offered by the ultimate frontier of space" (external pressure to maintain faulty mindset).
7. The plan to mention the teacher-in-space program in President Reagan's State of the Union address on the evening of the scheduled launch may have contributed to the feeling that *Challenger* had to be launched on time (implied external pressure).

It would be difficult to pinpoint any of these reasons as the primary ones for the *Challenger* disaster. But taken together, they constitute a groupthink situation. The groupthink syndrome can attack any group, no matter how prestigious or successful. NASA's reputation had always been that it erred on the side of caution. Delays in the launching of flights had been common. But success can breed complacency, and that may have been the most serious symptom of all.

Sources: "Anatomy of a Tragedy," *IEEE Spectrum*, February 1987, *24*, 44–51. James Jaksa, Michael Pritchard, and Ronald Kramer, "Ethics in Organizations: The *Challenger* Explosion," in *Communication Ethics: Methods of Analysis*, edited by James Jaksa and Michael Pritchard (Belmont, Calif.: Wadsworth, 1988).

The group displays its closed-mindedness in one of two ways: members engage in collective rationalizations or stereotyping of outsiders. *Collective rationalizations* include any failure by group members to attend to information or heed warnings that would deter the group from its present course. Such warnings are often brushed aside with such comments as "We can handle that," even though no mention of how the difficulty will be handled is ever mentioned. Group members are also amazingly closed-minded about the capabilities of those they view as adversaries. Discussions frequently are filled with unchallenged *stereotypes of outsiders*, leading the group to believe that the opposition will pose no serious threat.

Four characteristics of groupthink are related to the pressures members place on themselves and each other: self-censorship, an illusion of unanimity, direct pressure on dissenters, and self-appointed mind guards. *Self-censorship* takes place when members begin to belittle their own criticisms and doubts about the emerging consensus in group thought. Members refute their own arguments before they get to meetings and as a result fewer and fewer criticisms of the group's plan are available for discussion. With most members censoring their own criticisms and others interpreting their silence as approval, an *illusion of unanimity* develops. Everyone believes that everyone else agrees. On those occasions when someone does venture a criticism, others are quick to apply *direct pressure on dissenters*. The pressure may take the verbal form of rationalizations or even a solid persuasive argument. But the real message is nonverbal: through body language and tone of voice, members repeatedly remind the dissenter that he is not being loyal. A final symptom is the emergence of *mind guards*. These are self-appointed members who, believing the group's course of action to be correct or morally superior, try to protect the group from any ideas or information that might threaten the status quo. In the Watergate incident, President Nixon's inner circle of advisers kept from him the widely held view that impeachment was a real possibility. Without addressing such adverse information, groups continue down the same path they started on, unaware of the potential dangers.

The major consequence of a group that harbors these symptoms is a defective decision-making process. In particular, Janis noted seven observable aspects of this inferior process:

- Inadequate survey of alternatives
- Incomplete survey of objectives
- Failure to examine risks of preferred choice
- Failure to reappraise initially rejected alternatives
- Poor information search
- Selective bias in processing information at hand
- Omission of contingency plans

In short, groupthink prompts overconfident members to take an overly simplistic approach to their task. They fail to do what every successful group must do: engage in a critical testing of ideas, information, and alternative choices.

Managing Groupthink Tendencies

What can be done about a negative tendency such as groupthink? Recognizing symptoms is one thing; doing something about them is another. Fortunately, Janis's studies have led him to a number of conclusions about how groupthink can be prevented. However, he cautions that these remedies can be just as bad as the cause if the group (and especially its leadership) employs them with anything less than a wholehearted desire to eliminate the problem. The following list is a capsule summary of Janis's recommendations to curb the influence of groupthink:

- Place a high priority on communicating doubts and objections.
- The leader (especially if highly respected) should remain impartial and not indicate his or her preferences at the outset.
- Organizations should routinely assign more than one group to evaluate the same policy question.
- The group should frequently divide into two or more subgroups when surveying alternative solutions to make sure each one is thoroughly investigated. Then the whole group can review all of them.
- Each member should periodically discuss group issues with a trusted colleague and report their reactions to the group.
- Bring outside experts to meetings and encourage them to challenge the group's assumptions.
- Assign the role of devil's advocate to at least one member every meeting.
- Whenever issues involve a significant rival, time must be set aside to assess the rival's warnings and intentions.
- Once a major decision has been reached, hold a second-chance meeting and encourage members to rethink the entire issue before finalizing the decision.

If your group follows Janis's suggestions and designs its ground rules around them, and if members are alert to the conditions and symptoms of groupthink, you can minimize its effects while you fortify your group process.

Summary

This chapter has focused on two types of group discussion processes that undermine quality decisions. Polarization is the tendency for a group to decide on a more extreme version of the decision choice that most of the members favored initially. It is sometimes, but not always, the result of careful thinking and thorough analysis of the facts. More often, it is the product of shared cultural values, a competitive social comparison process, and the feeling that no one will be held responsible for the outcome.

Groupthink is the tendency for a group to let down its guard and fail to critically test its most favored solution options. As a result, the group makes decisions based on unrealistic and untested assumptions. We identified several conditions that encourage groupthink, including a high level of group cohesion, highly stressful or crisislike circumstances, and a lack of impartial leadership. In addition, eight symptoms of groupthink were discussed to help you recognize when your group is dangerously close to it or in its grasp. Finally, we identified a range of strategies for reducing the chances that groupthink will take hold in your group.

In effect, this chapter is something like the "Don't Walk" signs that remind us to beware of dangerous traffic conditions. Here the warnings are to alert us to subtle group pressures that will encourage us to believe our group can reach great heights even while it restricts discussion to the most superficial levels.

GroupQuests: Discussion Questions

1. Which of the explanations for the polarization tendency make the most sense to you? What kind of discussion topics might be prone to polarization?
2. Discuss some of the decision-making groups in which you participate. Are there any conditions (high cohesion, structural faults, stressful contexts) that suggest a group might be ripe for groupthink? Try to think of recent discussions that may have involved some symptoms of groupthink.
3. Try to relate topics discussed in previous chapters to the phenomena of groupthink or polarization. For instance, how is the style of leadership related to groupthink? Is a group that is socializing several new members more likely to engage in polarization?

GroupWorks: Group Activities

1. When is the polarization tendency (risky and cautious shifts) likely to be beneficial or harmful to the group process? Review the various situational contingencies from Poole's model (Figure 11.2) and the Groupthink model (Figure 12.1). Discuss each contingency and how it would relate to a risky or cautious shift. Would a shift in choice under these conditions likely be beneficial? Harmful? Or would it make little or no difference?
2. How can you alert a group to the possibility that it is engaging in groupthink? If one of the symptoms of groupthink is "collective rationalizations," is not the group likely to shrug off any critical comments or warnings? Look at the symptoms listed in Figure 12.1. What would you say to a group when you saw signs of a specific symptom (and how would you say it)?
3. For a term paper assignment, read one of the available chronicles of the Iran-Contra affair (for example, John Tower, Edmund Muskie, and Brent Scowcroft, *The Tower Commission Report* [New York: Random House, 1987]). As you read the sequence of events and summaries of major meetings among the principal participants, try to identify any symptoms of groupthink engaged in by the inner circle of advisers such as North and Poindexter. Be sure to document your observations with evidence (verbal statements or actions) that indicates a condition or symptom of groupthink.

GroupActs: Practical Applications

Assign one member the role of silent observer for the next group meeting. Armed with a list of all of the symptoms of groupthink, this member should take notes during the meeting, identifying any interactions that resembled one of the symptoms. At the conclusion of the meeting, spend a few minutes discussing these observations. Take appropriate steps to counteract any major symptoms.

CHAPTER 13

The Cultural Level: Groups in Their Natural Habitats

Imagine an American business organization being managed according to the following rules:

- Every job in the organization is designed to be performed by a *team* of workers; there are no individual job descriptions.
- A primary criterion for the selection of new personnel is their ability to work in groups; when possible, entire groups that have worked together previously will be *hired as a group*.
- All personnel will be *trained as a group;* all group members will be trained to perform all major tasks to maximize comprehension of the task and flexibility of individual assignments.
- Personnel will be *paid and promoted as a group;* bonuses, promotions, and salary or wage increments will be tied to the performance of the group as a whole.
- The *personnel will be fired on a group basis*, based on poor group performance or elimination of the group's functions.

In 1975, Harold Leavitt, a highly respected organizational theorist, proposed a system like this.[1] Leavitt contended that groups are not taken very seriously as a fundamental unit for building and maintaining organizations. If they were, he argued, we would see more institutions with rules like those just mentioned. Instead, most organizations in our culture are organized around the individual worker. Individuals are hired, trained, promoted, and fired—not groups.

As we noted in Chapter 1, American industry is slowly coming to the realization that teamwork is essential and that the small group can be a very effective way to organize and make decisions. However, making such fundamental changes in the way we conduct and evaluate work involves changing some of our most-cherished cultural attitudes and values. This shift will not be easy, and any organization that wants to become more team-oriented will have to pay close attention to how the organization itself influences the way group members communicate and work together. As long as the career path in an organization is viewed as single members climbing up the corporate ladder, for instance, there is little incentive for members to work together as a team.

Why are individuals so highly prized when much of an organization's work is done by groups? The answer lies in our cultural and institutional assumptions about human nature and in our perceptions of how things really get done. In this chapter, we take a look at the concept of culture and how it influences the way people behave in groups. We are concerned that culture, because it is left largely unexamined, can act as a set of blinders and limit our vision of the options available to us as group decision makers. A far-reaching concept, culture can refer to something as large as a hemisphere (East versus West) or as small as a family group. For our purposes, we will examine two particularly significant cultural contexts that influence much group decision making: the general American culture (and its Western heritage) and the more specific organizational culture that most groups operate within.

Cultural Influences on Groups

A *culture* may be defined in its simplest terms as a shared system for *thinking*, *communicating*, and *organizing* the actions of a group of people.[2] How can we identify the patterns of thinking, talking, and organizing characteristic of our own culture? How can we know which ones work for us and which may, on occasion, work against our efforts at group decision making? Most aspects of culture remain outside the awareness of an individual until that person encounters another culture and notices how its people think, talk, or act differently from members of his or her own culture. One way to be aware of these characteristics is to look at American culture in terms of how it contrasts with other cultures in these three ways.

Cultural Patterns of Thinking

One of the important ways that cultures differ is in terms of how people within the culture think—how they perceive what is important and what they take for granted as reality. Much has been written about the differences in patterns of thought between Eastern and Western cultures. We do not have the space here to do justice to the complexities of many cultures or to note the exceptions to the rule. But a quick review of some essential differences will help us locate a few of our own cognitive tendencies.

Views of Nature: Harmony Versus Domination According to the philosophers of most Eastern cultures, humans are an intricate part of the nature of things. There is a basic harmony between human beings and nature such that nature is to be revered and accommodated. In the Western view, the theme of the individual versus nature tends to dominate our thinking. Edmund Glenn explains the origins of these patterns in the differing concerns that preoccupied the early philosophers in both cultures.[3] Eastern thinkers were concerned primarily with how human life could be regulated and sought to pass on traditions that would remain relatively unchanged by succeeding generations. Western philosophers, on the other hand, focused their energies on the search for truth, for the reality of nature. Ultimately, this led to a scientific outlook on life, with each attempt to explain nature serving as a revision of an earlier generation's beliefs. In the process, knowledge of nature became a way to dominate it, and the exploitation of nature provided a constant source of new ideas and social change.

How does this outlook affect a decision-making group? Because of our emphasis on action and change, we often assume that we *have to act* to solve a problem. We seldom look for the benefits that might accrue if we do nothing, or if we simply change our perspective on the problem. Similarly, we are more likely to dismiss the importance of tradition and make decision-making mistakes like Coca-Cola's near-fiasco with Classic Coke (see Box 2.1).

Another difference is that Eastern cultures emphasize the *process* of life, whereas Western culture stress the *product* or end result of an endeavor. In the emphasis on process, great concern is devoted to how life should be lived, with less emphasis on what ultimate goals should be achieved. Westerners tend to be very goal oriented and often tinker with the process in an effort to be more efficient and productive. Because we, as a culture, tend to be more action oriented and less reflective, we often find it difficult to attend to the group process and do task work at the same time. We are not, on the whole, very process oriented.

Views of Society: The Group Versus the Individual Much moreso than Western cultures, Eastern cultures are group centered and value stability over change. Much has been written about Japanese organizations and their great emphasis on group consensus in decision making. Their culture teaches them to value loyalty to the group and to see family and work relations as permanent bonds that must be carefully nurtured. They are conditioned to view social life as a web of highly defined situations that involve mutual dependencies and obligations to be repaid. One of the major social concepts in Japan would be translated in our language as a sense of indebtedness that exists between people. Americans, on the other hand, are more individually centered.

We are taught to value such things as self-reliance, independence, and standing out in the crowd. We like to assign responsibility to the individual; we are not very comfortable with the idea of group responsibility. Take a poll of your classmates and ask how many prefer to work alone or in a group, especially when a grade is at stake!

What does this mean for us? For one thing, it means that we are not, as a culture, especially effective in groups. We have to work at it more than do members of many other cultures. We worry too much about things like someone else getting credit for our ideas, having to trust others to get their work done on time, or making sure we do not get lost in the crowd. Another implication is that knowledge of other cultures can increase our awareness of optional ways of doing things. Of course, this does not mean wholesale adoption of another culture's methods. American organizations, for instance, cannot simply mimic the practices of Japanese companies; too many cultural differences have to be taken into account. But many American companies are successfully *adapting* some of the techniques of Japanese corporations.[4] Broaden your own cultural spectrum by reading about the decision-making practices of other cultures.

Cultural Communication Codes

Perhaps the most obvious of all cultural differences is language. But according to one estimate, as much as 80 to 90 percent of the information in a message is conveyed by means other than language.[5] Much of this information is carried in the nonverbal behavior, the material artifacts, and the shared assumptions that people bring to a given situation. For Edward T. Hall, the noted anthropologist, culture can be defined as "a system for creating, sending, storing and processing information."[6] Hall has identified a continuum for evaluating the differences among cultural communication codes—that is, how a culture processes information.[7] At one end of the spectrum is the *high-context culture*. In this culture, most of the information in a message is already present in the physical context or has been internalized by the person. Members of the culture can assume a large pool of shared meaning because of a common, well-defined, stable set of traditions. Within a high-context culture, even strangers can assume that they will both know the common rules of etiquette, the subtle signs of each other's social status, and the important events of their cultural history. This shared knowledge will enable them to communicate easily; they will not have to use a lot of words to explain themselves. China is considered to be a very high-context culture. Its written language and many of its customs have changed little in the past three thousand years.

At the other extreme is the *low-context culture*, in which the verbal message itself must do most of the communicative work. Messages must be highly explicit in this culture, because the shared pool of knowledge members can assume is quite small. Americans tend to fall toward this end of the continuum. One recent critic of the American educational system, E. D. Hirsch, argues essentially that we are becoming more of a low-context culture all the time. In *Cultural Literacy*, Hirsch claims that educators have failed to provide students

Organizational cultures that value uniformity may discourage individual expression, which is valuable in decision-making groups.

with a common vocabulary for conducting intelligent conversations as national citizens. A number of surveys have documented that Americans cannot even count on each other to have a basic grasp of geography, history, literature, politics, or democratic principles.[8]

There are at least two ways in which you should assess how this continuum can affect your group's decision making. First of all, you should look at the cultural background of each member of your group. Try to ascertain the gaps in cultural knowledge that separate group members. Do not limit yourself to the obvious ethnic differences, but try to focus on which aspects of the larger culture the entire group shares and which ones it does not. For instance, do all members seem to understand the literary or political references made during discussions? Often a group member will be puzzled by a reference to an event or theory that he or she is unfamiliar with, but will be too embarrassed to admit it. A sensitivity to nonverbal behavior is necessary to catch and correct this by providing a little more context for the puzzled member. However, there is also a danger in providing too much information to someone who is already at the high-context end of the spectrum. You risk insulting their intelligence (or wasting their time) if you say far more than they need to know. The second factor relates to the target audience your group must report to, not the group itself. You need to do a similar assessment of the cultural gaps in knowledge between your group and its audience, if you want to be a successful communicator.

In addition to deciphering how much information is needed to provide a background for exchanging messages, you should also consider the cultural variables of time and space. Each culture (and subculture) has its own preferred pace for getting things done. Americans are rather fast paced, one reason we often get impatient with the group process. If your group is composed of members from different cultural backgrounds, the issue of pace may have to be dealt with when establishing meeting times and setting deadlines. Differences in pace may also be due to the more subtle cultural aspirations of group members. On many college campuses, students in different majors represent a subculture of their own and may have different time orientations. For instance, the pace of fast-track business majors may differ considerably from that of theater or history majors. For a slightly different perspective on how time (in the form of cultural history) can be used to a group advantage, see Box 13.1.

Other subtle cultural communication codes include the nonverbal use of space and habitual forms of touching. In some cultures, touching is a major form of communication; in others, it is largely forbidden. On the scale of world cultures, Americans avoid touching more than most do. We tend to keep our distance from one another in conversation and allow only mild forms of casual touching (a brush of the arm, a slight pat on the back). Again, there are subcultural variations within the United States to which you must be sensitive. It is not unusual to find group members repositioning their seats during a group discussion to get closer or move farther away from other group members. Usually this is simply a matter of maintaining a comfortable conversational distance, but it is often interpreted as disinterest or brashness. Pay attention to each other's subtle uses of space during group deliberations.

Cultural Patterns of Organizing

In spite of our culture's prejudice in favor of the individual, we still rely on groups to get the bulk of society's work done. Our democratic system, with its basic principle of majority rule, requires a lot of group effort to establish the will of the people. Groups are used to achieve the goals of our political system. Caucuses, political action groups, zoning commissions, parent-teacher groups, and Neighborhood Watch committees represent the typical American way to get things done. Many people spend much of their free time working with volunteer agencies and groups such as the United Way, Literacy Volunteers, or the Red Cross. Self-help groups such as Alcoholics Anonymous and Weight Watchers have produced astonishing results, as people find strength in groups to deal with personal problems. Some people live in communal groups. Society may be thought of as a complex web of small groups constantly pushing and pulling, each trying to increase its influence over the others. Some groups are more prominent and exert great influence, other groups affect our behavior in more subtle ways. Groups of the first type are called power groups, the second type are reference groups, and both types can have a measurable impact on your own group's decision making.

A *power group* can be defined as "a coalition of like-minded individuals

Box 13.1

Thinking in Time: How to Use History in Your Decision Making

Cultural history is rich with examples of poor and effective decision making. But according to Richard Neustadt and Ernest May of Harvard's Kennedy School of Government, very few groups use that history to their advantage. Neustadt and May have, for several years now, taught a course entitled "Uses of History" designed to help high-level public officials, business leaders, and their staffs to make more systematic use of history in their everyday decision making. What they found was "a host of people who did not know any history to speak of and were unaware of suffering any lack, who thought the world was new and all its problems fresh." As a result of the success of their course, Neustadt and May have written a book, *Thinking in Time: The Uses of History for Decision Makers*, which lays out their systematic plan of analyzing history for clues to current concerns or problems.

In most of the cases of poor decision making that they have analyzed, the authors found that the key people involved in the decision knew that something had gone wrong. The typical response was, "How in God's name did we come to do *that?*" Neustadt and May describe six ingredients in "usual" practice that contribute to such poor efforts: (1) a felt need to act quickly, (2) reliance on fuzzy analogies, (3) inattention to an issue's own past, (4) failure to reexamine key presumptions, (5) failure to refine stereotypes about the persons or groups involved, and (6) no recognition that the choices to be made are part of any historical sequence.

In response to these problems, the authors describe in detailed steps how to work through them. For instance, they suggest the following steps to help eliminate some of the fuzziness in a historical analogy: separating (and writing down) "the known" facts from "the unclear" and "the presumed" ones; quickly inspecting historical analogies that come to mind; reviewing the history of an issue, tracing how the specific concerns arose; and more thoroughly analyzing the analogy, identifying (and writing down) "likenesses" and "differences" between the two events. Other procedures are recommended for inspecting the history of an issue; for determining how historical events shaped the thinking of key participants; and for thinking in "time-streams" that view the present as part of the unbroken continuum between past and future.

One example will demonstrate how a lack of careful "thinking in time" produced a decision-making fiasco. In 1976, thirteen people at a crowded army camp were identified as having "swine flu." One of them died. Subsequently the new virus was identified as "chemically related" to a virus common among pigs and possibly related to a virus involved in the great influenza epidemic of 1918, which took the lives of a half-million Americans and twenty million more worldwide. The analogy between the two events

Box 13.1 (continued)

captivated the thinking of many senior officials in the federal government and public health organizations, eventually leading President Ford and the Congress to approve a very costly immunization program. The vaccine produced a rather serious neurological side effect and the administration of the flu shots was repeatedly delayed until the credibility of public health officials was almost destroyed. In addition, the feared epidemic never materialized.

Using their plan of analysis, Neustadt and May showed how a careful look at the likenesses and differences between the two "epidemics" made the analogy a weak one. They also identified a number of unexamined presumptions that became taken for granted as "knowns" and contributed to the ensuing difficulties, including:

1. Flu vaccine is safe and has no serious side effects.
2. One dose of the vaccine will be sufficient.
3. The vaccine can be administered through the usual channels.
4. Litigation problems of vaccine producers will not hinder efforts.
5. The medical and scientific communities will follow the lead of the Centers for Disease Control.
6. The mass media will do likewise.
7. Presidential sponsorship will facilitate public support.

In each case, the presumption proved to be wrong. Had the decision makers examined these issues carefully, they would never have embarked on the path they eventually chose.

Using the swine flu case and some thirty other historical cases, Neustadt and May show repeatedly the value of their simple analysis. To students of decision making, we strongly recommend that you add *Thinking in Time* to your "must" reading list.

Source: Richard E. Neustadt and Ernest R. May, *Thinking in Time: The Uses of History for Decision Makers* (New York: Free Press, 1986).

whose positions in society grant them real political clout."[9] The concept is similar to what sociologist Max Weber called a *veband*, first noted as a means by which small groups of aristocrats banded together to keep the king from taking away their land.[10] As a member of a small decision-making group, you may need to assess those power groups on campus or in your organization that might be opposed to the solutions you champion. Power groups that represent the status quo often oppose any changes that threaten their power base. Because their influence is so extensive, your group cannot simply pretend that they do not exist. A better approach is to target the power group as a major audience and try to convince its members that your proposals are beneficial to them. If that strategy is not likely to work, you must anticipate the power group's opposition and try to find ways of countering or minimizing its influence. At any rate, you should always size up the external groups that will be affected by the decisions you make and try to implement.

Reference groups are the other groups to which members already belong or aspire to join. Some of the norms held by these other groups become standards that affect the behavior of members when they are present in your own group. For instance, a member may frequently take a position during discussion such that he or she is actually representing the interests of a reference group. Sometimes this behavior will be intentional. When it is, and especially when the member is trying to mask the behavior as unintentional, we say that member is pushing a "hidden agenda." The numerous charges of "influence peddling" in the nation's capital are examples of supposedly hidden agendas at work. More often than not, the influence of reference groups is unintentional. A new member of a local community club may find himself or herself repeating an opinion expressed at the last meeting and not even be aware of where the opinion originated. Scrutinize the intentional and unintentional influences of reference groups. It is worth the extra time and effort to get to know group members well enough to identify the reference groups they pledge allegiance to.

In summary, culture influences and acts as a context for group decision making in three major ways:

1. Culture structures our habitual ways of thinking, which can limit our perception of problems and creative solutions to those problems.
2. Culture has an impact on how we process information and create messages. Group members frequently talk down to or past one another because they make different assumptions about how much information needs to be explicitly coded into their messages.
3. The values and norms of external reference groups and the naked influence of power groups can help your group immensely or spoil its efforts.

To forget that these cultural influences exist is to give up much of the impact your group's decisions can have in furthering the aims of society.

Institutional Influences on Groups

While the general culture serves as perhaps the largest and most pervasive context in which groups interact, the organization is one of the most observable contexts. An organization is a hierarchically arranged group of groups, a miniculture in and of itself. Group members may identify with particular power groups and reference groups within the organization as well as outside it. The hierarchy also usually indicates how your group fits into the total picture. If your group has been appointed by a high-ranking senior executive, chances are greater that the group's recommendations will be considered. But as influential as the formal organizational chart is, it is not always the most important factor. To most inside observers, the corporate culture and the patterns of interaction within the organization are equally important aspects of organizational life.

Types of Organizational Cultures

An *organizational culture* is a distinctive social reality consisting of shared beliefs and values, created through common practices such as jokes, stories, myths, and rituals. It is the culture of an organization that makes particular messages and behavioral exchanges meaningful to insiders, yet somewhat perplexing to outsiders. Many researchers today believe that organizational members create and sustain a particular culture through verbal and nonverbal communication practices.[11] In other words, culture is not something that an organization has; culture is the values and symbols that members express in their talk and everyday behavior. At one time, an organization may have a strong culture that is well-defined and highly shared; at another time, members may have fragmented or competing visions of what the organization is all about. Whatever the vision, the culture's impact is felt throughout an organization, including any place a group meets to make decisions.

Every corporate culture is unique. Yet many cultures share a number of features and can be grouped according to types. In their book *Corporate Cultures*, Terrance Deal and Alan Kennedy describe four different types of cultures they have encountered in the business world: the tough-guy macho, the work-hard/play-hard, the bet-your-company, and the process culture.[12] Before we look at these four types of corporate culture, a note of caution is in order. Typologies are inherently simplified versions of any organizational culture you will encounter under real circumstances. Do not interpret these four types as the only or even the most common forms of organizational culture. Nor should you believe that corporate cultures are static. They are not. As with any social process, cultures evolve and change in subtle ways every day. Over a period of time, the culture in an organization may change dramatically. As you read about these four types, view them simply as examples of what a particular organizational culture at a particular time might be like. Then imagine how such a backdrop might affect the decision-making effort of groups operating within such a culture framework.

Members of the *tough-guy macho culture* are highly individualistic and work under intense pressure to succeed. The pace of work in such a culture is frenetic and all but the heroes are likely to burn out at some point in their careers. Internal competition among members is stressed and risk taking is highly valued. The physical or financial stakes are usually very high in companies that develop this kind of culture. What kinds of organizations might boast a tough-guy image? The more obvious ones are police and fire departments and construction crews—especially those working with explosives. But often advertising agencies, sports teams, and television network organizations develop a similar type of culture. One strength of this kind of culture is that its hard work and risk taking often pay huge dividends. Its weaknesses include a short-term orientation, a frequent lack of cooperation, and a bent toward superstitious behavior (for example, the baseball player who goes through the same ritual every time he goes to bat).

Deal and Kennedy refer to the *work-hard/play-hard culture* as "the world of small risks and quick feedback." Its prototype is the sales organization where persistence pays off ("One more phone call, one more sale") and where the customer comes first. Sales contests and promotions, company picnics, and exaggerated claims of success or carousing are rites and rituals typical of this culture. The company literally works in spurts—periods of intense work followed by a day or two to blow off steam. As with the tough-guy culture, a lot of work gets done, but members often suffer the same short-term vision of the world ("Sales are up this quarter"). The culture tends to allow volume to replace concerns for quality. Loyalty to the company is also in short supply; one of the culture's rituals is moving on to greener pastures.

In contrast to the work-hard/play-hard culture, loyalty is everything in the *bet-your-company culture.* Such organizations as NASA, Boeing, Exxon, and the various divisions of the military invest their time and money in projects that require years of development, testing, and deployment. The risks are extremely high, but the results may not be known for decades. As you might expect, members communicate in ways that reinforce the importance of good ideas, stamina, respect for authority, accuracy and deliberateness, the ability to tolerate ambiguity, and a strong belief in the future. Meetings are the most prominent rituals in this culture because long-term planning dominates the thinking. The culture tends to produce exceptionally high-quality work in the form of inventions and scientific breakthroughs, but it is also at the mercy of the market or federal budget cuts.

Many businesses and industries are regulated by the federal government. Banks, the pharmaceutical industry, and especially the government itself are subject to a myriad of rules and regulations. As a result, a corporate culture may develop that prizes detail and order, procedures and red tape, and lots of paperwork. The heroes in such a *process culture* are the positions on the bureaucratic chart, not necessarily the people who happen to hold those positions at the moment. When following the rules is highly rewarded behavior, the focus of members is likely to be on the process itself—on *how* things are to be done, not on *what* is to be done. The strength of such a culture is its predictability. Once you know the rules (and if the rules are fair for most of the people most of the time), you will seldom be surprised by what happens. On the downside, the public does not like bureaucratic organizations very much. It is unlikely that people outside the company are going to congratulate you about the work you do.

The institutional culture in which you work or study is probably similar in some ways to one of these four cultures. One of the most important considerations of organizational culture, however, is knowing what to look for to make sense of the way the culture works. You are in the best position to identify the key aspects of your organization's culture.

1. *What does the physical setting suggest?* The layout of office space usually indicates what type of relationships are desired or expected among employees. Are there status symbols such as a corner office that members strive to attain?
2. *What images and values does the institution project in its official publications?* To what extent are those themes (or different ones) emphasized in memos, in-house reports, performance evaluations, and other forms of internal communication?
3. *What do the stories and anecdotes that people exchange say about the organization?* What conversational themes run through the interactions of people on their coffee breaks or between classes? How do members talk about the company and their feelings toward it? What stories circulate about the early history of the organization? What types of people are described as heroes? What cultural values do they embody?

The material and symbolic themes of organizational talk and behavior are the stuff out of which corporate cultures are made. Let us look now at how those cultural elements influence group decision-making processes.

The Corporate Culture's Impact on Group Decision Making

There is no way a group can escape the influence of the corporate culture of which it is a part. And it will feel the influence in many ways. The culture creates expectations or demands about when the group's work must be completed, as well as the quantity and quality of work it must do. Many of the organization's routine work habits will be carried over to the group. For instance, a decision-making group within a process culture will be expected to document the steps it follows (in triplicate). If the group proposes a new policy or practice, it will probably spend an inordinate amount of time on implementation (for example, creating the proper forms to fill out). In a work-hard play-hard culture, the group will probably work intensively, including a week or two of late-night sessions. The decision-making processes will be compressed, and the social dimensions of group interaction may be put on hold until the project nears completion. Afterward, the company is likely to reward the group—say, with a weekend ski party to Vermont—giving members a chance to socialize.

The function of group meetings can also differ from culture to culture. In some cultures where member participation is a norm, group meetings are frequent and the decisions made in them make a difference in the way the company does its business. In many cultures, meetings are a superficial cosmetic touch. Groups go through the motions of making decisions, only to have them overruled by higher powers. In still other cultures, it is routine to have meetings for sharing information. No decisions are made, but people are kept informed through the ritual of meetings. Knowing how an organization typically uses groups will tell you something about how the information and decisions your group provides will be treated.

The group decision-making process is likely to inherit most of the weaknesses of its company's culture. The short-term orientation of both the work-hard/play-hard and the tough-guy cultures will push a group in the direction of quick fixes rather than thorough analysis and long-term solutions to problems. A process orientation may result in a group tackling an issue of little or no real concern. "If it ain't broke, don't fix it" has little meaning in this type of culture. The most deliberate decision-making culture is the bet-your-company culture. Deal and Kennedy indicate that a typical meeting to evaluate a ten-page report may take up to two hours per page! In contrast, they have seen meetings in fast-feedback cultures where a document of two hundred pages was approved in a two-hour meeting.

The small group is much like a fish in the waters of its organizational culture. The culture surrounds it on all sides and seems natural to all but outsiders or newcomers. A group must identify those aspects of its culture that may negatively affect its decision-making process and consciously fight off those cultural tendencies.

Organizational Communication Networks

The organizational culture permeates everything a group does, but another, more specific feature of the organizational context will affect how well your group performs. This feature is the web of networks that loosely connects people and groups and keeps information flowing throughout the organization. Members of your group must be tied into the various networks if you want your work as a group to influence the whole organization.

The Nature of Communication Networks A *communication network* is a regular pattern of message exchange among organizational members and groups. You can view an organization as a system of loosely connected groups, striving to achieve some superordinate goals. Ideally, the communication network enables groups to work in concert. Messages exchanged via the network can keep groups informed about each other's activities and plans. Maintaining contact can also help minimize misunderstandings during intergroup conflicts as well. The communication network may be *formal*, as with an organizational chart that specifies to whom particular types of information should be directed. Or it could be *informal*, as in the case of janitors who exchange notes on what they find in the wastebaskets of the executive suites. Some of this information may be passed on to a secretary at lunch, who tells his or her boss, and so on. The network includes those people who regularly keep in touch with one another and exchange relevant information about organizational matters. Among the different kinds of networks in an organization, the "grapevine" is common, as is the "old boy" network (usually limited to white, Anglo-Saxon males who have been with the company for years). Some organizations have informal "innovations networks" of people who keep abreast of the latest ideas or technology in their field and like to talk to others who are interested in the same things.

Some networks are very loosely structured, or decentralized, meaning that almost anyone who took an interest could be included in the flow of information. There is no prescribed path for information to flow; one member is as likely as another to get the message first. Other networks are more tightly managed, restricting membership to an elite inner circle. The network may also be very centralized, in that messages are directed initially to one or two members, who then pass them on to the rest of the group. Some companies require strict adherence to the formally established networks; others seem not to care if members bypass the official lines of communication on occasion.

Key Features of Communication Networks You may need to keep track of many aspects of a network. Three key features that are likely to crop up repeatedly in the groups you work with include loyalty to the primary group, intergroup tensions, and the role of linking pins.

The formal units of an organization constitute the most obvious networks. Members of the accounting department usually interact more with each other than they do with people in sales or production. As a result, most organizational members retain a strong loyalty to their formal unit. This is especially important to remember when working on a task force whose membership includes people from different units within the company. Each member of the task force will probably try to protect the interest of his or her primary group. Sometimes people will admit this up front. Usually they will not. You need to know what hidden agendas members might bring to meetings. Group members need to respect each other's loyalties, without letting them create too much divisiveness. Bear in mind that the aspirations of some members to move up the corporate ladder may affect where their true loyalties rest.

If people have strong loyalties to their primary groups, the logical conclusion is that they will be leery of other groups in the organization. One group distrusts the motives of another, and all are competing for a bigger bite of the budget. This often makes it difficult for groups in large organizations to act in concert. In spite of the obvious goal that the company must succeed as a whole, groups will protect their own turf and sabotage the efforts of other groups. One way to get the edge over a competing group is to forge company policies that favor some groups over others. Where are company policies usually created or modified? In small task forces or policy-making committees. You must always keep group tensions in mind when conducting group decision making. Your group's final decision or policy statement must be reviewed in terms of how it will be perceived by various groups and factions. Will it be seen as a fair policy or does it favor a particular group? These concerns will be part of the organizational culture's response to your group's efforts. In addition, intergroup tensions may mean you will need to stress the group's superordinate goal and show how the task group's goal transcends the concerns of the various primary groups represented.

One way to minimize intergroup tensions is to include people in the task group who are perceived as having no particular loyalties or as having frequent contact with or who participate in more than one group. Such a person is called a *linking pin* because he or she transmits information from one group to another. There are basically two types of linking pins: the liaison and the bridge.

A *liaison* has frequent interactions with members of a wide variety of groups, but does not belong to any one particular group. Liaison positions are sometimes formally appointed for the express purpose of linking several important groups and their functions. Research on liaisons indicates that they are perceived as having high status, good connections, and a lot of influence within the power structure.[13] A *bridge*, on the other hand, is a person who does have a primary group membership, but also interacts a great deal with members of other groups. This level of interaction outside his or her own group gives the bridge a broader perspective of organizational issues and also reduces the perception that his or her main concern is the primary group. Both types of linking pins make effective task group members. It is vital to have group members who are well connected in various organizational networks. They have good ears and good influence.

Summary

In this chapter we have identified some of the aspects of culture that influence group decision making. National or regional culture affects decisions in ways that we often take for granted. Culture structures our thinking, our communication, and our ability to act in ways that will make a difference to society. More specifically, cultural similarities such as values and habitual ways of thinking can limit a group's perception of possible creative alternatives to problems. Subcultural or regional differences in the use of language or nonverbal expressions can create misunderstandings or relational tension among members. Finally, the reference groups and power groups that members identify with can influence the degree to which they support or argue against a particular proposal.

At a more observable level, the organizational culture in which a group functions exerts an influence. The culture of an organization refers to the creation and maintenance of a common core of values, beliefs, and methods of operation that influences virtually everything that members do and say. The corporate culture and the particular networks of communication within that culture tend to limit or enhance the effectiveness of a group's decisions. We described four different types of corporate cultures and provided examples of how each could influence the group decision-making process. We also noted that culture is created and sustained through communication, making observation of communication practices essential to understanding an organization's culture. To help hone your observational skills, we suggested that you pay special attention to the status symbols, stories, and conversational themes in group interaction. The more you tune yourself into the organizational culture, the better chance your group has to leave its mark on that culture.

GroupQuests: Discussion Questions

1. The chapter opens with Harold Leavitt's vision of an organization that really takes the idea of groups seriously. What do you think of this vision? In your opinion, what advantages would such an organization have?
2. Imagine that you have just met a new member of the organization you work for or a new student on her first day at your school. What could you tell that person about the corporate or college culture he or she is about to encounter? Try to identify common habits of thought or attitudes; acceptable, unacceptable, or potentially confusing ways that people in the culture communicate; and the power groups and the most popular referent groups.
3. Aside from what you have read in this chapter, what common values of the U.S. culture do you think promote effective group decision-making practices? Which values do you think hinder effective decision making?

GroupWorks: Group Activities

1. In groups of four or five, discuss and describe the "corporate culture" of your college or work organization. Although you can compare your own campus culture to the four types discussed in the chapter, try to think of a label that best describes the culture. List the common values and the specific rites and rituals that serve as evidence of the culture. Next make a list of how the culture could influence a decision-making group either positively or negatively. When finished, share the cultural description, the list of evidence, and the positive and negative influences with the rest of the class.
2. Form groups of five or six. To illustrate the concepts of high- and low-context cultures, plan a skit in which a typically high-context group must translate its messages into a low-context code. For instance, you might depict a dormitory group (whose members share a lot of inside jokes and know each other well) discussing the pros and cons of members of the opposite sex on campus. To change a message from its implicit, high-context code to an explicit, low-context code, you must verbalize everything necessary to convey the meaning to a cultural outsider. How would you, for example, make explicit the meaning of the term *hunk* used to describe a male of the species?
3. Try to think of groups or subcultures within our own culture that interact in ways similar to that of a high-context or a low-context culture (for example, communal groups, fraternities and sororities, ethnic groups). If you can, observe one of these groups and record examples of information that is either implicitly or explicitly coded into their messages. What information do members take for granted? How do they remind each other of the context in which a message should be interpreted? Write a short paper describing your observations and any problems you think the group encounters with the larger culture.
4. Identify two groups on your campus that seem to exhibit intergroup tensions. Describe the goals that each group appears to strive for and why you think they

dislike members of the other group. Next think of one or more superordinate goals (review Box 1.1) that, if brought to both groups' attention, would help reduce the tensions between them.

GroupActs: Practical Applications

This assignment is for groups that are involved in a term project concerned with some type of on-campus problem or policy. Prior to your next meeting, have all members complete Discussion Question 2. Review each person's responses in round-robin fashion, compiling a master list of cultural influences. Then as a group, decide how you can minimize the negative cultural influences on your campus and maximize the best of those influences. Would any power groups pose a difficulty in gathering information or proposing solutions? Also talk about the communication networks on campus, and determine if it is possible to place members of your group in strategic places within any of these networks. For example, would it benefit your group if a member were to volunteer to work on a particular committee? Can some members begin establishing themselves as bridges to other important groups? Your goal for this discussion is to find ways to manage your cultural surroundings as much as possible. At the very least, you want to know how the culture is likely to affect your group.

Part IV

Future Directions

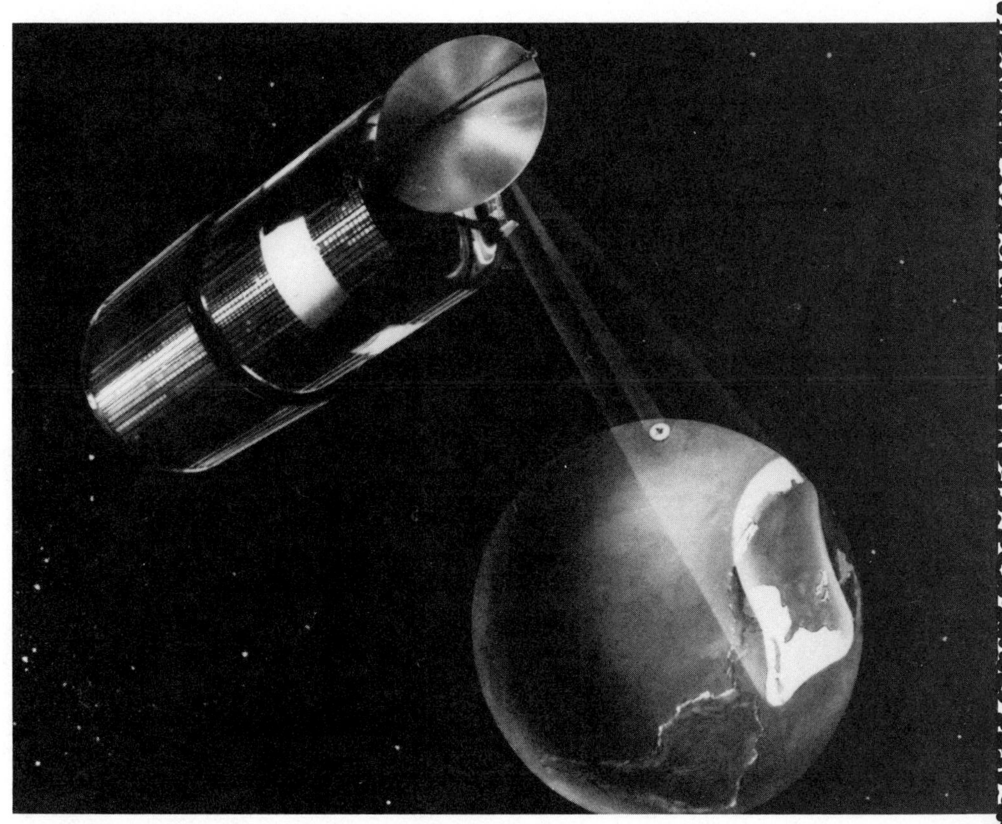

CHAPTER 14

Group Communication Technologies

This chapter title may conjure up images of groups using machines and electronic gadgets. If so, the image is correct but not complete. There are technical innovations in group communication that have nothing to do with equipment. *Technology* is derived from the Greek word *technologia*, meaning systematic treatment. The root of *technology* is *technique*, which means "the method of procedure (with reference to practical or formal details), or way of using basic skills, in rendering an artistic work or in carrying out a scientific or mechanical operation."[1] A technology is a systematic method to achieve an end product. Notice that there is no mention of equipment. We consider electronic and designed group procedures technologies because they are both systematic approaches to conduct group communication for making decisions.

The preceding thirteen chapters indicate a growing body of theoretical and practical knowledge on group communication, which has provided guidance in developing practices for group communication. At the same time, these practices are providing a basis for research on the effectiveness of group technologies and establishing premises underlying their development and use. Communication theory and practice are partners in the development of effective group decision making. This partnership has not been developed much. Although there are numerous practices for aiding decision-making communication, there is little empirical research assessing their effectiveness.[2] But observational information, user testimonials, and some research affirm the usefulness and effectiveness of group communication technologies.[3]

Group communication technologies are interventions designed to establish a systematic approach to efficient decision making. Their ultimate goal is to support the achievement of high-quality decisions while maintaining member satisfaction and group cohesion. The technologies do so through designing procedures and practices that promote productive and satisfying task and relationship group communication.

The technologies described in this chapter reflect numerous avenues for enhancing such communication. Some technologies are designed for particular situations (for example, group size, types of problems, information load). All share common design features regarding participation, information management, episode sequencing, group control of content, and specific practices for making decisions. To familiarize you with their uses, we will examine two types of technologies: group process designs (based on a system of communication procedures) and electronic group decision support systems (based on procedures designed for interactive media applications).

Group Process Design Technologies

A *group process design* (GPD) is a formal system of communication procedures, rules, and roles designed for conducting problem-solving meetings.[4] A formal GPD is typically complete and closed—it scripts the steps and techniques of the problem-solving process and typically is not open for modification by participants. GPDs govern the procedural dimension of meetings; the problem-solving content is the responsibility of the group members. All members must use the formal design, but a procedural facilitator usually initiates and monitors it. In some cases, the facilitator can contribute to the content of the task, but may be restricted to procedural issues, depending on the rules governing the facilitator's role.

Alternatively, a formal design can be partial and open. In this case, certain rules and procedures are prescribed, while others are left to the group's discretion. The group project facilitator at the end of Part II is an example of a partial and open GPD.

Design Features

GPDs share three features: role specialization, procedures and rules, and support media. They separate the procedural and decision-making functions by designating procedural responsibility to the facilitator and decision making to group members. Some designs provide further role specialization for generating ideas, recording minutes, and managing information.

Role Specialization GPDs usually establish several separate specialized roles to ensure effective role performance. This is accomplished by designating a single role to an individual or separating sequences of specific role behaviors

Process Facilitator Role Functions

Selection	*Implementation*
Introduction: Initiate discussion on procedure selection; Justify procedure choice	Guide group through steps and activities; Monitor compliance with process
Instruction: Review procedure rules	Intervene to maintain or change process

Figure 14.1 The role functions of the facilitator are specified in the group process design (GPD), a formal system of communication procedures, rules, and roles for conducting problem-solving meetings.

performed by members. The typical roles are facilitator, recorder, and member. However, implementation of these roles may vary considerably. Facilitation may be conducted by a neutral third party, a group member or manager, or all members of the group. Some GPDs require the facilitator to perform more than one role. More specific role behaviors, such as information sharing, coordinating, evaluating, and harmonizing, are not limited to any one group member, but may be designed to occur during a particular step of an activity or during a meeting involving, for example, high tension or defensive behavior.

The facilitator has two basic procedural role functions: selection and implementation (see Figure 14.1). Selection, the introduction of and instruction on a procedure, involves initiating, justifying, and describing a procedure for use. For example, suggesting the use of brainstorming for an activity could involve a rationale for its use and instructions on the procedure's steps and rules. The implementation function facilitates the group's use of the selected procedure. Implementation is characterized by guiding, monitoring, and intervening. Once a procedure is selected, message behaviors function to get it started, watch over its maintenance, acknowledge when the rules are broken, and reinstate or change the procedure. For instance, if brainstorming is selected, a facilitator or member could start the procedure by reminding the members to behave appropriately. Their actions will be monitored for compliance and followed by an intervention if a member fails to follow the communication rules of a step.

Procedures and Rules All GPDs provide procedures and rules for conducting meetings that directly shape communication behaviors. They structure group meetings by providing or requiring a *process agenda* irrespective of the meeting's goal. All designs establish some, if not all, of the meeting procedures. Most rules are specified for particular roles and activities. An activity such as brainstorming may have several rules for all participants (for example, idea generating followed by evaluation), or rules may be limited to specific activities for certain roles (for example, the facilitator instructs participants on procedures).

Some rules may operate throughout the meeting for all members regardless of the activity. These are usually designed to enhance relational communication. For example, a no-attack rule may be established to reduce defensive communication and interpersonal conflict. Guiding members' behavior, the rule would be enforced by the facilitator or members at all times.

Support Media GPD support media record, process, and manage meeting information. The most common are simple: easels, large notepads, markers, and tape. More sophisticated media involve overhead projectors, computer-based systems, copying machines, and even meeting rooms specially designed to display and rearrange many ideas. The use of these more sophisticated media is largely determined by the group's goal and task demands. Complex unstructured problems in large groups require methods that can manage a large volume of information and perform complex information processes rapidly. The types of operations to be performed on it and reproduction for immediate distribution also require specialized and sophisticated media.

In summary, the essential features of a GPD are operationalized through roles, rules, and support media. The success of a GPD largely depends on the appropriate match among the design and the group's task and situation, participants' understanding and acceptance of the design, and the fulfillment of the design by the facilitator and members.

Types of Group Process Designs

Factors such as group size and the type and complexity of the problem influence the design of procedures, roles, and rules and use of support media. The following six GPDs reflect these considerations. Note the specific purpose of each, the structure of steps, the activities used, and the ways they implement the basic design features. Consider ways you might improve the designs or adopt features in groups you belong to.

Interaction Method This process was introduced in Chapter 5 as a method to manage effective decision-making meetings in general.[5] It is mainly designed to handle four common meeting problems: unfocused discussion, inappropriate procedures, lack of member involvement, and personal criticism. Each problem is managed through a combination of rules and roles designed to govern the meeting. Although the designers provide information on tools for problem-solving activities, the procedures are intended to manage a meeting.

The facilitator and group members determine the procedures for solving problems.

To handle the problem of unfocused discussion, a focus rule requires the group to establish a specific topic or task for discussion at all times during the meeting. To avoid the problem of inappropriate procedures, group members consider the best procedure or tool for conducting each selected focus. To involve members, a consensus rule requires all members to make decisions. To prevent personal criticism of members, the no-attack rule dictates that members refrain from such behavior at all times.

Although any member can acknowledge a breach of the four rules of the interaction method, the facilitator initiates and monitors them. The facilitator must keep out of the meeting content, but may seek permission to contribute if circumstances appear appropriate. Because there are no specified procedures for various meeting activities, the consummate interaction method facilitator needs to be knowledgeable about a variety of communication and decision-making techniques such as those reviewed in Chapter 6. Both the facilitator and recorder roles should be performed by neutral third parties to ensure effective meeting procedures and allow members to concentrate on the meeting's content and activities.

Group Project Facilitator This GPD is designed to guide college students' group projects in critical decision making. Unlike most GPDs, the group project facilitator requires all group members to play the facilitator role and requires the group to identify and assign other key roles before beginning the project.

The procedures of the GPF are based on communication rules, instruction on various activity tools, and essential group project phases. The process requires groups to adopt three communication rules to enhance a positive communication climate and participation. The instruction on tools provides guidelines for ways to share information, generate ideas, and make decisions. The project steps are divided into four phases: forming the group, identification, analysis and information search, and project synthesis and delivery.

Of all the GPDs reviewed here, this is the most open. The group determines the selection and implementation of procedures, rules, and roles. The group project facilitator is a menu of options that the group can select or add to in orchestrating the project process.

GPDs that are partial and open emphasize the design of meeting episodes. They usually describe steps and recommend specific activities but leave the choice to the group. Complete and closed GPDs prescribe both episodes and activities thus detailing procedures and limiting choices. The following GPDs are examples of this type.

Rational Management Charles Kepner and Benjamin Tregoe developed an elaborate procedure to help managers become better problem solvers, but Rational Management is readily adaptable to conducting problem-solving

Phases and Principles of Rational Management

Problem analysis phase:

1. Establish the expected standard of performance or desired outcome. What should be achieved or performed?
2. The problem is a deviation from the standard. What should be? What is?
3. Identify, locate, and describe the deviation; what, where, when, or to what extent?
4. Determine and note when and if the deviation is not occurring. When is or is not the deviation occurring?
5. Look for the change that has produced a distinctive feature, mechanism, or condition producing the unwanted deviation. What has changed or occurred that might have caused the deviation?
6. Deduce the causal relationship of the change or condition associated with the deviation. Could the change or condition account for the deviation?
7. Determine whether the most likely cause of the deviation accounts for all the deviations from the standard. Do the characteristics of the change or condition account for the deviation?

Decision-making phase:

1. Establish the objectives of a satisfactory decision (solution). What are the requirements for an acceptable solution?
2. Determine the importance of each decision objective. Which priorities are "musts" and which are "wants"?
3. Develop alternative solutions to the problem. What are possible ways to fulfill the objectives?
4. Compare alternative choices with decision objectives. Which alternatives fulfill the "musts" and "wants"?
5. Select the alternative that best fulfills the decision objectives . Which alternative satisfies all the "musts" and the most "wants" with the fewest disadvantages?
6. Review the selected alternative to determine its future impact. What are the consequences if the alternative is implemented?
7. Identify actions to prevent adverse effects of the alternative. What can be done to eliminate or minimize new problems?

Figure 14.2 Kepner and Tregoe's rational management procedures can help groups as well as managers solve problems. [From Charles H. Kepner and Benjamin B. Tregoe, *The Rational Manager: A Systematic Approach to Problem Solving and Decision Making* (New York: McGraw-Hill, 1965).]

meetings.[6] The process has two distinct phases: problem analysis and decision making. The problem analysis phase involves problem clarification, cause-and-effect analysis, cause verification, and problem identification. The decision-making phase establishes standards, generates and selects alternatives, and assesses implementation consequences.

Seven principles govern each of the phases, which are the foundation for a prescribed series of questions. The seven principles establish phase episodes, and the questions direct activities by establishing the purpose and focus of discussion (see Figure 14.2).

Rational Management is the least elaborate GPD in that it does not require role specialization beyond the manager as facilitator or prescribe procedures or rules for the relationship dimension of group communication. It only addresses the task dimension of group problem solving. More recent GPDs include roles, procedures, and rules to support and enhance the relationship dimension of group communication.[7] This additional dimension is addressed in the next three GPDs.

Quality Circles *Quality circles* (QCs) are small groups of employees organized to meet periodically to identify, solve, and present management with solutions to job-related problems.[8] The QC process is an organization-wide project that focuses on setting up the QC groups and training their members in procedures and rules for conducting effective problem-solving meetings.

Quality circles were instituted in American manufacturing and service industries to enhance employee involvement in decisions to improve production.[9] QCs tap employees' firsthand experience in the production process and aim to motivate higher levels of performance through involvement in decisions related to their immediate working conditions.

There are three key QC group roles: facilitator, leader, and members. The facilitator coordinates the various QCs and trains the leaders in the QC process design. The leader, preferably a supervisor or manager, recruits members, schedules and plans meetings, trains members while facilitating problem-solving meetings (on-the-job training), helps with problem-solving activities, and records and documents meeting progress. The members are the main information resources and problem solvers, although the leader can also participate and outside experts can be consulted. The members and leader are responsible for recommending solutions to work-related problems to management.

The QC design is based on the typical problem-solving model designating specific activities for each episode. For example, brainstorming is used for identifying work-related problems and generating solutions, cause-and-effect analysis is used to analyze problems. Additionally, procedures and techniques are provided for data collection and display and presentation management.

The relationship dimension of group communication is established in three ways. First, the leader is trained in group dynamics, supportive communication, and motivation skills. Second, the members are required to develop a "code of conduct" to guide behavior in meetings. Third, some of the activity procedures—for example, brainstorming—incorporate relationship supportive practices. The comprehensiveness of the GPD reduces procedural ambiguity, which can reduce tension and confusion while its use provides a way to identify common goals and solutions.

Business organizational culture exerted an interesting influence in the design of QCs. The hierarchical nature of organizations, with their emphasis on status and control, appears to underlie the emphasis on the supervisor as the initial leader, although leadership can rotate to another employee once the QC design is well in place. We conjecture that some organizations use QCs to alter authoritarian cultures to more participatory cultures. The failure of many QC programs has been attributed to the clash between the organization's authoritarian culture and the participatory principles of QC groups.[10] It is hard to teach an old dog new tricks.

Synectics Synectics, a highly specialized GPD, uses a small group in an atypical manner for tackling difficult problems creatively.[11] Synectics applies creative problem-solving practices to problems that fail to be solved using expert knowledge and analytic approaches. In this respect, Synectics is a solution-centered approach because it emphasizes activities to find solutions rather than analyze problems.[12] It requires participants to use metaphors to create unfamiliar and unusual perspectives to the problem in order to find new and creative directions for solutions. It is most applicable to open-ended problems with no apparent solution. Synectics works best on "thing problems" (for example, how to make a light, compact frame for a portable solar mirror), although it can be used on "people problems" (how to reduce a work force without reducing morale).[13] It is particularly useful on problems concerned with inventions, research, and innovations.

Synectics involves three specific roles: client, facilitator, and participants. The client is most typically the person with the problem, perhaps an expert such as an engineer with an invention problem or manager with an operational problem. The client is responsible for defining the problem, providing background, and evaluating and selecting solutions.

The facilitator makes sure that the prescribed procedures are adhered to and ideas are displayed. The key duties are to instruct, guide, and monitor the client and participants. Thus the facilitator must know what is going on during the session at all times in order to keep members in their roles and conduct the procedures appropriately. This is the critical challenge for the facilitator of all GPDs.

The participants are strictly idea generators who use prescribed activities designed for this task. The participants and facilitator are ideally persons who have no particular expertise or connection to the client's problem. Creative idea generation is enhanced when group members are not versed in the problem domain and are not subordinates of the client.

The process begins with a preliminary meeting between the facilitator and client to review the synectics process and the "problem as given"—its background and desired outcome. During the synectics session, the client presents the problem in a how-to form (for example, how to make a light, compact frame

Every year telecommunications trade shows display the latest developments in group decision support system hardware and software.

for a portable solar mirror). This is followed by an analysis episode in which the client is asked: Why is this a problem for you? What has been tried to solve it? What have you thought of? What do you want from the group? The participants listen intently for implied wishes and goals and note any questions they may have while the client is presenting the analysis. While they are listening they are idea writing how-to statements based on their perceptions of the client's explicit and implied problem, desires, and goal. The how-tos are highly metaphorical solution-seeking statements (how to use a sky hook or an umbrella, for example). They are used to escape the routine associations of the problem field to reframe and trigger new associations that might stimulate novel solutions.

The facilitator moves the group into the next episode by listing their how-to statements on newsprint before the client. The client is then asked to select a favored how-to statement and if he or she has any ideas for making it into a solution. If not, the participants are asked for ideas on solving the given problem sparked by the how-to statement. A participant must start with an idea that draws from the how-to statement's metaphorical context. Other participants can build on the idea but cannot shift the direction. Typically two or three additions are permitted before the facilitator asks the client to paraphrase the idea. The client is then asked to identify all the attributes he or she likes about the idea and then any perceived obstacles in a proactive form ("I would like to see"). The participants listen and write down how-tos while this is taking

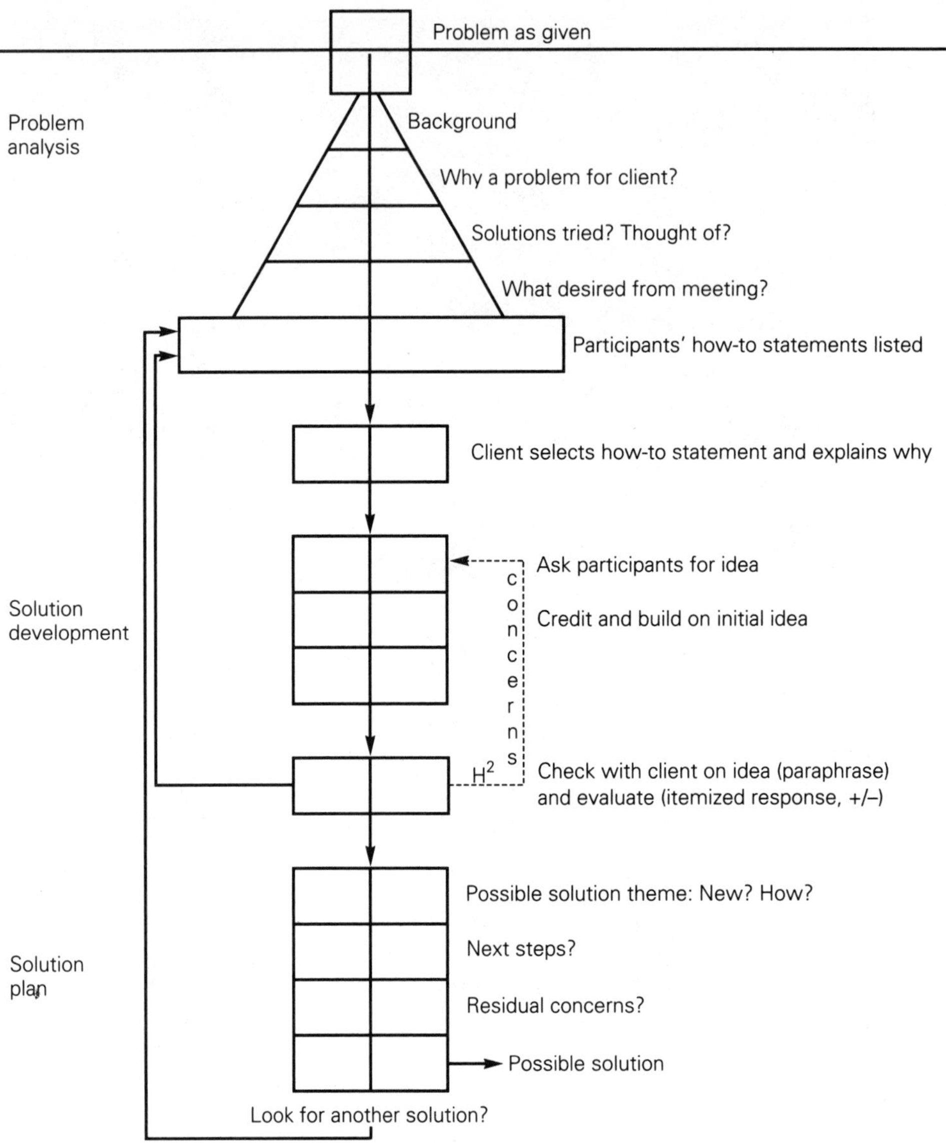

Figure 14.3 Diagram of the synectics process.

place. The obstacles are then subjected to a repetition of this same cycle in an effort to find solutions.

When an acceptable solution is developed, the client is asked to review the steps for implementing the idea. When this is achieved, the client has a possible solution and continues seeking solutions by selecting another how-to statement (see Figure 14.3).

Synectics exemplifies a complete and closed GPD in that it is totally prescribed. No deviations are permitted in this process, with the exception of introducing techniques to overcome mental blocks. The excursion technique—an imaginary vacation or a walk through a supermarket—is used to take a break from the problem and can help spark novel ways of looking at problem solutions.

Interactive Management The Interactive Management (IM) approach is designed for complex problem solving—policy development, organizational redesign, strategic planning—requiring the involvement of relevant parties.[14] It provides a mechanism for an in-depth examination of a primary goal to establish a comprehensive understanding of the problems and possible solutions. A major value of IM is its thorough exploration of the problem domain. It establishes a comprehensive picture of problem and solution relationships to arrive at strategic solution priorities based on the participants' knowledge and experience.

An elaborate and incisive GPD, IM provides a sequence of steps or consensus methodologies involving one or more activities.[15] The process requires a facilitator, participants, support staff, and selected technologies. The facilitator works with the client group representative to establish the primary goal for the sessions and helps in identifying the appropriate participants. During the IM sessions the facilitator orients the participants to the meeting's goal and instructs them on the rules governing each consensus methodology as they occur in sequence. The facilitator also records ideas during information-generating activities of various methodologies. The support staff set up the room and equipment and perform computation, reproduction, and display activities using simple and sophisticated technologies.

The consensus methodologies establish discrete episodes spanning several group sessions. It is not unusual for IM to take up to ten days to complete. The methodologies structure the sequence of activities and guide the manner and focus of participants' involvement (see Figure 14.4). Each methodology maximizes task and maintenance functions through activities that require input, joint decision making, and supportive communication behavior.

The information management demands of the complete IM process require a designated room designed to accommodate the various support media and the participants. Modified versions of IM have been conducted off-site.

IM is a complete and largely closed GPD. The specific sequence and types of steps and activities can be modified to serve specific client constraints usually determined by time limitations, the problem, or unanticipated information needs. In this respect, the overall GPD can be somewhat open to address specific needs and circumstances of the client group, but is adhered to when implemented.

GPDs and Group Productivity

Scant research directly addresses the relationship of GPDs to group productivity. However, available group research and field observations by practitioners have provided information on the utility of GPDs.

Interactive Management Consensus Methodologies

Methodologies[a]	Activities	Functions
Nominal group technique	Individual idea generation, round-robin for master list, clarification, and ranking of items	Information sharing and idea generating
Interpretive structural modeling (ISM)	Pairwise comparison of selected items, voting on preference, computer computation and display	Analysis of interrelationship among items using one of six transitive relationships
Delphi[b]	At distance idea generation by participants/experts using trigger question followed by tabulation and distribution of results	Information gathering or idea generating by sources outside of meeting
Options field method[c]	Pairwise comparison of solution options,clarification, vote on preference, computer computation and display, label option clusters, pairwise comparison of clusters, clarification, vote on preference, computer computation and display	Construction of solution field
Options profile method[c]	Small groups select solution options within and across option categories and report to group	Construction of one or more solution profiles
Trade-off analysis[c]	Review and analyze developed option profile(s) for implementation feasibility, adjust priorities if needed	Selection of preferred solution profile

a. All methodology activities require member's participation.

b. Delphi is used to obtain task specific information relevant to continuing the decision-making process. It can involve nonparticipant information experts.

c. An inherent function of these methodologies is to reveal and identify embedded issues, constraints, or needed information relevant to critical decision making.

Figure 14.4 The Interactive Management approach is a group process design that calls for a sequence of steps, called consensus methodologies, each of which includes one or more activities. The approach is especially effective for groups solving complex problems. [From Joseph C. Chilberg, "A Review of Group Process Designs for Facilitating Communication in Problem Solving Groups," *Management Communication Quarterly*, *3*, 62–63.]

Individuals without knowledge of or experience with GPDs or lacking basic tools for task group meetings (reviewed in Chapter 6) may view the use of GPDs with skepticism. We have already emphasized the task and relationship communication functions of GPDs. Additionally, GPDs promote problem-solving meeting efficiency and effectiveness and maximize group-centered decision making. A closer look at how GPDs fulfill these communication issues will establish a rationale for their use.

Task and Relationship Communication Ivan Steiner conjectures that groups risk productivity if they lack a clear and precise process that corresponds to the task and maximizes resources.[16] Research indicates that when tasks are divisible, groups need to divide them into discrete activities and establish coordinated patterns of interaction to enhance group productivity. Additionally, groups perform better when members' roles are designated and matched with activities. However, the probability of an effective division of labor is lower when groups are left to divide a task into subtasks and match individuals with subtasks.[17] GPDs that establish division of tasks, division of labor via roles, and coordination of task and relational behaviors could contribute to group productivity.

Harold Guetzkow contends that the successful problem-solving group requires the integration of task and maintenance functions and group structure.[18] GPDs integrate the task and relationship functions by establishing group structures through role specialization and shared task procedures and rules. At the same time, they reduce the potential for relational conflict through complementary role structures, supportive relationship behaviors, and clear procedures. This can contribute to a more efficient use of group effort and time, especially for zero-history groups that do not have established role relationships.

Efficient and Effective Decision Making The elaborate and detailed activities of process designs frequently take a lot of time to complete. This is an artifact of critical task activities and should not be confused with inefficiency. In actuality, the systematic activities of GPDs increase critical decision-making efficiency, especially in view of increased participation.

Design features also enhance decision-making quality by drawing upon all members' resources to increase the quantity and variety of information. At the same time, this increases the problem of "bounded rationality," or information overload. Members "cannot handle logistically all of the knowledge available in working with complex issues."[19] By separating mental activity into distinct activities and steps, GPDs provide ways to reduce the total cognitive load that the members must manage when addressing complex problems. Research indicates that greater group productivity can be achieved through the conscious separation of decision-making activities.[20]

Role specialization can reduce the number of tasks any one member must perform at a given time, and it ensures the appropriate performance of procedures. Establishing clear and separate roles and role behaviors improves

Box 14.1

Using a GPD: The Empowering Powwow

My first experience with Interactive Management occurred as an observer during a off-site application with a Midwestern Indian tribe. The tribal council was experimenting with the IM process to identify obstacles and solutions for implementing a self-sufficiency plan. The tribal council of eighteen members met for two days to work on this task until the available time was exhausted.

The IM team, a facilitator and four support staff, set up the meeting room for easy display of information. The easels, personal computer, printer, copier, computer projector, and cables were readied for the first day's meeting. A reception followed in which we met many of the meeting participants. I was skeptical about the possible success of IM after observing and speaking with tribal council members. Some members were clearly suspicious of outsiders and the chief's motives for bringing us in. I could not blame them after all the disappointment the white man has brought to their lives. In fact, the tribe was experiencing conflict and had already had an unsuccessful attempt with another group intervention using a conflict management process. The tribal chief believed it failed because it reinforced an adversarial climate by identifying conflicting positions and did not promote consensus, the traditional way of tribal decision making. In view of the conflicts, skepticism, outsiders, and lack of participant experience with a highly structured meeting process, it seemed unlikely that IM would work in this situation.

During the first day of meeting, participants generated a master list of ranked obstacles using the nominal group technique. Interpretive Structural Modeling (ISM) was then used to establish the priority and relationship of the list of seventy-one obstacles. ISM required the group to compare pairs of all the obstacles with each other in terms of relative priority. The PC and computer projection system were used to display each pair of obstacles for the participants to discuss and jointly decide on the relative priority. The pair decisions were transmitted using a modem to a mainframe computer, which used a transitive inferential algorithm to minimize the number of pair judgments required by the group and calculate overall obstacle relationships.

The second day began with a graphic display of the computed results of the ISM, showing participants' judgments in the form of an "obstacle map." This structural map showed obstacle priorities and relationships. The map provided a comprehensive picture clarifying what was previously a complex and confusing plethora of issues. The obstacle map seemed to infuse the group with energy and a desire to continue.

At the end of two days, the participants had developed an integrative picture of problems facing their efforts to become self-sufficient and several

Box 14.1 (continued)

solutions for each of fourteen key problems. Virtually every participant expressed a strong sense of achievement and satisfaction with what *they* had accomplished. This stands in direct contrast to the cautious attitude and negative climate that prevailed before the sessions began.

The participants found the first day of the IM process tedious and uninspiring. It was not until the second day, when the obstacle map was displayed, that the participants saw the insightful fruits of their labor. The feedback on the use of IM indicated its capacity to help members present and discuss divergent views, overcome substantive misunderstanding, learn about the tribe and its problems, reach consensus, provide direction for tribal action, and recognize a shared purpose. At the end of the IM process, the tribal council was more informed, energized, and optimistic about becoming self-sufficient. Several members expressed interest in making IM available to their and other tribes for future problem-solving forums. They felt united, capable, and empowered to tackle their future.

team effectiveness.[21] Furthermore, the regular use of role-based procedures and practices can clear up misunderstandings before they disrupt relations among members.

Steiner claims that the quality of group decisions is based on the process used.[22] Current research on the functional perspective of group communication has found no difference between the presence of key decisional functions in groups using a specified problem-solving agenda and those without such agenda.[23] The quality of decisions was related to the presence of four critical decision-making functions, regardless of procedures used. Follow-up studies found that groups that effectively assess: "(1) the problematic situation, (2) the requirements for an acceptable choice, (3) the positive qualities of alternative choices, and (4) the negative qualities of alternative choices are more likely to arrive at high quality decisions than groups that do not."[24] At the same time, there is no evidence linking the quality of interaction in the performance of the critical decision functions to high-quality decisions. Even though the quality of interaction in relation to decisions produced through using the GPDs reviewed here has not been determined, they nonetheless require the performance of critical decision functions. There is reason to believe GPDs enhance the quality of performance of these critical functions, which may translate into higher quality decisions.

An added advantage of GPDs can be attributed to reducing, if not eliminating, the amount of communication devoted to procedural decisions.

The more energy a group devotes to establishing operating procedures, the less it expends on useful task functions. Recent research on decision-making development has shown that groups go through periods of disorganized activity, especially when the task is complex and difficult.[25] Thus adopting ready-made procedures not only enhances the performance of critical task activities but also increases the amount of time devoted to them. Furthermore, meetings using GPDs are very task centered, reducing the occurrence of social interactions unrelated to the task. Group facilitation designs help groups overcome some of the inherent disadvantages of the group development process and reduce disorganized activity, which is unproductive and costly to organizations.[26]

Group-Centered Communication Group-centered communication is crucial to maximizing the value of groups for problem solving, which resides in the ability of a group to surpass its most expert member or the sum of its members' knowledge. Additionally, the *law of requisite variety* stresses the need for identifying all relevant aspects and issues of a problem to maximize the development of appropriate solutions. Thus contributions from all members of all relevant information is crucial to effective problem solving, especially as a problem's complexity and the number of relevant parties increase.[27] As we have stressed throughout this book, participation by all members instead of leader-centered communication is critical to the effective use of groups for making decisions.

A GPD facilitates the development of group-centered communication in several ways, particularly in establishing opportunities and a climate for participation. A GPD also promotes group-centered communication through adopting a shared goal and meeting procedures that can promote cohesion and morale.[28]

Another useful practice of GPDs that enhances group-centered communication is the use of group memories to record and display meeting proceedings. They provide a common focus that draws members' attention to the meeting's flow and progress. This facilitates concentration on the meeting's content, the product of collective communication inputs. Additionally, group memories and support media provide easy access to this information, which enhances members' satisfaction.[29] Practices and conditions that increase satisfaction, morale, and group cohesion can in turn reinforce group-centered communication.

Adopting GPDs

There is no conclusive evidence regarding the quality of decisions or meetings using the GPDs we have reviewed. Our personal experience and testimonials indicate satisfactory, if not exceptional, results. The few experiences we have had with unsuccessful use of GPDs appeared to result from an unclear or misunderstood problem, lack of a shared meeting goal, personal or hidden agendas, lack of commitment to the adopted procedures, and unskilled facilitation. These situations are harmful to the success of any group problem-solving effort.

The payoffs of a GPD are not without cost. There are expenses associated with obtaining a third-party facilitator or training to install the GPD in an organization. Installation of a GPD will likely require a commitment of personnel to serve as facilitators and requires support staff.

The more difficult and demanding costs are those associated with the human factors. Group leaders will be faced with working as members and will not have the freedom to do what they want, when they want. They will have to share decision making and authority in meetings. Many organizations and managers are not comfortable with group ownership of the meeting and third-party interventions. Group members may be reluctant to assume responsibility for decision making, especially if there is an atmosphere of distrust, a closed communication climate, or lack of confidence.

The organized, rational, and systematic practices of GPDs may not suit some members' decision-making style or may interfere with personal goals. Such conditions can lead to uncooperative behaviors and overt efforts to undermine the GPD process. Even though the facilitator must rectify such situations, they still threaten group effectiveness.

Given the number of groups in public and private organizations, the use of GPDs is by no means widespread. This is in part due to a lack of information on GPDs and their purposes. Cultural values may contribute to resistance to them, especially because our culture emphasizes individualism, competitive interpersonal styles, and hierarchical relationships—all of which are antithetical to the collaborative values inherent in GPDs.

Electronic Group Decision Support Systems

A host of traditional and new electronic technologies have been and are being developed to support the display, storage, duplication, analysis, and exchange of information. The more common group support technologies use familiar electronic devices such as telephones and broadcast media (TVs, video cameras, phone lines, microwave relays, satellites). The newest developments in electronic group support use computers.

Robert Johansen has classified three major ways in which computer-based systems aid group decision making: face-to-face meeting facilitation services, support for electronic meetings, and support between meetings.[30] Although his categories were developed for computer-based group technologies, other electronic media applications fit within this classification.

Face-to-Face Meeting Facilitation Support

Technological applications developed to support various decision-making activities are primarily computer based and augment group activities during meetings. The various applications emphasize information display, organization, analysis, and storage functions. The most common electronic devices are the personal or mainframe computer, computer projector, and large screens. The applications are based in computer software, which may involve a standard word-processing program or may be specifically designed for a particular activity. A common application is for idea-generating activities such as brainstorming. A facilitator at a central terminal in the meeting room records members' ideas, which are displayed on a large screen for common access. The ideas can be modified, aggregated, and stored for future access. Systems with printers and duplicating devices can provide instant hard copies for distribution. In a modification of this application, each member has a computer terminal. Meeting information is displayed on each member's video display terminal. This arrangement typically provides capabilities for group editing, ranking and voting, data access and retrieval, and information analysis and search features.

For the Interactive Management GPD, a computer-augmented group activity uses a personal computer linked to a mainframe computer and a computer projector to display and analyze comparisons of ideas in pairs (Interpretive Structural Modeling). Members must decide which item of a pair is more important or preferred. Each decision is recorded and computed by the mainframe computer using an algorithm that calculates and maps the relationship of all the previous decisions comparing pairs. The group takes a break and the map of the ideas is ready for review when it returns. This computer application provides a sophisticated service that could not be done quickly without a computer. The design of interpretive structural modeling not only serves a sophisticated analysis function but also facilitates group interaction by focusing discussion and decision making.

Support for Electronic Meetings

Electronic meetings or teleconferencing is simply the use of electronic media, most commonly the telephone, for group interaction. Teleconferencing technologies enable members of a group who are geographically dispersed to conduct a meeting without being face to face.

The use of teleconferencing for meetings has its advantages and disadvantages.[31] The more common advantages involve savings on travel costs, immediacy of access, and task-centered meetings. Teleconferencing requires some, if not extensive, procedural guidelines to facilitate interaction and decision-making tasks. Rules and roles cannot be ignored. The same considerations used in developing a GPD are involved in the design of teleconferencing meetings, with the addition of factors involving specific media capabilities and limitations (visual code capabilities, response time, and interaction patterns, for example). Common disadvantages are reduced access to nonverbal cues, lack of skills and familiarity with electronic mediated meetings, and lack of ease of learning and use. Research literature "emphasizes that acceptance, use, and consequences of group media are created from complex interactions of the medium (system design as well as coding attributes and interactivity), task, individual traits and motivations, group size and structure, group rules and rewards, access to alternative media, conduct of the group's meetings, and the organizational environment and goals."[32]

This plethora of variables appears to discourage adoption of teleconferencing modes for meetings, especially the newer computer-based technologies. However, future projections indicate significant expansion in the development of teleconferencing by U.S. organizations.[33] For example, 84 percent of the Fortune 500 companies plan teleconferencing installations soon, with a 90 percent projected growth by 1995. Fifty million dollars was spent on teleconferencing in 1980, and that amount is expected to increase to $900 million by 1990. Organizations are seeking a competitive edge in an era characterized by a global economy and fierce competition. The role of communication—particularly group communication—in organizational effectiveness will stimulate development and adoption of electronic meeting technologies.

Teleconferencing is not a single innovation, but comes in four modes with a variety of electronic device configurations within each mode.[34] The four modes are audio, audiographic, video, and computer based. A brief look at each mode will give you an idea of the present state of electronic meetings.

Audio Conference Telephone conferencing, the most common, simplest, and least expensive mode of teleconferencing, can be created through several methods.[35] The easiest is speakerphones in two locations for interaction among three or more people. Modern switching systems can also be used to add one or more parties to a phone conversation using dial-up conference or bridging services. Computer-based telephone extensions can build on commercial networks, private branch exchanges within or between organizations. Some sophisticated systems use accompanying screens to show the speaker. The screens can also be used to present data or graphics, creating a new technological form: audiographic teleconferencing.[36]

Telephone conferencing is an easy and timely way of conducting a meeting but poses limitations. Phone-based interaction requires high-quality sound reproduction to maximize communication effectiveness. Also, the absence of visual nonverbal cues reduces social information that can be important to participants involved in sensitive discussions or negotiations. Research indicates that the absence of nonverbal cues in interaction involving opinions and conflict reduces the balance of influence among members. Vocal cues were found to be most important in balancing influence, while visual nonverbal cues enhanced positive interpersonal evaluation in mediated interactions.[37] From these limited findings, telephone conferencing appears to be appropriate for information sharing, coordination tasks, and perhaps negotiation, if the group is already cohesive and relationship satisfaction is not a high priority.

Audiographic Conference This mode of teleconferencing adds a visual component to the telephone conference by using additional telephone lines or other carriers, for example, optic fiber cable or microwave relay. Fax machines, telewriting devices, computer displays, slow-scan/freeze-frame video, and video annotation systems can provide the graphic portion of the audio conference.[38] The visual capacity of audiographic systems is limited to graphic materials. It cannot use full-motion video images of participants or prerecorded videocassettes.

Graphic transmission devices vary in speed of transmission, interactivity, and types of graphics materials they can handle. For example, fax machines can send text and graphics in ten seconds, but machine feeding and transmission delays slow down meeting interaction involving these materials. Telewriting devices can be used to create and modify materials developed during a meeting, but cannot transmit existing documents.

Combinations of various graphic devices promise to enhance the versatility of audiographic conferencing by providing features needed for rapid meeting interaction and manipulation of shared information. According to Lynne Svenning and John Ruchinskas, "Scratch pad annotation systems are being linked with freeze-frame video allowing almost real-time annotations of existing documents, objects, and maps from each location."[39] The increased interactivity and ability to annotate meeting documents will likely increase the already popular use of audiographic teleconferencing, especially because such systems are less expensive and easier to implement than full-motion interactive video conferencing.

The obvious advantage of audiographic conferencing is the capacity to transmit and manipulate visual information. Although it does not provide visual nonverbal cues of participants, it does display visual information. Thus we assume that factors that hold true for audio conferences also hold true for audiographic conferences. However, electronic meetings involving the exchange of graphic information that leads to opinions on modifications would find relationship factors important when deciding on the appropriateness of this mode of teleconferencing. Talking over a phone while manipulating shared textual information that involves controversy may be very disconcerting and interpersonally uncomfortable, affecting decision quality, participation, and group satisfaction.

Video Conference Video conferencing uses broadcast TV technologies to conduct small and large group meetings. It provides full-motion video where participants can see speakers while they talk. It is the closest electronic meeting format to a face-to-face meeting because it provides some visual nonverbal cues of the participants. Video conferencing lends itself more readily to meetings involving opinions, negotiations, and conflict.

There are two predominant forms of video conferencing: point-multipoint and two-way video. Point-multipoint conferencing uses two-way audio and one-way video of the main presenter. It is used mainly in large groups for training, sales meetings, orientation programs, and other situations where information needs to be disseminated to multiple locations. Two-way interactive video comes in two formats, continuous presence and voice switched. Continuous presence provides images of all participants within camera range at each site, while voice-switched video shows the person speaking using a voice-activated device. Evaluations conducted with potential users indicate a preference for continuous presence because it provides visual cues of all meeting participants, similar to a face-to-face meeting.

Video conferencing, particularly two-way video, requires extensive equipment and specially designed rooms. Many organizations rent facilities from vendors, making access inconvenient. Speaking to a camera is awkward to most users, tending to inhibit contributions and create stilted interaction. This is largely because of the medium's physical characteristics. Systems that use digital compression and satellite transmission create a half-second delay between a message sent and seeing and hearing the distant respondents reply. This characteristic is most apparent when participants try to interrupt each other or make a humorous comment. (It appears as if the joke was not funny.) Having to wait for reactions is a prime reason users report reduced spontaneity and give-and-take during meetings.[40] At the same time, research indicates that video conference affects the process of meetings, making them more formal, task oriented, and shorter than face-to-face meetings, with mixed findings on users' perceptions of meeting effectiveness.[41]

Computer Conference This electronic meeting mode is the newest type of teleconferencing receiving attention from vendors, organizations, and researchers.[42] The computer terminal and personal computer are becoming as common as the phone in work settings because of the variety of tasks they can perform (word processing, data management, graphic production, desk-top publishing). Distant interaction is possible with computers connected to a computer network. Software vendors are developing electronic meeting programs and including them in computer software packages. Although there is no wide use of electronic meeting products yet, there is promise of expanded use as the software improves and is diffused into the network of computer users.

We discussed the use of E-mail in Chapter 6 for conducting activities outside of meetings. It allows members to communicate without being present at the same time—in an *asynchronous* mode. E-mail is not a true electronic meeting in that participants cannot interact with each other at the same time—in a *synchronous* mode.

Computer conferences (CCs) are conducted at a distance in real time, although they may be augmented with asynchronous interaction between meetings. This mode of teleconferencing has the unique capacity for instantaneous exchange of textual messages in real time and access to shared group files. Unlike other electronic meeting modes, CC is presently restricted to text-graphic messages, which as we will see later, creates several interesting consequences for group dynamics.

The central component of CC technology is the software shell. It provides functions to exchange, store, edit, scan, and print messages. Group specific features include on-line voting and decision-making procedures (risk analysis, preference weighting, and ranking, for example). In this respect, the software is very much like a GPD that establishes procedural choices and guidelines via the software. The software features facilitate decision-making activities and group interaction as a human facilitator would. For example, CC software can provide a group with a menu of problem-solving steps with several choices of activities. The selected activity, such as brainstorming for idea generation,

```
Joe,
here is my current glossary of e-mail affect codes that you
requested:  Lean your head toward your left shoulder . . .

:-)     happy-bitnetting
:-(     mourning, sadness
.-)     flirting
 -)     dreaming
:-()    astonishment
 -(     wouuu! bad joke
:-)))   belly laugh
:-S     frustration
:-o     whistling
|:-o    very shocked! (note raised eyebrows)
|:-(    ow! something's in my eye . . .

Sample:

Hi, Joe! :-)
it was nice running into you in the parking lot the other day.
-( :-))) Seriously, these symbols can be used to enhance and
reinforce the emotional content of a message.  Similar to
using italics, underscoring, capitals for EMPHASIS, for ex-
ample.  By the way, did you see the Bills game Sunday! :-()  A
great play in the last few seconds, :-o, after so many missed
opportunities :-S.  Take care, Andrea :-)
```

Figure 14.5 Groups that meet via computer conferences have developed graphic and verbal codes to overcome the fact that teleconferencing offers no nonverbal cues between group members. These codes are employed by Bitnet users. [From Andrea Domst, Department of Chemistry, State University of New York College at Fredonia.]

would direct the group through each step of the process. The members' messages are entered at will (and can be sent anonymously) and are available to all conference participants. The type of message would be guided by the sequence of the selected activity (generate ideas, clarify, then rank).

Unlike other modes of teleconferencing, CC is virtually cueless. No nonverbal behaviors are displayed; messages are textual. The main source of emotional display and relationship message cues is drastically reduced by this mode of mediated interaction. However, users have adopted graphic and verbal methods to overcome this limitation. Research indicates that CC users tend to be more emotionally expressive than are those in other teleconferencing modes. They express emotions graphically in what has been called "flaming": @+#%*&!!!!, ????!!!!, ☺ . Furthermore, findings indicate that users send more negative social messages in this communication mode. A community of users often develops a catalog of specific symbols for various emotional expressions. (See Figure 14.5.)

The first generation of research on CC's effects on group communication has produced some obvious and interesting findings:

- CC interaction takes more time than face-to-face interaction because of typing and reading textual messages.
- CC interaction produces more choice shift and less agreement than face-to-face interaction does.
- CC interaction is less inhibited (a negative and positive effect).
- Use of computers reduces social and status cues, which contributes to equalizing participation, and lessens member dominance compared to face-to-face groups.
- CC interaction is more task oriented with a higher incidence of procedural messages and fewer social messages than face-to-face groups have.
- CC groups are less effective in managing conflict than are face-to-face groups with access to the same conflict management procedures:[43]

Research on CC communication is in its infancy, with no conclusive evidence regarding CC decision-making effectiveness and satisfaction. Factors such as group members' familiarity with the system; software design, features, and flexibility; and actual use of software features pose difficulties in assessing CC effects. Evidence indicates the group use of CC technology mediates its impact. This is influenced by the task, the software features, and the effects group social interaction has on using software features.[44] Unlike a GPD, which uses a formal process facilitator to actualize the process design, CCs provide the process design and depend on the group's members to select and use it. All members or a designated member must raise procedural task issues to capitalize on decision-making advantages of software features.

Support Between Meetings

Computer technology offers numerous software features to aid group work and interaction between meetings. These features are easily included in CC software, which can handle meeting scheduling, record keeping, group document development, and information filing and search protocols. Robert Johansen identified several software products used to conduct group work between meetings:[45]

- *Project management software.* Keeps records of tasks, subtask breakdowns, assignments, and schedules; also organizes and reminds members of deadlines.
- *Calendar management of groups.* Helps group members schedule meetings and organize meeting times.
- *Group authoring software.* Provides centralized draft of documents with comments, author's name, and retention of various versions or additions.

- *Conversational structuring.* Provides explicit forms of communication for particular task interactions to reduce ambiguity.
- *Group memory management.* Store-and-search software based on shared information structures. Can include flexible search protocols to help find relevant information from text of previous group meetings.
- *Computer-supported spontaneous interaction.* Reinforces informal and spontaneous interactions (like what occurs around the water fountain or coffee pot) by informing a group member on the computer when another member has signed onto the computer.

The entry of the computer to the communication scene has not only added a major technology to group communication but has also altered other electronic meeting technology configurations. We can expect improvement in computer hardware and software for group communication. Although the advancements will be ahead of large-scale adoption by potential users in the near future, the rate of adoption will increase as more people become computer literate, systems become easier to use, and organizations adopt a more critical approach to task group processes.

Group Technologies in the Future

There are forces and circumstances that create a rather complex web of factors influencing the future adoption of group technologies. The most fundamental condition that hinders adoption is the lack of critical attention to the meeting as an organization tool. Despite a body of literature on effective meeting communication practices, little has been implemented in organizations. Like communication, meetings are taken for granted. Practical and cultural forces contributing to this condition stem largely from a lack of knowledge and education. Most executives and managers know little about effective meeting practices, let alone sophisticated meeting technologies. Add implementation costs, the inability to assess contributions to the bottom line, and the emphasis on authoritarian versus participatory management styles and it is easy to understand why new group technologies are not widely adopted. Certainly, our culture's emphasis on individualism poses difficulties in situations requiring cooperation and commitment.[46] The role and use of groups to serve personal, group, and societal ends is at the center of this quandary.

As the century draws to a close, Marshall McLuhan's "global village" is becoming more a reality every day, with electronic communication drawing distant countries, organizations, and groups into a seemingly smaller world.[47] The radical changes for democratization and economic participation in the Soviet Union and Eastern Europe indicates the importance people place on access to information and participation in making decisions to improve their life. Telling signs in our country are the wide adoption of quality circles, management literature devoted to participatory decision making, teamwork, and the commercial development of group technology products and services.

All organizations depend on groups to serve their goals. This dependence is increasing as organizations implement team approaches to improve productivity. The emphasis on decentralized decision making, use of task forces, and evaluating group performance and productivity has increased critical attention to group decision-making practices. Peter Drucker projects that the organization of the future will require the development of professionalism through task forces.[48] The group will become a main format for organizational work and productivity, creating a need for group technologies to increase communication access and participation and provide methods for effective decision making.

We anticipate increasing demand for various group technologies as the global economy continues to develop and interdependence across organizations increases. Task forces, typically composed of members from different departments or organizations, will need electronic technologies for timely and rapid communication.

Group technologies will continue to provide opportunities to improve traditional group situations. Weekly staff meetings, community action groups, large classes in schools, and team coordination situations indicate recognition of the benefits from adopting group technologies. The Interaction Method for structuring systematic and participatory meetings has been successful in numerous group settings. E-mail is being used in educational settings to increase student-teacher interaction in large lecture courses, coordinate project groups, and provide college courses at a distance.[49] The use of E-mail is rapidly becoming as common as the telephone for interaction between meetings and task coordination in organizations.

The most critical advantage of group technologies lies in opportunities to use procedures that support and improve task and relationship practices. Task efficiency and effectiveness is advanced through practices promoting the exchange, management, and display of information. Additionally, they create more task-centered meetings and emphasize the performance of critical decision-making functions. Task effectiveness is also supported by practices that enhance positive and productive relationships. Technologies can improve participatory decision making through increasingly timely interaction, promoting involvement, equalizing power, and reinforcing constructive interpersonal communications.

The future of group communication technologies lies in the larger societal and world context. Improving decision-making and problem-solving communication is one thing; the problems to be solved are another. The challenge is in using such technologies to solve critical organizational and social problems. Nations, nature, and economics clearly are intertwined in complex interdependencies. Problems facing mankind are increasing in complexity, requiring more sophisticated ways to manage and solve them. Group technologies are responding to this challenge. The future of our world will hinge on the application of knowledge and the adoption of practices that contribute to solving personal, organizational, and global problems. Group communication technologies promise to play a significant role in helping us solve these problems.

GroupQuests: Discussion Questions

1. A GPD is a prescription that guides group communication. Do you believe that GPDs interfere with the group development process discussed in Chapter 2? Explain your views and consider the advantages or disadvantages.
2. Review your experience in your present or recent group project. Note the specific task and interaction practices that hindered group morale and cohesion and high-quality task outcomes. What could have been done to design more effective group meetings? Examine the GPD features to help you develop possible strategies.
3. Review your experience in your present or recent group project. Note the various meeting tasks (check meeting notes or minutes) that took place across the project meetings. For which group tasks could you have used E-mail? Would this have provided any advantage to you or the group? If your group did use E-mail, what tasks did it use it for and what tasks could it have been used for? To what advantage?

GroupWorks: Group Activities

1. Discuss with the members of your project group its procedural effectiveness during and between meetings. Note specific problems with task efficiency and effectiveness and relationship communication. How did the procedures used or not used contribute to the problems? What procedures or practices could have been followed to manage or eliminate the problems?
2. Conduct a discussion in your project group on the merits and problems with using E-mail for interaction between meetings. If your group used E-mail, assess the benefits or problems and reasons why. If your group did not use E-mail, identify various tasks E-mail could have made more efficient or communication problems that it might have alleviated. What would have been required of the group to obtain these benefits? Would they have been worth it?
3. Identify the computer programs available through your campus mainframe and personal computer software. Look at the various features of each program, and note the programs that appear to provide useful electronic support for group meetings or tasks. Request a demonstration of the program or specific feature. In what way would the program or feature contribute to your group's effectiveness? Would it pose any problems or disadvantages? Explain your views.
4. Find a campus or community group that uses a GPD for conducting its meetings. (Parliamentary procedure is a GPD.) Seek permission to observe one or more of its meetings. Before the meeting, solicit information on the specific purpose, procedures, rules, and roles of the GPD. At the meeting, note the use of the GPD and how it contributes to participation, interaction, and task efficiency and effectiveness. Review the notes of your observations and determine the GPD's effectiveness in achieving its purpose.

GroupActs: Practical Applications

1. Organize a video panel-forum (two-way audio, one-way video point-to-point or multipoint) through your campus media center. Organize a panel discussion around a topic of interest or controversy. (See procedures for panel and forum discussion in Chapter 5.) Telecast the panel discussion to your class or another campus audience. After completing the video panel-forum, solicit feedback from the participants and audience on their impressions of the telepanel-forum. Ask the respondents to identify advantages and disadvantages.

2. If your campus computer system has a local area network (LAN) and software that permits synchronous interaction, schedule a demonstration of it. Practice using the system to interact and conduct a real or simulated meeting activity such as brainstorming. Upon completing the activity, use the system to discuss your experience, focusing on what you liked and disliked about using the CC mode for group communication. What features could improve the CC program for group use?

Notes

Notes for Chapter 1

1. Rodney Napier and Matti Gershenfeld, *Groups: Theory and Experience*, 3rd ed. (Boston: Houghton Mifflin, 1985), p. 519.
2. "The Payoff from Teamwork," *Business Week*, July 10, 1989, p. 57.
3. Ibid.
4. Georges Duby, ed., *A History of Private Life, Vol. II: Revelations of the Medieval World* (Cambridge, Mass.: Belknap Press, 1988), p. 509.
5. Marvin E. Shaw, *Group Dynamics: The Psychology of Small Group Behavior*, 3rd ed. (New York: McGraw-Hill, 1981), pp. 8–11.
6. R. E. Pittinger, C. F. Hockett, and J. J. Danehy, *The First Five Minutes: A Sample of Microscopic Interview Analysis* (Ithaca, N.Y.: Paul Martineau, 1960), p. 223.
7. R. D. Mann, "A Review of the Relationship Between Personality and Performance in Small Groups," *Psychological Bulletin*, 1959, *56*, 241–270.
8. *The American Heritage Dictionary* (Boston: Houghton Mifflin, 1976), p. 582.
9. Sarah Trenholm and Arthur Jensen, *Interpersonal Communication* (Belmont, Calif.: Wadsworth, 1988), p. 5.
10. Edward de Bono, *Six Thinking Hats* (Boston: Little, Brown, 1985).
11. Richard Heslin and Dexter Dunphy, "Three Dimensions of Member Satisfaction in Small Groups," *Human Relations*, 1964, *17*, 99–112.
12. F. B. Chaney, "Employee Participation in Manufacturing Job Design," *Human Factors*, 1969, *11*, 101–106.
13. L. R. Hoffman and Norman Maier, "Valence in the Adoption of Solutions by Problem-Solving Groups: Concept, Method and Results," *Journal of Abnormal and Social Psychology*, 1964, *69*, 264–271.
14. B. Latané, K. Williams, and S. Harkins, "Many Hands Make Light the Work: The Causes and Consequences of Social Loafing," *Journal of Personality and Social Psychology*, 1979, *37*, 822–832.
15. Clovis R. Shepherd, *Small Groups: Some Sociological Perspectives* (San Francisco: Chandler, 1964), pp. 94–95.
16. Fredric Jablin, "Cultivating Imagination: Factors That Enhance and Inhibit Creativity in Brainstorming Groups," *Human Communication Research*, 1981, *7*, 245–258; Fredric Jablin, David Siebold, and Ritch Sorenson, "Potential Inhibitory Effects of Group Participation on Brainstorming Performance," *Central States Speech Journal*, 1977, *28*, 113–121; Gerry Philipsen and David Dietrich, "The Effects of Social Interaction on Group Idea Generation," *Communication Monographs*, 1979, *46*, 119–125.
17. Dean Hewes, "A Socio-Egocentric Model of Group Decision-Making," in *Communication and Group Decision-Making*, eds. Randy Hirokawa and Marshall Poole (Beverly Hills: Sage, 1986), pp. 265–291.
18. Ibid., p. 282.
19. Jablin et al.

Notes for Chapter 2

1. B. Aubrey Fisher, *Small Group Decision Making*, 2nd ed. (New York: McGraw-Hill, 1980).
2. Daniel J. Boorstin, *The Discoverers: A History of Man's Search to Know His World and Himself* (New York: Random House. 1983).
3. John Dewey, *How We Think* (New York: Heath, 1910).
4. James L. Adams, *The Care and Feeding of Ideas: A Guide to Encouraging Creativity* (Reading, Mass.: Addison-Wesley, 1986), pp. 192–193.
5. Thomas Scheidel and Laura Crowell, "Idea Development in Small Discussion Groups," *Quarterly Journal of Speech*, 1964, *50*, 140–145.
6. David M. Berg, "A Descriptive Analysis of the Distribution and Duration of Themes Discussed by Task-Oriented Small Groups," *Speech Monographs*, 1967, *34*, 172–175.
7. Dennis Gouran, "Inferential Errors, Interaction, and Group Decision-Making," in *Communication and Group Decision-Making*, edited by R. Y. Hirokawa and M.S. Poole (Beverly Hills, Calif.: Sage, 1986), pp. 93–112.
8. Fisher, *Small Group Decision Making*, p. 132.
9. Ibid., p. 9.
10. B. Aubrey Fisher, "Decision Emergence: Phases in Group Decision-Making," *Speech Monographs*, 1970, *37*, 53–66; Bruce W. Tuckman, "Developmental Sequence in Small Groups," *Psychological Bulletin*, 1965, *63*, 384–399; Robert F. Bales and Fred L. Strodtbeck, "Phases in Group Problem-Solving," *Journal of Abnormal and Social Psychology*, 1951, *46*, 485–495.
11. Ernest G. Bormann, *Discussion and Group Methods: Theory and Practice*, 2nd ed. (New York: Harper & Row, 1975).
12. Fisher, "Decision Emergence."
13. Bormann, 1975.
14. Fisher, "Decision Emergence."
15. Marshall Scott Poole, "Decision Development in Small Groups I: A Comparison of Two Models," *Communication Monographs*, 1981, *48*, 1–24; "Decision Development in Small Groups II: A Study of Multiple Sequences in Decision Making," *Communication Monographs*, 1983, *50*, 206–232; "Decision Development in Small Groups III: A Multiple Sequence

Model of Group Decision-Making," *Communication Monographs*, 1983, *50*, 321–341.

16. Irving Janis and Leon Mann, *Decision Making: A Psychological Analysis of Conflict, Choice, and Commitment* (New York: Free Press, 1977), p. 11.
17. Janis and Mann, chap. 14; Randy Hirokawa and Roger Pace, "A Descriptive Investigation of the Possible Communication-Based Reasons for Effective and Ineffective Group Decision-Making," *Communication Monographs*, 1983, *50*, 363–379.
18. W. Barnett Pearce, personal communication, 1980.
19. Edward T. Hall and Mildred Reed Hall, *Hidden Differences: Doing Business with the Japanese* (New York: Anchor Press, 1987), p. 7.
20. W. Barnett Pearce and Vernon Cronen, *Communication, Action and Meaning: The Creation of Social Realities* (New York: Praeger, 1980).
21. John J. Gumperz, "Introduction," in *Directions in Sociolinguistics: The Ethnography of Communication*, edited by J. J. Gumperz and D. Humes (New York: Holt, Rinehart & Winston, 1972), p. 17.
22. Fisher, *Small Group Decision Making*, p. 43.

Notes for Chapter 3

1. James L. Adams, *Conceptual Blockbusting: A Guide to Better Ideas*, 2nd ed., (New York: W. W. Norton, 1979), p. 14.
2. Frank Barron, "The Psychology of Imagination," *Scientific American*, September, 1958, 151–166.
3. R. Summers, "A Phenomenological Approach to the Intuitive Experience." Doctoral dissertation, California School of Professional Psychology, 1976. Cited in Carol Nalbaandian, "Using Intuition in Decision-Making: A Management Skill." (Paper presented at the International Communication Association convention, May 1983.)
4. R. A. Cosier and J. C. Aplin, "Intuition and Decision Making: Some Empirical Evidence," *Psychological Reports*, 1982, *51*, 275–281; J. C. Henderson and P. C. Nutt, "The Influence of Decision Style on Decision Making Behavior," *Management Science*, 1980, *26*, 371–386.
5. H. S. Kindler, "The Influence of a Meditation-Relaxation Technique on Group Problem Solving Effectiveness," *Journal of Applied Behavioral Science*, 1979, *15*, 527–533.
6. B. Aubrey Fisher, *Small Group Decision Making*, 2nd ed. (New York: McGraw-Hill, 1980), pp. 266–267.

Notes for Chapter 4

1. Seymour Wishman, *Anatomy of a Jury: The System on Trial* (New York: Times Books, 1986), pp. 235–236.
2. These nine principles are derived largely from Randy Hirokawa, "Group Communication and Problem-Solving Effectiveness I: A Critical Review of Inconsistent Findings," *Communication Quarterly*, 1982, *30*, 134–141, and Randy Hirokawa and Roger Pace, "A Descriptive Investigation of the Possible Communication-Based Reasons for Effective and Ineffective Group Decision Making," *Communication Monographs*, 1983, *50*, 363–379.
3. Dennis Gouran, "Variables Related to Consensus in Group Discussions of Questions of Policy," *Speech Monographs*, 1969, *36*, 387–391.
4. Charlan J. Nemeth, "Dissent, Group Process, and Creativity: The Contribution of Minority Influence," *Advances in Group Processes*, vol. 2 (Greenwich, Conn.: JAI Press, 1985), 57–75.
5. Ralph G. Nichols and Leonard Stevens, "Listening to People," *Harvard Business Review*, 1957, *35*, 85–92.
6. Kenneth Benne and Paul Sheats, "Functional Roles of Group Members," *Journal of Social Issues*, 1948, *4*, 41–49.
7. John Cragan and David Wright, *Communication in Small Group Discussions: An Integrated Approach*, 2nd ed. (St. Paul: West, 1986), pp. 158–165.
8. Robert Bales and Philip Slater, "Role Differentiation in Small Decision-Making Groups," in *The Family, Socialization, and Interaction Process*, eds. Talcott Parsons et al. (New York: Free Press, 1955), pp. 259–306.
9. Stephen Wilson, "Some Factors Influencing Instrumental and Expressive Ratings in Task-Oriented Groups," *Pacific Sociological Review*, 1970, *13*, 127–131.
10. Randy Hirokawa and Dennis Gouran, "Facilitation of Group Communication: A Critique of Prior Research and Agenda for Future Research," *Management Communication Quarterly*, in press.
11. Ibid.
12. Randy Hirokawa, "Group Communication and Problem-Solving Effectiveness: An Investigation of Procedural Functions." (Paper presented at the annual meeting of the International Communication Association, Minneapolis, May 1980.)
13. Randy Hirokawa, "Group Communication and Problem-Solving Effectiveness II: An Exploratory Investigation of Procedural Functions," *Western Journal of Speech Communication*, 1983, *47*, 59–74.
14. B. Aubrey Fisher, *Small Group Decision Making*, 2nd ed. (New York: McGraw-Hill, 1980), p. 170.
15. Ibid., p. 172; John Baird, Jr., and Sanford Weinberg, *Communication: The Essence of Group Synergy* (Dubuque, Iowa: Wm. C. Brown, 1977).

Notes for Chapter 5

1. Ivan D. Steiner, *Group Process and Productivity* (New York: Academic Press, 1972), p. 9.
2. John Brilhart, *Group Discussion*, 5th ed. (Dubuque, Iowa: Wm. C. Brown, 1986).
3. William Fawcett Hill, *Learning Through Discussion*, 2nd ed. (Beverly Hills, Calif.: Sage, 1986).
4. Henry M. Roberts, *Robert's Rules of Order, Newly Revised* (Chicago: Scott, Foresman, 1981).
5. Michael Doyle and David Straus, *How to Make Meetings Work* (New York: Wyden Books, 1976).
6. Jack R. Gibb, "Defensive Communication," *Journal of Communication*, 1961, *11*, 141–148.

Notes for Chapter 6

1. A. F. Osborn, *Applied Imagination* (New York: Scribners, 1957).

2. Carl M. Moore, *Techniques for Idea Building* (Beverly Hills, Calif.: Sage, 1987), pp. 40–47.
3. T. J. Bouchard, "Personality, Problem-Solving Procedure, and Performance in Small Groups," *Journal of Applied Psychology Monograph*, 1969, *53*, 1–29; T. J. Bouchard, "Training, Motivation, and Personality as Determinants of the Effectiveness of Brainstorming Groups and Individuals," *Journal of Applied Psychology*, 1972, *56*, 324–331; and J. P. Campbell, "Individual versus Group Problem Solving in an Industrial Sample," *Journal of Applied Psychology*, 1969, *52*, 205–210.
4. Morris O. Edwards, *Doubling Idea Power: Workbook*, (Reading, Mass.: Addison-Wesley, 1975), p. 22.
5. Jay Hall, "Decisions, Decisions, Decisions," *Psychology Today*, November, 1971, pp. 51–54, 86–87.
6. Kenneth Williams, *The Practice of Creativity* (New York: Harper & Row, 1970); George Prince, *The Practice of Creativity: A Manual for Dynamic Group Problem Solving* (New York: Macmillan, 1972).
7. Francis L. Ulschak, Leslie Nathanson, and Peter G. Gillan, *Small Group Problem Solving* (Reading, Mass.: Addison-Wesley, 1981), pp. 85–96.
8. Arthur B. VanGundy, *Managing Group Creativity* (New York: Amacom, 1984), pp. 204–206.

Notes for Chapter 7

1. Thomas F. Crum, *The Magic of Conflict* (New York: Simon & Schuster, 1987), pp. 19–49.
2. Ernest Stech and Sharon A. Ratliffe, *Working in Groups* (Skokie, Ill.: National Textbook Company, 1977), p. 6.
3. Joseph P. Folger and Marshall Scott Poole, *Working Through Conflict* (Chicago: Scott, Foresman, 1984), p. 4; Joyce Hocker Frost and William W. Wilmot, *Interpersonal Conflict* (Dubuque, Iowa: Wm. C. Brown, 1978), pp. 9–14.
4. Lewis Coser, *The Functions of Social Conflict* (New York: Free Press, 1956), pp. 48–55.
5. Morton Deutsch, *The Resolution of Conflict* (New Haven, Conn.: Yale University Press, 1973), pp. 158–60.
6. Ronald B. Adler, *Communicating at Work*, 3rd ed. (New York: Random House, 1989), p. 93.
7. E. Sieburg, "Confirming and Disconfirming Communication in an Organizational Setting," in *Communication in Organizational Setting*, eds. J. Owen, P. Page, and G. Zimmerman (St. Paul: West, 1976), pp. 129–49.
8. Jack R. Gibb, "Defensive Communication," *Journal of Communication*, 1961, *11*, 141–148.
9. Deborah Borisoff and David A. Victor, *Conflict Management* (Englewood Cliffs, N.J.: Prentice-Hall, 1989), pp. 29–57.
10. Ibid., pp. 45–46.
11. Ronald B. Adler, *Communicating at Work*, 3rd ed. (New York: Random House, 1989), pp. 101–102.
12. Sharon Bowers and Gordon Bowers, *Asserting Yourself: A Practical Guide for Positive Change* (Reading, Mass.: Addison-Wesley, 1976), pp. 90–95.
13. Louise R. Pondy, "Organizational Conflict: Concepts and Models," *Administrative Science Quarterly*, 1967, *12*, p. xx.
14. Folger and Poole, *Working Through Conflict*, pp. 20–23.
15. Ibid., p. 60; R. Walton, *Interpersonal Peacemaking: Confrontations and Third Party Consultation* (Reading, Mass.: Addison-Wesley, 1969), p. 105.
16. Folger and Poole, *Working Through Conflict*, pp. 65–77.
17. Ibid., p. 68.
18. Roger Fisher and William Ury, *Getting to Yes* (Boston: Houghton Mifflin, 1981), pp. 3–57.
19. Ibid., pp. 58–83.
20. Linda Putnam, "Conflict in Group Decision-Making," in *Communication and Group Decision-Making*, eds. Randy Y. Hirokawa and Marshall Scott Poole (Beverly Hills, Calif.: Sage, 1986), pp. 185–188.
21. Ibid., pp. 185–186.

Notes for Chapter 8

1. Gordon Allport, *Personality: A Psychological Interpretation* (New York: Holt, Rinehart & Winston, 1937).
2. John Kihlstrom and Nancy Cantor, "Mental Representations of the Self," in *Advances in Experimental Social Psychology*, vol. 17, edited by Leonard Berkowitz (Orlando, Fla.: Academic Press, 1984), pp. 1–47.
3. Edward E. Jones and Richard Nisbett, "The Actor and the Observer: Divergent Perceptions of the Causes of Behavior," monograph, General Learning Press, 1971.
4. Mark Snyder and William Ickes, "Personality and Social Behavior," in *The Handbook of Social Psychology*, vol. 2, 3rd ed., edited by Gardner Lindzey and Elliot Aronson (New York: Random House, 1985), pp. 883–947.
5. John C. Turner, "Social Categorization and the Self-Concept: A Social Cognitive Theory of Group Behavior," *Advances in Group Processes*, 1985, *2*, 94.
6. Ibid., pp. 85–89.
7. Robert F. Bales and S. P. Cohen, *SYMLOG: A System for the Multiple Level Observation of Groups* (New York: Free Press, 1979).
8. Julian Rotter, "Generalized Expectancies for Internal versus External Control of Reinforcement," *Psychological Monographs*, 1966, *80* (1, whole no. 609).
9. W. L. Gregory, "Locus of Control for Positive and Negative Outcomes," *Journal of Personality and Social Psychology*, 1978, *36*, 840–849.
10. Steven Alderton, "Attributions of Responsibility for Socially Deviant Behavior in Decision-Making Discussions as a Function of Situation and Locus of Control of Attributor," *Central States Speech Journal*, 1980, *31*, 117–127; Dennis Gouran and P. H. Andrews, "Determinants of Punitive Responses to Socially Proscribed Behavior: Seriousness, Attribution of Responsibility, and Status of the Offender," *Small Group Behavior*, 1984, *15*, 525–543.
11. William C. Schutz, *FIRO: A Three-Dimensional Theory of Interpersonal Behavior* (New York: Holt, Rinehart & Winston, 1958).
12. Theodore W. Adorno, E. Frenkel-Brunswik, D. J. Levinson, and R. N. Sanford, *The Authoritarian Personality* (New York: Harper & Row, 1950).
13. W. W. Haythorn, A. Couch, D. Haefner, P. Langham, and L. F. Carter, "The Behavior of Author-

itarian and Equalitarian Personalities in Groups," *Human Relations*, 1956, *9*, 57–74.

14. A. H. Roberts and R. Jessor, "Authoritarianism, Punitiveness, and Perceived Social Status," *Journal of Abnormal and Social Psychology*, 1958, *56*, 311–314; I. D. Steiner and H. H. Johnson, "Authoritarianism and Conformity," *Sociometry*, 1963, *26* 21–34.
15. Adorno et al.; Milton Rokeach, *The Open and Closed Mind* (New York: Basic Books, 1960).
16. R. Christie and F. L. Geis, *Studies in Machiavellianism* (New York: Academic Press, 1970).
17. F. L. Geis, "Machiavellianism in a Semi-real World," *Proceedings of the 76th Annual Convention of the American Psychological Association*, 1968, *3*, 407–408.
18. Christie and Geis, *Studies in Machiavellianism*.
19. Mark Snyder, "The Self-Monitoring of Expressive Behavior," *Journal of Personality and Social Psychology*, 1974, *30*, 526–537.
20. Mark Snyder, "Self-Monitoring Processes," in *Advances in Experimental Social Psychology*, vol. 12, edited by Leonard Berkowitz (New York: Academic Press, 1979), pp. 96–97.
21. D. L. Rarick, G. F. Soldow, and R. S. Geizer, "Self-Monitoring as a Mediator of Conformity," *Central States Speech Journal*, 1976, *27*, 267–271.
22. Schutz, *FIRO*.
23. William C. Shutz, "What Makes Groups Productive?" *Human Relations*, 1955, *8*, 429–465; "On Group Composition," *Journal of Abnormal and Social Psychology*, 1961, *62*, 275–281; W. B. Reddy and A. Byrnes, "The Effects of Interpersonal Group Composition on the Problem Solving Behavior of Middle Managers," *Journal of Applied Psychology*, 1972, *56*, 516–517; see also M. E. Shaw and S. A. Nickols, "Group Effectiveness as a Function of Group Member Compatibility and Cooperation Requirements of the Task," technical report 4, ONR Contract NR 170-266, Nonr-580(11) University of Florida, 1964 (cited in Shaw, *Group Dynamics: The Psychology of Small Group Behavior*, 3rd ed. [New York: McGraw-Hill, 1981] p. 231).
24. Howard Giles and Richard L. Street, Jr., "Communicator Characteristics and Behavior," in *Handbook of Interpersonal Communication*, edited by Mark L. Knapp and Gerald R. Miller (Beverly Hills, Calif.: Sage, 1985), pp. 205–261.
25. Albert Mehrabian, "The Development and Validation of Measures of Affiliative Tendency an Sensitivity to Rejection," *Educational and Psychological Measurement*, 1970, *30*, 417–428.
26. James C. McCroskey, "Oral Communication Apprehension: A Summary of Recent Theory and Research," *Human Communication Research*, 1977, *4*, 78–96.
27. Gail Sorensen and James C. McCroskey, "The Prediction of Interaction Behavior in Small Groups: Zero-History versus Intact Groups," *Communication Monographs*, 1977, *44*, 73–80.
28. James C. McCroskey and D. W. Wright, "The Development of an Instrument for Measuring Interaction Behavior in Small Groups," *Speech Monographs*, 1971, *38*, 335–340.
29. Arthur Jensen and Peter Andersen, "The Relationship among Communication Traits, Behaviors, and Interpersonal Perceptions." Paper presented at the International Communication Association convention, Philadelphia, May, 1979.
30. Judee Burgoon, "Unwillingness to Communicate as a Predictor of Small Group Discussion Behavior and Evaluations," *Central States Speech Journal*, 1977, *28*, 122–133; Morton Lustig and Theodore Grove, "Interaction Analysis of Small Problem-Solving Groups Containing Reticent and Non-Reticent Members," *Western Speech Communication*, 1975, *39*, 155–164.
31. Frederic Jablin, "Cultivating Imagination: Factors That Enhance and Inhibit Creativity in Brainstorming Groups," *Human Communication Research*, 1981, *7*, 245–258.
32. Barbara Eakins and R. Gene Eakins, *Sex Differences in Human Communication* (Boston: Houghton Mifflin, 1978).
33. Linda L. Putnam, "Preference for Procedural Order in Task-Oriented Small Groups," *Communication Monographs*, 1979, *46*, 193–218.
34. Michael Burgoon, "Amount of Conflicting Information in a Group Discussion and Tolerance for Ambiguity as Predictors of Task Attractiveness," *Speech Monographs*, 1971, *38*, 121–124.
35. Randy Hirokawa, Richard Ice, and Jeanmarie Cook, "Preference for Procedural Order, Discussion Structure and Group Decision Performance," *Communication Quarterly*, 1988, *36*, 217–226.
36. Robert Norton, *Communicator Style: Theory, Applications, and Measures* (Beverly Hills, Calif.: Sage, 1983).
37. Timothy Leary, *Interpersonal Diagnosis of Personality—A Functional Theory and Methodology for Personality Evaluation* (New York: Ronald Press, 1957).

Notes for Chapter 9

1. Richard Heslin and Dexter Dunphy, "Three Dimensions of Member Satisfaction in Small Groups," *Human Relations*, 1964, *17*, 99–112.
2. Julia T. Wood, Gerald M. Phillips, and Douglas J. Pederson, *Group Discussion: A Practical Guide to Participation and Leadership*, 2nd ed. (Boston: Houghton Mifflin, 1986), pp. 79–81.
3. Ralph Stogdill, "Personal Factors Associated with Leadership: A Survey of the Literature," *Journal of Psychology*, 1948, *25*, 35–71.
4. L. F. Carter, "Recording and Evaluating the Performance of Individuals as Members of Small Groups," *Personnel Psychology*, 1954, *7*, 477–484.
5. B. Aubrey Fisher, *Small Group Decision Making*, 2nd ed. (New York: McGraw-Hill, 1980), pp. 194–195.
6. For a summary of this research, see Marvin Shaw, *Group Dynamics*, 3rd ed. (New York: McGraw-Hill), pp. 326–331.
7. L. L. Rosenbaum and W. B. Rosenbaum, "Morale and Productivity Consequences of Group Leadership Style, Stress, and Type of Task," *Journal of Applied Psychology*, 1971, *55*, 343–348.
8. Marvin Shaw, "A Comparison of Two Types of Leadership in Various Communication Nets," *Journal of Abnormal and Social Psychology*, 1955, *50*, 127–134.
9. Fisher, *Small Group Decision Making*, p. 196.

10. Fred Fiedler, *A Theory of Leadership Effectiveness* (New York: McGraw-Hill, 1967).
11. Paul Hersey and Kenneth Blanchard, "A Situational Framework for Determining Appropriate Leader Behavior," in *Leadership Development: Theory and Practice,* edited by R. N. Cassel and R. L. Heichberger (North Quincy, Mass.: Christopher Publishing House, 1975), pp. 126–155.
12. Julia T. Wood, "Leading as a Process of Persuasion and Adaptation," in *1976 Group Facilitators' Annual Handbook*, edited by J. William Pfeiffer and John Jones (LaJolla, Calif.: University Associates, 1976), pp. 132–135.
13. Linda Smircich and Gareth Morgan, "Leadership: The Management of Meaning," *Journal of Applied Behavioral Science*, 1982, *18*, 257–273.
14. Fisher, *Small Group Decision Making*, pp. 203–207.
15. Ibid., pp. 205–206.
16. Wood, Phillips, and Pederson, *Group Discussion*, p. 73.
17. B. Aubrey Fisher, "Leadership: When Does the Difference Make a Difference?" in *Communication and Group Decision-Making*, edited by Randy Hirokawa and Marshall Scott Poole (Beverly Hills, Calif.: Sage, 1986), pp. 197–215.
18. Karl Weick, "The Spines of Leaders," in *Leadership: Where Else Can We Go?*, eds. M. McCall and M. Lombardo (Durham, N.C.: Duke University Press, 1978), pp. 37–61; Fisher, "Leadership," pp. 197–215.
19. Fisher, "Leadership," p. 205.
20. F. Dansereau, G. Graen, and W. J. Haga, "A Vertical Dyadic Linkage Approach to Leadership within Formal Organizations," *Organizational Behavior and Human Performance,* 1975, *13*, 46–78.
21. Julia T. Wood, "Leading in Purposive Discussions: A Study of Adaptive Behavior," *Communication Monographs*, 1977, *44*, 152–166; R. Hamblin, "Leadership and Crises," in *Interpersonal Behavior in Small Groups*, edited by R. Ofshe (Englewood Cliffs, N.J.: Prentice-Hall, 1973), pp. 466–477.
22. G. Lloyd Drecksel, "Interaction Characteristics of Emergent Leadership," Ph.D. dissertation, University of Utah, 1984.

Notes for Chapter 10

1. Bob Woodward and Scott Armstrong, *The Brethren: Inside the Supreme Court* (New York: Simon & Schuster, 1979), pp. 241–242.
2. Ernest G. Bormann, "Symbolic Convergence: Organizational Communication and Culture," in *Communication and Organizations: An Interpretive Approach*, edited by Linda Putnam and Michael Pacanowsky (Beverly Hills, Calif: Sage, 1983), p. 100.
3. Leon Festinger, "Informal Social Communication," *Psychological Review*, 1950, *57*, 274.
4. James C. McCroskey and Thomas McCain, "The Measurement of Interpersonal Attraction," *Speech Monographs*, 1974, *41*, 261–266.
5. Marvin E. Shaw and J. C. Gilchrist, "Repetitive Task Failure and Sociometric Choice," *Journal of Abnormal and Social Psychology*, 1955, *50*, 29–32.
6. Leon Festinger, Stanley Schachter, and K. W. Back, *Social Pressure in Informal Groups* (New York: Harper & Row, 1950).
7. For a review of the literature on attraction in groups, see Marvin E. Shaw, *Group Dynamics: The Psychology of Small Group Behavior*, 3rd ed. (New York: McGraw-Hill, 1981), pp. 86–91.
8. T. D. Schaible and A. Jacobs, "Feedback III: Sequence Effects. Enhancement of Feedback Acceptance and Group Attractiveness by Manipulation of the Sequence and Valence of Feedback," *Small Group Behavior*, 1975, *6*, 151–173.
9. F. A. Blanchard, R. H. Weigel, and S. W. Cook, "The Effect of Relative Competence of Group Members upon Interpersonal Attraction in Cooperating Interracial Groups," *Journal of Personality and Social Psychology*, 1975, *32*, 519–530.
10. Richard Heslin and Dexter Dunphy, "Three Dimensions of Member Satisfaction in Small Groups," *Human Relations*, 1964, *17*, 99–112.
11. K. W. Back, "Influence through Social Communication," *Journal of Abnormal and Social Psychology*, 1951, *46*, 9–23.
12. *The American Heritage Dictionary*, 2nd college ed. (Boston: Houghton Mifflin, 1982), p. 639.
13. Tracy Kidder, *The Soul of a New Machine* (Boston: Little, Brown, 1981).
14. Ernest G. Bormann, "Symbolic Convergence Theory and Communication in Group Decision-Making," in *Communication and Group Decision-Making*, edited by Randy Hirokawa and Marshall Scott Poole (Beverly Hills, Calif.: Sage, 1986), p. 221.
15. Ibid., pp. 221–231.
16. Ivan Steiner, *Group Process and Productivity* (New York: Academic Press, 1972), p. 171.
17. J. A. Jackson, "Structural Characteristics of Norms," in *Current Studies in Social Psychology*, eds. Ivan Steiner and Martin Fishbein (New York: Holt, Rinehart & Winston, 1965), pp. 301–309.
18. Charles Kiesler and Sara Kiesler, *Conformity* (Reading, Mass.: Addison-Wesley, 1969), p. 2.
19. Herbert Kelman, "Compliance, Identification, and Internalization: Three Processes of Attitude Change," *Journal of Conflict Resolution*, 1958, *2*, 51–60.
20. Robert K. Merton, *Social Theory and Social Structure* (New York: Free Press, 1957).
21. Edwin Hollander, "Conformity, Status and Idiosyncracy Credit," *Psychological Review*, 1958, *65*, 117–127.
22. Cheryl Tromley, "The Strategies Groups Use to Deal with Deviant Members," Ph.D. dissertation, Yale University, 1984.
23. Our definition of socialization is combined from definitions provided by Kay Deaux and Lawrence Wrightsman, *Social Psychology in the 80s*, 4th ed. (Monterey, Calif.: Brooks/Cole, 1984), p. 495, and Richard Moreland and John Levine, "Socialization in Small Groups: Temporal Changes in Individual-Group Relations," in *Advances in Experimental Social Psychology*, vol. 15, edited by Leonard Berkowitz (New York: Academic Press, 1982), p. 139.
24. Moreland and Levine, "Socialization in Small Groups," pp. 137–192.
25. Ibid., p. 148.
26. Ibid., p. 149.
27. Ibid.

Notes for Chapter 11

1. Robert Bales and Fred Strodtbeck, "Phases in Group Problem-Solving," *Journal of Abnormal and Social Psychology*, 1951, *46*, 485–495.
2. Bruce Tuckman, "Developmental Sequence in Small Groups," *Psychological Bulletin*, 1965, *63*, 384–399.
3. B. Aubrey Fisher, "Decision Emergence: Phases in Group Decision Making," *Speech Monographs*, 1970, *37*, 53–66.
4. Marshall Scott Poole and Jonelle Roth, "Decision Development in Small Groups IV: A Typology of Group Decision Paths," *Human Communication Research*, 1989, *15*, 325.
5. Marshall Scott Poole, "Decision Development in Small Groups I: A Comparison of Two Models," *Communication Monographs*, 1981, *48*, 1–24; Marshall Scott Poole, "Decision Development in Small Groups II: A Study of Multiple Sequences in Decision Making," *Communication Monographs*, 1983, *50*, 206–232; Marshall Scott Poole, "Decision Development in Small Groups III: A Multiple Sequence Model of Group Decision Development," *Communication Monographs*, 1983, *50*, 321–341; Poole and Roth, "Decision Development . . . in Small Groups IV;" Poole and Roth, "Decision Development in Small Groups V: Test of a Contingency Model," *Human Communication Research*, 1989, *15*, 549–589.
6. Poole and Roth, "Decision development . . . IV," p. 328.
7. Ibid., p. 328.
8. Poole and Roth, "Decision development . . . V."

Notes for Chapter 12

1. S. Moscovici and M. Zavalloni, "The Group as a Polarizer of Attitudes," *Journal of Personality and Social Psychology*, 1969, *12*, 125–135.
2. James Stoner, "A Comparison of Individual and Group Decisions Involving Risk," master's thesis, Massachusetts Institute of Technology, 1961. (Cited in M. A. Wallach, N. Kogan, and D. Bem, "Group Influence on Individual Risk Taking," *Journal of Abnormal and Social Psychology*, 1962, *65*, 75–86.)
3. Roger Brown, "Further Comment on the Risky Shift," *American Psychologist*, 1974, *29*, 468–470.
4. Barbara Kiernan, "Risky Shift and Polarization," unpublished manuscript, Graduate School of Communication, Fairfield University, 1988. Used with permission of Barbara Kiernan.
5. M. A. Wallach, N. Kogan, and D. Bem, "Diffusion of Responsibility and Level of Risk Taking in Groups," *Journal of Abnormal and Social Psychology*, 1964, *68*, 263–274.
6. Rebecca Cline and Timothy Cline, "A Structural Analysis of Risky-Shift and Cautious-Shift Discussions: The Diffusion-of-Responsibility Theory," *Communication Quarterly*, 1980, *28*, 26–36.
7. Roger Brown, *Social Psychology* (New York: Free Press, 1965).
8. L. K. Hong, "Risky Shift and Cautious Shift: Some Direct Evidence on the Culture-Value Theory," *Social Psychology*, 1978, *41*, 342–346.
9. D. G. Myers and M. F. Kaplan, "Group-Induced Polarization in Simulated Juries," *Personality and Social Psychology Bulletin*, 1976, *2*, 63–66.
10. M. A. Wallach and N. Kogan, "The Roles of Information, Discussion, and Consensus in Group Risk Taking," *Journal of Experimental Social Psychology*, 1965, *1*, 1–19.
11. Eugene Burnstein and Amiram Vinokur, "What a Person Thinks upon Learning That He Has Chosen Differently from Others: Nice Evidence for the Persuasive-Arguments Explanation of Choice Shifts," *Journal of Experimental and Social Psychology*, 1975, *11*, 412.
12. Irving Janis, *Victims of Groupthink* (Boston: Houghton Mifflin, 1972).
13. Janis, *Groupthink* 2nd ed. (Boston: Houghton Mifflin, 1982).

Notes for Chapter 13

1. Harold J. Leavitt, "Suppose We Took Groups Seriously, . . ." in *Man and Work in Society*, edited by Eugene L. Cass and Frederick G. Zimmer (Western Electric Company, 1975).
2. Edmund S. Glenn, *Man and Mankind: Conflict and Communication Between Cultures* (Norwood, N.J.: Ablex, 1981), p. 8.
3. Glenn, *Man and Mankind*, p. 230.
4. Randy Y. Hirokawa, "Improving Intra-Organizational Communication: A Lesson from Japanese Management," *Communication Quarterly*, 1981, *30*, 35–40.
5. Edward T. Hall and Mildred Hall, *Hidden Differences: Doing Business with the Japanese* (New York: Anchor Press, 1987), p. 3.
6. Ibid.
7. Edward T. Hall, *Beyond Culture* (New York: Anchor Press, 1977), p. 91.
8. E. D. Hirsch, Jr., *Cultural Literacy: What Every American Needs to Know* (Boston: Houghton Mifflin, 1987).
9. George Crane, personal communication, Graduate School of Communication, Fairfield University.
10. Max Weber, *The Theory of Social and Economic Organizations*, translated by A. M. Henderson and T. Parsons, edited by T. Parsons (New York: Oxford University Press, 1947).
11. Michael Pacanowsky and Nick O'Donnell-Trujillo, "Communication and Organizational Cultures," *Western Journal of Speech Communication*, 1982, *46*, 123.
12. Terrance Deal and Alan Kennedy, *Corporate Cultures: The Rites and Rituals of Corporate Life* (Reading, Mass.: Addison-Wesley, 1982.)
13. Donald F. Schwartz, "Liaison Roles in the Communication of a Formal Organization," in *Communicating in Organizations*, edited by Lyman W. Porter and Karlene H. Roberts (New York: Penguin Books, 1977), pp. 255–271.

Notes for Chapter 14

1. David B. Guralnik, ed., *Webster's New World Dictionary* (New York: Williams Collins & World Publishing, 1974).

2. Randy Y. Hirokawa and Dennis S. Gouran, "Facilitation of Group Communication: A Critique of Prior Research and an Agenda for Future Research," *Management Communication Quarterly*, 1989, *3*, 72.
3. See citations in Joseph C. Chilberg, "A Review of Group Process Designs for Facilitating Communication in Problem-Solving Groups," *Management Communication Quarterly*, 1989, *3*, 51; Ronald Rice and associates, eds., *The New Media* (Beverly Hills, Calif.: Sage, 1984), pp. 129–154, 217–248; Robert Johansen, *Groupware* (New York: Free Press, 1988).
4. This material is largely adopted from Joseph C. Chilberg, "A Review of Group Process Designs for Facilitating Communication in Problem-Solving Groups," *Management Communication Quarterly*, 1989, *3*, 51–70.
5. Michael Doyle and David Straus, *How to Make Meetings Work* (New York: Wyden Books, 1976).
6. Charles H. Kepner and Benjamin B. Tregoe, *The Rational Manager: A Systematic Approach to Problem Solving and Decision Making* (New York: McGraw-Hill, 1965).
7. S. A. Olsen, "Background and State of the Art," in *Group Planning and Problem-Solving Methods*, edited by S. A. Olsen (New York: John Wiley, 1982), p. 9.
8. Discussion largely drawn from Donald L. Dewar, *Quality Circle Handbook*, (Red Bluff, Calif.: Quality Circle Institute, 1980).
9. Jane P. Elvins, "Communication in Quality Circles: Members' Perceptions of Their Participation and Its Effects on Related Organizational Communication Variables," *Group and Organizational Studies* 1985, *10*, 479–507.
10. E. Lawler and S. Mohrman, "Quality Circles after the Fad," *Harvard Business Review*, Jan.–Feb. 1985, 65–71.
11. This version of Synectics is from George M. Prince, *The Practice of Creativity* (New York: Harper & Row, 1970).
12. Ben Gray, "Synectics: A Solution-Centered Approach to Problem Solving," Ph.D. dissertation, School of Communication, Ohio University, 1982.
13. J. H. McPherson, *The People, the Problems, and the Problem-Solving Methods* (Midland, Mich.: Pendell Co., 1967).
14. John N. Warfield, *Societal Systems* (New York: John Wiley, 1976); David B. Keever and Alexander N. Christakis, "Management's Quest for New Solutions," unpublished manuscript, Center for Interactive Management, George Mason University, 1984.
15. John N. Warfield, "Principles of Interactive Management," Proceedings of the International Conference on Cybernetics and Society, Bombay and New Delhi, 1984); Benjamin Broome and David B. Keever, "Facilitating Group Communication: The Interactive Management Approach," paper presented at Eastern Communication Convention, Atlantic City, 1986.
16. Ivan D. Steiner, *Group Process and Productivity* (New York: Academic Press, 1972).
17. Shirley A. Olsen, "Framework for Selection and Implementation," in *Group Planning and Problem Solving Methods in Engineering Management*, edited by Shirley A. Olsen (New York: John Wiley, 1982), pp. 23–75.
18. Harold Guetzkow, "Differentiation of Roles in Task-Oriented Groups," in *Group Dynamics*, edited by Darwin Cartwright and Alvin Zander (New York: Harper & Row, 1968), pp. 512–526.
19. Warfield, "Principles of Interactive Management," 1976, p. 50.
20. Olsen, "Framework for Selection," 1982, pp. 23–75.
21. Ibid.
22. Steiner, *Group Process*, p. 9.
23. Randy Y. Hirowkawa, "Discussion Procedures and Decision-Making Performance: A Test of a Functional Perspective," *Human Communication Research*, 1985, *12*, 203–224.
24. Randy Y. Hirowkawa, "Group Communication and Decision-Making Performance: A Continued Test of the Functional Perspective," *Human Communication Research*, 1988, *14*, 512.
25. Marshall Scott Poole and Jonelle Roth, "Decision Development in Small Groups IV: A Typology of Decision Paths," *Human Communication Research*, 1989, *15*, 323–356.
26. Benjamin Broome and David B. Keever, "Next Generation Group Facilitation: Proposed Principles," *Management Communication Quarterly*, 1989, *3*, 113.
27. Broome and Keever, "Next Generation," p. 114.
28. Olsen, "Framework for Selection," pp. 23–75.
29. Ibid.
30. Robert Johansen, *Groupware: Computer Support for Business Teams* (New York: Free Press, 1988), pp. 12–44.
31. Lynne L. Svenning and John E. Ruchinskas, "Organizational Teleconferencing," in *The New Media*, eds. Ronald E. Rice and associates (Beverly Hills, Calif.: Sage, 1984), pp. 217–248.
32. Ronald E. Rice, "Mediated Group Communication," ibid., p. 130.
33. Svenning and Ruchinskas, "Organizational Teleconferencing," p. 218.
34. Ibid., p. 219.
35. Discussion of characteristics of four modes of teleconferencing largely adopted from Svenning and Ruchinskas, pp. 220–226.
36. Johansen, *Groupware*, pp. 18–19.
37. Rice, "Mediated Group Communication," p. 134.
38. For more detailed description of these devices, see Rudy Bretz, *Media for Interactive Communication* (Beverly Hills, Calif.: Sage, 1983).
39. Svenning and Rushinskas, "Organizational Teleconferencing," p. 222.
40. Lynne L. Svenning and John E. Ruchinskas, "The Impact of Video Conferencing: The Case of ARCOvision," presented at International Communication Association Convention, Nov. 1, 1985.
41. Svenning and Ruchinskas, "Organizational Teleconferencing," p. 16.
42. Materials for this section were derived from Ronald E. Rice, "Mediated Group Communication," in *The New Media*, edited by Ronald E. Rice and associates (Beverly Hills, Calif.: Sage, 1984), pp. 129–156; Jane Siegel, Vitaly Dubrovsky, Sara Kiesler, and Timothy W. McGuire, "Group Processes in Computer-Mediated Communication," *Organizational Behavior*

and Human Decision Processes, 1986, *37*, 157–187; and Gerardine DeSanctis and R. Brent Gallupe, "A Foundation for the Study of Group Decision Support Systems," *Management Science*, 1987, *33*, 589–609.

43. Marshall Scott Poole, Michael Holmes, and Gerardine DeSanctis, "Conflict Management in a Computer-Supported Meeting Environment," paper presented at the International Communication Association Convention, San Francisco, May 1989.

44. Poole, Holmes, DeSanctis, *Conflict Management*, p. 35.

45. Johansen, *Groupware*, pp. 12–44.

46. Robert N. Bellah, Richard Madsen, William M. Sullivan, Ann Swidler, and Steven M. Tipton, *Habits of the Heart: Individualism and Commitment in American Life* (Berkeley, Calif.: University of California Press, 1985).

47. Marshall McLuhan, *Understanding Media: The Extensions of Man* (New York: McGraw-Hill, 1965).

48. Peter F. Drucker, "The Coming of the New Organization," *Harvard Business Review*, Jan.–Feb. 1988, pp. 45–53.

49. Joseph C. Chilberg and Delann Williams, "Implementation and Evaluation of Electronic Mail for the Development of a Student-Centered Large Lecture Course," paper presented at the Speech Communication Convention, San Francisco, Nov. 1989; Gerald M. Phillips and Gerald M. Santoro, "Teaching Group Discussion via Computer-Mediated Communication," *Communication Education*, 1989, *38*, 151–161; Roger Boston, "Remote Delivery of Credit Courses Via Computer Modem," presentation at Second Annual Conference on Interactive Technology and Telecommunications, University of Maine, Aug.–Sept. 1988.

Index